QUEER JUDGMENTS:
HOMOSEXUALITY, EXPRESSION,
AND THE COURTS IN CANADA

Chapter 15 of Canada's Charter of Rights and Freedoms now states
that it is unconstitutional to discriminate on the basis of race, class, or
sexual orientation. Although the letter of the law has been changed
with regard to homosexuality, has the spirit of the people who implement the law been transformed as well?

Judicial response to cases concerning the rights of lesbians and gay
men – decisions and the language used in the ruling – has a profound
impact on social perceptions. Bruce MacDougall sifts through hun-
dreds of reported and unreported cases of the past four decades in
order to uncover the subjective assumptions and biases operating in
the courts. In his examination of issues including gay bashing, homosexuality and the school system, outing, and pornography, the author
exposes the insidiousness of homophobia in society. MacDougall also
assesses the impact individual judges have on Canadian society.

This study examines the rhetoric of judicial expression in connection
with a vast array of material on the subject of homosexuality. Mac-
Dougall's style is refreshingly conversational, and *Queer Judgments*,
with its critical perspective, celebrates the reforms that have been
achieved and suggests strategies for social change.

BRUCE MACDOUGALL is Associate Professor in the Faculty of Law at the
University of British Columbia.

BRUCE MACDOUGALL

QUEER JUDGMENTS
Homosexuality, Expression, and the Courts in Canada

UNIVERSITY OF TORONTO PRESS
Toronto Buffalo London

ISBN 0-8020-0951-4 (cloth)
ISBN 0-8020-7914-8 (paper)

Printed on acid-free paper

Canadian Cataloguing in Publication Data

MacDougall, Bruce, 1960–
    Queen judgements : homosexuality, expression and the courts in Canada

    Includes bibliographical references and index.
    ISBN 0-8020-0951-4 (bound)   ISBN 0-8020-7914-8 (pbk.)

    1. Homosexuality – Law and legislation – Canada.   2. Gays – Legal
status, laws, etc. – Canada.   3. Judicial process – Canada.   I. Title.

    KE4399.M32 1999   349.71′086′64   C99-931833-0
    KF4483.C576M32 1999

This book has been published with the help of a grant from the Humanities
and Social Sciences Federation of Canada, using funds provided by the
Social Sciences and Humanities Research Council of Canada.

The University of Toronto Press acknowledges the financial assistance to its
publishing program of the Canada Council for the Arts and the Ontario
Arts Council.

We acknowledge the financial support of the Government of Canada
through the Book Publishing Industry Development Program (BPIDP) for
our publishing activities.
Canadä

A Berardino Domenico Brancatini

Contents

Acknowledgments

I am grateful to a number of people for their support, criticisms, and ideas while I was working on this book. At the risk of omitting someone, I particularly want to thank Robert Wintemute, Don Casswell, Brad Anderson, Brad Bemis, Sean Carley, Paul Clarke, Keith Farquhar, Bill Flanagan, Sheena Fleming, Jack Forbes, Simon Fothergill, Andrei Godoroja, Isabel Grant, Victor Janoff, Louise Langevin, Mark Lawson, Rod Macdonald, Wayne Morgan, Philip Moxlow, Shannon O'Byrne, Jonathan Oliphant, Brian Parsons, Bob Paterson, Walter Quan, Doug Sanders, Quentin Spetifore, Doug Stollery, Almut Suerbaum, and Ross Waring. I also want to thank the approximately three hundred students at UBC Law School who have taken my Sexuality and Law course for their challenges and input. Allyson May has been a superb copyeditor and I thank her. My partner, Gustavo Febres-López, was there to provide special encouragement.

Two of the chapters in this book appear in shorter and earlier forms. Chapter 3 is an elaboration on an article entitled 'Silence in the Classroom: Limits on Homosexual Expression and Visibility in Education and the Privileging of Homophobic Religious Ideology,' which appeared in *Saskatchewan Law Review* 61 (1998), 41. Chapter 5 is an expanded and updated version of my article entitled 'Outing: The Law Reacts to Speech about Homosexuality,' *Queen's Law Journal* 21 (1995), 79. Those journals have kindly consented to modified versions of the articles appearing as chapters in this book.

BRUCE MACDOUGALL

QUEER JUDGMENTS:
HOMOSEXUALITY, EXPRESSION,
AND THE COURTS IN CANADA

Introduction

This book is concerned with expression of and about homosexuality and how the courts have been implicated in that expression. Its subject is the way in which judges in Canada, particularly in the period 1960 to mid-1997, have constructed homosexuals and homosexuality and how they have betrayed their assumptions about both in their decisions. It also examines the courts' reaction to the expression of others about homosexuality, in particular, their reaction to homophobic expression and instances of outing. Such reaction is as revealing of judicial attitudes, as is the courts' direct expression of opinion.

Queer Judgments is not about the 'black-letter' law on homosexuality or anything else. Its focus is not on decisions the courts have made in cases relating to homosexuality; it is not about *ratios*. If it were, the news would be reasonably good. In cases that are squarely about homosexual rights, Canadian courts have on the whole established quite good track records in recent years. Canadian law and especially the Canadian judiciary are considered to have had a positive influence in the achievement of equality for homosexuals. Without doubt, the legal lot of gays and lesbians has improved in the past four decades. The judiciary has read sexual orientation into section 15 of the Charter, although some judges have been reluctant to do so. In perhaps a typically Canadian manner this protection was confirmed by the majority of the Supreme Court of Canada not in ringing tones but somewhat grudgingly, in a case in which the court also recognized that Parliament could discriminate against gays and lesbians in any event.[1] Thus while there was no cause for great celebration, at the end of the day, protection was confirmed in principle. Furthermore, many other courts have taken steps to ensure benefits to same-sex couples and to ban discrimination at the private level whenever possible.

At the same time the legislatures of most jurisdictions have added sexual orientation to the protections offered by the various human rights statutes. True, this protection has not been extended across the board, but those jurisdictions that do not offer such protection have become the oddities, rather than the other way around. And while the protection granted is subject to many exceptions, that is equally the case for the other protections provided in human rights legislation. It has become the 'done thing' to acknowledge equality for gays and lesbians, even if its implementation is not always wholehearted. Despite these legislative changes, however, most of the initiative towards the implementation of equality for homosexuals has come from the judiciary. There is a popular idea that the courts are the preferred agents of change over the legislature, which is capricious and prone to pander to hateful tendencies in the public at large. It is to the courts, then, that it is now customary to look for guarantees of equality.[2]

Despite the progress made, the marginalization and inferiorization of homosexuals and homosexuality continues, not only in society generally and in legislative bodies, but also at the court level. Homosexuality is still very much 'other' in the eyes of judges. The focus of this book, then, is not so much on the good news, but the bad news that circumscribes it. Judges continue to treat homosexuals as different from heterosexuals, not equivalent to heterosexuals, and sometimes as a threat to heterosexuality. The tenacity of stereotypes and assumptions about homosexuals and homosexuality among the judiciary exists in large part because judges do not pause to examine what these attitudes are or how messages are sent in the manner of their expression as well as in the ultimate decisions taken. The casualness of judicial expression is at least as much at fault in the perpetuation of negative assumptions about homosexuals and homosexuality as any intentional disparagement.

The language that judges have used to achieve some of the advances for gays and lesbians is not conducive to an atmosphere of real equality. Gays and lesbians continue to be other – they are the objects of the law and not at the heart of the law's concern. Homosexuals are always knocking at the door of a heterosexual court asking for its benevolence. In many instances, it is true, support has been forthcoming. The judiciary itself, however, is definitely *not* part of the homosexual community. Criminals are similarly the object of the law's attention but the judicial community is decidedly not constructed as part of the criminal community. They are mutually exclusive. The judiciary can do 'favours' for the criminal community but it is not (nor does not want to be) perceived as working in a sort of partnership with criminals for their mutual benefit. Compare this situation with, say, that involving the corporate community and the courts. Those two overlap; they work together; they need each other. The judiciary adjudicates issues involving the corporate community but would not think to pass value judgments on it or its members in a general way. That community is simply accepted as part of the core of society; no evidence is needed to prove its existence, its value, or its entitlement to respect or attention. Likewise, neither the heterosexual community nor the religious community are ever obliged to justify their existence or value. They are simply accepted. My concern is that the courts ensure the equality of homosexuals and homosexuality in such a way that it does not appear to be a favour or a concession to homosexuals.

In this book, my focus is on the role judges play in making decisions, and, in particular, in expressing the reasons for their decisions. I do not believe that judicial change is irrelevant or unimportant absent a change at the legislative level. Judicial decisions and attitudes matter; the bench is a crucial part of any movement towards equal treatment for homosexuals and homosexuality. Judges are not alone, of course, in formulating the law. As Robert Martin argues: 'While the judiciary bears primary responsibility for ensuring that justice is seen to be done, the bar, the academy, and the mass media all play supporting roles in the great ideological drama that is the legal system.'[3] The legislatures and the bureaucracy are of course important components of the legal system, but in this study I concentrate on the judiciary. The reader, I trust, will be alive to the fact that judicial attitudes and expression grow out of and are manifestations of more general social and legal attitudes and expression, which I leave to others to explore.[4] While this book examines judicial manifestation of legal attitudes towards homosexuals and homosexuality, I do not address in any detailed way its more broadly social and political causes. I argue that judicial attitudes can change, accepting that judges are not primarily at 'fault' for the development of those attitudes. I expect, therefore, a great deal from judges. While judges by no means embody the entirety of those involved in the law, they are its primary mouthpiece. Judicial expression influences the attitudes of the public, legislators, bureaucrats, and other judges.[5] The judge, by virtue of his or her position, has greater authority than, for instance, a bureaucrat who is also in theory impartial and may similarly be charged with setting standards. John Bell comments:

> The *enunciation of public standards* is not confined to the task of determining rules for the future, but may have an important place in authoritative exposition of the law during the course of the judicial task. 'Lectures' given to miscreant criminals or in the findings of civil wrongs are addressed not merely to the persons affected, but to the public as a whole. From the charge to the Assize jury onwards, the judge's authority as a state officer has put him in a position to deliver statements about conduct on behalf of society. As a spokesman for the community, he purports to propound its requirements for particular situations. Some bureaucrats, such as trading standards or environmental health officers, may exercise similar authority with regard to particular sections of the community. With them, the judge shares an official position, but his authority is also based on the functions performed in other tasks and the impartiality associated with them.[6]

The influence of judicial expression can be internal as well. A judge's attitudes towards a particular subject in one context must influence the way in which he or she will treat the subject in another context. Thus, judicial speech generally about homosexuality will influence or at least provide a good indication of how a court will react to the speech of others about homosexuality and homosexuals. Similarly, a judge who uses racist language can hardly be expected to be sympathetic to those who seek to overcome racism. If judges speak negatively of women, society can legitimize its hostility towards women and not expect strong judicial or other legal disapproval.

A court is not, of course, merely a neutral sounding board or the provider of a level playing field for litigants and resolving disputes with justice.[7] A court and the law it dispenses provide a standard for social conduct. The judiciary is one of the great social agencies (perhaps *the* great agency) for determining right and wrong, for deciding what is good and what is bad, for approving and for disapproving. The courts are institutions based on principle, which distinguishes them from legislatures: 'Unlike a legislature, which is under no obligation to display any consistency in its decisions as to which grounds it includes in anti-discrimination legislation, and which is free to respond to political pressures on a purely *ad hoc* basis, a national court or international human rights tribunal should strive to provide a coherent, principled basis for finding that some grounds are prima facie prohibited and some are not.'[8]

Courts and judges are not, whatever they might desire, passive agents simply reflecting the law. Contrary to what Montesquieu maintain, a judge is not 'but the mouth which pronounces the words of the law.'[9] Judges have a political and social role.[10] A judge is part of an evolving process, called the law, which is shaped and moved forward as much or more by judges as by anyone else. The judiciary has an activist role, which can be intentional or unintentional.[11] In an intentional activist role a judge takes proactive measures that are not traditionally thought of as within the domain of the common law courts. For example, the court might 'read in' sexual orientation as a ground for nondiscrimination in a human rights statute,[12] or it might order 'bussing' to try to break historical, systematic racial segregation in schools.[13] In other cases the activist role might be much more traditional, in the granting of an order of specific performance or an injunction. The unintentional activism of the courts, however, is in many ways more interesting and powerful because it is not consciously prescriptive. This unintentional activist role includes how judges talk about, that is to say, construct, subject matter and, often absent any legislative direction to do so, pass judgment on the object of their speech. Expression in positive terms about something will send a positive message about that thing to the rest of society. If a judge calls something beautiful, then it must be so.[14] If a judge describes something as abnormal then it must be so. That is the job of the judge: to put labels on things and people and concepts for the benefit of society.[15] The judge judges.

The law is all about words, in particular, labels. Judges sometimes explicitly recognize this fact. For example, in a Federal Court of Appeal case (1994) that turned on whether a provision in the Income Tax Act was discriminatory contrary to section 15 of the Charter, Hugessen JA said, in agreeing that it was: 'The appropriate description of the ground of discrimination to which separated custodial parents are subject would, it seems to me, be "family status." I consider it to be almost self-evident that such status has historically been, and is still, used as a basis for stereotyping. One has only to call to mind such traditional expressions as the "happily married man," "old maid," "gay" [Hugessen JA adds here the note, "In the traditional sense of that word"], "bachelor" or "merry widow" to find examples.'[16]

How a court says something is often as important as what it says.

The popular mythology of the law is that it consists of 'technicalities,' definitions, and designations. Judges are criticized for how they say something as often as for the actual decisions they make.[17] Judges should be 'judicious.'[18] Judges do not, therefore, have freedom of expression, at least while speaking from the bench.[19] While speaking from the bench, judges are not at liberty to state what they personally think the law or society should be unless such expression conforms with their constitutional role, including that of upholding the equality ideals of the Charter.[20] As some judges have acknowledged, a judge does not speak simply for him- or herself.[21] Mr Justice William A. Esson has written: 'I agree with those who say that judges should stay out of public debates and should accept narrow constraints on their freedom of speech. We all come to the bench as captives, in some degree, of our backgrounds. We all continue to have personal views and prejudices. That is unavoidable. But our duty is to do justice according to the law. That requires that we decide the cases before us without allowing our personal views to enter into the process of making decisions. We will be better able to do that if we refrain from publicly expressing personal views.'[22]

Part of the judicial exercise is, however, to recognize what those personal views are. A judge should determine what preconceptions he or she brings to bear in any situation. Having dealt with those 'personal' issues, the judge should then consider the social context of any given situation. Broader issues than just those of the litigants before the court must be considered. 'Wise judicial choicemaking must necessarily require the court to envisage in terms of *the whole community* all claims likely to be affected by the alternative precepts considered, and not only those of the parties immediately adversary.'[23] The judge speaks for the state and for society. Basic societal aspirations, including those in the constitution, are not inappropriate subjects for judicial expression. The converse is also true. As A. Wayne MacKay notes: 'A demand that judges refrain from sexist, racist or homophobic speech is not a call for "political correctness" but rather a call for conformity with the *Charter.*'[24] Such is the importance of the role of the judge that what a judge says and the way in which it is said can take on a significance, even a mythology, of its own. For example, the Privy Council decision in *Re Section 24, B.N.A. Act,*[25] the 'persons' case, has taken on a somewhat mythical dimension in Canada, the idea being that women were not thought of, for any purposes, as persons before this case.[26]

Freedom of expression is one of the most valuable freedoms recognized by society.[27] Many pressures are put on this freedom today, sometimes in the guise of reactionary rant about 'traditional' values, at other times in the form of what is sometimes called 'political correctness.' In many cases, however, freedom of expression can only be ensured when the judiciary is not too free in its own speech about any particular subject matter. The language of judges is rightly the subject of the highest scrutiny. There are many instances in which judges have been taken to task in the press for their choice of language.[28]

It is thus appropriate to examine how judges talk about homosexuality in order to determine the (perhaps unintentionally) activist role the judicial system plays in establishing the place in society that homosexuals are thought fit to occupy. It will be a much less significant development when courts make decisions in favour of gay and lesbian rights if the language in which those conclusions are expressed is filled with negative stereotypes and pejorative usage. If judicial language carries the implication that homosexuality is wrong and that homosexuals should stay in the closet, then it is little wonder that, for example, speech about who is a homosexual (i.e., 'outing') is fraught with apprehension. Can there truly be freedom of expression about homosexuality, the kind of liberty that outing demands, if judicial expression about homosexuality is rife with condemnation, marginalization, and inferiorization? Can judges really help tackle the problem of homophobic expression, as manifested in, for instance, a gay bashing, if such expression is not recognized as homophobic and instead viewed only as assault?

Judges ought to be aware of the difficulties of language and terminology in dealing with homosexual issues or with homosexuals. The courts must acknowledge both their own history of homophobic language and the continued existence in society at large of stereotypes about homosexuals. Judges must also be conscious of their position as role models. In Canada, legal issues relating to homosexuals and homosexuality can be situated in the context of the constitution, in particular, the Canadian Charter of Rights and Freedoms, which is interpreted to prohibit discrimination on the basis of sexual orientation.[29] The Charter prohibits discrimination on many bases, including race and sex. While there is no shortage of racists or misogynists in Canada, their views ought not be reflected in judicial speech; such speech would be an affront to the ideological aspirations of the Canadian state. Through its Charter of Rights and Freedoms, Canada has adopted a rights-based model for judges in deciding cases. Justice D.G.

Blair of the Ontario Court of Appeal has said: 'The *Charter* presents opportunities and challenges to the judicary as well as problems. Judges recognise that the *Charter* is a manifestation of the faith of the Canadian people in them. The people look to judges to defend and advance their rights and freedoms, both ancient and modern.'[30] Even when a case is not directly a Charter case, Charter values should have an influence in that a judge should not say or do in that case that which is contrary to the spirit of the Charter. Judges are charged with the responsibility of upholding the ideals of equality and inclusion and accommodation; they cannot simply throw up their hands in despair at not being able to right all the wrongs of the world. It is true, as La Forest J has said, that not all rights can be equally protected.[31] But the fact that not all can be righted in practice is no excuse for giving up the struggle.

Queer Judgments covers cases from a defined period. Given the remarkable consistency of attitudes and assumptions over that time, I assume that many of them will continue for some time in some form. Judges are, however, capable of changing their attitudes and of taking into account factors they have previously overlooked. I am an optimist with respect to what Canadian courts are capable of achieving. The fact that this book takes issue with how judges express themselves more than with the actual decisions they reach is the best evidence of what Canadian judges can and have achieved. To a large extent, I subscribe to what has been criticized as the 'progressive hypothesis' of Canadian law.[32] There is a great deal to be done and in all likelihood it will never be completely achieved. But this book is meant, despite its at times very critical tone, to indicate how much more is possible; it is not a polemic against using the courts to fight for equality and changes in attitudes. The book is descriptive, but often prescriptive as well.

In conducting my research I looked at all reported and unreported Canadian cases I could find from 1960 to mid-1997 (and a few before) that dealt with or referred to homosexuality or had some homosexual aspect, however minor, in their facts.[33] In all, I studied about eight hundred cases.[34] These cases were analyzed by asking questions such as: Does the case directly decide anything about homosexuals or homosexuality? What assumptions did the judge make about homosexuals or homosexuality? Were these assumptions based on any material before the court? What language did the judge use in dealing with homosexuals and homosexuality? In what way, if any, was homosexuality treated as 'other'? Were social attitudes to homosexuals and homosexuality considered and, if so, how were those social attitudes explained and were they considered to be of a particular period or somehow timeless? What attitudes about the judicial role are revealed in the treatment of homosexuals and homosexuality? How did homosexuality relate, in the judge's mind, to other aspects of the case before the court, including other aspects of a homosexual person? In some cases, my task was relatively easy because the court was quite explicit in stating what it thought or assumed. In other cases, a judge said little, but often that little was very revealing. Much of the most telling expression about homosexuality comes in cases where homosexuality is only a very incidental aspect of the case. Here, judicial assumptions or 'candid' responses to the expression of others about homosexuality are more evident than when homosexuality is centrally in issue.

I chose 1960 as a rough starting point because it allows for sufficient time to see any change in judicial attitudes and expression. Once the body of cases had been compiled, I examined the cases first in chronological order, and only later reassessed them in particular categories of subject matter, for example, gay bashing, custody, education. As I will discuss in Chapter 2, there has been a remarkable persistence of general judicial attitudes towards homosexuality, even if the details of those attitudes change. Beginning in 1960 allows for comprehension of cases decided when both the Bill of Rights and the Charter of Rights were in effect. It also covers the period when cases are better indexed: the researcher is consequently better able to decide whether the case has, in fact, a homosexual aspect. Finally, 1960 is the year in which I was born and thus it provides a very subjective significance to me, having been – from an essentialist view, at least – a homosexual since then. This is what judges have said and thought about me. The first of June 1997 was chosen as the endpoint for no particular reason, except that the bulk of the research was then complete. Some major (and minor) cases have since appeared, which have not been taken into account except in the conclusion. The problem with any law book, especially in areas as active as those covered here, is that it is never as up to date as the author would like. Where it is helpful to situate a case, I indicate the year of the court's decision in the text.

Occasionally, I mention a foreign (English or American) case but my focus is on what has happened in the Canadian legal culture in the last (almost) four decades. I am strongly of the view that there is a distinctive Canadian legal culture, part of a distinctive Canadian approach to socio-political problems. There are, however, relatively few French-language cases in this study. Those that were included are those cases in which judges said something deliberate about homosexuality or where equal treatment for homosexuals was squarely an issue before the court. The more casual references in French-language cases were usually excluded, because it is rather difficult to determine whether they have exactly the same significance as a seemingly equivalent casual remark in an English-language decision. There are limits to how much can legitimately be concluded from remarks made in two separate languages.

I emphasize again that *Queer Judgments* is not intended in any way to set out the black-letter law on any given topic. Other works do that.[35] I am not particularly concerned about specific *ratios* or whether a case was later followed, distinguished, or even overruled. Nor does the fact that a judge was dissenting or belonged to a lower level court make much difference to this study. Sometimes I concentrate on the language and reasons in a case that was overturned on appeal. On the whole, I treat the Canadian judiciary as a single unit. What each judge says, how he or she says it, and what attitudes are expressed are important. However, comments made by a Supreme Court of Canada judge obviously have a greater potential impact and consequently sometimes I deviate from my professed intention to treat judges equally. It is remarkable how generally consistent judicial expression about homosexuals and homosexuality is in the period I cover, wherever the judge is from, whatever the court, and whether the judge speaking is in the majority or the minority. As I mention in Chapter 1, however, it is extremely rare for a female judge to make negative assumptions about homosexuality. I did not attempt any other analysis of judges on the basis of, for instance, religion, ethnicity, or age.

The expression examined in this book is not judicial expression alone but expression about homosexuality generally, so long as there is a (potential) judicial response to it. That is to say, the book deals not just with judicial expression about homosexuals and homosexuality but also with judicial reaction to expression about homosexuals and homosexuality. As will be most obvious in Chapter 4, I have given the broadest possible interpretation to 'expression.' Expression can be words or action or deliberate silence or inactivity that is intended to convey a message. Exclusion of a group from a parade is as much expression as writing a letter to a newspaper urging such exclusion. The breadth of this definition is not without legal basis. The Supreme Court of Canada has lent its support to a broad interpretation of the idea of expression in section 2(b) of the Charter. In *Irwin Toy* (1989),

Dickson CJC, Lamer and Wilson JJ said: 'if the activity conveys or attempts to convey a meaning, it has expressive content.'[36]

On another definitional matter, some readers will be troubled by my use of the words 'homosexual' and 'homosexuality' instead of terms such as 'gay,' 'lesbian,' or 'queer,' which I use infrequently. The problem of terminology is dealt with in Chapter 1 and, to a lesser extent, in Chapter 5. 'Homosexual' and 'homosexuality' were preferred as less cumbersome than 'gay men, lesbians, and bisexuals'; they are also more common, at least in legal usage, than 'queer' and 'queerness,' though I have no 'problem' with those terms, which are in fact often the most effective.[37] Some writers have obvious difficulties with the use of 'homosexual' instead of 'lesbians and gay men,' since they take judges to task for such usage.[38] Don Casswell makes this comment in relation to the Supreme Court of Canada in *Egan*: 'Iacobucci J was the only justice who appeared comfortable using the words "lesbian" and "gay" to refer to lesbians and gay men. His Lordship's use of "homosexual," "lesbian," and "gay" reflected the current practice among many lesbians and gay men themselves. "Homosexual" was used as an adjective as, for example, in the expression "homosexual relationships," but when referring directly to lesbians and gay men, His Lordship used the nouns "lesbians" and "gays."'[39]

I am not sure that homosexuals use homosexual as an adjective any more than they use it as a noun. I prefer it here both as an adjective and a noun perhaps primarily because it has the advantage of being understood by everyone and used by no one on a day-to-day basis. It is generally unloved.[40] Also, the equivalent terms heterosexual and bisexual are available, which, especially in the case of heterosexual, are equally unused by people on a day-to-day basis.[41] For some, 'homosexual' has negative connotations as a word forced on homosexuals because 'gay' was unacceptable.[42] But many terms have been reclaimed from a negative origin. Another reason to choose 'homosexual' over 'gay and lesbian' is to avoid the real issue that I – obviously – have no personal experience with the lesbian perception of the issues discussed in this book. Sometimes a given situation might be the same for lesbians as for gay men. I am often not a good 'judge' of that, and some will no doubt be right in assigning or limiting some of the statements in this book to the gay male experience. At times I might be overly rash in assuming that the same situations or conclusions can apply equally to women as to men.[43]

There is, of course, a school of thought that lesbians should be separated from discussion of gay male sexuality.[44] It is true that lesbian theory generally tends to identify lesbians quite strongly with women as a whole, whereas gay theory decidedly does not identify gay men with men as a group. Much of the hostility for both arises from the threat that lesbians and gay men appear to pose to the position of men and women in the world, particularly to the privilege of males and the image of cohesiveness and self-importance in that group.[45] Gay men are reviled because they are perceived as having given up being men, or thought to be weak because they act in a 'womanly' way by submitting to other men.[46] Or, they are perceived as wanting other men, instead of women, to submit to them sexually. Lesbians are in a sense doubly estranged from the dominant because not only are they 'not-men' but they are perceived as 'not-needing-men' or, worse, 'wanting-to-be-men.' This perception of lesbianism might be used as a tool to try to separate lesbians from other women. The fusion of lesbian issues with women's issues generally may be valuable to prevent this divide-and-conquer approach. The nondifferentiation of lesbians from women may be important and positive because of the problem of 'lesbian baiting,' which Cynthia Petersen describes in a summary of Diana Majury's work as 'a common tactic used by men to inhibit solidarity between lesbian and non-lesbian women, to discredit feminist activists, and to silence women's discontent.'[47] Majury argues that there is a 'need to present and analyse lesbian discrimination as sex discrimination.'[48] Yet she concludes that, 'Strategically, it is probably not advisable to leave lesbian inequalties to be addressed exclusively through the prohibition of sex discrimination.'[49] What links both lesbians and gay men is the historic oppression by straight-male-dominated society and norms, including judicial and legal norms. Possible differences do not mean that the lesbian experience can never inform the gay male experience and vice versa. The positions of both are similar in many ways. In choosing the terms 'homosexual' and 'homosexuality' I can say with some confidence that they apply to male homosexuals and homosexuality, while they 'might' apply to lesbians and lesbianism. I often use 'homosexuals' and 'homosexuality' somewhat interchangeably because, as will become obvious, no distinction between being a homosexual and the phenomenon of homosexuality is usually made by the courts, homosexuals, or society in general. That said, I admit that the easy use of such terms (by me as by others) obscures the fact that these concepts are fairly recent and result from certain social processes, attitudes, and assumptions.[50]

Queer Judgments explores the issues of expression about homosexuals and homosexuality and judicial involvement in it in five contexts. In the first chapter, 'What's in a Name?,' I examine the problems of terminology in more detail and argue that the discussion of why homosexuals and homosexuality exist should be less important than a consideration of what follows from the application of such terms. The second chapter, 'Censoriousness and Censorship,' studies the way in which judges have participated in censoring homosexuals and homosexuality. Censorious attitudes towards homosexuals and homosexuality must affect the courts when they come to judge acts of censorship and the censoriousness of others. In the third chapter, 'Scholastic Silencing,' I examine how the silencing of homosexuals and homosexuality in academic settings, especially the schools, has been assisted by judicial silence on the subject. Religious traditions and prejudices are allowed to effect the separation of children from homosexuality, which is contrary to the inclusive-accommodative ideal of Canadian society. The fourth chapter, 'Homophobic Expression,' also looks at the way in which the judiciary responds to expression about homosexuals and homosexuality by others. In this chapter, I examine the multitude of forms homophobic expression takes. While the courts have been fairly good at responding to individual instances of homophobic expression such as, for example, instances of assault or a killing, they have generally failed to identify the homophobia that connects the various forms of expression. Judicial responses to 'outing' are explored in the fifth chapter, which, given the paucity of cases in this area, is more prescriptive than descriptive compared with the previous chapters. Judicial response in this instance is to expression about homosexuality that most often comes from homosexuals themselves, by way of identifying another as homosexual, and it is here, rather than in the context of homosexual issues in a scholastic setting, that the courts should remain silent.

1

What's in a Name?

Terminology and Contingency

Words and meaning are everything in the law. Lawyers have the reputation of being nitpickers and difficult conversationalists because of their obsession with precision (or, more usually, imprecision) in language. Terminology is always important, legally.[1] In dealing with the topic of expression in the legal context, terminology becomes particularly important. If a judge talks about homosexuality or homosexuals or gays or lesbians or sexual orientation, what does he or she mean? In this chapter, rather than attempting to provide anything approaching conclusive meanings, I want to explore the ambiguities and contingency of these terms. It is as important in legal contexts to recognize ambiguities in meaning as it is to provide precise definitions. Applying a particular word is not just a matter of deducing the appropriate label from a given state of affairs; the application of that word can also induce certain consequences or assumptions about what those consequences will be. If a judge uses the term 'homosexual,' he or she should be alive not only to the deductions made in deciding to apply it but also to the consequences that will or may follow from its application.

This chapter thus discusses labels and definitions, where they come from and how they are used. In the first part of this chapter, I describe the long common law tradition of discrimination against what we now call homosexuals and homosexuality and how this tradition forms the context for the particular period examined in this book. I also deal, to a limited extent, with how the 'homosexual' has been seen as 'other' than the judicial. The second part of the chapter examines how, despite the long-standing homophobic tradition in society, there is remarkable ambiguity with respect to what 'homosexual' and related terms mean. There has similarly been little legal exploration of what it means to use the term 'homosexual,' either as an adjective or as a noun. By way of avoiding the necessity of defining such terms, the law has preferred to restrict particular acts that are considered emblematic of homosexuals and homosexuality, rather than directly to restrict homosexuals and homosexuality themselves. This approach, however, raises the problem of the stereotypical association of homosexuals and homosexuality with those particular acts or characteristics. In the third part of the chapter I turn to the essentialist/constructionist debate of recent decades on the question of what, precisely, (a) homosexual is. After reviewing the debate I then study how judges have, unwittingly, taken a side in it. Judges often assume that there is some 'cause' to homosexuality and thus, might be called 'rudimentary constructionists.' For this reason, and given the unhappy legal history of homosexuals and homosexuality, it is sometimes argued that an essentialist approach to homosexuality is more helpful, legally. I suggest that while a consideration of the essentialist/constructionist debate might lead to some understanding of the social or even scientific causes for labelling, it results in the debate being sidetracked into a relatively unimportant issue, for legal purposes. What flows from the use of the term 'homosexual,' in particular what assumptions are made, what stereotypes are applied once the label is assigned, is much more significant. The application of stereotypes and the control of their content and use is the subject of the final section of the chapter. What follows from identification as 'homosexual' is the principal subject of this book and it should become clear that judges have been reasonably content to allow the consequences to be determined by stereotypes, on the whole negative and marginalizing stereotypes, the content of which has not been defined by homosexuals. In this chapter, then, I examine preliminary definitional issues in a legal context – the history of homophobia, what 'homosexual' means, and why the more important issue is not the 'why?' of homosexuality but the 'what then?'

History and Homophobia

Particularly in a legal context and most particularly in a precedent-based legal context, as is the common law system used in all Canadian jurisdictions but one,[2] the past is important. The law's current treatment of homosexuality and homosexuals is grounded in a long tradition of social (including legal) assumptions and attitudes. While this study looks only at judicial treatment, and that only within the period 1960 to 1997, it cannot be forgotten that this treatment is situated within a broader legal and social treatment and for a long period before 1960. Homophobia and heterosexism in society have deep historical roots, of which I will give but a few examples.[3] Often there has been a tension between a desire to regulate homosexual activity rigorously but at the same time not discuss such a loathsome subject. The examples to select from are numerous.[4] In 1562,[5] an earlier statute of Henry VIII[6] dealing with buggery was revived because 'since [the] repeal [of the statute by Mary] so had and made, divers evil disposed persons have been the more bold to commit the said most horrible and detestable vice of buggery, aforesaid, to the high displeasure of Almighty God.'[7] Sir Edward Coke called buggery 'a detestable, and abominable sin, amongst christians not to be named, committed by carnall knowledge against the ordinance of the Creator, and order of nature, by mankind with mankind, or with brute beast, or by womankind with bruite beast.'[8] He blamed the introduction of buggery on the Lombards, a wealthy class of bankers who were banished from England during the reign of Elizabeth. As Alex Gigeroff has noted, Coke spent more time on these offences than he did on rape.[9] Blackstone also employed a string of negative adjectives and phrases to describe sodomy. He called it a 'crime not fit to be named' – even though there was a statute that dealt with it.[10]

Blackstone and Coke were not alone. Homosexuality has often been referred to as the 'unspeakable vice,' the 'love that dare not speak its name,' or some other epithet.[11] This attitude towards homosexuality is ancient and is usually accompanied by a reference to sodomy.[12] It lingers in the way in which homosexuality is often never mentioned. People will ask 'Is she so?' or 'Is he?' followed by some gesture indicating queerness. Knowledge about homosexuality is based on assumptions; until very recently, it has not been discussed. The silencing of homosexuality has also taken more sinister form, in the killing of homosexuals. Many died in Nazi concentration camps, but homosexuals were the only group denied monetary compensation from the federal German government after the war and they are often excluded from commemorations of the Holocaust.[13] It is noteworthy that even the more positive treatments of homosexuality have involved secrecy. Thus, the sessions of the British Committee on Homosexual Offences and Prostitution that produced the Wolfenden Report in 1957[14] were all held in private, because it was thought that that was the only way that people could speak freely.[15]

The silencing of homosexuality is deemed suitable in part because homosexuals have long been thought to undermine society. Homosexuals are charged with threatening society's very existence by their refusal to procreate and with wanting to convert people (especially children) from normalcy. It is not surprising that 'sodomy' is derived from the name of a society that, according to myth, was destroyed. 'Buggery' is derived from a reference to an eleventh-century 'Bulgarian' sect that practised heresy and to whom 'abominable practices' were ascribed.[16] The accusation that homosexuals are prone to convert and subvert is strange, given that homosexuals have never been in a socially dominant position, certainly not in a position to determine general attitudes about themselves. As Robert Wintemute says, the gay, lesbian, and bisexual minority 'is a minority in every country in the world, unlike particular racial or religious minorities, which are usually the majority in at least one country. This may reduce the potential for empathy on the part of the heterosexual majority, who cannot imagine the tables being turned.'[17]

The historical meanings and effects of the label 'homosexual' and its equivalents are important for purposes of recognizing the deep-rooted obstacles to the achievement of equality for those or that to whom or which the label was affixed.[18] As social constructionists tell us, it is misleading, in a certain sense, to talk about the 'historical' treatment of homosexuality (and especially 'homosexuals') outside of the past one hundred years or so. Even within that period meaning has changed drastically. On the other hand, history is simply a perception of the past and the interpretation for the present of what we regard as important. What may not have seemed terribly significant or unusual (or usual) at any given time can subsequently assume importance, as much for what it is taken to represent as for what it actually was, assuming that can be determined. Thus, early Europeans might have had no consciousness of being part of a nation or have thought nationhood insignificant, to the extent that they had a very abbreviated vocabulary to describe what we would call nationalism. But in the nineteenth and twentieth centuries 'historical events' took on profound significance as nationalism was constructed. The same is true of much modern thinking about race or gender. History is continually reinterpreted to make the past relate to today and to be defined in today's terms. This process applies equally to sexuality and sexual orientation. The ancient Greeks, in what is regarded by some male homosexuals as a golden era, would have been confused and probably alienated by today's 'gay' cultures,[19] but that does not mean that they cannot be interpreted as homosexuals or that events or attitudes in and of that period cannot be said to involve homosexuality.[20] It is acceptable, therefore, to look at homosexuals and homosexuality in history, to impose current analysis on past events and attitudes. This includes analysis of what judges said and the courts did in the past, especially where the common law maintains the idea of a continuous common law. I will not attempt anything so sweeping as an analysis back to the Greeks or even Blackstone, however; in this book, the past extends back only some forty years, but the longevity of homophobia in legal history should be remembered. As Gary Kinsman says: 'Examining historical experiences and practices can help us understand from where lesbian and gay oppression and, more generally, oppressive sexual regulation has come, where it may be going, and the possibilities for transformation.'[21]

Historically, the effect of the label 'homosexual' and its related terms has been, as social constructionists would have it, to render the activity or the people to whom the label is applied beyond the pale of acceptability. The use of the label homosexual and its various historical and modern equivalents has been, for the most part, an exercise in marginalization.[22] The opprobrium attached to homosexuality has been called 'homophobia.'[23] Few writers today, aside from those at the unthinking fringe, actually attempt to devise a coherent theory justifying, in a sense, homophobia, as John Finnis has done.[24] Finnis would agree that while the details of implementation have changed, the general public policy of disparaging homosexuality and homosexual acts remains: 'The standard modern position differs from the position which it replaced, which made adult consensual sodomy and like acts crimes per se. States which adhere to the standard modern position make it clear by laws and policies such as I have referred to that the state has by no means renounced its legitimate concern with public morality and the education of children and young people towards truly worthwhile and against alluring but bad forms of conduct and life. Nor have such states renounced the judgment that a life involving homosexual conduct is bad even for anyone unfortunate enough to have innate or quasi-innate homosexual inclinations.'[25] Finnis's assessment embodies much of the historical and modern judicial attitude. There is often, at best, a pitying of homosexuals and homosexuality. Homosexuality is associated with that which is not worthwhile, and condescension towards it is palpable. Homosexual conduct is 'bad'; homosexuals are 'unfortunate'; homosexuality is an issue of 'public morality' and something to be kept from children and young people.

Homophobia takes many forms and like all forms of judgmentalism, is not always easily recognized for what it is. The more obvious forms – gay bashing, for example – are difficult to mistake. However, more muted and more commonplace distinctions based on sexual orientation can also fall within this category. Homophobia is a result in part of the invisibility of homosexuals. It is a natural result of the silencing of homosexuality, which reinforces stereotypes rather than producing knowledge about homosexuality and homosexuals.

This historical cycle of silence and assumptions can be broken only by expression and engagement. Gregory Herek argues that contact with homosexuals is the way to reduce prejudice, but not every kind of interaction will have that effect. According to Herek, to lessen hostility towards homosexuals it is important that: 1) the contact experience be intimate and ongoing rather than superficial and momentary; 2) the contact involve people who share many beliefs and values aside from those concerning sexuality; and 3) the contact occur under conditions that foster cooperation and shared goals rather than competition.[26]

In the judicial context, the persistence of prejudice plays out in part as a judicial distancing of itself from homosexuality. Homosexuality is 'other' and something that has always been judged. The judiciary never gets to 'know' homosexuals in the way Herek suggests is important. Historically a homosocial institution itself, the judiciary has reflected the irrational fears of homosexuals and homosexuality that other homosocial organizations still evince.[27] Extremely few judges are identified by themselves (or others) as gay.[28] Would they be accepted?

The judiciary, having excluded homosexuals like sports teams regularly (think they) do, not surprisingly sometimes uses only slightly more elegant speech about homosexuals than might be heard in the locker room. If the judiciary were to be open to and about homosexuality within its own ranks, its speech and attitudes would change.[29] Can one imagine a judge who was openly gay or lesbian requiring proof of the normalcy of homosexuality, as was required in the *Knodel* case (1991)?[30] Would a judge question the maleness of a male homosexual (1976) if that judge's colleague was openly gay?[31] It is inconceivable that an openly gay or lesbian judge would speak of an 'abnormal desire to indulge in homosexual practices' (1957).[32] Curiously, as far as I can tell, female judges have not made any of the negative comments that form the subject of this book. In part, of course, this owes to the comparative scarcity of women in the judiciary, but some of the most sensitive reasons have been given by female judges.[33] Awareness of their own group's treatment by (male) judges in the past may make female judges more sensitive to the language used to describe and attitudes towards other historically disadvantaged groups, like homosexuals.[34]

What Is (a) Homosexual?

What do the terms homosexual and homosexuality – and terms like them – mean? In this section, I do not attempt to arrive at any definitive conclusions; I want merely to problematize something that the courts and others often simply assume to be straightforward: the language that forms the basis for the subject matter of this book.

It is easy to operate in absolutes, to prefer black-and-white analysis and to unthinkingly categorize the world as us and them, heterosexual and homosexual.[35] Many people do this without either defining those terms or considering a middle position. Such polarization pervades much thought in this area.[36] Eve Sedgwick writes: 'many of the major modes of thought and knowledge in twentieth-century Western culture as a whole are structured – indeed, fractured – by a chronic, now endemic crisis of homo/heterosexual definition, indicatively male, dating from the end of the nineteenth century.'[37] It is out of this insistence on either/or that the definitional difficulties of homosexuality arise. Human activity and desire are so diverse that they cannot really be slotted into one of two pigeonholes. Opening up the choices, to include, say, bisexuality, does not provide much help because there are then still only three choices for the whole of human experience. In fact, of course, the homo/heterosexual categorization historically is not so much an effort towards proper labelling as it is a generalized two-tier ranking. It is not meant to provide a sensitive assessment of a person so much as a blunt assessment of whether that person is 'one of us' or 'one of them.' The person has to be one or the other, normal or abnormal, acceptable or unacceptable.

Accepting, nonetheless, as the law does, that there is a category of 'homosexual,' the opposite or other of 'heterosexual,' what does it mean to say somebody is (a) homosexual (or gay or lesbian)? Despite a long tradition of homophobia and homophobic expression there has been little in the way of an exploration (especially among the judiciary) about what the terms used in this context actually mean. The term 'homosexual,' coined in 1869, has never had one meaning.[38] It is often thought of as describing a person who is not heterosexual, but heterosexuality is defined by reference to homosexuality, which is the earlier term.[39] Quite apart from the definitional tension with heterosexuality, homosexuality has internal definitional issues. The words 'homosexual,' 'gay,' 'lesbian,' 'queer,' and so on have slightly different meanings.[40] As I mentioned in the Introduction, some writers have noted with satisfaction the use by judges of words like 'gay' instead of 'homosexual.' Obviously to them such differentiation in terminology is significant. For the purposes of simplification, however, I have chosen generally to use the term 'homosexual' in this book, admittedly giving the term a breadth and modernity it has really never had.

All we can say with certainty is that 'homosexual' is a contingent concept.[41] Many explanations and definitions have been proffered, none of them particularly satisfying, as their authors would probably be the first to recognize. Forbidden or problematical sex[42] with or desire for a person of the same gender is usually part of the concept of homosexuality. For a long time, homosexuality and prostitution were seen as 'products of undifferentiated male lust.'[43] The Wolfenden Committee was thus set up to examine both.[44] Although its assumptions and recommendations look particularly dated, the committee did have a surprisingly progressive grasp of certain issues. For example, it easily disposed of the idea that there was some significant difference between what Richard Posner has recently (and anachronistically) called 'real homosexuals' versus 'opportunistic homosexuals.'[45] The Wolfenden Report thought such a distinction, at least for legal purposes, unhelpful; a distinction between the 'invert' and the 'pervert' was not 'very useful.' Such a distinction 'suggests that it is possible to distinguish between two men who commit the same offences, the one as the result of his constitution, the other from a perverse and deliberate choice, with the further suggestion that the former is in some sense less culpable than the latter.'[46] The committee doubted the validity of such a distinction. Still associated with the phenomenon of homosexuality, however, is the idea of 'culpability' and a link with the forbidden and even the criminal.

The law has tacitly recognized the difficulty of defining homosexuality, and especially of identifying 'a homosexual,' by historically avoiding overt regulation of homosexuality and homosexuals per se. It has been far easier to regulate sodomy, sexual touching, cunniligus, and so on when the law wishes to define or marginalize or punish homosexuals. Society may not approve of gays or lesbians, but it is much easier to define and condemn them by proscribing their supposed activities rather than their status. This is a relatively common approach. If we want to marginalize or regulate Sikhs, we do not exclude them; we ban turbans. If we do not like Central Americans, we ban 'loitering' in public places; if we do not like teenagers, we ban skateboarding or loud music. True, not all Sikhs wear turbans, not all Central Americans like to socialize out of doors, and not all teens are loud, but these are accepted stereotypes or constructions and by regulating these activities the whole group can be seen to be put in its place. A woman who considers herself a Sikh is inferiorized by a ban on turbans, even though she does not wear a turban. Similarly, while not all gay men engage in sodomy, and perhaps many homosexuals might not have sex at all, the stereotype is that gays and lesbians have sex as often as possible and with as many different partners as possible. Thus society can attack gays and lesbians by restricting their sexual activities and assumes that it need not define gay or lesbian any further.

Various acts thus become emblematic of hetero- or homosexuality. That so much could turn legally on the fact that a man has anal intercourse with his wife as opposed to another man says a great deal about the capacity of humans to make a lot turn on very little. The ability to find all sorts of rationales as to why this distinction is significant while others are not is a testament to human mental agility. It is truly remarkable that defenders of the distinction can resort to a dubious prohibition in the Bible, written thousands of years ago, while blithely ignoring other 'killjoy' prohibitions in the same book. Furthermore, this obsession with particular acts has meant that the acts are not thought to have a value in their own right. Masturbation, vaginal intercourse, caressing a breast, all must have some other meaning in order to give them value. As Jeffrey Weeks says: 'Our culture has all too readily justified erotic activity by reference to something else – reproduction or the cementing of relationships usually – and has ignored the appeal of the erotic as a site of freedom, joy and pleasure.'[47] One man touching another man's penis is not just engagement in pleasurable activity – he is in danger of becoming (or being) 'a homosexual.'[48]

Homosexuality, however, is generally agreed to go beyond a particular sex act. It is now thought of as a type of sexual orientation and a person with that orientation is described as 'homosexual' and usually 'a homosexual.' Robert Wintemute has usefully identified four ways of looking at sexual orientation: 'Any statement that a specific person is heterosexual, bisexual, gay, or lesbian could refer to (a) the direction of the person's attraction, (b) the direction of their conduct (taken as a whole), (c) the direction of a specific instance of their conduct, or (d) their 'identity' (i.e. whether they consider that the direction of their emotional-sexual attraction or conduct serves in part to define them both as a unique individual and as part of a group or community of similar individuals).'[49] The range of choice of definition makes the legal handling of the terms difficult. Nonetheless, the issue of whether somebody is correctly called homosexual often comes back to the emblematic importance of acts. Are acts necessary and, if so, what acts?

Although the law, in Canada at least, has sought to avoid a definition of homosexuality beyond making particular acts unlawful or illegitimate, homosexuality and the homosexual have played significant parts in the judicial imagination. As will become evident, the courts have, especially in criminal and family contexts, come across people and situations rightly or wrongly labelled 'homosexual.' And they have been forced to deal with more than just specific inferiorized acts. More recently, human rights legislation has made the concept of 'sexual orientation' important. Far from simplifying matters, this new term has rendered the definitional problems for judges more complex. Is attraction alone not enough to make a person homosexual (or heterosexual)? People can be attracted to many people without ever acting to manifest the attraction.[50] Some religions would have us distinguish between having homosexual feelings and acting on those feelings, the second being a graver problem or sin than the former.[51] Is only the actor really 'gay' or 'lesbian,' that is, 'bad'? Is it possible to distinguish between a homosexual status, which of itself is unfortunate or, at best, neutral, and a homosexual activity, which should be discouraged? Finnis assumes the position that it is all right to be homosexual, but not to engage in homosexual acts: 'The phrase "sexual orientation" is radically equivocal. Particularly as used by promoters of "gay rights," the phrase ambiguously assimilates two things which the standard modern position carefully distinguishes: (I) a psychological or psychosomatic disposition inwardly orienting one *towards* homosexual activity; (II) the deliberate decision so to orient one's public *behavior* as to express or *manifest* one's active interest in and endorsement of homosexual *conduct* and/or forms of life which presumptively involve such conduct.'[52]

Since Finnis is an apologist for the orthodoxy of the present conservative Roman Catholic Church, his position is not surprising. He goes on to say, in a somewhat shocked tone: '... "gay rights" movements interpret the phrase as extending full legal protection to *public* activities intended specifically to promote, procure and facilitate homosexual *conduct*.'[53] Finnis would argue that mere attraction is sufficient to make a person 'homosexual,' but he categorizes good and bad homosexuals, the former not acting on their attractions. This refusal to recognize that respect for sexual orientation must be interpreted to include deeds as well as desires is quite common in the judgments discussed below. The double standards this constructs are usually passed over. It is unlikely that Finnis would say that the law should respect his right to orient towards Catholicism but not protect a manifestation of his Catholicism. If there is legal respect for religious beliefs, then, except where it directly adversely affects an unwilling other, implementation as well as inclination must be respected. Sexual orientation, however, is thought to be less benign than religion and more than suitable for regulation similar to that provided to check the behaviour of criminals. We would probably attempt not to prevent or control a 'criminal mind' but only criminal acts. In such situations, the status is regarded with pity at best and identification of a person as having that status is somehow impolite or even offensive. The act, however, must be controlled rigorously, even using publicity as discouragement.

The acceptance of a valid distinction between sexual orientation and sexual activity seems to be common,[54] but there is rarely any analysis (especially logical analysis) of why this should be so. Is the person who lives solely with fantasy and dreams of persons of the same sex any less of a threat to society – that is, any less 'gay' – than someone who regularly engages in sexual activity with a person of the same sex? If what is required to be beyond the pale is actual physical sex with someone of the same sex, what constitutes sex? If Joseph kisses a man or hugs him a moment too long, is this sex? The question of what constitutes a homosexual act was raised in *Gaveronski v. Gaveronski* (1974),[55] where Mrs Gaveronski and a Mrs F caressed each other's breasts. The court said that sometimes a 'friendly caress of the bosom of one female by another may not be homosexual,' but in this case it was. Can we call Mrs F a lesbian because she once caressed another woman's breasts? If having sex even once with a person of the same sex makes both people involved homosexual then it might not be all that 'abnormal.' The courts do, however, continue to invest a 'homosexual' action with considerable importance. Outside of human rights cases, judges only use the word 'homosexual' to describe someone who has done an act that is thought to be reprehensible, or at least open to a negative interpretation.

Whether homosexuality relates to sexual attraction, sexual action, or both, it is sometimes given an absoluteness it cannot bear. It is, in fact, inaccurate to say that Adam is attracted to males or Mary is attracted to females. Adam will not be attracted to most males. Mary will be attracted to individuals with many characteristics, one of which is that that individual is female. Furthermore, once the label 'homosexual' or 'lesbian' or such like is applied, the people within those categories cannot be treated as a monolith. Surely there are differences between a First Nations homosexual and an Asian-Canadian homosexual, for example. Their experiences – even as 'homosexuals' – must be dissimilar. The most significant division is arguably that between male and female homosexuals. The distinction between gay men and lesbians ought not be forgotten, because the effect of the labelling can be quite different.[56] Gay men have historically (if I can treat them as a historical continuity for a moment) been treated as analogous to women, and many of the terms for gay men are derived from pejorative terms for women.[57] The status of gay men is somewhat akin to that (historically) of women. Lesbians, already women, are considered to be further debased. Their position is inferior to that of women generally. The division between heterosexual and homosexual can also be seen as a very male division in that it focuses to a considerable extent on a particular set of sexual acts, largely centred on the penis, to determine whether a person is one or the other. Lesbians were for a long time beyond the reach of the law because it was thought that they did not have the necessary anatomy to do anything. Doing was much more significant than thinking or feeling. Similarly celibate priests were not categorized because of the myth that they did not use their penises and therefore were not sexual at all. However the conclusion is reached, we know that some people are or define themselves as homosexual. That should be sufficient to raise the concern that, by virtue of this labelling, these people are not treated with inequality. There is, however, a strange obsession with and an alarming amount of energy spent on trying to determine how many people are homosexual.[58] The idea seems to be that the more numerous homosexuals are, the more deserving they are of equality, which fits in neatly with the beliefs of those who are convinced that the law is designed to protect majoritarian interests. It also perhaps accounts for the liveliness of the debate over what makes a person 'homosexual.' Some are motivated to maximize the numbers while others have the opposite motivation.[59] This is of course a travesty of the justice and fairness principles of the law, according to which it should not matter whether there are 100 or 100,000 Sikhs, seventy-five-year olds, or homosexuals. Given the difficulty of defining 'homosexual,' the numbers game becomes permanently inconclusive. Apart from justifying equality the other purpose of the numbers game is to establish a sense of security as a community. Although it is important for legal institutions to help create security for homosexuals, the courts should not do this by perpetuating the myth that, somehow, the more numerous a group is the more secure it can be in its legal protection.

What about heterosexuality? While enormous amounts of time and ink have been spent studying the origins, meanings, and implications of homosexuality, the concept of heterosexuality is seldom examined.[60] It remains unstated or appears as an afterthought. For something that is the norm, heterosexuality is very little defined.[61] One of its privileges is not to be thought of as requiring close examination. Homosexuality is problematized, glamorized, demonized, fetishized, but heterosexuality is left uninvestigated. Gays and lesbians might well be concerned that we have to deconstruct homosexuality but never heterosexuality. Where homosexual identity has to be scrutinized, the dominant one is not questioned. As Jan Schippers says: 'Many people fear constructionism will be applied to homosexuality only, leaving the construct of *heterosexuality* unchallenged. In this way it could take away the long-fought-for security a supportive gay subculture provides.'[62] 'Why?' is frequently asked about homosexuality and never about heterosexuality. On the other hand, the consequences – the 'what then?' – of heterosexuality are treated much differently from those of homosexuality. The consequences of heterosexuality are never predictable, never generalized; heterosexuality leaves open a myriad of possibility. The consequences of homosexuality are, however, on the whole left to stereotypes. While the causes of homosexuality are the subject of exhaustive study, the consequences are usually left to assumptions and generalizations. Care is taken to ensure that the right acts have occurred before the label 'homosexual' is applied to a person or a situation, but little time is spent assessing the effects of that label.

The ambiguity involved in all these questions reflects debates that are going on within the homosexual community itself. There has been considerable discussion over the past couple of decades about whether 'homosexual' is an essential characteristic or a constructed one. Implicated in that debate are many other issues, such as assimilation, gender identity, lesbian versus gay male interests, race and ethnic and 'multiple oppression' issues. Once identified as 'homosexual,' how should a person behave? What is expected of him or her? I cannot even try to address or resolve those issues in their general context here, but I want to suggest that the judiciary should at least be more alive to their existence in the context of cases that come to court and not assume a certainty or exactitude or inevitability that simply does not exist. The questions and complexities raised above have judicial and legal ramifications. That does not mean, however, that there can be no legal resolution of cases involving these questions. I am certainly not suggesting that, in problematizing terms such as 'homosexual,' 'gay,' and 'sexual orientation,' judges are prevented from making decisions or investing meaning in terms. Some courts are quite capable of recognizing the imprecision of terms such as 'sexual orientation' but do not let that imprecision prevent them from reaching a fair decision. In one case of hate propaganda (1996),[63] for example, the applicants argued that 'sexual orientation' was too broad a category to be the basis of a prohibition on hate expression. Joyal J noted that counsel for the applicants argued that the expression covered all forms of sexual activity. These activities might not include only those in which adult gays and lesbians were engaged, but paedophilia, incest, date rape, bestiality, and other forms of sexual behaviour as well. Joyal J rejected the idea that the inclusion of 'sexual orientation' in the definition of discrimination was tantamount to legitimizing or legally protecting acts of paedophilia or bestiality. He said, instead, that 'sexual orientation' was 'a precise legal concept as it deals specifically with an individual's preference in terms of *gender.*'[64] It is no more possible to give an exhaustive list of what is included in sexual orientation than in, say, 'religion.' The judge recognized that while there might be grey areas in a definition, they should not be allowed to trigger judicial paralysis. It is curious that those who raise the spectre of sexual orientation as undefinable, as encompassing all sorts of nasty phenomena and beliefs – and therefore of no legal use for ensuring rights protection – have no difficulty accepting that religion can be a protected category, even though one or two religions might espouse truly despicable views. Sexual orientation, homosexuality, and the like are no more contingent terms than many others. At the same time, however, a court should not make casual assumptions about them, especially when those assumptions are based largely on historical stereotypes.

These issues of what a homosexual is, what constitutes a sexual orientation and how many lesbians there might be are all questions that go to the 'cause' of homosexuality. As I have argued, too much attention is placed on the questions of why homosexuality or homosexuals exist and how they come into existence, at the expense of considering what happens once their existence is determined or assumed. The biggest problem that has faced homosexuals in the legal context has not been so much one of labelling but of the stereotypes attached to the label. Why somebody is called a homosexual is not as important as what it means practically to be called a homosexual. Judges should, of course, consider their choice of labels and the implications of the label chosen; a judge who simply uses a 'loaded term' without thinking about the ramifications of the choice of label acts recklessly. But, rather than avoiding a particular label, he or she should consider whether it is possible to change an unfair meaning or stereotype associated with it. In the context of a child custody case, for example, where one parent is arguing that the other should not have custody on the basis that he is 'gay,' the judge should consider, before automatically adopting the term, a number of things. Is it in fact necessary to affix such a label? Why is it thought important to know anything about that quality in any event? What does it mean to say that a person is 'gay'? What assumptions, that is, stereotypes, might be made by the court or by others if the label is applied? There are many examples of situations in which judges have accepted that a person is 'homosexual' but given little thought to why that information is relevant or to their unthinking acceptance of certain stereotypes that follow from the application of the label. What, for example, does the choice of the following judicial language imply? '[The mother] does not flaunt her homosexuality,' or, 'She does not seem to be biased about Lynn's [the child's] sexual orientation and seems to assume that Lynn will be heterosexual' (1980).[65] 'Flaunt,' 'homosexuality,' 'sexual orientation,' 'biased,' and 'heterosexual' are what I call 'loaded terms' and although the judge might use them casually, such usage implies all sorts of assumed answers to the questions I have just posed. Only rarely does a judge challenge the stereotypes, that is, the consequent meanings, associated with those words.

The fluidity and contingency of meaning of terminology associated with homosexuals and homosexuality ought not to be an excuse for inactivity on the part of the courts. We cannot say that, absent clear terminology, there can be no clear legal response and therefore that no legal response should be made. If we cannot agree on the meaning of homosexuality or if it is impossible to define sexual orientation with exactitude, does that mean that it is legally impossible to take either into account? Of course not. The fluidity of meaning is the lifeblood of the law and gives rise to most of the matters barristers and therefore judges deal with. 'Homosexual' is no more contingent than race, religion, gender, disability, ethnicity, and so on. Like sexual orientation, these statuses have ambiguous meanings. They are simply grey areas, areas in which a judge should be cautious about terminology and especially cautious about the consequences flowing from the terminology.

Essentialism versus Constructionism

Undoubtedly the liveliest debate in recent decades about terminology as it relates to sexual orientation and homosexuality is the essentialist/constructionist debate.[66] That debate is now rightly seen as, on the whole, of limited use because it leaves so much unaccounted for. It is an academic rendition of the old debate that plays out on the street in the form of opinion as to whether people are 'born homosexual' or 'choose to be homosexual.' Why should it matter which is correct, so long as at the end of the day it is clear that at least some people are homosexual? Whether one is born black or chooses to be black, born Catholic or chooses to be Catholic has little practical relevance; the important thing is that people *are* black or Catholic and particular consequences flow from that identification. But homosexuality is thought to be more 'acceptable' if people are born that way. The person affected is not acting on a whim and should, therefore, somehow be excused. His or her homosexuality is more than a 'lifestyle' choice. Homosexuality cannot be 'wrong,' or at least not entirely wrong, if the homosexual was born that way. That the argument is even started, however, concedes to a certain extent the point that there is a right/wrong component to the question.

The essentialist and the constructionist both take on the question of why someone is homosexual, although in somewhat different forms. In its essentialist guise, the question is whether the person could be anything but homosexual; in its constructionist guise, the question is what factors lead to the conclusion that the person is homosexual. The selection of factors involves a choice. It is probably fair to say that more lesbians than gay men would say that there is an element of choice in their homosexuality; lesbians are more 'naturally' constructionists. More gay men than lesbians would argue that they are born that way. Gay men tend to be essentialists.[67] This potential source of division within the homosexual community can be avoided if the essentialist/ constructionist debate is put to one side as of little interest for legal purposes. The question of 'why' gets dangerously close to the issue of prevention as opposed to that of equal treatment.

Yet the causation of homosexuality has been taken up by the courts, sometimes obliquely, sometimes not. Why a person is homosexual is implicitly important to the judge who thought that sexual assault of a boy by a man 'might lead to future paedophilia or homosexuality' (1986),[68] to the judge who described a woman as 'a neophyte in the lesbian world' (1986),[69] and to the judge who said, in defending nonrecognition of same-sex marriages, that 'Some homosexuals do marry' (1993).[70] Judicial consideration of the cause of homosexuality is connected to concern about how it might be got over or caught, as though it were as illness. Homosexuality has been medicalized, treated as an abnormal phenomenon. Scientists, especially in the medical field, have made a fortune out of studying why people are homosexual and how they might be (if at all) cured,[71] and the courts have tapped into this well of 'knowledge.' An example of how homosexuality is seen as a fit subject for scientific study which is then brought into court can be found in R v. Neve (1994),[72] where the court considered a great deal of expert evidence in a case of a woman charged and convicted of a brutal assault and robbery of another woman, who was stripped of her clothing and left naked in the cold. The evidence of one expert was described in part as follows: 'A systematic study of psychopaths as a group has not begun. He fairly conceded that though the profession has some knowledge of male homosexual brain wave patterns, it does not in the case of female homosexuals.'[73] It was not thought problematic to admit evidence on 'homosexual brain wave patterns.' Neither male or female 'heterosexual' brain wave patterns are ever, however, the subject of any court interest.'[74] The cause of homosexuality and homosexual activity alone is of interest.

As I have argued, the question of what flows from the attachment of the label 'homosexual' to a person or a situation is much more relevant than debates about causation. However, I do want to consider the extent to which judges have been involved in the essentialist/constructionist debate. It should be noted from the outset that judges enter this debate more or less at the level of the street discussion; the nuances of either a sophisticated constructionist or essentialist approach are rarely found in judicial consideration of the question.

Constructionism

The social constructionists look at the history of homosexuality and note that all the terms we use now in connection with it are relatively recent.[75] Homosexuality, as we know it, is a modern phenomenon; particular homosexual activity always existed but 'the homosexual' is a recent being. How we view homosexuality and the homosexual is a contingent phenomenon very much of today.[76] It serves modern requirement for the regularization (or irregularization) of sexual activity and desire. The essentialist, on the other hand, argues that although the terminology is new, the concept of a person who is attracted sexually to his or her own sex is as ancient as humankind. Whether that person is called a sodomite, a bugger, or a sapphist, the idea has existed from time immemorial, because the phenomenon is an essential, that is, an innate, characteristic of the person.

To make the constructionist point, take the analogy of race. One is born with a particular coloration. However, what it means to 'be black' or who exactly counts 'as black' is very much socially determined. One person with a particular genetic make-up in terms of colour might not use the label 'black' whereas another with the same genes might. 'Being black' carries all sorts of different meanings and significance. When a person adopts the term he or she might well consciously have to process what it means to 'be' 'a black.' In another place or another time being black had another meaning or perhaps it meant nothing to be black. Furthermore, it is more obvious that some people are more 'black' than others. Some fulfil the superficial categories so completely that they in fact have little choice in this society but to 'be black.' Others might have more of a choice. The availability of choice might also depend on where the person lives: a person who might be assumed to be black in Canada would have more 'choice' in, say, the Dominican Republic. Similarly, where homosexuals are concerned, there might well be some biological factor at work, but the labelling, the identity process is a social construction, a product of the person's place and times. Some people simply cannot be homosexual, just as some people simply cannot be black, because the fundamental (perhaps biological) building blocks are not there. There is a certain essentialist element in this, therefore, but it is not 'black' or 'homosexuality' but the building blocks that are essential. The race analogy is also a good one because it demonstrates the fluidity of language. The terms 'coloured,' 'Negro,' 'black,' 'African-American,' and 'nigger' mean different things. Their meanings are constructed differently, just as 'homosexual,' 'gay,' 'lesbian,' and so on are differently constructed.

The constructionist view is politically charged, given its dependence on definition in order to gain admission to the club of homosexuality. It is an intrinsically unstable method of classification because it embodies the idea of definitional flux and accepts that a person or thing might pass into and then out of the definitional space of homosexuality. The constructionist approach is inherently ambiguous. Is homosexuality a personal choice or a label attached by society after a person passes certain 'tests'? Is a man who leads an average suburban existence except for the fact that he has sex with other men 'a homosexual'? Is a man 'a homosexual' when he takes his 'boyfriend' on his honeymoon with him?[77] The grey areas such as these are especially important when the law makes the status of 'homosexuality' relevant, as it used to be for divorce or immigration purposes and still is for human rights purposes.

The constructionist claims that there is nothing inevitable or permanent about 'homosexual.' 'Homosexual' is just a state that society brings into existence in order to label a collectivity of activity or being that it sees as abnormal or negative. The idea that homosexual labelling is an instrument of social control is decades old. In 1968, Mary McIntosh, an early social constructionist, wrote: 'The practice of the social labeling of persons as deviant operates in two ways as a mechanism of social control. In the first place it helps to provide a clear-cut, publicized and recognizable threshold between permissible and impermissible behaviour ... The creation of a specialized, despised and punished role of homosexual keeps the bulk of society pure in rather the same way that the similar treatment of some kind of criminals helps keep the rest of society law-abiding.'[78]

The reason that there is so much said about homosexuality – so much so that a person can become a homosexual – when so little is said about heterosexuality is that a particular set of acts or desires has been, for whatever reason, rendered 'bad.' Homosexuality is constructed, it is argued, because it is thought socially necessary to relegate to social opprobrium a particular set of acts or characteristics. We need to know which people are bad and why – that is, what they (probably) have done or what they might be prone to do. As I will discuss in Chapter 2, judges reflect this negative characterization of homosexuality in generalized language in a way they never do about heterosexuality. Thus, judges can talk about 'a homosexual liaison, depicted in all its manifestations – even the most disgusting' (1978)[79] or about 'the female counterpart of homosexuality, with all its sensual and disgusting behaviour and gratifications' (1968).[80] A set of actions and desires becomes distinguishable because of a wish to exclude those acts or desires from what is socially acceptable. This set of acts and desires takes on a life of its own by being set apart and a person who is implicated in that set of acts or desires becomes identified himself or herself by that labelling.[81] A person who performs a homosexual act or a series of such acts becomes 'a homosexual.' This sort of construction and passage from an adjectival quality to a noun happens elsewhere in the law, especially in the criminal context. At one time the courts could label a person who had a record of convictions for gross indecency with other men a 'dangerous sexual offender.'[82] If society thought it unremarkable that one man would desire to have sexual relations with another there would be no need to label the person as 'homosexual.' However, homosexual acts are not treated as having no significance beyond the particular act. The act can lead to a labelling of the person. This labelling process works at all levels of speech. Some things – otherwise adjectival – become so significant that they infuse the person. Compare a person who speeds or drinks and drives; that individual does not thereby become known as a speeder or a drunk driver. Those characteristics are not seen as infusing his or her entire existence. However, a person who steals or kills might well become known as 'a thief' or 'a murderer'; the negative quality has isolated and become that person. There is no label for a person who scratches his or her elbow from behind rather than in front, or who desires to do so, because the phenomenon is thought to be unremarkable. There is no need to construct it into a category that has broad social significance or to take the activity that has an adjectival quality in describing the person and turn it into a noun to sum up someone who engages in such activity.

Judicial Constructionism

Judges have historically eschewed an essentialist view, but not as the result of any systematic consideration of the essentialist and the constructionist approaches, of which most judges remain unaware. Rather,

judges have simply stumbled into their own construction of homosexuality.[83] Judges were early constructionists, although their particular
constructions can often be criticized for their crudeness. Perhaps one of
the reasons for the popular appeal of the essentialist perspective for
homosexuals is the legacy of intolerance, in part judicial, that has been
created by a choice-based vision of homosexuality, which is thought to
be a near relative of more complex constructionist attitudes. Judicial
constructionism, however, bears little resemblance to academic constructionism. There is rarely consideration of the social desire to marginalize in the labelling process and there is little sensitivity to the
contingency of terminology, over time. Judicial construction of homosexuality usually boils down to three issues. First, homosexuals choose
to be that way and could equally choose to become heterosexual once
more. Second, homosexuality is a problem of confused gender identity.
Finally, homosexuals and homosexuality are remarkable while heterosexuals and heterosexuality are not. I return to the judicial construction
of homosexuality in Chapter 2; here, I want simply to look at mark-
ers that demonstrate the judicial attitude that homosexuality is a construction rather than an innate or fundamental aspect of a person and
judicial indications that homosexuality is a contingent but aberrant
phenomenon, one which deserves to be labelled in a way that makes it
'other.'

Homosexuality as Changeable

To the extent that judges deal with the question of the cause of homosexuality it usually involves a bald statement that assumes capriciousness rather than social factors. A judge often simply assumes that a
person's homosexuality or homosexual behaviour is the result of
choice. The judge is in a sense living up to the worst concerns of the
essentialist that homosexuality will be trivialized. Judges quite commonly evince this potted version of construction – that is, homosexuality as somewhat fickle choice. There have been some exceptions to this
attitude, although they are often to be found in minority or dissenting
judgments.[84] Fortunately, the exceptions are also more recent than not.
    I have already mentioned that the courts often see homosexuality as
something that is 'caused,' much like a disease, and therefore treatable.
Like a disease, it is true, homosexuality has something of an essential
quality, but it can be got rid of;[85] like the flu, with the proper cure, it
can be remedied. In a 1961 case, a Manitoba magistrate said, 'The

accused are confirmed homosexualists and have not indicated that they intend to fight off this disease.'[86] Some three decades later, in *R. v. Veysey*, a man was accused of gross indecency with teenage boys. In considering the case (1989), Finlayson JA said: 'The appellant, the [presentence] report states, is an avowed homosexual and is not disposed towards any treatment for his homosexuality ...'[87] Likewise, in *Partland v. Partland* (1960),[88] the question arose of the availability of maintenance for a woman whose husband admitted he was homosexual, wanted his 'boyfriend' on their honeymoon, and refused to give up his 'way of life.' McRuer CJHC said: 'The appellant has elected to pursue his homosexual life in preference to living with his wife as her husband in fact as well as in law.'[89] The most elaborate statement of the idea that homosexuality is an 'acquired condition' comes from *R. v. Lupien* (1969), where Hall J said:

> Homosexuality is not a disease of the mind nor a mental illness nor a condition arising out of mental incapacity or deficiency. It is a sexual attraction and interest between members of the same sex. There are all gradations of the condition from those at one end of the scale who have never had a normal sexual impulse to those at the other end who are only homosexual under exceptive conditions, *e.g.*, when they are totally segregated from the opposite sex, and in their case their homosexuality generally disappears as soon as they return to a normal environment. In between, others have both homosexual and heterosexual impulses and are known as 'bisexuals.' In whatever category the homosexual falls, his condition is an acquired aberration from the normal state. No one is destined at birth to be a homosexual any more than any given individual is earmarked to be an alcoholic or a drug addict. Heredity plays a part in the development. Environment is said to be the decisive factor.[90]

Inherent in the idea that homosexuality can be 'treated' is the idea that it could equally be spread, especially to children. Homosexuality as a contagious condition that will affect children is not confined to the family context; judges fear that children who have been sexually assaulted by a person of the same sex will end up being tainted by homosexuality.[91] The idea that homosexuality is contagious has been reinforced by the use of experts to analyse it. Thus, in *R. v. Roestad* (1971), the court heard evidence that suggested that homosexuality (which the court equated with paedophilia) could be caused by a sexual experience in childhood.[92] Graburn Co. Ct J noted, for example, that one expert said 'that "potential homosexuality is the most adverse cause and effect result". He also said that in his practice he had met many respectable fathers who were seduced in the past and at 40 the homosexual life reasserted itself and threatened the family and loss of job.'[93]

In the construction of homosexuality, homosexuality as a choice carries all sorts of baggage. Homosexuals do not live in ordinary situations; they have 'lifestyles' and form odd groups. In *Children's Aid Society of the District of Thunder Bay v. T.T.* (1992), the court described a young man who 'was introduced into a ring of homosexuals and ended up living with one of them.'[94] One never hears of a 'ring' of heterosexuals. In *Anderson v. Luoma* (1986), the court considered whether one lesbian had an obligation to support her former partner and her two children, born during the relationship between the two women. In describing the plaintiff, Dohm J said: 'My impression of the plaintiff is that she is sincere and forthright but quite naive. She was a neophyte in the lesbian world. She wanted to believe that her new found life was really no different from the one she just left. This keen desire of wanting things to work out and to develop and be part of a 'family unit' very much clouded the plaintiff's judgment.'[95] It is clear that the woman was thought to be making a (hopelessly misguided) lifestyle choice in becoming a lesbian. The idea that homosexuality is not a profound, essential quality of a person can apply not just to homosexuality per se but to other aspects of a homosexual existence. In *Egan* (1995),[96] La Forest J justified common law heterosexual couples receiving benefits because: 'Many of these couples live together indefinitely, bring forth children and care for them in response to familial instincts rooted in the human psyche.'[97] Homosexual couples were excluded from eligibility for the same benefits whether or not there were children involved. A homosexual union is apparently not rooted in the human psyche.

Homosexuality as a Gender-Identity Problem

Society persists in believing that a gay man is not really a man and that a lesbian is not quite a woman. A male person desires only the sexual companionship of a female and vice versa; if the person has no such desire then he or she is not genuinely male or female. Judges at times appear to accept this social construction by equating maleness and femaleness (and normalcy) with heterosexuality. In *Re Board of Gover-*

nors of the University of Saskatchewan and Saskatchewan Human Rights Commission (1976),[98] a homosexual education student was told that he would not be allowed to supervise practice teaching in the public schools. Johnson J said: 'Mr Wilson is an admitted homosexual. He also admits his male gender.'[99] The court appeared to have questioned whether a male homosexual could admit to a male gender.[100] Similarly in *R. v. Fraser* (1980),[101] a defence of provocation was offered to a murder charge. After drinking in the accused's home, the deceased supposedly made what were called 'homosexual' suggestions and advances towards him.[102] The trial judge found as a fact that there was a 'homosexual attack' on the accused: 'I am of the opinion that the accused perceived this as a real threat and as a danger to him, both physically and emotionally, in his perceived image of himself as a male person.'[103] Real men are not gay. They are, however, it seems, under a threat from homosexuals who might undermine their gender identity, just as homosexuals' own gender is questionable. Female homosexuals are likewise abnormal. 'La lesbienne n'est ni une femme ni un homme.'[104] In *Morrison v. Morrison* (1972),[105] there was a divorce action on grounds of a homosexual act, namely a wife having sex with another woman. Nicholson J called it an 'unnatural relationship.'[106]

Transvestism is also identified with homosexuality and as abnormal.[107] Some of these associations can be seen in the custody case of *H.I.M. v. W.A.M.* (1994), where deVilliers Prov. Ct J said that the father acknowledged that he was a transvestite but, when asked, denied that he was a homosexual. The questioning was continued by Ms Christie. The judge said: 'In answer to her question whether he had a sexual relationship with K. he evasively enquired what period of time she was referring to, and then denied it. K. testified, somewhat emotionally, that he and the father are close friends, but that they do not engage in sexual intercourse. I accept his evidence, and find that the Father probably has latent homosexual tendencies, but that he does not practise sodomy.'[108] The court here appeared to think that an admitted transvestite who had a close male friend must be a 'homosexual' of some sort. Once 'homosexual tendencies' were suspected, sodomy naturally came to the judge's mind.

Homosexuality as Remarkable

There are any number of judicial examples of the general attitude that homosexuality is remarkable and noteworthy while heterosexuality is not. Homosexuality is constructed as an aberration. This is particularly common in sexual assault or 'homosexual panic' cases. Homosexuality is identified, despite its irrelevance to the case at hand and where heterosexuality would not be mentioned in an equivalent case. Thus, in one case (1986),[109] Philp JA described a situation in which an accused 'made homosexual advances to the complainant, a young man 19 years of age,' who was a gas station attendant.[110] In another (1988),[111] the court spoke of: 'The relevant background facts pertaining to police investigation of the homosexual activities taking place in the men's public wash-room at the Silvercreek Park ...';[112] '... this public place had been taken over by a group of men for homosexual activities ...'[113] Likewise, in yet another criminal case (1995), we are told that 'The respondents have been separately charged ... of offences suggestive of homosexual activity in the men's public washroom at Shell Park in Oakville'[114] and that 'homosexual graffiti adorned the walls in the stalls.'[115] In a case (1989) in which there were disciplinary proceedings against a doctor charged with six counts of professional misconduct involving sex with minor patients,[116] Gerein J said: 'I am here confronted with alleged homosexual acts of a physician upon individuals who, with one exception, were minors at the time.'[117] In *R. v. Caskenette* (1993),[118] a case of sexual assaults on boys by a man, Hollinrake JA set out what he called 'incidents of homosexual activity'[119] and Hutchinson JA referred to 'uninvited homosexual advances' in *R. v. Hansford* (1987).[120] In *R. v. Kluke* (1987), we are told about the deceased who 'went to Victoria Park, known to be a rendezvous for men with homosexual interests.'[121] In *R. v. Ryznar* (1986),[122] the court considered a defence of provocation to a charge of murder; it commented that the deceased 'followed a homosexual life-style' and referred to a 'local club frequented by those of homosexual persuasion.'[123] The tone of the language evinces the court's disapprobation of and condescension towards homosexuality.[124] Also evident is a sense of the threat posed by homosexuality and a sense that homosexuality is mostly about taking up evil habits. This setting aside of homosexuals and homosexuality as abnormal and remarkable is common in other situations. Women are often identified as such when men would not be; racial minorities are often singled out in judicial comments. It would not be surprising, for instance, to find a court say that a person followed an 'Asian' lifestyle or went to a 'local club for blacks.' So it is with homosexuality. In *Re L. (R.)* (1981), the court dealt with an off-duty police officer charged with discreditable conduct for having allegedly picked up a male hustler and giving him a blow job in his car. Throughout, the court uses terms such as 'payment in advance for homosexual services,' and 'guilty of the homosexual act.'[125] These were not just 'sexual' services and acts; they were worse – they were 'homosexual' services and acts. In an appalling case (1997) of sexual abuse of boys at a 'youth ranch,' the court referred to 'homosexual activity' and 'homosexual behaviour.'[126] This litany of examples only scratches the surface of the instances to be found in the jurisprudence.

In none of situations described above does the word 'homosexual' add anything that the simple word 'sexual' would not convey, except apparently to reaffirm that homosexuality is wrong and to imply that a homosexual advance is more shocking than a 'simple' sexual advance. In *R. v. Ruby* (1986), Mifflin CJN said: 'We are not here dealing with a homosexual who enticed or forced a young person of good character to have anal sex with him.'[127] It is not clear why 'homosexual' is used instead of 'person.' The generous use of the words in these negative situations provides a striking contrast to the attitude of the law, as we will see, in the outing context, where the use of the label 'homosexual' as a neutral (or even a positive) term is discouraged.[128] Negative stereotypes of homosexuals and homosexuality are reinforced when outing is the only permissible legal context in which the terminology of homosexuality is acceptable.[129]

Part of the remarkability of homosexuality is that this sole characteristic is all we are allowed to see of the person. There is no need for any other aspect of that person to be described, and little consideration is accorded to the racial, ethnic, economic, or religious background of the person involved. From legal judgments, we simply cannot tell how different the impact of particular situations might be on different categories of homosexuals. Male homosexuals are treated as a monolith. As Mary Eaton argues: 'In short, legally speaking, there is no race to homosexuality. This racelessness might be understood as being synonymous with colorlessness. However, given the tendency under conditions of white supremacy to regard whiteness as a norm to which no racial reference need be made, I prefer to read this erasure as signifying that homosexuality has been legally coded as white, or to put matters conversely, that race has been legally coded as heterosexual.'[130]

On the other hand, with respect to female homosexuals, all we often see is the femaleness rather than the homosexuality. Few of the cases examined for this book involve lesbians. This is owing in part to the fact that women as a whole are not involved in perpetrating some of the offences that unfortunately make up so much of this study – killing, sexual assault, and abuse of authority. With a few exceptions, women identified as lesbians are jurisprudentially ghettoized into cases involving children. There are no doubt many other cases involving lesbians than those identifiable as such from the case reports, but their lesbianism is lost or subsumed in their femaleness. As in the past, the law continues to be dismissive of lesbianism. It can be ignored for the most part. Homosexuality is an issue for men to sort out – those who are male and those who are not-so-male.

Essentialism

The idea that somebody is born 'homosexual' is a reasonably recent phenomenon. The essentialist viewpoint, given that it does not have any proponents who claim the label 'essentialist,' is badly understood. The constructionist invents a person ('the essentialist') who simply says that a homosexual is born a homosexual and would be a homosexual in any society or at any time. This oversimplifies the essentialist position. John Boswell, while not calling himself an essentialist, defends the idea that characteristics do not change over time, that there is an essential element to them even though the language used to describe those characteristics might change. He takes the analogy of religion: 'Does this mean that there was no "religion" in Rome, and that historians are distorting reality by talking and writing about "Roman religion"? Should some new word, free of the contaminants of modern concepts, be coined to characterize the veneration of Roman deities and the cult of Cybele? No. There was obviously "religion" in Rome, including Christianity itself – which gave us our sense of 'religion.' That Romans viewed it somewhat differently does not demonstrate that it was, in fact, a different entity.'[131]

Nobody, not even the essentialist, would deny that homosexual is a loaded term and that certain things take on a significance today that did not possess that significance elsewhere or at a different time. What the essentialist stresses most is that the person's homosexuality is not a foible – a fickle or easily changed characteristic. It is of the very essence of the person. It is not trivial and it is not something that might have gone away or could go away or that could be fundamentally altered by putting the person in a different environment. It is not anybody's 'fault.'

Judicial Essentialism

It is rare for judges to express what might be called an essentialist view. To the extent that it exists, such expression is quite recent and arises in the context of antidiscrimination cases where legislation is interpreted as mandating an essentialist approach. To the extent that judges have seen homosexuality as an essentialist quality, it is often not viewed as terribly significant. Thus, in *Layland v. Ontario (Minister of Consumer and Commercial Relations)* (1993),[132] where a same-sex couple applied for a marriage licence, Southey J said: 'The law does not prohibit marriage by homosexuals, provided it takes place between persons of the opposite sex. Some homosexuals do marry. The fact that many homosexuals do not choose to marry, because they do not want unions with persons of the opposite sex, is the result of their own preferences, not a requirement of the law.'[133]

The idea of homosexuality as essential appears in immigration and refugee cases, like other rights cases, because of the peculiar requirements for status-based claims. Thus the Supreme Court of Canada, in *Canada v. Ward* (1993),[134] said that sexual orientation is a ground on which a refugee claimant could claim membership because it is an innate or unchangeable characteristic. The Federal Court took this same approach in *Veysey* (1989), where Dubé J said: 'Presumably, sexual orientation would fit within one of these levels of immutability.'[135] La Forest J subsequently reinforced his view in *Ward* in *Egan* (1995), where he said that sexual orientation 'is a deeply personal characteristic that is either unchangeable or changeable only at unacceptable personal costs.'[136] Essentialism works best for status arguments. To be protected, one must be a member of a particular group based on immutable characteristics, but that does not necessarily mean that particular behaviour is protected along with the status. Although *Egan* was not directly about protecting behaviour as opposed to status, La Forest J did accept in that case that homosexuals were protected under section 15 of the Charter. But he then concluded that that protection meant little in terms of acquiring benefits equal to those available to heterosexuals.[137] Perhaps, then, with such an approach, protection under section 15 is protection of status alone, rather than of any behaviour or action.

Critique of the Judicial Approach to Constructionism and Essentialism

There are problems with both the constructionist and the essentialist approaches. With a constructionist approach, of course, much depends on the construction itself, on whether the judge constructs 'homosexual' identity simply as a whim that could be changed at will. In terms of equality litigation, the difference between an essentialist and constructionist approach can be important for the purposes of deciding whether a person is a member of a group that is protected from discrimination. If the courts insist on an essentialist interpretation of a classification – the person had no choice, the person was born that way – before granting human rights protection, and if homosexuality is a social construction involving an element of choice and contingency, no protection will be available. Furthermore, if homosexuality is a construction how does one establish being homosexual? A scientific, medical, or sociological element is added to homosexuality that is not there for other characteristics like race and gender which (however wrongly) are assumed to be essential. Can anyone who claims to be homosexual be accepted as such? The task of determining homosexual status will result in litigation becoming that much more costly and time consuming. And the government is in fact given more tools with which to defeat the goal of equality with a constructionist approach. Construction, an inherently divisive approach to homosexuality and equality, can be used to retard the project of equality more than to advance it.

From a legal perspective, there are real strengths to the essentialist position, in particular because it does not lend itself to the foible quality many judges assume about homosexuality. While a thoughtful understanding of the constructionist approach does not in fact lead to this conclusion, unfortunately judges (like many others) will search only for the essence of constructionism in which contingency will be construed to mean simply 'choice' and 'changeability.' Many involved in the fight for equality for homosexuals have consequently found the essentialist approach more useful. It clearly posits that homosexuality is an immutable characteristic of individuals. Stychin notes that 'despite its limitations, the use of essentialist rhetoric retains a strategic usefulness in constitutional rights discourse.'[138] In part this is owing to abuses and misunderstanding of the constructionist approach. Eve Kosofsky Sedgwick has expressed concern that:

> ... a social fact deeply embedded in the cultural and linguistic forms of many, many decades is being degraded to the blithe ukase that people are 'free at any moment to' (i.e. must immediately) 'choose' to adhere to a

particular sexual identity (say, at random hazard, the heterosexual) rather than to its other ... To the degree – and it is significantly large – that the gay essentialist/constructivist debate takes its form and premises from, and insistently refers to, a whole history of other nature/nurture or nature/culture debates, it partakes of a tradition of viewing culture as malleable relative to nature: that is, culture, unlike nature, is assumed to be the thing that can be changed; the thing in which 'humanity' has, furthermore, a right or even an obligation to intervene.[139]

Sedgwick is concerned that the constructionist approach can easily be turned against homosexuals and used to attempt to erase homosexuality from society. Essentialism, in contrast, provides a bulwark against the cultural malleability that constructionism can lead to, a malleability that 'continues by inventing an ethical or therapeutic mandate for cultural manipulation; and ends in the overarching hygienic Western fantasy of a world without any more homosexuals in it.'[140] Essentialism offers resistance to this threat 'by conceptualizing an unalterably *homosexual body*, to the social engineering momentum apparently built into every one of the human sciences of the West ...'[141]

An essentialist approach may not be the answer either, however. The problem with essentialism is, as I noted above, that it might protect a status but not an action. A constructionist approach makes some active element (mental or physical) a component of identification as homosexual. The constructionist approach admits a social role to status as homosexual. In her critique of the *Canada v. Ward* decision, Nicole La Violette criticizes the court's emphasis on 'particular social group' because it fails 'to recognize that sexual orientation is fundamental to human dignity.'[142] As she says: 'The implication in *Ward* is that some personal characteristics deserve refugee protection only as long as individuals are unable to change.'[143] Part of human dignity is that it is not just one's status that is valued but also what one can do as a result of that status. La Violette goes on to conclude: 'A sounder approach would have been to recognize that gay men and lesbians deserve international protection because the common social identity of the group is ascribed an inferior social status by society and the state. This formulation shifts the focus of the legal test away from the causes of homosexuality towards the central issue: whether the sexual orientation of a group of people makes those people discernible to the general population, and if so, whether that group is considered by society and the state to be undesirable.'[144]

A combination of essential and constructed factors is possible. The Canadian Immigration and Refugee Board has granted refugee status to an Argentinian man on the basis of his persecution in Argentina for being 'a homosexual.'[145] The tribunal found (1992) that homosexuals constitute a particular social group, relying on *Veysey v. Commissioner of the Correctional Service of Canada*[146] to the effect that homosexuality was at least as immutable as race, national or ethnic origins, colour, age, religion, and so on. According to the IRB, however, even if homosexuality were considered a voluntary condition, it was so fundamental to a person's identity that he could not be compelled to change it.[147] Thus the court neatly combined the conceptions of homosexuality as immutable and as a choice.

Asking Different Questions

Trying to combine an essentialist and a constructionist approach might be somewhat useful, but it really only perpetuates the notion that establishing the cause of homosexuality is of some importance. The essentialist/constructionist debate is, in fact, fairly unhelpful with respect to homosexuals and homosexuality; it concentrates too much on why homosexuality and therefore homosexuals occur. As I have argued, for legal purposes at least, what flows from that designation is much more significant. What is important is the consequential meaning placed on a particular term. Why are some things regarded as negative, so as to entail inferior characteristics or consequences? Can negative be made positive or at least neutral? Why somebody is homosexual is relevant only if it is thought that what follows will be different than if the person were not so labelled.

Some writers have moved from a focus on fixed polarity of view in the constructionist/essentialist debate. Eve Kosofsky Sedgwick, for example, prefers not to enter into it, referring instead to 'minoritizing' versus 'universalizing' understandings of homosexuality. She claims that that distinction, as opposed to the constructionist/essentialist one, helps record and respond to the question: 'in whose lives is homo/heterosexual definition an issue of continuing centrality and difficulty?' Kosofsky Sedgwick's 'minoritizing'/'universalizing' approach relates much more to the effect of a labelling process rather than to the reason the labels are attached in the first place. More important is the issue raised by Jeffrey Weeks, who argues: 'The real problem does not lie in whether homosexuality is inborn or learnt. It lies instead in the question: what are the meanings that this particular culture gives to homosexual behaviour, however it might be caused, and what are the effects of those meanings on the ways in which individuals organize their sexual lives. That is a historical question. It is also a question which is highly political: it forces us to analyse the proper relations which determine why this set of meanings, rather than that, are hegemonic; and poses the further question of how those meanings can be changed.'[148]

What is important, then, is the extent to which a practical meaning of inferiority or marginalization is allowed to attach to these terms, however they become applied in the first place. This is where the law comes in – as one of the regulators of society. The courts are part of the machinery that decides on the significance of a particular label. To date the courts have not spent a great deal of time on the question of why somebody is given or deserves the label homosexual. Rather, outside specific human rights contexts, they have tended to jump to easy assertions about people being homosexual based on abnormality, gender confusion, or capriciousness. While I have criticized such rudimentary, constructionistlike assumptions, I am not arguing that judges should spend more time exploring why somebody is or deserves to be labelled homosexual. Instead, when the label is applied, the court should reflect on the consequences that have flowed, do flow, or should flow from that situation.

Stereotypes, Control of Identity, and Equivalency of Treatment

The problem to be addressed is not so much that there are only two categories of sexual orientation or indeed whether the source of these categories is essential in nature or socially constructed. What needs to be addressed, at least for legal purposes, is the consequential meanings that accompany the terms. The focus of both heterosexuals and homosexuals on cause rather than consequence leads to a situation in which the practical implications of 'being homosexual' remain invisible and stereotypes flourish to fill the vacuum of real knowledge.[149] The consequences of homosexuality, the consequences for homosexuals, are dictated by stereotypes or assumptions about what must follow from the application of the label. These stereotypes can take on a life of their own and be believed even by those to whom they apply. For example, homosexuals often have unstable relationships in part because that is the accepted stereotype.[150]

Particular care must be paid to the use of assumptions and stereotypes about homosexuals. Few other groups can have had so little control over what is assumed about them. How we are perceived or constructed by others is terribly important to homosexuals. Identity (including self-worth) may come from within but it takes its cue from external representation. Film studies scholar Richard Dyer says: 'How a group is represented, presented over and over again in cultural forms, how an image of a member of a group is taken as representative of that group, how that group is represented in the sense of spoken for and on behalf of (whether they represent, speak for themselves or not), these all have to do with how members of groups see themselves and others like themselves, how they see their place in society, their right to the rights a society claims to ensure its citizens.'[151] Judges influence the way in which people see themselves.

The problem is not really the existence of stereotypes, but the content of those stereotypes. A stereotype is simply a generalization and the world, with all its complexities, demands that we use generalizations or stereotypes. We know what a festive Christmas celebration entails and what smart business attire looks like because of stereotypes. These are generally helpful stereotypes. Stereotypes about a group of people can be a positive reinforcement to the members of the group if they have been created and perpetuated by that group. We can make jokes about 'Americans,' 'Germans,' 'Englishmen,' and 'men' in general because those groups have been sufficiently in control of their own image that the stereotypes are somehow reinforcing and complimentary. People in other groups might be more sensitive if the same things were said about them because they have not been and do not feel in control of the terminology and imagery being used to describe them, and perceive the comments made as a put-down. These different reactions can happen in the same person who belongs to different groups. Thus a Jewish-American man who is called 'loud' might take it as a compliment if he thinks it refers to his maleness or Americanness, those groups having cultivated the idea of loudness as a positive thing. If, however, he thinks it refers to his Jewishness, he might feel threatened because that description of Jews was not developed by Jews but was ascribed to them as a negative stereotype. So, too, with homosexuality. An English homosexual might have different reactions to being described as 'fastidious' depending on whether he thought it described his Englishness or his homosexuality. A group does not necessarily want to eliminate stereotypes about it; its members merely want to have some say in what those stereotypes are, or at least not have the

state give its imprimatur to a negative stereotype that has been historically imposed. People who use stereotypes in any official way, as
judges do, should be aware of the differing impact of stereotypes,
depending on the group. A judge cannot simply assume that all
groups are similarly robust in their reactions to stereotypes.

The judiciary should be cognizant of the historical and social context
of a given stereotype. Duncan Kennedy, in an article on judging, calls
'social and historical stereotypes' 'the stock in trade of legal argument.'[152] He notes that judges can reverse a stereotype by expanding
the factual basis surrounding its subject. A judge must recognize that
certain terms are 'loaded' for members of some groups while not for
others. For example, 'aggressive' can invoke very different feelings
depending on the group it is used to describe.[153] When a judge talks of
'aggressive homosexual inmates' (1991),[154] he conjures up and uses the
image of the predatory homosexual.[155] It is important, therefore, not to
generalize in this way.

Part of the questioning of stereotypes involves abandonment of the
standard of formal equality. This sets up its own stereotype of a single
standard for all to conform to if the expectation of protection from discrimination is to be realized. In several cases where the courts have
considered the meaning of family or relationship in the homosexual
context, for example, they have looked for virtual identity with the heterosexual model.[156] To be questioned is the assumption that heterosexual stereotypes of family or relationship are the only ones that are
worth protecting. It is important to remember that part (though not all)
of being a homosexual is *homo*-sexuality. Homosexuality by its very
nature is never going to be formally equal to heterosexuality, and vice
versa. Furthermore, decisions involving homosexuals should not
incorporate sexist terminology. Male homosexuals need not be 'real
men' or lesbians 'real women.' Tests developed by the courts must be
examined carefully for heterosexist bias. If they are used to preserve a
particular vision of society, does this vision exclude homosexuals?
Does it only accept homosexuals if they conform to the heterosexual
model of roles and identities? Are the people who administer the tests
even aware of homosexuals or homosexuality beyond their own pre-
existing stereotypes? For example, in the context of obscenity, a test
framed in terms of domination of one sex by the other is inherently
heterosexist, as is an analysis that assigns to the couple in a same-sex
relationship a male role and a female role. This is the case in *Butler*
(1992) where the Supreme Court of Canada accepted a heterosexist

MacKinnonesque approach in its test for obscenity.[157] Domination of one gender by another is not a principal concern of gay and lesbian pornography. It is true that some gay and lesbian pornography depicts 'male' or 'female' roles, but this occurs infrequently. Gay men, for instance, who are getting fucked should not be thought of as women or as representing another gender from the man who is fucking. Nor should it be thought that sexual intercourse in a gay male context necessarily implies a power dynamic – sometimes it does and sometimes it does not.

A more satisfying approach is to look for equivalents between groups rather than identity. Judges are quite capable of achieving this in the homosexual context. For example, in *M. v. H.* (1996), Charron JA for the majority said:

> The inquiry in this case inevitably leads to a comparison between same-sex and opposite-sex cohabitees. While it is perfectly legitimate and indeed necessary to make comparisons between the two groups since, after all, equality is all about comparisons, it is important to keep the basis of discrimination firmly in mind when going through this analysis. The requirement cannot be that same-sex relationships be 'just like' heterosexual relationships in all respects to qualify for equal legal recognition because this would amount to a requirement that the claimant lose the identity for which protection is claimed in order to achieve equality. This is the antithesis of equality. For example, this is precisely where the analysis would lead us if procreation were viewed as the operative distinction between the two groups since same-sex relationships, by their very nature, cannot be procreative. And, it is this very characteristic – sexual orientation – which forms the basis of the discrimination.[158]

It can be difficult, however, to know how to educate judges about the reality of gay and lesbian existence, that is, what constitutes an equivalent situation,[159] when judges refuse to listen. For example in *M. v. H.*,[160] Finlayson JA, disapproved of 'several affidavits from various representatives of the homosexual community, describing same-sex relationships.' Finlayson JA said: 'I do not believe that this evidence is sufficiently reliable to be instructive. Unlike most social science evidence adduced in Charter motions, this evidence does not consist of objective, replicable studies of statistical data. Rather, it is replete with personal accounts prepared for the specific purpose of supporting M's position in these proceedings.'[161] Why homosexuals should not know how their relationships work and why some medical expert would be better is incomprehensible. The failure to hear stories from homosexuals themselves about homosexual life may itself reflect another stereotype about homosexuals, namely, their untrustworthiness.

As I will explore further in Chapter 2, judicial insistence on identity rather than equivalency and judicial disinclination to hear homosexuals' own stories results in the felt need of homosexuals who go before the courts to pretend to be other than themselves. They cannot simply set out their situation and expect to receive a judgment that does not include a judgment of their 'lifestyle' and who they are. The homosexual participant in the legal process must appear to be as heterosexual as possible in order to attract the sympathy of the court, which entails the suppression of the sex and sexuality of that person. The homosexual person becomes 'sanitized' or regularized. Janice Ristock has discussed this phenomenon in the context of a Winnipeg woman, 'Maryann,' who was in court in connection with a sexual assault charge against her partner. Describing the scene in court Ristock comments: 'Maryann looked very different in court than when she had talked with me dressed in black leather urban dyke clothes. Her court clothes were stereotypically feminine, her hair was loose and long. In fact she was a bit embarrassed by her outfit but said that she thought she would have a better chance of succeeding if she looked "virginal."'[162] This forced conformity has analogies in other areas. Paul Siegel, quoting Ellis Close, writes: 'The assumption of black dangerousness forces upon African-Americans a coping style that makes it "folly to compete for a taxi on a street corner with whites. It means realizing that prudence dictates dressing up whenever you are likely to encounter strangers (including clerks, cops, and doormen) who can make your life miserable by mistaking you for a tramp, a slut, or a crook." The crucial point again is that these "strangers" are reacting not to "benign" racial features but rather to behavioral attributions based upon those features.'[163]

In the remainder of this book I explore the way in which judges have participated in the inferiorization and problematization of homosexuals and homosexuality. Through the way in which judges express themselves, they have participated in the perpetuation of stereotypes about homosexuals, stereotypes over which homosexuals themselves have had no control. Homosexual expression or expression by homosexuals has been constrained because homosexuals cannot just be themselves, but have to operate instead in a context of behavioural attributions and assumptions in which judges, for the most part, have been implicated. The history of homophobia, including the development of 'the homosexual' and a simplistic 'homosexual' construction of capriciousness and changeability, continues in the present in the form of a legacy of assumptions and generalizations about homosexuals and homosexuality that affect what judges say and take into account in making decisions in cases that have a homosexual element.

2

Censoriousness and Censorship

While there is today much less overt censoriousness and censorship of homosexuality and homosexuals and of expression by and about them, even compared with a decade ago, there remains a constant and consistent affirmation of the otherness of homosexuality. As I discussed in the previous chapter, assumptions are made about homosexuality that would not be made in the equivalent heterosexual context. Homosexuality is feared and exoticized, stereotyped and eroticized. It is kept hidden, while knowledge about it is simply assumed. These attitudes are themselves a form of censorship of expression about homosexuality and certainly constitute a censoriousness of homosexuals and what they supposedly represent. Furthermore, these attitudes are as typical in the judiciary as they are of society at large. Judicial censoriousness must necessarily affect the act of judging censorship of homosexual expression and censorious attitudes toward homosexuality. In this chapter I begin by examining what constitutes censorship and censoriousness and how such actions have an impact beyond the immediate parties. Then, I summarize the B.C. Supreme Court decision in *Little Sisters*, which I return to frequently as an example of the connection between judicial censoriousness and censorship and the censoriousness of others. After establishing the similarities between a censorship system and the judiciary we arrive at the core of the chapter: an examination in five parts of how judges have, fairly consistently, adopted censorious attitudes towards homosexuals and homosexuality. The chapter concludes by arguing that, while it is not an easy task to challenge these attitudes, efforts made in this direction are worthwhile and necessary.

The Nature of Censorship and Censoriousness

Censorship and censoriousness are forms of passing (negative) judgment on the expression of others. Censoriousness can extend to the others' very existence, but I will treat that existence as a form of expression. The goal of censorship and censoriousness is to make something or somebody invisible, that is, to make expression by or about them disappear. Censorship in its paradigmatic form is the determination by a third party of whether or how my expression will be received by you. It involves, for legal purposes, the state or some organization or individual with statelike powers. For example, a religious body might purport to censor books for its members or even prevent the public at large from reading them. The statelike function can also be located within some sort of family unit – so that the 'head of the family' might well control, as one of the means of power over the others, what those people read or watch or say. Such paternal censoring of expression is invariably done in the 'interests' of the 'good' of others. Father knows best. Sometimes, however, censorship is of one's own expression, usually to prevent incurring the wrath of others, which might hurt the financial or social position or the security of the communicator. Self-censorship flows from that other constraint of expression, censoriousness.

Censoriousness is one of the tools used to try to accomplish censorship, often self-censorship, by others. It can take the form of direct criticism but it might instead occur in the form of ridicule or disparagement or trivialization. Censoriousness can even be effected by exclusion, where the opposite of something is indicated or assumed. It is much more difficult to circumscribe and address censoriousness than censorship, because of its more amorphous nature. Censoriousness involves the passing of a (negative) judgment on expression without directly preventing that expression. It qualifies the expression as bad, as less worthy expression. Some things are best left unsaid. Censoriousness, unlike censorship, does not inherently involve a statelike function but it certainly contains a paternalistic element. It also involves a sense of one person's judgment being superior to that of another. Censorship can lack this element of superiority, which is replaced by a sense of duty or constraint.

Censoriousness and censorship are based on the idea that humans are powerfully subject to suggestion and may be unable to control their actions after certain types of suggestion. They will be irreparably harmed by certain expressions and, after being harmed, will in all likelihood become new sources of that which needs to be censored. Thus the old tests for obscenity looked for a 'tendency to deprave and corrupt.'[1] This idea is also the basis of the notion that some things – like homosexuality – are or ought to be unmentionable. There is a schizophrenic apprehension that some 'unnatural' things are both contagious and corrupting. Expression about homosexuality or sodomy can affect the mental processes of others; formerly ignorant of such things, they might become desirous of investigation or conversion after exposure to such expression. How, exactly, this susceptibility through contagion or corruption can be squared with the unnaturalness of homosexuality is never satisfactorily explained. Most censorship and censoriousness, however, is not explained. It proceeds on simple, strong assumptions of badness. The assumption is made and justified after the fact, if at all.

Censorship and censoriousness divide the world into good and bad expression, in the broadest sense of the term. If a book is not allowed in a school library because it contains a description of how to make bombs, the conclusion to be drawn is that bomb-making (at least by school students) is bad. It falls outside the paradigm of that which is identified as good. So, too, if a book that describes a same-sex couple or homosexuality neutrally or positively is excluded, the message is sent not merely that this particular book is bad but that all such books and all such expression is bad. The impact of censorship and censoriousness is compounded when the 'opposing' image or expression is given free rein and thereby sanctified as good, so that, for example, all images of couples are of opposite-sex couples.

The message of censorship and censoriousness has a different impact on members of two different groups of people: those who are not immediately implicated in the expression and those who are. The latter category is more seriously affected. Within this category the impact differs again as between, first, the (would-be) speaker and the (non-) recipient, who have had their liberty curtailed (their liberty to express at all in the case of censorship and their liberty to express without a sense of constraint in the case of censoriousness) and second, all of the people who would fit, in some way, into the content of the censored expression. Thus, if a neo-Nazi is prevented from or made to feel guilty about using a hate-line to send or receive messages then his or her liberty and that of the (would-be) recipient have been restricted. But, all neo-Nazis, even those not a party to the particular censored communication, have also had their liberty restricted. Likewise when expression with homosexual content is censored or subject to censoriousness, the

freedoms of all homosexuals are affected in a way that nonhomosexuals' freedoms are not. It is not just the content of the expression that
is being judged, but the nature of the content of the expression and that
or those who share in that nature. The content of the expression is
rendered negative, worthless, or inferior and likewise those who could
in some way be assimilated to the content of the expression are rendered negative, worthless, or inferior. Those not immediately implicated in the expression are affected by being given a sense of this
negativity or inferiority of the others. The members of the 'other' group
might be perceived to be small in numbers, but threatening and contagious nonetheless, and therefore deserving of containment.

Because of the negative impact of censorship and censoriousness,
there is a natural tendency to want to be included in the nonimplicated
group rather than in the group of 'others.' A person might tend to
eliminate or minimize aspects of himself or herself that would tend
towards implication in the content of the censored communication. 'I
am not a neo-Nazi ... Those neo-Nazis are more extreme than me.' 'I
am not homosexual – what I do is not homosexual.' 'My anal sex with
my girlfriend is normal. What those perverts do is disgusting.' In a
more extreme form, this elimination of negativity by self-inclusion in
the nonimplicated group can take the form of 'passing'; in its less
extreme form it can be simple rationalization. That little sexual encounter with another man was just an aberration; only people who do
it all the time and really want to and need to do it are disgusting.
Censoriousness encourages this gradation by making frequency an
exacerbation of the badness. While committing one homosexual
act is bad, engaging in many homosexual acts is worse. Worst of all is
self-identification with the adjective, so that the person becomes 'a
homosexual.'

Censoriousness and censorship can thus operate on two levels, the
general and the specific. At the specific level they operate to forbid or
constrain or condemn a particular instance of expression. At the general level they disapprove of anybody who might be associated in
some way with the particular censored expression and expect at least
self-censorship from that person. The specific can also be general in the
sense that it has a symbolic meaning. Thus, for example, an instance of
sodomy may be a symbol for something larger: male homosexuality.
Even if I do not engage in sodomy or a particular act of sodomy, it is
taken to represent my sexuality. Any censoriousness or censorship of
sodomy, therefore, is a censoriousness or censorship of my sexuality.

The clearest example of this process is the long-time banning of pornography that depicted 'lesbianism.'[2] The censorship of these particular instances of lesbianism was a symbolic censoriousness of all lesbianism. For those who identified or were identified with lesbianism, their existence itself was the subject of censoriousness.

Beyond the division into general or specific, the types of censorship and censoriousness are varied. In some instances of censorship the action is direct and directly involves the law. It is thus easily monitored and challenged. For example, in terms of Customs' inspection of books and films coming into the country there is a process (of sorts) in place to implement censorship. The system has its faults, as was found in the *Little Sisters* case,[3] but at least the evident legal process provides an obvious target for legal or political challenge. In other situations, the act of censorship or censoriousness is clear, but the process is more political than legal, which, given arguments based on democracy, however flawed they may be, makes these acts less easy to identify and challenge. For example, a municipality's decision to ban gay and lesbian material from its libraries involves a legal procedure and probably the passing of regulations, but it is the political process that is really 'at fault' for the discrimination in censorship that follows.

In still other situations, the act of censorship or censoriousness is less obvious. This is particularly true of censoriousness, which is more insidious, often involving noninclusion or marginalization rather than outright condemnation. Censoriousness is much more difficult to tackle than overt censorship in that it ostensibly involves an opinion or feelings rather than direct action. An individual act of censoriousness, as opposed to an individual act of censorship, is difficult to respond to legally. When censoriousness falls into a pattern, however, it may also be identifiable and, therefore, possible to address.

Can censorship and censoriousness, particularly of something like homosexual expression, be supportable on some democratic principle? If the bulk of the people want certain expression censored, prohibited, or confined then should not the wishes of the majority be respected? Legal tests usually appeal to this democratic principle in some way, often under the guise of 'public interest' or 'community standards.'[4] But there are several problems with this approach. Censorship and censoriousness are never, in fact, implemented in a democratic way. Censorship is always done by nameless people (often bureaucrats) in the best interests of the people rather than at the behest of the majority; censoriousness is meted out without any polling or scientific testing. In fact the whole idea of censorship and the censoriousness that leads to it is the prevention of the majority of the population from having much or any exposure to the expression involved, without which they can hardly decide for themselves whether they want or accept it. Democracy is based on the idea that people know what is best for themselves; censorship cannot therefore be based on the democratic principle. It is based instead, as I said earlier, on a paternalistic principle. Furthermore, few ideas or other expression ever have the support of over half of the population. It is nonsensical in most instances to say that expression has the 'support' or 'approval' of any segment of society. Most political expression is not 'approved' or 'accepted' by the bulk of society. Most academic or religious expression is likewise not subject to tests of acceptability. It would be farcical to assume that they could be. Perhaps people 'approve' of the broad category of political or religious expression, but then it must be assumed that they approve of the broad category of sexual expression, since most fiction would fall within it. Besides, having the support of the majority for every decision is not the essence of democracy. The Canadian electoral system regularly places in power a group of people who do not have the support of over 50 per cent of the population. Most people would prefer to have the governing party *not* govern, but they govern in any event. Even our most basic power arrangements are based at best on a modified democratic-majority principle. In any event, to the extent that communication and expression are individual-based rights, the democratic principle should be a minor concern. For gays and lesbians of course, the democratic principle, even if we take it to be something less than majoritarianism, could always be potentially fatal unless homosexuality is reduced to an innocuous characteristic of passing interest at best. Even the most optimistic assessment of homosexuals or homosexuality in society would always make homosexuals a small minority.

The courts are intimately and inextricably involved in issues of censorship and censoriousness. Their implication in censorship is obvious, but they may also be called upon to adjudicate issues arising from censoriousness, for example, when a decision is made to exclude a particular group from funding because the members of that group are not 'deserving.' This chapter leaves for others a consideration of the ways in which the courts may or may not intervene in cases involving censorship and censoriousness.[5] What I explore here are the courts' own instances of censorship and censoriousness, sometimes in the context of censorship cases and sometimes not, as they affect homosexuals and homosexuality. The extent of judicial involvement in censorship and censoriousness is a gauge of just how dispassionate the courts really are in reviewing or implementing decisions that involve such actions and attitudes. A pattern of judicial censoriousness (and at times even censorship) has remained remarkably fixed over time. For all the vaunted neutrality of the courts, the judiciary has repeatedly passed a negative judgment on homosexuals and homosexuality, in much the same way as others have done.[6] This attitudinal pattern forms the judicial construction of homosexuals and homosexuality.

Judicial attitudes towards and constructions of homosexuals and homosexuality have been quite consistent over time, even though the courts are occasionally aware of how the implementation of standards of acceptable expression (particularly about sexual matters) changes. In one Customs censorship case (1979),[7] the judge expressed wistful frustration about the changes in society: 'I cannot fail to be aware that hardly a day passes when my senses are not assailed, in magazines, in films, in books, on the television and on the street, with the exploitation of nudity and of human sexuality and its quirks and foibles ... So rapid is the change which is taking place, so quickly are the standards retreating against the constant pressures of those who would test the community's tolerance to and beyond its limits, that material which only 10 years ago would have been clearly immoral, indecent or obscene, may be found today within the permitted limits.'[8] While judges are aware of changes in attitudes towards sexual matters and towards homosexuals and homosexuality (which are perceived as sexual matters),[9] the censorious attitudes and constructions are, first, enduring and, second, not deliberately or thoughtfully explored by more than a handful of judges. In the cases discussed below, it is noteworthy how often patterns of construction about homosexuality have survived over the past four decades. They appear even in the context of decisions that are, in their result, progressive and positive towards homosexuals and homosexuality. As such, those decisions become (grudging) concessions more than (enthusiastic) acknowledgments of equality.

Little Sisters: Judicial Sensitivity to Homosexual Expression?

Censorship issues as they arise in the context of homosexuality were recently given careful consideration by the B.C. Supreme Court in *Little Sisters Book and Art Emporium v. Minister of Justice* (1996).[10] The case is described in reasonable detail in this section, as I will come back to this decision case frequently in the subsequent discussion to show how, even in the most sympathetic of judgments, the old themes of censoriousness of homosexuals and homosexuality return in a new context. They occur in more palatable form, but they are still present.

In this case, Little Sisters, a gay and lesbian bookstore, challenged Canada Customs' continued detention of materials destined for the bookshop[11] and the constitutionality of the legislation prohibiting the importation of obscene materials. The bookstore argued as well that it was being unconstitutionally singled out for unfair treatment by Customs by virtue of the regularity of seizures of material destined for the store. An enormous number of experts presented evidence on the nature, effect, and significance of homosexual literature and its seizure. The judge dealt with the relevance of much of this evidence early on and established that the court would use a common sense approach. Smith J said:

> Over the two months taken up by this trial this court heard from artists, writers, sociologists, anthropologists, psychologists, teachers, book distributors, magazine publishers, booksellers, librarians, customs officers, police officers, and ordinary citizens, many of whom testified most eloquently. The subject of their discourse is a matter at the core of our fundamental democratic values – the right to speak and read and write fluently. Their testimony illuminated and explored the historic tension between that right and state censorship. The court's function, though, is not to attempt to resolve that tension as a philosopher or political scientist might, not to decide whether censorship by the state is a good thing or bad. Rather, the court must determine the legal and factual issues presented by the parties to this action, which question the constitutional validity of the customs legislation by which Parliament prohibits the importation of obscene material into Canada.[12]

The court established early on in its analysis that its role was limited. The court must not venture too far; it could only ensure that what might, conceivably, be a bad thing was administered appropriately. The law was seen as a practical tool rather than an ideal one. The rule of law was based not on an aspirational model of what the law might be or what a court might strive to do, but on a common sense model of what realistically can be made to work. In such a model the court will inevitably not go much beyond what the 'reasonable person' thinks.

Judicial hesitation to take strong stands in cases involving homosexual equality issues will be met again in the context of the issues discussed in the later chapters of this book: issues involving homosexuals and homosexuality clearly make judges nervous.

Despite its no-nonsense approach, the court in *Little Sisters* was able to paint a damning picture of the arbitrary and chaotic 'procedure' used by Customs in the case of a seizure of material. The Customs officers were not well trained. Apparently the work of dealing with obscenity was thought to be 'undesirable' by Customs employees and they did not spend long at it.[13] Testimony by a Crown witness who had done a study of the effects on Customs officers of reviewing pornography also revealed personal bias. Twenty per cent of the officers were personally homophobic; over 70 per cent of them appeared to find 'homosexual acts' repulsive.[14] Moreover, the judgment pointed out that the people doing the inspection 'do not have sufficient time available to consistently do a proper job.'[15] They had many items to consider. Despite the fact of cursory determinations, 'Few decisions to prohibit are challenged, and few challenges succeed.'[16] One of the bases for detaining goods had been 'anal penetration' but this had been deleted – just before trial – because 'departmental policy' had been changed 'as a result of evolving jurisprudence.'[17]

Notwithstanding the paucity of challenges that had been made to determinations of obscenity by Customs, Smith J found that 'a great many of the classifications are qualitatively questionable':[18] 'decisions are made by such expedients as thumbing through books, choosing pages at random to read, and fast-forwarding videotapes to count the number of offending scenes.'[19] The judge concluded that 'Many publications, particularly books, are ruled obscene without adequate evidence.'[20] He also admitted a heterosexist bias in the system, such that, '... a book of photographs entitled *Sex*, produced by the popular entertainer known as "Madonna", was approved by admission on an advance review of the Prohibited Importations Directorate, despite the fact that it contains many depictions that, considered discretely, violate Code 9956(a).'[21] This procedure was unavailable for homosexual material. Smith J was thus sympathetic to Little Sisters with respect both to the double standard applied and to the expectation of self-censorship that Customs obviously thought warranted. He said:

> Little Sisters has experienced difficulties with Canada Customs since its inception. Anticipating such difficulties, Mr Deva and Mr Smythe [the

store's owners] approached Canada Customs to seek a way to smooth the passage of their importations into Canada. They were told that they should submit, for advance review, one copy of each item they intended to import, a suggestion they understandably found to be unacceptable. The delays inherent in that procedure would have been costly to the business. As well, they found the suggestion offensive as they believed that books dealing with heterosexual topics were not handled in that way when imported by traditional bookstores.[22]

The store had to be circumspect in its orderings and it was 'uncomfortable with this self-censorship.'[23] The court noted that there was a high rate of wrong decisions made on first determination in situations involving Little Sisters and said that 'Such high rates of error indicate more than mere differences of opinion and suggest systemic causes.'[24] '[T]raditional bookstores,' as the court noted, did not have problems importing the same books.[25]

The judge in *Little Sisters* was aware that the effect of the work of Customs went beyond the bookstore:

The customs regime affects artists and writers as well as commercial bookstores. For example, Persimmon Blackridge, a local artist with impressive credentials and an international reputation, was embarrassed and upset by customs' decision to prohibit re-entry into Canada of photographs produced by her and two colleagues as part of an internationally recognized work dealing with lesbian sexuality. Jane Rule, a renowned author who received the prestigious award for best Canadian novel in 1978, spoke eloquently of her feelings as a lesbian and the hurt and shame she felt when she learned that her award-winning novel had been suspected of contravening Code 9956 (a) and was detained for inspection by customs.[26]

In the end, the court found that although the obscenity law did not infringe the Charter, the application of it in this case to matter containing homosexual expression did.[27] Despite its conclusion that the obscenity laws do not per se infringe the Charter, which was disappointing to the plaintiffs and others who seek to import sexually explicit material, the judgment is significant as it relates to censorship practices applied to homosexual expression. Some of the factors the judge recognized in the application of the law by Customs include: the use of a double standard by Customs, whereby heterosexual material is judged less severely than its homosexual counterpart; the assumption that homosexual expression was excessively sexual and should be assumed to be aberrant; the pervasiveness of negative stereotypes among the censors about homosexuals and homosexuality, the expectation that homosexuals (including the Little Sisters bookstore) should self-censor their activities; the disinclination of Customs to enquire into individual instances of expression and its tendency instead to treat them as all the same and to use a broad-brush approach. Customs was criticized for not having drawn more on 'experts' to educate them about the importance of homosexual expression, and the judge alluded to the unaccountability of the censorship system employed by Customs.

Judicial and Censorial Commonality

All of the assumptions about homosexuals and homosexual expression noted in *Little Sisters* are characteristic not only of the censorship system used by Customs but of the judiciary itself. Parallels can be found between the official systems of censorship and censoriousness (such as Customs) and the (censorious) assumptions made by judges themselves when dealing with homosexuals and homosexuality; in fact, many of these characteristics are evident even in the *Little Sisters* decision. For example, homosexuals and homosexuality are treated as other – the court needs experts to understand them. The court is resolutely heterosexual. Homosexuals can be treated as sharing common characteristics such that a broad-brush approach can be used in description of them. Homosexuals are unusually preoccupied with sex and sexual imagery. Different standards are appropriate when dealing with homosexuality than with heterosexuality. Furthermore, the judiciary is at least as anonymous as the Customs censorship system. Who is Smith J? By his own statements, it is clear that homosexual people went before him to tell very intimate and difficult things about themselves and their sexuality. They had to explain themselves. Homosexuality was open for examination.[28] The judge and the court were not.

There are three particular aspects in which parallels can be found between the judiciary as a system and a system of censorship: facelessness and systemic attitudes, heterosexuality of the decision maker, and difficulty in identifying expression. It is not, of course, possible to change the judicial system radically to avoid these parallels but a court might become more 'judicious' if it were aware of them, particularly in a case involving censorship or censoriousness.

Facelessness and Systemic Attitudes

One of the difficulties with cases of censorship (and to a lesser extent of censoriousness) is the facelessness of the individuals who make the decisions. The actual person who decides to censor a homosexual-theme book, for example, is not known. We know nothing about that person's background or beliefs. Rarely do we know the real reaction he or she had to the material excluded or to groups like homosexuals, whose interests are adversely affected by the decisions made. The judge in *Little Sisters* noted these issues as well as the poor training received by the censor. In another censorship case, in which some books and magazines were stopped because they depicted 'lesbianism,' the court expressed frustration about the secrecy of the situation. Freedman JA said in *R. v. Prairie Schooner News Ltd. and Powers* (1970): 'How does the Customs Deparent function in this regard? Do they follow a sampling method or do they scrutinize everything? If the latter method is impractical and sampling is resorted to, how can we know whether the public actions in question were the subject of actual examination? Indeed how can the accused know about that? Or do they simply believe without knowing? Finally, by what standard does the Customs Department make its determination? Is it by the same standard as the Court? We do not know, and the record before us furnishes no answer.'[29]

While many of these answers were provided in the *Little Sisters* case, we still have no sense of who the actual people are who are taking these important decisions for the public. This facelessness is justified on the basis that the censor is simply effecting state policy and not making a purely personal decision. This justification, however, obscures a real problem. In the censorship context, the bureaucrat is not simply deciding whether to issue a building certificate or to allow a tax deduction. This individual is deciding what ideas we will hear and how they will be heard. He or she is charged with filtering expression. Sometimes in a literal sense, that person is screening our calls for us and opening our mail. The censor usually acts within very broad guidelines. We would expect that a call screener or a mail opener would be known to us; we would expect to know that person's prejudices and the basis for his or her decisions on what is good and what is bad. The person should at least be accountable in detail for every decision made, especially a decision to exclude and be censorious of certain ideas or expression.

The facelessness of censorship and censoriousness can cause difficulties for the legal processes that are designed to scrutinize it. In a sexual harassment case, despite its other difficulties, at least there is usually an individual person whose actions or words (or inaction) can be challenged legally. In a censorship case, the person who made the decision is screened behind the only known party, namely, the governmental structures and individuals that might be known colloquially as 'the system.' The problem is even greater when the censorship or censoriousness is not in fact the product of just one person but is indeed a product of *the system.* Much censorship and censoriousness in the homosexual context is systemic. Canada Customs is not the only censor. Most television stations exclude gays and lesbians or stereotype them; most bookstores marginalize or exclude works on homosexual themes. Similarly most schools and school boards exclude gay groups and information from the schools. Given this situation systemic discrimination begins to appear normal. It cannot be otherwise or not everybody would be acting so.

The faceless and systemic nature of the process are not just issues that judges have to contend with as part of the factual background of a legal case on censorship or censoriousness. They are characteristic of the judicial system itself. We do not know who the judge is or what personal factors may motivate his or her decision. Did he have a bad 'homosexual' experience once? Does she have strong religious beliefs that disapprove of homosexuality? Does he have a daughter who is a lesbian and is ashamed of that fact? The judge is not called upon to reveal such matters. True, unlike in many cases of censorship, we do at least know the judge's name and might do some investigation to find out a little more. But beyond that, we remain unaware of what motivates a judge to assume a particular attitude about something like homosexuality. Furthermore, the judiciary in general is affected by a systemic censoriousness of homosexuals and homosexuality. Particular instances can be identified and subjected to particular criticism, but in a sense it is hard to fault a particular judge when what he or she does (that is, says) is part of a long tradition of censoriousness of homosexuality. That is not to say that judges' lives should be an open book or that judges should necessarily be held personally accountable for censorious statements. But the judiciary needs to be aware of the systemic censoriousness and censorship where homosexual issues are concerned so that these attitudes are not (thoughtlessly) perpetuated.

The Decision Maker as Heterosexual

Aside from the actual censoriousness of the courts with respect to homosexuality, which will be discussed shortly, it is noteworthy that the courts sometimes feel a need to distance themselves from homosexuality. Judges and the courts are heterosexual and we need reminding of that fact sometimes. No Canadian judge has ever decided a case involving homosexuality (or anything else) by identifying with homosexuality. A judge never makes the sort of personal identification that a female judge might in deciding a case involving women. Homosexuality is always the object and never the subjective identity of the law. In *Little Sisters*, for example, homosexuals are always 'they' and homosexual expression is 'their art and literature.' The ramifications are manifold. Judges need 'experts' to explain homosexuality. Thus, in *Little Sisters* an enormous amount of time and money was spent teaching the judge about things that would be assumed in any heterosexual context. Great care is used not to call somebody or something homosexual 'recklessly.' Judicial notice will rarely be taken of factors relating to gays and lesbians. This judicial distancing from homosexuality is part of the reason why judges can put forward positive and negative views of homosexuality and treat them as equally valid. In *Nielsen v. Canada* (1992),[30] in denying a right to benefits for same-sex couples, Muldoon J could say: 'It is a well-known fact, of which the Court takes notice, that Canadian society is deeply riven over the question of homosexual behaviour, the course and direction of the applicant's sexual orientation.'[31] McClung JA took comfort from similar 'controversy' in *Vriend* (1996).[32] Only a judge distancing himself from homosexuality could make these kinds of remarks. Even judges reaching decisions favourable to homosexuals are careful to distance themselves so as not to be tainted and themselves made suspect.

Some judges are more flippant in their rendering of homosexual as 'other.' In *Re Priape Enrg.* (1979),[33] the judge said: 'The homosexual community (which, for reasons which escape me, calls itself "gay") has exercised constant pressure upon the public consciousness and has gained for itself a high degree of tolerance, if not acceptance.'[34] The judge is quite clearly not a member of that lot whose customs are baffling to the court. As I discuss at greater length in Chapter 4, a homosexual is not an 'ordinary person.' In a gross indecency case (1988) involving a consenting fifteen-year-old boy and an older man, the court asked itself whether the ordinary Canadian citizen would consider the action a very marked departure from the decent conduct expected of the average citizen. MacDonald Co. Ct J said: '... who are these people, these ordinary citizens? They are, among other things, mothers and fathers, family members. They are people, generally, with an understanding of and experience in life, and I would add the basic sense of decency.'[35] Given the exclusion of homosexuals from the family context and the myth that gays and lesbians are not parents, a homosexual cannot be the ordinary person. It is this distancing of itself from homosexuality that allows the judiciary to be censorious of homosexuality.[36] It is difficult (albeit possible) to be censorious of something that you are. This distancing from homosexuality also creates the parallel between the court system and the system of censors. That a censorship system is heterosexual is self-evident. One does not put convicts in charge of the prison system. 'Lesbianism' could not have been a basis for designating expression obscene if the censors were lesbian.

Recognition of Expression

Following from the self-identification of judicial and censorial systems as heterosexual comes a difficulty in recognizing some homosexual actions as having (valuable) expressive content. The task of the censor is to evaluate potential candidates for protection under the rubric of freedom of expression. Some actions are not deemed worthy of protection – they are not valued as expression and have no expressive content that warrants noninterference. Both judges and censors are given the job of assessing whether something is or is not expression that can be valorized. One of the difficulties in ensuring freedom of expression, not just for homosexuals, but generally, is judicial ambivalence with respect to what constitutes expression. I have taken a very broad approach in defining expression, but judges do not always do so. Some actions are clearly expressive but others are not always recognized as falling within the ambit of expression. For some homosexuals, for example, any sexual act is expression because it conveys a powerful message, even beyond that conveyed to the other party to the sexual act. Both the censor and the court, however, might have difficulty understanding the expressive significance of homosexual expression.

The courts appear to accept that there is a hierarchy of things that might or might not be expression. Words are at the top of the hierarchy, followed by pictures. Actions come last. In *Prairie Schooner News*

(1970),[37] Freedman JA of the Manitoba Court of Appeal accepted a distinction between writing and photos. He said that 'community tolerance of the printed word is greater than of pictorial presentations': 'A book requires some understanding and the exercise of the imagination; a photograph at once tells its story to all, even to the illiterate. A book demands an expenditure of time and effort; a picture conveys its message swiftly and easily. A description in a book of an erotic scene, no matter how luridly written still remains only a description; the same scene presented in the form of a vivid photograph instantly rivets the attention, whether its effect is to shock, stimulate or amuse.'[38]

The court put a premium on effort at understanding as something that enhances the value of expression or indeed makes something expression. In a heterosexual world where homosexual imagery and certainly homosexual actions are rare and in places non-existent, a picture or an action can have an expressive content that is more complex and message laden than any written description. The affirming and political nature of homosexual imagery can, it is true, 'convey its message swiftly and easily' while a written description will take 'an expenditure of time and effort.' Why, however, the latter should more easily than the former be expression worthy of protection is a mystery.

In R. v. LeBeau; R. v. Lofthouse (1988),[39] the court considered whether some forms of sexual conduct could be a form of 'expression' within section 2(b) of the Charter.[40] The court said that while it might be argued that some forms of sexual conduct may involve 'making a statement,' if any constitutional right is implicated it would more reasonably be a form of 'liberty' protected by section 7 of the Charter. That is to say that the sexual act was more a matter of privacy than of expression. The problem with making a portrayal of a particular (homosexual) action an issue of privacy rather than expression is that it can then be categorized as protected in the 'private' sphere but not necessarily in the 'public' sphere. Homosexuality should be kept private, where it might be acceptable, but publicly it will perhaps be banished. It is not expression and therefore it has no business being seen or heard. It does not have the *freedom* of expression. My kissing a man in public is however, a matter not just of privacy but also of expression because of the messages it will send. And it *does* send direct messages beyond the parties involved, unlike a man kissing a woman. Even, as in the *LeBeau* case, having sex in a public washroom with another man is a matter of expression, not just privacy. If we call it expression, then we can squarely address the issue at hand, which is what expression we wish to censor – perhaps including sex in washrooms, where others can see it. There is an expression as well as a privacy aspect to the situation. Admitting the existence of that aspect allows a frank assessment of what expression is acceptable and when; it acknowledges that the message sent is the concern of the regulation. These problems of deciding whether or not there is in fact expression and whether the expression is to be valued are faced by both the judiciary and the censor. There is no simple answer, but again a court can act more constructively if it is at least aware of the parallel.

Facets of Judicial Censoriousness

In addition to these structural or functional similarities, courts resemble the censor in the context of homosexual expression by virtue of their attitudes towards homosexuality. The censor obviously censors; a court might also censor, but what a court does is more likely to take the form of censoriousness. Five facets of censoriousness, which have changed little over time, appear again and again in judicial speech about homosexuality:

1 a double standard is acceptable when dealing with homosexuals and homosexuality;
2 homosexuals are sexually obsessed;
3 homosexuality should be desexualized as much as possible to make it palatable;
4 homosexuality can be both unnatural and seductive; and
5 homosexuals and homosexuality can be treated in a two-dimensional and uniform way.

The way in which these assumptions, these aspects of censoriousness, are brought to bear by the courts change over the years, but the assumptions themselves reappear with consistency. Sometimes, as in the *Little Sisters* case, the result of a judicial decision might appear to be to the advantage of homosexuals, but a closer examination reveals the existence of long-standing assumptions about homosexuals and homosexuality.

Double Standards

At times, the courts can be quite open about imposing a different standard with respect to homosexuality than it applies to heterosexuality. The clearest recent examples of the express double standard for homosexuals are perhaps found in the same-sex benefits cases. Here, homosexual relationships are rendered something less than heterosexual relationships. In the decision of La Forest J in *Egan v. Canada* (1995),[41] the reasons given for permitting the denial of same-sex benefits are completely nonsensical unless one accepts a double standard on faith. Heterosexuality is elevated into a sanctified realm and part of that sanctity owes to the status of marriage. La Forest J said: 'Suffice it to say that marriage has from time immemorial been firmly grounded in our legal tradition, one that is itself a reflection of long-standing philosophical and religious traditions. Part of its ultimate *raison d'être* transcends all of these and is firmly anchored in biological and social realities that heterosexual couples have the unique ability to procreate, that most children are the product of these relationships, and that they are generally cared for and nurtured by those who live in that relationship. In this sense, marriage is by nature heterosexual.'[42] There are, of course, no 'biological and social realities' that heterosexual couples *do* procreate or that a homosexual who is part of a couple (or not) *cannot* procreate. La Forest J continued: 'I fail to see how homosexuals differ from other excluded couples in terms of the fundamental social reasons for which Parliament has sought to favour heterosexuals who live as married couples. Homosexual couples, it is true, differ from other excluded couples in that their relationships include a sexual aspect. But this sexual aspect has nothing to do with the social objectives for which Parliament affords a measure of support to married couples and those who live in a common law relationships.'[43]

The judge did not consider whether his statements were true for heterosexuals, let alone for homosexuals. La Forest J was evidently determined to exclude homosexual couples from being considered to have relationships equivalent to heterosexual ones even if logic lost out as a result. His interpretation of what Parliament intended, however, was probably correct. Parliament probably *did* intend to privilege heterosexual over homosexual couples. The court, to the extent of support for the views of La Forest J, accepted this discrimination. La Forest J is not judicially alone in his views on such a distinction – but neither is he alone in being unable to provide a justification for the distinction that is based on anything other than a straightforward double standard. An acceptance of the double standard is required in order to believe that Marceau JA gave a valid justification for finding that two men did not constitute a family in the case of *Re Attorney-General of Canada and Mossop* (1990).[44] He said: 'It seems to me that what was done by the tribunal was to take some attributes usually ascribed to families, such as mutual love between members, mutual assistance, joint residence, emotional support, sharing of domestic tasks, sexual relationships, and treat them as being of the essence of the concept itself being signified. There is a difference between being, in certain respects, functionally akin to a family and being a family.'[45] If everything else is the same between the two would-be families, then the only thing that prevents the same-sex couple from being recognized as a family is a double standard that will never permit that recognition. If a flower has all the characteristics of a rose, why must it be 'functionally akin' to a rose rather than being a rose? Such a conclusion can only be reached because of a simple determination not to reach any other conclusion.

The courts sometimes express astonishment that a same-sex couple could even consider that its relationship would be the equivalent of an opposite-sex relationship; a judge can be quite genuinely surprised that anyone could be so naive. This astonishment can be seen in the judgments of La Forest J and Marceau JA discussed above. Judicial bemusement is also evident in *Anderson v. Luoma* (1986): the court stated that the plaintiff, who was 'forthright but quite naive' and 'a neophyte in the lesbian world,' actually 'wanted to believe that her new found life was really no different from the one she just left.'[46] The plaintiff, if one is to accept the court's logic, was a fool to think that a lesbian relationship could be anything but doomed to failure and unhappiness.

Sometimes the disinclination to recognize a homosexual relationship as equivalent to a heterosexual one affects heterosexual couples. In one Ontario case (1990), the court considered whether one person in an opposite-sex couple, who was still legally married to a third party, could claim spousal immunity from giving evidence against her new partner. The court said no. Part of the reasoning of Farley J was: 'What would be the logical reason for excluding homosexual lovers who cohabit as a couple from the exemption if they asserted that they had a quasi-marital relationship?'[47] This possibility, although it had nothing whatever to do with the case before the court, was something that had to be kept in mind as a result to be avoided at all costs. The homosexual couple was analogized to an adulterous couple. The idea that a homosexual couple could have a marital relationship was not even considered to be a possibility.

Not surprisingly, the judicial double standard is taken to heart by some same-sex couples, who consequently go out of their way to show that their relationship *is* like that of an opposite-sex couple. The hope is that the court will be unable *in their case* to apply the double standard. There is a certain tacit acceptance of the double standard in such behaviour. The litigants accept that perhaps homosexual couples have not generally been good enough to qualify for recognition or for benefits and must try harder to have 'better' relationships.[48] In doing so, they put unnecessary pressure and artificiality on their relationship and indirectly sabotage equal recognition for other homosexual couples. Some judges at least would spare same-sex couples this more onerous burden of the double standard. Two of the Supreme Court of Canada judges in *Egan v. Canada* (1995) went out of their way to acknowledge the double standard that otherwise exists and to say that the homosexual quest to establish the perfect relationship for the approval of the court was not necessary. Cory J said: 'In this case, a great deal of time was spent demonstrating the nature of the warm, compassionate, caring relationship that very evidently existed between the appellants. In passing, it is, I think, worth mentioning that this need not be done in every case. It is not necessary that the evidence demonstrate that a homosexual relationship bears all the features of an ideal heterosexual relationship, for the relationship of many heterosexual couples is sometimes far from ideal. The relationships between heterosexuals must vary as infinitely as do the personalities of the individuals involved.'[49] Iacobucci J agreed and said that 'Whereas there is a presumption of interdependence in heterosexual relationships, there is a presumption against interdependence in same-sex relationships. The latter presumption is not only incorrect, but it is also the fruit of stigmatizing stereotypes.'[50] Progress is thus not impossible.

The double standard exists not just for homosexual relationships but for homosexual relations in general and especially for homosexual sex. Some judges have been quite unabashed in their censoriousness of homosexuality, comfortably setting out and then applying a double standard. In *Re Priape Enrg.* (1979),[51] for example, where the court had to decide whether certain publications aimed at a gay audience were obscene, Hugessen ACJQ said:

'Gay' rights movements flourish; 'gay' publications can be found in bookstores and newsstands, and 'gay' bars, clubs and self-help groups advertise daily in the newspapers. It remains, however, that, in my opinion, the community standard of contemporary Canada is less tolerant with regard to overt homosexual acts that with regard to similar acts committed between people of opposite sexes. By way of simple example, a young man and a woman lying on the grass in a sunny city park, at lunch hour, kissing and embracing one another, will draw hardly a passing glance. The same conduct in the same place by two men together would almost certainly lead to a disturbance and to the police being called. As I understand the law, I have to take account of these differences in community standards of tolerance. I would only add that in doing so I do not think that I am giving judicial sanction to any kind of discrimination, for there is a real difference between what one may have the right to do in private and what the community is prepared to tolerate to be published, imported or distributed.[52]

Hugessen ACJQ did not, therefore, see his role as facilitating a challenge to this double standard. In fact, in his view, his job was to take them into account. The court's role was to perpetuate, not prevent them. Nor did the judge see any reason to analyse *why* exactly it is 'normal' that two men embracing each other would lead to a disturbance and police intervention.[53] David Dyzenhaus has criticized the judicial approach that looks to public offensiveness as a determinant in expression cases. Of the situation involving two men displaying affection in public, he says: 'Surely in this situation homophobic people can say that their distress is caused by public indecency? It will not matter to the homophobes that they are not exposed to even more physical manifestations of affection. What matters is that in public they are forced to confront clear evidence of what is likely happening in private.'[54] As Dyzenhaus concludes, the upshot of this double standard is to '... force the un-conformist to hide his or her non-conformity in the closet, which is surely an effective and harmful sanction.'

Having excused himself from being a party to an approval or application of any kind of discrimination, the judge in *Re Priape* went on to use the double standard in his decision. Of one of the categories of materials, he said: 'In App. D, I have listed 16 magazines which consist largely of photographs, again in clinical detail, of homosexual couplings, but with only two participants. It is in this group where I think the distinction between community tolerance for heterosexual activities and acts involving persons of the same sex comes into play. Many of the activities portrayed would be at, or just within, the limits of tolerance if the persons shown were opposite sexes. They are not, and I am satisfied that contemporary community standards would judge this material to be immoral or indecent.'[55]

This decision is resonant with a much earlier case (1957), in which two men were charged with gross indecency for having sex in a car, when it was still dark, in the early hours of the morning, in a remote place. [56] Egbert J said: 'An act which in itself is indecent cannot become decent because of the circumstances surrounding its performance.'[57] He distinguished this situation from that which might apply if the two had been a man and a woman. The judge cited earlier authority that said that sex between a man and a woman is 'natural and normal' and 'not indecent at all,' even if the man and woman are not married. The process of reasoning here is the same as that used by La Forest J in *Egan* and Marceau JA in *Mossop* and it extends from an acceptance of the inherent inferiority of the homosexual as opposed to the heterosexual. The judge does not accept that there is an analogy to be drawn between the heterosexual and the homosexual.

Just as in *Anderson v. Luoma*, where the court appeared to think that application of the double standard with respect to family status was somehow a favour to the 'naive' young lesbian, so a court can manage to construe a law that embodies a double standard with respect to homosexual sex (as opposed to heterosexual sex) as a favour to homosexuals. How else can we make sense of what Charles Prov. Ct J said in *R. v. Mason* (1981)?[58] In that case, 'married and unmarried couples resorted to the home of the accused and indulged in a variety of sexual activities, normal, perverted, deviant and totally heterosexual, including sexual activities between three or more parties of both sexes.' We are assured that 'There were no homosexuals at the parties given by the accused ...'[59] The judge then considered section 158 of the Criminal Code, which said that the sections of the Code relating to buggery or bestiality and acts of gross indecency respectively did not apply to acts committed in private, privacy being a situation where there was no third party involved. He said that: 'An act of gross indecency, as contemplated by the *Code*, includes an act between homosexuals whether done in private or in public. Section 158 was designed to protect homosexuals, so long as they performed their acts in private and not in the presence of a third party.'[60] An act of gross indecency, as contemplated by section 158, could not be committed by heterosexuals. Homosexuals, though, are supposed to be seen as 'protected' by having a double standard applied to them. Charles Prov. Ct J emphasized the difference in treatment when he decided that it was 'difficult to attribute to

Parliament any such quixotic and deadening purpose as would render group sex among persons of different sex in privacy of a private dwelling-house, be it normal or deviate, an indecent act ...'[61] Heterosexuals are given a degree of tolerance unavailable to homosexuals. Homosexuals should be thankful that they are allowed to do things in private with one other person. The judge said that: 'Sex is still considered by its opponents as being something which is dirty, not nice to speak about or discuss, whereas I think the average reasonable citizen in Canada considers it as the ultimate in a very tender and loving relationship *between persons of different sex.*'[62]

Of course, a different standard could be applied to homosexuals so as to give them an 'advantage' unavailable to heterosexuals. This might be seen as 'protection' for homosexuals. The *Little Sisters* case is an example of a situation in which different treatment for homosexual erotica and pornography was construed as protection for gays and lesbians. In deciding whether the law allowing Customs to seize material was discriminatory under section 15 of the Charter, Smith J said:

> The defining characteristic of homosexuals – the element that distinguishes them from everybody else in society – is their sexuality. Naturally, their art and literature are extensively concerned with this central characteristic of their humanity. As attested by several of the plaintiffs' witnesses, erotica produced for heterosexual audiences performs largely an entertainment function, but homosexual erotica is far more important to homosexuals. These witnesses established that sexual text and imagery produced for homosexuals serves as an affirmation of their sexuality and as a socializing force; that it normalizes the sexual practices that the larger society has historically considered to be deviant; and that it organizes homosexuals as a group and enhances their political power. Because sexual practices are so integral to homosexual culture, any law proscribing representations of sexual practices will necessarily affect homosexuals to a greater extent than it will other groups in society, to whom representations of sexual practices are much less significant and for whom such representations play a relatively marginal role in art and literature.[63]

The judge put sexual depictions at the heart of homosexuality. He explicitly distinguished this from the heterosexual situation, in which erotica is 'marginal.' Brenda Cossman and Bruce Ryder, in their examination of this aspect of *Little Sisters*, conclude that: '... the premise that homosexual expression generally, and material imported by Little Sisters specifically, contains a disproportionate share of obscenity strikes us as implausible and certainly not sustainable on the evidence presented.'[64] They say that this must overlook the abundance of material depicting sexual violence, child sexuality, and sexual degradation.[65] It is true that depictions of homosexuality (including homosexual sex, which category is *not* co-extensive with the category of depictions of homosexuality) probably has a more powerful expressive content in many cases than a depiction of heterosexuality. The expressive significance is not just for homosexuals but for everyone; it is, in fact, arguably more significant for heterosexuals than for many homosexuals. Smith J went beyond that conclusion, however, and accepted in essence that homosexuals could get away with more explicit sexual imagery than could heterosexuals. The argument that was accepted by the judge was made by counsel for Little Sisters to evade the problems posed by the heterosexist obscenity ruling in *R. v. Butler* (1992).[66] It entails, however, the acceptance of a double standard and a need to consider homosexual sex as different from heterosexual sex for legal purposes. Is this not just censoriousness in another form of double standard? Though neither erotica nor pornography should be seen as inherently bad, the identification that the judge made was censorious because it generalized in a way that is in practice perceived to be negative. Homosexuals are treated as oddities. While trying to be understanding, in his expression the judge was ultimately patronizing, and he rendered all homosexuals as uniform and subject to oversexualization. Although it is true that homosexuals have been historically unable to gain access to homoerotic images in the same way that heterosexuals have had access to heteroerotic images, the court did not stop at that point on this matter. Rather than looking at how equivalency between the heterosexual and the homosexual positions might be attained, the court treated homosexuals, in an absolute and arguably permanent way, as different. Where heterosexuals can do without erotica, homosexuals are addicted to it.

Is the establishment of a counter double standard, as suggested by Smith J in *Little Sisters*, really the route to equality? While such approach might be a 'favour' to homosexuals in that case, it introduces double standards, the use of which usually works against homosexuals. More helpful might be an approach that looks not to whether gays or lesbians find erotica (or depictions of sex) more 'important' than do heterosexuals but rather to whether the standards of obscenity or other basis for censorship have a more onerous impact on homosexuals than on others. The most obvious examples are the prohibitions that have existed against depictions of 'lesbianism,' 'sodomy,' or 'anal intercourse.' The first one obviously has broader impact on gay women. The second and third prohibitions, because of their symbolism for gay men, will have a broader impact on gay men. Here the effect of censorship goes beyond mere censorship in a given instance and becomes symbolic of censoriousness of the whole group. That sort of finding does not constitute the judicial imposition of a double standard, whereas the idea that homosexual erotica is 'more important' to homosexuals as a group while heterosexual erotica is just 'entertainment' *does*.

Sexual Obsession

A second aspect of the censoriousness of homosexuality and homosexuals by the courts takes the form of the notion that homosexuals are abnormally obsessed with sex. As sex is generally thought to be a negative thing, any indication of an obsession with it will be looked upon with suspicion. But the fact that gay or lesbian sex is so unusual gives the courts greater reason to be especially censorious of it. We have just seen that even the judge in *Little Sisters*, who was on the whole sympathetic to homosexuals, accepted the equation of homosexuality with a propensity to need imagery of sex.[67] Homosexuals are portrayed as being obsessed with sexual imagery in a way that the judge appeared to believe heterosexuals are not. The constant barrage of romances, marriages, infidelities, and 'families' on television, in print, and in music (mostly heterosexual) does not, it would seem, constitute sexual imagery. Or, at least, it is not 'important' to heterosexuality. Thus, Smith J can say, without any consciousness of a double standard: 'Since homosexuals are defined by their homosexuality and their art and literature is permeated with representations of their sexual practices, it is inevitable that they will be disproportionately affected by a law proscribing the proliferation of obscene sexual representations.'[68]

The idea of the permeation of homosexuality with obscene sexual representations is reflective of other judgments in which the court accepted a heightened sexual view of homosexuals to less 'welcome' results. For example, in *Vriend v. Alberta*, another 1996 case, McClung JA, for the majority, reached back to stereotypes linking homosexuals inextricably to sodomy, which of course never has a heterosexual manifestation, and therefore to 'unnatural' sex. The case concerned a man losing his job because of his sexual orientation. Although we know nothing about Mr Vriend's sexual activities, McClung JA appeared to think that he knew what Vriend was up to, by virtue of his sexual orientation alone. McClung JA said: 'I am unable to conclude that it was a forbidden, let alone a reversible, legislative response for the province of Alberta to step back from the validation of homosexual relations, including sodomy, as a protected and fundamental right, thereby, "... rebutting a millennium of moral teaching".'[69] With the theme of aberrant sexual practices firmly in mind, McClung JA leapt to make an association with other 'bizarre' sexual practices. How else can we explain the judge's sense that it was relevant to the case to say: 'It is pointless to deny that the Dahmer, Bernardo and Clifford Robert Olsen prosecutions have recently heightened public concern about violently aberrant sexual configurations and how they find expression against their victims.'[70]

McClung JA's views, which I will elaborate on further in Chapter 3, are part of a long judicial tradition that links homosexuality with excessive and aberrant sexual practices. There is an expectation that homosexual sex will take place in strange places and in strange ways.[71] In *R. v. Salida* (1968), F.K. Jasperson QC, magistrate, defined 'lesbianism' as 'the sexual relationship between females, the female counterpart of homosexuality, with all its sensual and disgusting behavioural gratifications.'[72] In *R. v. Duthie Books Ltd.* (1966),[73] in which the court dealt with whether the book *Last Exit to Brooklyn* was obscene under the Criminal Code, Bull JA said that the events in which men engaged in sex with each other are 'all told in unsavoury detail.'[74] The language of the court with reference to homosexual sex assumed a more mocking tone in *R. v. Pinard and Maltais* (1982),[75] where the court found that there was gross indecency in a gay bathhouse. The tone of the judges' comments make clear their distaste for what went on in the bathhouse. Monet JA said: 'The purposes of these encounters has nothing to do with psycho-juridical studies on "sexual orientation," terms which the Quebec legislator added ... to the *Charter of human rights and freedoms* ...'[76] This was homosexual sex and therefore fell somehow outside of propriety. A need to examine why there was a lack of a heterosexual equivalent to such a crime, why men might need a bathhouse for sexual release, or why society thought it had an interest in patrolling such places did not occur to the judge. Some answers to these questions may in fact have been found in the 'psycho-juridical studies' that were dismissed. Monet JA instead made some sport of the homosexual sex involved. Consistent with the view that homosexuals are uncontrollably addicted to sex, the judge said: 'The evidence ... establishes that the clients of David Sauna did not lack enthusiasm.'[77] The court also appeared to approve of the somewhat farcical idea of a hierarchy of sexual acts, sometimes depending on where they take place. Malouf JA commented: 'In the present case, I have no doubt that the accused who introduced his finger into his anus committed an act which is intrinsically one of gross indecency. However, I am not ready to find that the act of masturbation committed by the second accused is in itself an act of gross indecency. However, in the circumstances and the location in which it was committed, it was an act of gross indecency.'[78] One assumes that the homosexual association of the finger in the anus is what distinguishes it from masturbation *simpliciter*, and that masturbating in a gay bathhouse is worse than doing it at home alone.[79]

The courts are most alarmed and disapproving of the link they make between unnatural sex and homosexuality when it comes to custody of children cases. There are numerous examples of the courts exhibiting their disapproving alarm at the combination of children and unnatural sex, which will be dealt with in more detail in the next section and in Chapter 3. One example will suffice here. *Saunders v. Saunders* (1989) was an access case in which the father was in a homosexual relationship.[80] The judge was alarmed by the fact that the father and his partner did not keep their relationship a secret from the child. Wetmore Co. Ct J said: 'This child [a boy] has a normal, stable home in which there are only the normal environmental circumstances for maturity to develop. Surely it cannot be argued the exposure of a child to unnatural relations is in the best interests of that child of tender years. While it is an impossibility to protect a child from many undesirable situations, even when they are very young, the prudent parent does not voluntarily and deliberately expose a child to any environmental influence which might affect normal development.'[81] The judge apparently assumed that the two men would be flaunting their (abnormal) sexual activities in front of the child. There was also an assumption that a heterosexual household would not host such a flaunting of (normal) sex.

Given the hostility of the courts to homosexual sex, it is not clear that the linking of homosexuality with a need for erotica, as in *Little Sisters*, is a positive development in jurisprudence as it affects homosexual issues. It is in fact an extension of the tradition of associating homosexuality with sex. Sex is not seen as a positive form of expression in our society. While this is lamentable, a fostering of the association of homosexuality with sex is unlikely to change this situation. In fact, it will serve only to confirm the 'other' status of homosexuality.

Desexualizing Homosexuality and Homosexuals

The opposite response to sex and homosexuality – to desexualize homosexuals – is of course just as censorious. Here the sex in homosexual is censored. It is either obliterated or rendered into an unimportant aspect of homosexuality, or at least an unimportant aspect of being homosexual. The effect is to separate doing from being. It is acceptable for people to be homosexual but they must not engage in homosexual activity. This approach mimics at least one religious approach whereby we are encouraged to love the sinner (in this case the homosexual) but not the sin (the homosexual act) and the sinner ought to be assumed to avoid the sin as much as possible. The courts will thus give the benefit of the doubt to people who are homosexual (or who might be homosexual) by avoiding implicating them in an actual homosexual act. The homosexual act is thereby rendered a negative thing. The court censors the homosexual act and is censorious of those who would do such a thing.

The most common example of the desexualization of homosexuals is the refusal to make an analogy between a same-sex couple and a heterosexual married couple, which we have already seen as an aspect of the double standard applied to homosexuality.[82] The court avoids the necessary sexual implications of their relationships by equating them with asexual couples.[83] The sexual relationship is thus censored by the court. The desexualizing of homosexuals and their relationships was something of a theme in the *Egan* case at all levels. At first instance (1991), the judge said: 'The plaintiffs as a homosexual couple, just as a bachelor and a spinster who live together or other types of couples who live together do not fall within the traditional meaning of the conjugal unit or spouse.'[84] He went on to say: 'The homosexual couple is one of the larger class of same-sex non-spousal couples who live together.'[85] The Court of Appeal judgment in *Egan* (1993) contains the view of Mahoney JA in the majority, who compared same-sex couples to 'cohabitation by siblings.'[86] Linden JA, dissenting, noted the effect of this desexing of same-sex couples: 'To treat lesbian and gay relationships like all other non-spousal relationships is to rely on and perpetuate the prejudiced view of the legitimacy and worth of those relationships.'[87] La Forest J (1995) resurrected the old view that gays and lesbians, as couples, are just like other couples 'such as brothers and sisters or other relatives, regardless of sex, and others who are not related, whatever reason those other couples may have for doing so and whatever their sexual orientation.'[88] La Forest J did, it is true, admit that there is a sexual element to same-sex relationships, but this sexual element was to be excluded from consideration because it was not socially valuable.

Egan by no means stands alone. There is a tradition of treating homosexuals as a couple of maiden aunts living together.[89] Thus, in *Re Andrews and Minister of Health for Ontario* (1988),[90] McRae J compared homosexual couples to 'heterosexual couples of the same sex, brothers and brothers, sisters and sisters, brothers and sisters, cousins, parents and adult children and any combination of them.' [91] The emotional-sexual bond of a same-sex relationship is either non-existent or not as strong as that found in an opposite-sex relationship.

Related to the desexing of a homosexual relationship is the idea that homosexual sex is simply a manifestation of capriciousness on the part of those who identify themselves as homosexual. In Chapter 1, I discussed the judicial idea that homosexuality is a choice that could be reversed. Homosexuals could stop if they wanted to and in fact, they should stop. People in a same-sex relationship are given judicial encouragement to be normal and enter opposite-sex relationships. In *Layland v. Ontario (Minister of Consumer and Commercial Relations)* (1993) the court had to determine whether section 15 of the Charter was infringed when a same-sex couple was denied a marriage licence.[92] The majority trotted out the old end-of-society fears and said that the denial did not infringe the Charter because: 'One of the principal purposes of the institution of marriage is the founding and maintenance of families in which children will be produced and cared for, a procedure which is necessary for the continuance of the species ...'[93] Southey J then said: 'The law does not prohibit marriage by homosexuals, provided it takes place between people of the opposite sex. Some homosexuals do marry. The fact that many homosexuals do not choose to marry, because they do not want unions with persons of the opposite sex, is the result of their own preferences, not a requirement of the law.'[94] As Donald Casswell says these words 'ring with cruel contempt.' This approach denies 'their very identities as lesbians and gay men.'[95]

The idea that homosexual activity is something that can be given up or changed easily so as to allow the person to conform to societal norms appears quite frequently in custody cases, where the court makes clear that its view of custody might change if the homosexuality were to cease.[96] There is in such cases no conception that a same-sex relationship might be important to the homosexual parent who seeks custody. In *Elliott v. Elliott* (1987), the court had to decide whether custody of a daughter should be with the mother, who was in a lesbian relationship. The mother had been in a cohabiting relationship with Mrs Whittle earlier, as a result of which custody had been granted to the father. The mother regained custody upon stating that she had ceased cohabiting with Mrs Whittle. However, circumstances had now changed again. MacKinnon J thought it 'particularly significant' that the mother had resumed cohabitation with Mrs Whittle shortly after she had obtained custody of the two girls on the grounds that she had terminated the cohabitation. He said: 'It is, in my view, relevant and significant that the mother would risk losing custody of the girls rather than terminate her cohabitation with Mrs Whittle. She knew the basis of the order of Macdonell J. It was she who sought the variation on the grounds of terminating the cohabitation. In resuming it, she left no doubt as to the priority of her relationship with her companion. It was the paramount consideration. She wanted custody. It was, however, not at the sacrifice of the homosexual relationship.'[97] The 'sacrifice' of the homosexual relationship was something expected. The court was incredulous that the same-sex bond could be so strong that the mother would want it to persist even though it jeopardized her custody of the children.

The court sometimes offers a gay parent a bribe in the form of hope by implying that if the parent abandons his or her homosexuality, the result of a custody case might be different. In one case of a homosexual father wanting access (1985),[98] the father lived with his lover, which is all we are told about either of them. The mother, it appears, did not oppose access, but she was 'very concerned that the children [two girls] be exposed to a life-style that is very confusing, disruptive and contrary to their moral upbringing,' and she was particularly concerned about overnight access. McIntyre J said: 'I can readily understand and I share Mrs Worby's concern about overnight access because it could be harmful to the children while his present life-style continues.'[99] The court ordered: 'Peter Worby will not be awarded overnight visits with his children while his present life-style continues.'[100] The court would, it seems, prefer the father to lie about his sexual orientation. It hoped and in fact expected that he would give up his homosexuality,[101] which was not seen as fundamental to his existence.

Where the homosexual parent is not expected to give up on homosexuality altogether, he or she is at least expected to hide it from the children. Homosexuality is not, apparently, an essential part of the person, but rather something of a nasty hobby that can be concealed from children: *pas devant les enfants*. Self-censorship is a good thing for homosexuals. This matter usually arises in custody and divorce cases. For example, in *K. v. K.* (1975),[102] there was an action for divorce and custody of the children. The mother was a homosexual; the court granted her custody but took into account that there was no sexual contact in front of the children. The judge appears to have accepted the view of a Dr Brown, who said that there would only be a problem if the mother 'preached the joys of lesbianism.' He also felt that separate accommodation of the two women – 'Or, at least, separate bedrooms' – would provide a 'better situation.'[103]

A similar outcome was reached in *D. v. D.* (1978).[104] The court found, somewhat grudgingly, that the father was probably in a homosexual relationship. It awarded him custody but said that:

It has not been established that Mr D's sexual preferences exclude members of the opposite sex. He describes himself as bisexual. He is discreet. He has not indulged in unusual exhibitionistic behaviour in the presence of the children, although there was evidence led which sought to establish that he did. His sexual orientation is not known outside his immediate circle; he does not flaunt it. Visitors to his house include married couples, mainly. He has never exhibited any missionary attitude or inclinations toward militancy in this difficult area of homosexual behaviour. He disclaims membership in any club although he admits to having frequented a bar which has earned the reputation of having become a meeting place for people with homosexual leanings.[105]

The court approved of his self-censorship of homosexual activity and encouraged the interest in the opposite sex. Some visitors were obviously better than others, and heterosexual visitors were definitely better for the children. The father should never talk about his sexual orientation and militancy was definitely beyond the pale. [106]

In another case (1988), the court appeared to be favourably disposed to a father because of his negative feelings towards his sexual orientation. Felstiner Prov. Ct J said: 'I felt [the father] was sincere when he said on cross examination that if he could have controlled the situation, he would not have chosen to be homosexual. He added that he wishes his children to be heterosexual.'[107] If an individual cannot give up homosexuality, he or she is at the very least expected to wish that it were possible to do so.

Aside from expecting homosexuals to refrain from homosexual sex, the other form of judicial 'wishing away' of homosexuality is the occasional refusal to identify homosexual activity where it quite obviously exists. It is defined out of existence. One of the most striking (and amusing) instances of a court censoring homosexuality by refusing to believe it could be happening occurs in a 1964 New Brunswick case.[108] There, at 11:30 p.m. and in front of a restaurant, two sailors were spotted lying on the ground entwined somehow and they were charged with gross indecency. The lower court convicted the appellant on the basis of the evidence of the principal witnesses for the Crown, a 'police recorder' and his wife. The Appeal Division refused to consider such a possibility and thought it better to accept the evidence of the appellant and Roberts, the other man. According to their testimony they and some companions had been drinking for four hours and the two of them, having got some chicken and chips, leaned against the mud guard of a car. The appellant, they said, slid off and fell to the sidewalk and in endeavouring to assist the appellant to his feet, Roberts fell beside him. They denied that their clothing was disarranged. Ritchie JA said: 'Having some knowledge of the behaviour of service men out for a night on the town, I have no difficulty picturing an intoxicated giggling sailor sliding off the rear mud guard of an automobile so as to lay prone on the sidewalk and an intoxicated giggling companion going to his assistance and ending up on the sidewalk beside his friend. I cannot picture the act of gross indecency described by the Garners being committed on the sidewalk of a busy street in full view of anyone passing by. That just does not happen.'[109] The court – having some expertise with the navy! – could not countenance homosexuality among sailors having any public form of expression. Such an occurrence simply could not be contemplated, and was therefore removed from the realm of possibility. This involved disbelieving a police recorder and his wife and believing instead two sailors who, although they had been drinking for over four hours were able to remember that their clothes were not 'disarranged.'[110]

Perhaps more so than with men, courts are disinclined to construe activity between women as homosexual if there is any way possible to avoid such a construction. The desire to desexualize homosexuality by eliminating the lesbian option is evident in *T. v. T. and W.* (1975), in which there was a petition by a husband for divorce based on the 'homosexual act' of the wife.[111] The problem was that there was no evidence of a specific act, just words about a relationship and opportunity for homosexual acts. The court refused to imply them. Dewar CJQB clearly distinguished what the court was willing to contemplate in a heterosexual situation versus in a homosexual situation: 'Evidence of familiarity and opportunity is commonly offered in proof of adultery, commission of the act being a matter of inference influenced by human experience that, as between male and female, natural or normal sexual conduct will probably occur. The same influence does not operate in proved circumstances of familiarity and opportunity involving two people of the same sex where the sexual conduct to be inferred is unnatural or abnormal.'[112] Even though the women involved said they were having an affair, the court preferred to close its eyes to the situation. It did say that the relationship between the women 'may well be an inverted one, the expression of propensity or preference on the part of each of them for a person of the same sex.'[113] But it refused to draw conclusions as to sexual acts on that basis. The sexual act is censored out of the relationship unless it is absolutely necessary. This is reminiscent of *Gaveronski v. Gaveronski* (1974).[114] This was the case in which the court said, in the context of a divorce action based on a homosexual act committed by the wife, that in some instances, 'a friendly caress of the bosom by one female of another' might not be homosexual, although in that particular case it had been.[115] The court did not elaborate on how, exactly, friendly caresses of another woman's breast might not be homosexual.

Judicial scepticism about acts possibly being homosexual in nature (along with the contrary police tendency to assume homosexual activity) was evident in a rather unorthodox fashion in *Re L. (R.)* (1981).[116] There, an off-duty police officer was charged with discreditable conduct for allegedly picking up a male hustler and giving him a blow job in a car in Ottawa. The accused was observed picking up 'O' on a street well known for male hustlers. They then drove together to a nearby parking lot. 'O,' who admitted he was a male prostitute, said they were engaging in sex when he noticed an approaching car. He testified that when he told this to the accused, the accused stopped giving 'O' a blow job and tried to do up his own trousers. The court chose to disbelieve 'O' on the basis that he had a history of lying and in this case had lied about his age and whether he had been paid. The other police officers (who had observed the incident) gave some rather general evidence about what had happened when they followed the accused's car that night. The two police officers' evidence 'was hesitant and uncertain and lacked that quality of precision and reliability one expects from experienced police officers.' The accused's version was that he had been drinking and drove past the pick-up area, picked up a hitchhiker, and pulled over into the parking lot because of the effects of drink. Although the court chose to disbelieve this version, it found that the charge of discreditable conduct based on an act of gross indecency was not made out.

The fact that sometimes courts assume that the 'worst' sexual antics are afoot when homosexuality is involved but at other times desexualize homosexuality testifies to a certain judicial schizophrenia about homosexuality. There is an uncertainty about how exactly to deal with it; it has either to be magnified or minimized. The bifurcated, contradictory judicial attitudes – homosexuality as rampant, homosexuality as impossible – mean that homosexuality is a fraught issue and in many contexts, as will be discussed in Chapter 3, one that is not appropriately justiciable. Homosexuality is not allowed to exist in a 'natural' state: it is always rendered into something bigger or smaller than it is. The slightest act with homosexual content takes on a significance as either the signifier of aberrant and excessive sexuality or a refusal to eliminate that which ought to be trivial. Public (homosexual) displays of affection are not acceptable, for example. They should be eliminated or at least kept 'private.' This attitude fits in with the tradition of tolerance of private expression of homosexuality so long as it remains private. This is the basis of the closet, the basis of the acceptance of gays and lesbians who 'pass,' even if known to be gay and lesbian. They are acceptable because they do not 'flaunt' their homosexuality. The Criminal Code rule against three people being involved in sodomy appears to be an attempt to keep the gay sex act as private as possible.[117] The Wolfenden Report is replete with the idea that homosexual sex is fine as long as it is kept quiet.[118] The U.S. military policy of 'don't ask – don't tell' is another manifestation of this attitude. And the refusal to recognize gay and lesbian marriages or to treat gay and lesbian relationships as of equal status with heterosexual ones is yet another form of the expectation of concealment and trivialization.

The discouragement of public homosexuality only drives it into areas in the remotest parts of the public domain – the washroom, the park trail, the pornographic video, and so on. One form of censoriousness of homosexuality, marginalization, leads to another: the assumption of aberrance and excess. Thus encouraged is the association of homosexual affection with darkness and furtiveness. The forbidden nature of homosexuality is eroticized.

Unnatural but Seductive

Despite their frequent assumption that homosexuality is unnatural and perverse, the courts at times also assume that it is contagious and must be controlled for that reason.[119] It is seductive while still being aberrant, and, like a contagious disease, imperils the health of society. The courts act as the guardians of civilization in this respect, in inhibiting the undue spread of homosexuality. For some reason, as I examined in the previous chapter, some people are thought to be peculiarly susceptible to conversion to homosexual 'lifestyles,' to socialization in 'rings,' to a perverse opting-out of a heterosexual union. Many refuse treatment.

As I have said, the concern about the spread of homosexuality is particularly strong in cases where the homosexual person could expose children to homosexuality. Thus, the courts are particularly censorious of homosexuality where a court's decision will possibly have that result. In *Saunders v. Saunders* (1989), one of the access cases in which the father was in a homosexual relationship,[120] the judge was very concerned about 'the exposure of a child to unnatural relations ... which might affect normal development.'[121] In *R. v. Noyes* (1986),[122] despite evidence from witnesses who seemed to doubt that a male child's having been sexually assaulted by a male adult 'might lead to future paedophilia or homosexuality in the victim himself,' Paris J thought it not 'unreasonable ... however, that a process of patterning of the child's sexual personality may take place, just as such patterning takes place in other areas of a child's personality, attitudes and beliefs during the crucially formative years of pre-pubescence and early adolescence.'[123]

The equation of homosexuality and disease is made easy for the courts with the prevalence of AIDS among gay men. While HIV and AIDS is not strictly a homosexual issue, it is constructed as such because of the large number of gay men who live with AIDS and the public association of homosexuality with AIDS. Censorship and censoriousness issues affecting the one, therefore, naturally have an impact on the other. Thus in the Quebec case of *Valiquette* (1991) the court could quite easily accept that revelation of a person's HIV status was also a revelation about his (homosexual) sexual orientation.[124]

Courts that are concerned about the contagiousness of homosexuality sidestep the peculiarity of such a conclusion in light of the unnaturalness of homosexuality, which the courts must also assume or they would not be 'concerned.' Perhaps the disease analogy makes the link unproblematic. A disease is 'unnatural' but apt to spread. Judges are usually careful to avoid the issue of how something so disgusting as homosexuality could be such a threat. The play of unnaturalness and contagion was, however, taken up by counsel for the appellant news company in the old case of *R. v. National News Co. Ltd.* (1953), where the company was charged with possession of obscene matter, including the novel *Women's Barracks*, which dealt with lesbianism. Counsel for the appellant argued that the books could not be obscene because 'They might affect abnormal persons, but not normal ones.'[125] He said: '"Women's Barracks" is more apt to arouse disgust and pity among normal persons than to excite their sexual passions, and it is for the public good that information as to lesbianism should be widely distributed.'[126] The court rejected the rather clever argument that the book could 'act as a warning against the dangers of lesbianism' and sought a compromise in this tension between the tendency of lesbianism to disgust and to corrupt. Pickup CJO said: 'Counsel contends that the tendency to corrupt and deprave should be related to normal persons only. If this means persons who are immune to immoral influence from obscenity, the legislation under consideration would not be necessary at all. On the other hand, I am not holding that matter is obscene which tends to corrupt and deprave only persons who are corrupted and depraved. Between these extremes there must be a large section of the public, young and old, whose minds are not corrupt and depraved but are open to immoral influences.'[127]

Two-Dimensional Uniformity

Perhaps a more insidious censoriousness of homosexuals and homosexuality by the judiciary comes not from establishing double standards or raising (or accepting) fears of aberrance and contagion but from the inability to see homosexuality as involving much in the way of complexity or homosexuals as individuals with feelings and stories rather than character types who can be stereotyped in a fairly two-dimensional and uniform way. I discussed the judicial tendency to stereotype homosexuals in the last chapter.[128] We are rarely informed about the ethnic, economic, or religious background of a person identified as homosexual. Those who have overcome judicial reluctance to characterize a situation as 'homosexual' are left with little more than the simple categorization as 'homosexual.' Homosexuality is used as a general term to include all sorts of (negative) characteristics and the courts fail to accord much complexity to homosexuals as individuals. Homosexuality pretty much sums them up. The nuances of their lives, especially their sexual lives, are censored; it is assumed that we do not want or need any information beyond the fact of homosexuality.

This diminishing of homosexuals by rendering their homosexuality an all-defining, all-encompassing, standardized characteristic is most clearly seen in family law cases. Thus, in custody cases, the homosexuality (per se) of one parent plays an enormous role in the court's decision as to whether custody will go to that parent. The homosexual parent is first and foremost a homosexual. The better the person can hide his or her homosexuality the better the chances are of getting custody. Thus in the *Worby* (1985) case noted earlier,[129] the description of the father is exhausted once we are told that he is homosexual and that he lived with his lover. The court did not discuss in any meaningful way what his 'homosexuality' meant. The fact that he had a same-sex lover was apparently sufficient; there was no sense of a loving (or non-loving) relationship being at all relevant. The court expected us to accept that the mere fact of his homosexuality justified its conclusion that 'overnight access ... could be harmful to the children while his present life-style continues.'[130]

This flatness of homosexuality, its lack of detail or texture, also appears in older divorce cases. As we have seen in *Partland v. Partland* (1960), for example, the wife sought maintenance from her husband on the ground of cruelty because he had refused to give up 'what he termed his "way of life".'[131] The court clearly expected this man to abandon his homosexuality and settle down to be a 'husband.' It gave no consideration at all to the feelings of the husband (or the boyfriend): they are censored out of the picture. The husband was rendered a somewhat obscene creature, too odious to have any genuine feelings, certainly not feelings of love or anything else positive. The wife, who appeared to have known about his homosexuality all along, was portrayed as something of a saint who suffered greatly. Her religiosity – supported by the judgment (she did not want a divorce) – only added to her aura of suffering and sanctity. Homosexuality was not worth discussing except as an affliction on a poor woman who wanted sex from a homosexual man so badly that she married him and could not let go because her religion forbade it. Likewise, in *King v. King* (1985), a divorce and maintenance case in which the husband had engaged in homosexual acts with the co-respondent, Matlow J, in the course of deciding the maintenance issue, said: 'The failure of the marriage is of course to be lamented from the wife's point of view ...'[132] The husband and his homosexuality were at fault and his feelings were not, therefore, apparently of much relevance.

The two-dimensionality and uniformity of homosexuality is not just an historic phenomenon; it arose again in the more sympathetic context of the *Little Sisters* case (1996), in the part of the judgment I have noted already. The importance of erotica and representations of sexual practices was simply assumed for homosexuals *as a group*.[133] Homosexuals were seen as suitable for categorization in a way that would not have been thought in the least appropriate for heterosexuals. While specific parts of the decision in *Little Sisters* might be welcome, the tools used to reach it were part of a much older tradition of judicial censoriousness of homosexuality that is lamentable.

Judicial reluctance to explore homosexuality as a complex phenomenon probably explains why the courts avoid making the issue even more complicated by considering other issues, such as race, gender, and national origin, along with homosexuality. Jody Freeman has studied how difficult it is to make what she calls 'interactive discrimination' arguments in court.[134] She comments: 'Conveying to a court how different 'kinds' of discrimination overlap and intersect is an enormous challenge. Jurisprudence and legal scholarship about discrimination have not, as a rule, been geared to determining how discrimination on the basis of race and sex, for example, work together. Equality analysis has paid scant attention to the ways in which discrimination may occur on multiple grounds. And yet, people often experience discrimination in precisely this way. They are denied a benefit or an opportunity because of their gender *and* their race, or their disability *and* their sexuality, or their race *and* their class.'[135]

Because of the perception that an argument based on homosexuality is as complicated as a court can accommodate, there may well be a disinclination on the part of the parties before the court to provide information that would allow it to go beyond a two-dimensional characterization. Furthermore, the apparent relative absence of lesbians from case law is probably a result of the same factors. In the case of a lesbian, it is simply easier to hide the homosexuality so as to focus on the femaleness of the person before the court. This may be the case in some situations involving gay men as well, where they are affected by another factor in addition to their homosexuality.

Challenging Censoriousness

It is not inevitable that a court bring into play these traditional censorious assumptions when hearing a matter that contains a homosexual element. Canadian courts have attempted to challenge established preconceptions in recent years. For all I have criticized it, the B.C. Supreme Court in *Little Sisters* should be applauded for the progressive steps it took in treating issues relating to homosexual expression. Shaking the established pattern of censoriousness about homosexuals and homosexuality will require a good deal of conscious effort on the part of the courts.

One of the challenges in tackling the censoriousness of homosexuality lies simply in identifying it. It is so pervasive as to seem natural. What is taken as commonplace or natural can be based simply on the irrational and the merely traditional. These factors are, however, among the most difficult to overcome. Behind censorship and censoriousness of homosexual content is a suspicion that homosexuality *is* in fact wrong or at least somewhat sinister, that it *is* contagious and does need to be contained and that, while it is not logical or desirable, it is seductive as well. There is the idea that homosexuality can be cured and possibly even eradicated.

These assumptions and suspicions have deep roots, which lead to an attitude that of course irregularizes gays and lesbians as a minority while negativity about them is regularized. Expression about homosexuality is particularly fraught because of the assumption that certain types of communication actually cause homosexuality and makes it proliferate: expression is the *cause* of homosexuality. People are converted to homosexuality. Censorship and censoriousness play, in this view, an important role because they are the primary methods to control and prevent homosexuality. Communication about homosexuality has always been problematized in a way that communication about other minorities has not. Homosexuality is the love that dares not speak its name. The courts, like others in society, consequently have difficulty dealing verbally with homosexuals and homosexuality in a straightforward manner.

The courts should also recognize that it can be difficult for homosexuals themselves to go to court to raise issues that reveal or relate to their homosexuality.[136] Many agents of censorship and censoriousness are able to take actions and positions against homosexuals and homosexuality because they are confident that their actions and words will go unchallenged. If Customs forbids a work from coming into the country to someone who has ordered it, they count on the lack of a challenge. It is difficult enough for an organization like Little Sisters to challenge a decision; an individual is not going to do so, probably not because of the cost or the time but out of fear of the potential for embarrassment and ridicule that is involved. Likewise it is difficult to take to task a censorious judge. How is a litigant to respond to the censoriousness of a judge like McClung JA in *Vriend*, particularly when, as this chapter reveals, those views are common in the judicial decisions of this country, despite a constitution that forbids discrimination on the basis of sexual orientation? The courts must try harder and review the language they use for the attitudes their words betray.

It is not only the courts that have to be taken to task for censoriousness of homosexuals and homosexuality; sometimes, homosexuals themselves and their 'friends' are guilty. Much of the evidence the courts use and the conclusions they reach come from submissions made by the homosexual party. The homosexual community lacks cohesion, to say the least, and often attitudes and positions are taken in court without much thought for their effect on others. This is particularly true in the context of issues involving expression, which can engender diametrically opposed views even within the same community. Why should I defend your right to express yourself in a way I find offensive? The argument that 'you might be next' is rarely effective in any context. If it were, there would probably be no discrimination, since everyone falls into some minority or other. Religious groups would be coming to the defence of homosexual books being kept out of school libraries; Reformers would be defending the right of police officers to wear turbans.

There is much condemnation, that is censoriousness, within the homosexual community of other parts of the community. Some homosexuals are too effeminate and flamboyant and embarrass the rest of the community; not all homosexuals want to be associated with such behaviour. There is criticism of leathermen and bondage fetishists, who bring shame to the group. 'Diesel dykes' are thought to provoke the anger of the general public, which must be somewhat justified in its hostility if it thinks we are all like that. The dominant groups can play on this internal division by using shocking images again and

again to advance an agenda of preserving the status quo. This is a typical propaganda position. If you dislike the seal hunt you present the
world with the most brutal images of it that you can find and claim
that they represent the norm.[137] It is difficult to counter such propaganda because the truth will lack the sensational appeal of the original
image. What often happens instead is that a person does not deny the
general validity of the stereotypes but seeks to have his or her own particular situation excluded from it. A homosexual litigant might, therefore, endeavour to show that, although there are bad homosexuals,
and perhaps even the majority of homosexuals are bad, this particular
litigant, while homosexual, falls outside the loathed group. Thus, in
Egan v. Canada (1995),[138] counsel for the plaintiffs effectively suc-
cumbed to the view that homosexual relationships are not as worthy as
heterosexual ones by emphasizing the perfection of the particular relationship in issue in that case, giving the court the opportunity to accept
that homosexual relationship, and perhaps others like it, but not more
unorthodox or imperfect ones. Fortunately, as I have mentioned, two
of the judges on the Supreme Court of Canada went out of their way to
say that this was not necessary.[139]

The involvement of homosexuals in the problem of the repetition of
stereotypes is discussed by Shelley Gavigan in the context of homosexuals who appropriate heterosexist ideas of family in legal disputes
when their own family has broken up and issues of property division
and support arise. Gavigan argues: 'We must be prepared to do more
than analyse the judges and lawyers. We need to look at the litigants
and the positions they take, and why (if we can discern this) they take
them. And, as academics, we must be prepared to take a hard look at
ourselves (as Eagleton has intimated, ideological thought, like halito-
sis, may be more readily detectable in another). We do not have the
luxury of idle critique. In other words, if we are prepared to be rigor-
ous in a decentering project, we will admit that the courts have not
been alone nor necessarily even principally implicated in the denial of
lesbian families.'[140]

Mary Eaton has criticized the tendency of homosexual litigants to
make status claims instead of practices claims.[141] Eaton points out that
despite the fact that the Supreme Court of Canada has moved from the
'similarly situated' test in equality rights,[142] many homosexual litigants
appear to want to continue this approach by showing just how similar
they are to heterosexuals. She advocates a more imaginative use of the
tools that the courts have given us, especially in the *Andrews* case (1989),

which 'has created the jurisprudential space to analyze "homosexual" sex, not as a site of difference but as a site of dominance.'[143] Eaton says that the dominance model of equality rights will give protection to acts and not just status. On the other hand, while the historical domination and marginalization is important, it is vital not to create or perpetuate a culture of victimization among homosexuals, which dominance (inferiorization) arguments can lead to. We might simply end up constructing a ghetto of victimization that needs to be populated and, with its filling, that becomes difficult to escape. Equality should also mean liberation. Litigants should consider arguments that neither betray the interests of other homosexuals nor ghettoize homosexuals as inevitable victims. They should also be careful to allow liberty *within* the homosexual community, not to exclude some from being valued and not to lump all homosexuals together unnecessarily in the way that we criticize courts and others for doing.[144] Some might take umbrage at Little Sisters, for example, for presuming to speak for the whole homosexual community in arguing that erotica is important to gays and lesbians in a way that it is not for heterosexuals. Speaking in such categorical ways does not necessarily help in building bridges. How can homosexuals complain about being the subjects of generalizations when they make generalized arguments about themselves in court?[145]

A related issue arises when those who might be expected to be 'friends' to homosexuality take legal positions that are detrimental to gays and lesbians. In the *Butler* case, the feminist legal organization, LEAF, made submissions that are widely regarded as homophobic. Janine Fuller and Stuart Blackley set out the circumstances in their book on the *Little Sisters* case:

> An infamous remark by Kathleen E. Mahoney, Calgary law professor and co-counsel in LEAF's *Butler* intervention, showed how LEAF had pandered, consciously or otherwise, to judicial homophobia. In the May/June 1992 issue of *Ms.* magazine, Mahoney told Canadian journalist Michele Landsberg how LEAF helped sway the Supreme Court: 'How did we do it?' said Mahoney, 'We showed them the porn – and among the seized videos were some horrifically violent and degrading gay movies. We made the point that the abused men in the films were being treated like women – and the judges got it. Otherwise men can't put themselves in our shoes.'[146]

Donald Casswell says: '... others have been severely critical of LEAF in respect of its involvement as an intervenor in *Butler*. LEAF has been accused of betraying lesbian and gay communities, aligning itself with the right on the porn issue, and having inadvertently contributed to an increase in attacks against already besieged lesbian and gay book-stores.'[147] As Casswell points out, LEAF appears to have lost itself in its introspective heterosexism and 'forgot' about the impact on homosexuals. The result is that the test *Butler* established is used most, perhaps, to seize homosexual pornography and not that involving violence against women.[148]

Given the historical treatment of gays and lesbians by the legal system it might well be questioned how any faith could be put in that system to ameliorate their unequal status and treatment. Judges have created a censoriousness of gays and lesbians and their expression and at times they have tolerated and even promoted censorship of homosexual expression. It is the legal system that has historically condemned homosexuality as punishable. Until very recently, homosexuals could be legally excluded. One has to go back in time for such blatant censorship of most other groups in this country. Most religious groups have been respected – at least formally – for some time. Women have always been 'accepted' by the law as having some sort of legitimate social role – though usually inferior to or subsumed in that of men. Perhaps one has to look to racial laws for the most recent analogies, though those too (formally) belong to the past. The law has been formally and practically hostile to gays and lesbians in ways it has not been for other groups, aside from the diseased or the criminal, for some time. The law, as we have seen, is still infused with language and attitudes of disapprobation for homosexuality and homosexuals. Given this history of censorship and censoriousness, how can gays and lesbians look to the law for any sort of solace or protection?

To begin with, the legal is the only generalized societal structure, other than the political, that can give that protection. Smaller societal structures can, of course, help provide some security and a sense of inclusion – whether that involves living in a safe city or a safe part of a city or having a job in a place that respects expression of and is respectful in its expression about homosexuality. However, the difficulty of relying on such structures is that they can create a siege mentality and ghettoization. Gay and lesbian life is notorious for its ghettoization. It is important for all people to feel integrated into the larger community, to feel part of society generally in an accepted way. The gay and lesbian community extends beyond locally safe protected zones. Those most in need of acceptance and those most often subject to censorship and censoriousness live outside protected urban and employment ghettoes and require the protection that only the general political and legal systems can provide. The legal system, including the judiciary, is not of course completely separate from the political and it is admittedly somewhat artificial to speak of it as such. The judiciary is, however, no small part of the picture and cannot lag behind the other legal and political parts. The judiciary can acknowledge or be sensitive to its role in the historical project of censorship and censoriousness of homosexuals and homosexuality. Judges can be careful not to assume the answer to the question 'what then' once the label 'homosexual' has been applied. Judicial restraint from censorious attitudes towards something (such as homosexuality) will not itself prevent censorship and censoriousness by others but it does delegitimize the censoriousness of others. If the judiciary actively or passively allows censorship and censoriousness of homosexuals and homosexuality, how can others fail to perceive their own censorship and censoriousness as legitimate? As I have said, I do not believe that the judiciary is incapable of effecting change or of being the logical source of reform. The judiciary can initiate change for the better. It cannot do this by blatant reverse discrimination, which only compounds the problem. The root of the problem is discrimination; its cure is not more discrimination. If homosexual expression has been unfairly targeted for censorship or censoriousness in the past, the cure is not to privilege it today over heterosexual expression but to ensure real equality of treatment. Not mere formal equality, but true equivalency. Equivalency of treatment and respect should begin in judicial discourse itself. I have given a number of examples, admittedly too often from dissenting judges, of situations in which judges have looked at the problem of expression in the homosexual context fairly and have been willing to assume a leadership role. Thus, Cory J in *Egan v. Canada* showed a real understanding of the implications of a legal decision when he said: 'The public recognition and acceptance of homosexuals as a couple may be of tremendous importance to them and to the society in which they live.'[149] The record of the courts is improving; there has been a somewhat decreasing frequency of censoriousness in judicial statements about homosexuals and homosexuality over the past couple of decades.

Judges ought to have more of an aspirational conception of the rule of law. It would be a scandalous legal structure that recognized and protected equality only when society in general had already accepted it. Society has yet to accept visible minorities (and women) as full participants but it would be outrageous if the courts did not provide full protection from discrimination on the basis that society had still not fully accepted the idea of racial and gender equality. A far better approach is that taken in *Re Haig and The Queen* (1992),[150] by the Ontario Court of Appeal. The court, speaking through Krever JA, said: 'The social context which must be considered includes the pain and humiliation undergone by homosexuals by reason of prejudice towards them. It also includes the enlightened evolution of human rights social and legislative policy in Canada, since the end of the Second World War, both provincially and federally. The failure to provide an avenue for redress for prejudicial treatment of homosexual members of society, and the possible inference from the omission that such treatment is acceptable, create the effect of discrimination offending s. 15(1) of the Charter.'[151]

The importance of legal protection is especially significant for a group that will always be a minority. In some respects the censorship and censoriousness of homosexual expression is similar to the restraints placed on women's expression in earlier days. Nonetheless, women at least had the numbers to hope that with time equal treatment could be achieved through political processes. The problem for gays and lesbians is that we will always be a minority and thus cannot rely on political processes entirely. The difficulty of getting the legislature to move to protect against discrimination makes that perfectly clear.[152] It takes court action to effect such changes and to ensure that they remain undisturbed. And the courts cannot truly address the illegitimate censorship and censoriousness acts of the legislature and society when they themselves are actively censorious.

3

Silence in the Classroom

The most important factor in the perpetuation of homophobia and marginalization of homosexuals, including self-hatred in homosexuals, is the intense indoctrination in heterosexism that children experience, a great deal of it in educational institutions. Society loses much of its rationality when it comes to homosexuality and children. Children are 'sheltered' from contact with homosexuality and homosexuals, who are presumed to prey on them.[1] The sheltering of children from homosexuality may make them more vulnerable to those few homosexuals who do prey on children. One man writes: 'For years I grew up thinking I was the only person in the world attracted to my own sex. And while I was never victimized myself, I can't help remembering the power the older, small-town homosexuals hold over terrified youth. The power comes from fear of "exposure." The old gay-boy and gay-girl network has a vested interest in keeping the scene illicit and underground. Otherwise their hold over the scared young kids would evaporate.'[2] Television, music, and literature generally teach children that boys fall in love with girls and not other boys. On the somewhat rare occasions when a boy (or more likely a man and less likely a girl or a woman) is depicted as having same-sex desires, this situation is treated as *different*, often accompanied by sensational news stories of its peculiarity.[3] Of particular importance for this chapter, religions historically have taught and often still teach children that homosexuality is wrong and undesirable and that gays and lesbians are 'bad' – unless perhaps they are ashamed of what they desire and repress their feelings. Fairy tales, told in early childhood, stress the importance of marriage and also the dependence of a woman on a man and the inevitability of a union between the two.[4] Girls and boys play the card game of 'Old Maid,' the goal of which is to avoid becoming the Old Maid. The worst insults on the playground are 'lezzie,' 'faggot,' 'queer,' and 'fruit.' While these terms are first used by children who probably have no full awareness of the meanings or implications of the words, by adolescence the implications are clear. Cooper Thompson, a coordinator of the Campaign to End Homophobia, described his experience when visiting a suburban U.S. high school to give a guest presentation on male roles:

> As a class we talked about the ways in which boys got status in that school and how they got put-down by others. I was told that the most humiliating putdown was being called a 'fag.' The list of behaviors which could elicit ridicule filled two large chalkboards, and it was detailed and comprehensive; I got the sense that a boy in this school had to conform to the rigid, narrow standards of masculinity to avoid being called a fag. I, too, felt this pressure and became very conscious of my mannerisms in front of the group. Partly from exasperation, I decided to test the serious-ness of these assertions. Since one of the four boys had some streaks of pink in his shirt, and since he had told me that wearing pink was grounds for being called a fag, I told him that I thought he was a fag. Instead of laughing, he said, 'I'm going to kill you.'[5]

This negativity is not balanced by positive or even neutral expression or images of homosexuals and homosexuality in schools, because homosexuality is silenced there and homosexuals are sometimes even excluded.

In this chapter I look at the role the courts have played in perpetuat-ing the inferiorization and marginalization of homosexuality. Exclu-sion of (positive) expression about homosexuality has found support in judicial decisions that involve young people and homosexuality. In the reasonably few education cases that have come before them, the courts have little by way of a track record of facilitating a positive pres-ence. Instead of protecting against discrimination on the basis of sexual orientation in the context of young people, the vested interests of the status quo and concerns about protecting religiously based attitudes are given priority. Because these interests and concerns are often anti-thetical to the interest of protecting against discrimination on the basis of sexual orientation, homosexuals and homosexuality – and in fact society in general – lose out. The judiciary has internalized much of 'traditional' religious dogma in this area and has tended to give precedence to conservative religious interests over the interests of equality of sexual orientation, especially when young people are involved. This judicial attitude is typically 'thoughtless' in the sense that it is rare for a judge to explore his assumptions or their appropriateness. It is also 'generalized' in that the judge rarely identifies a particular theology beyond 'religious values.' Education has long been associated with religion and it is difficult for sexual orientation protection to succeed in the education context when religious dogma in the generalized sense used by the courts stands squarely against such a thing. In the area of homosexuality and education – in fact, in many areas relating to homosexuality – the judiciary has failed to make much of an effort to ensure that the Canadian ideals of inclusion and accommodation are satisfied. As a recent example of this failure and as something of a paradigm of the situation, I will examine in particular the 1996 Alberta Court of Appeal decision in *Vriend*,[6] especially the reasons of McClung JA. The attitudes in this decision are not contrary to those found in earlier cases on homosexuality and education and in fact are substantially consistent with them. In this chapter I want to challenge the appropriateness of the religious basis that these attitudes manifest in the judicial context and to develop the idea that they are contrary to the inclusive-accommodative ideals better suited to guide judicial decision making in cases that involve pronouncements on values and equality. This chapter thus deals with the interplay in the legal context among the judiciary and education, homosexuality and youth, religion and homosexuality, religion and education, and religion and the judiciary. I structure the examination of these issues in seven parts and reach the following conclusions:

1 The education system often problematizes and excludes homosexuality and homosexuals from its domain.
2 The education system and the judiciary rarely have much to do with each other, even though they are the two principal systems for values inculcation and assessment in our society. Judges have a role in expressing the norms of society, including attitudes towards homosexuals and homosexuality.
3 That judges fail to fulfil this role in the context of cases involving education, especially where issues relating to homosexuality and homosexuals are involved, is exemplified in the majority reasons in the Alberta Court of Appeal case of *Vriend*. There, the court deferred to the status quo, including conservative religious tradition, in

deciding the appropriate response to a case involving homosexuality and education.

4 The judicial disinclination to defend homosexual equality interests in *Vriend* is consistent with a judicial tradition of viewing homosexuality and youth as incompatible or at least a dangerous combination.

5 Part of the tradition of keeping homosexuality and youth separated is keeping homosexuality and homosexuals out of the education system. Judges make half-hearted efforts at best to ensure nondiscrimination on the basis of sexual orientation in the education system, and, indeed, generally.

6 Judicial reluctance actively to protect homosexual equality interests and homosexual visibility and expression in the education context exists in large part because of judicial reliance on a generalized religious tradition that is hostile to homosexuality and homosexuals and insists on seeing such issues as ones of morality rather than equality. *Vriend* is an example.

7 Judges should resist reliance on generalized religious tradition when asked to make decisions involving homosexuality and education and should instead consider what I suggest is the Canadian ideal of ensuring inclusion and accommodation of members of various groups, including homosexuals. This approach would favour homosexual visibility and expression in the education context.

The Silencing of Homosexuality

The irrational fear that gays and lesbians will 'convert' children simply means that children who think they might be gay or lesbian grow up with nobody to look to as a role model except paedophile priests and their like, often prominently identified as 'homosexual' in news reports. Unlike most members of most other minorities, a lesbian or gay child very rarely grows up among other lesbians or gays. There is no family to seek refuge in from the hostile world outside. Many families in fact make it clear that for the child to be gay or lesbian is the worst possible news they could have and could result in exclusion from the family group. Where children are exposed to people who are homosexual, the details of their homosexuality are invariably hidden. Thus maiden aunts and uncles are portrayed as leading solitary existences. [7] The only gay character I ever encountered in thirteen years of public school was a paedophile in Hugh Garner's *Cabbagetown*, erotic enough for a child denied any other images of homoeroticism, but nothing compared to the thousands of depictions of heterosexual – 'normal' – sexuality I saw on television and in movies and read about in books. There are no homosexual public figures or historical figures, unless there is a report of a scandal. Gay and lesbian young people often feel terribly isolated even though they may well be part of a large number of homosexuals at their school or university.[8]

When it comes to dealing with issues of homosexuality, the educational system falls short. At both the school and the university levels, those who wish to silence expression about homosexuality and keep it as a dark, scandalous thing are most effective.[9] Heterosexuality reigns unchallenged and exalted.[10] There is an effective silence about homosexuality, except perhaps as a clinical topic to be examined in an acultural environment like a science class. This silence exists not just at the teaching level but at the level of access to resources. Students are not exposed to materials on homosexuality and cannot in many instances get access to them. This is the result of intentional decisions.[11] Imagine if the educational system had no information about heterosexuality – there would be no discussion of love, sex, marriage, or families. History would be reduced to the nonbiographical. Students could not date, have mixed dances, or Valentine's Day. Biology would be gutted, much art would not be studied. Teachers would not have the option of being called 'Mrs' and no reference would be made to spouses of any sort. Equivalent situations exist for homosexuality. Homosexuality is simply not allowed to express itself in an academic setting except as an absolute 'other.' Change at the school level will come very slowly, if at all, from political means. Efforts to introduce curriculum dealing fairly and evenhandedly with homosexuality are often rebuffed by parents' groups.[12] Representatives of homosexual groups are not treated as legitimate participants in curriculum reform.[13]

It is small wonder, then, that gays and lesbians grow up anguished by their feelings for members of their own sex.[14] It is not surprising that so many commit suicide when they realize that they are or might be a 'fag' or a 'lezzie.' Suicide, especially youth suicide, is higher among homosexuals or people who think they are homosexual than among others.[15] A young person will often fight his or her sexual urges by attempting to conform to 'normalcy' by finding a partner of the opposite sex. He or she strives to do everything possible to appear straight and is often the first to make homophobic comments or jokes. A young person who suspects that he or she is homosexual will often be the most vocal proponent of violence against gays and lesbians.

These attitudes are reinforced as people leave childhood and continue even to such 'enlightened' institutions as law schools. The problem is not quite so acute at universities as in schools, but universities are still often reluctant to encourage much homosexual content in studies. In a 1994 article, Cynthia Petersen recounts the frustration and angst of being an open lesbian teaching in an (often) hostile environment with inadequate tools. Petersen says: 'Occasionally, in the middle of a lecture, I am struck by fear. My heart starts to pound, I begin to sweat, and I think that if I dare utter the word "lesbian" one more time, then I will suffer some atrocity.'[16] In my own institution, probably the most homophilic of law schools, it can still be awkward for issues relating to homosexuality to be brought up by an openly gay professor. There was some resistance from students some years ago when I first taught a mandatory course on sexuality and the law to all first-year students. Even among those students who were not vocally annoyed by the course the sense of unease was palpable.

Education and Law Do Not Mix

Arguably too much is expected of our school, college, and university systems. Teachers, in North America, are expected to be role models.[17] The blame is placed on the schools for a decline in society; people continually question why such and such is not taught in the schools. Schools and universities carry a great deal of cultural significance. They are the primary vehicles for cultural continuity. In a secular society, they are the institutions in which values are to be found. Schools and universities are not supposed to teach 'bad' things, only what is 'good.' They are supposed to facilitate truth and to be enlightened. They are the great civilizing influence, in a culture where civilization is thought to be at the opposite end of a progression from chaos. It is thought to be incumbent on teachers in the schools to embody the values that this society wants continued. Michael Manley-Casimir says that the perspective of the teacher as a 'cultural custodian' goes beyond the embodiment in teaching of cultural and moral ideals: 'This perspective suggests that the teacher is expected to create cultural continuity by passing on to the next generation the valued aspects of the culture.'[18]

Schools and, to a lesser extent, colleges and universities, are the subject of constant political attention. Because they are institutions with which so many in society have an almost daily direct or indirect contact they are kept in the forefront of the public mind in the way that museums, churches, or sports and financial institutions are not. Because of the acceptance of their pivotal role in forming societal ideas and in inculcating those ideas they are naturally going to be subject to political change in a democracy where personalities and parties change on a regular basis. Institutions that once had more of a direct role in determining the standards of society now attempt to retain such a role through influencing educational policy. Religions thus fight hard to control and retain public funding for their own schools because of the propagandistic role the schools play. Religions, all of them proselytizing to some degree,[19] care little to have their own banks or hockey rinks because those institutions do not have the role of spreading or preserving ideas and values in the way schools and universities do. Religions, however, expend a great deal of energy to preserve or extend their hold on the school system.[20] Even in public school systems, religious bodies sometimes seek to extend their influence to cover all students in the school. If achieved, this is a most insidious form of religious control in that a school that is purportedly public and secular is subjecting its students to tuition that is heavily religiously constrained. Religious people, rarely overtly 'representing' a religious organization, are eager to have a school board reflect their religious views on science, sex education, literature, or art.[21] There is no balancing the other way; school curriculum and even university courses rarely if ever encourage a critical appraisal of religion, in the way that almost all other subjects can be the subject of criticism. Religion is either directly or indirectly taught or it is beyond critical scrutiny.[22]

The courts, on the other hand, show little inclination to become involved in influencing the course of educational policy. Issues involving education rarely come before judges to be litigated.[23] This has been attributed to the high costs and the delay in getting a final decision,[24] but I believe that it is also due to an assumption that such matters do not 'belong' in court. Disputes in the education context tend to be settled at the political and administrative levels.[25] This is not for lack of any jurisdiction by the courts to act. Actions by schools or school boards are state actions subject to Charter scrutiny. We will see that most of the cases involving homosexuality and education that have gone to the courts, including *Vriend*, have raised issues relating to the Charter or human rights statutes or both. These cases have involved a variety of topics, such as employment issues, school material issues, and school use issues. Curriculum issues have not tended to be litigated, although there is no reason to doubt that Charter and Human Rights Act arguments could not be made in that context. This absence of litigation in the curriculum area is no doubt partly the result of the lack of judicial receptiveness in those other areas where there has been litigation. Courts cannot intrude into an area of social or political life unless there is a complainant before the court, but no complainant will appear if the court is perceived to be uninterested in certain types of complainants or in certain types of cases. The judiciary has not created much in the way of a comfortable environment for these education issues to be dealt with. In part this is because students, especially elementary and high school students, are not significant in the judicial imagination.[26] They are seen as little more than appendages of their parents. Furthermore, a whole legal education could be had (and what would be thought a good one) without reference to any case involving a school or university – or a religious organization, for that matter. One could not imagine a similar absence of reference to a family, a bank, a company, a trade union, or a prison. The education system is thought, it would seem, to be extralegal in some sense, in a way that the family used to be so thought. Perhaps education is so obviously about values and their inculcation that the law (at least in the form of the courts) does not seem to be the appropriate place to deal with educational issues.

How odd. Much more expected perhaps would be that the two great institutions of values in our society, the law, as interpreted by the judiciary, and the educational system, would come into contact with greater frequency. [27] But the courts tend to avoid educational issues and schools and universities infrequently touch upon the courts and the legal system in a way that represents their significance in the life of the community. The schools appear content to leave instruction about these processes to television and media generally. To a large extent, discussion about the law in universities is left to law schools, which are usually isolated physically and intellectually from the rest of the university. Anyone who has taught in a law school can attest to the enormous misconceptions incoming students have about the law and the legal system – and these are supposedly the best informed among their peers about that system. Law students are allowed by the educational system to arrive with misconceptions that have no equivalent in any other discipline, whether it be medicine, other sciences, or the arts or commerce.

Education is an area in which the courts can make a difference. They will not, of course, eliminate homophobic taunts on the playground, but they can symbolically try. Canadian ideals, as manifested particularly in documents like Human Rights Acts, in section 15 of the Charter, and in various multicultural policies, are of inclusion and accommodation. The judiciary plays a role in facilitating these ideals. The agencies of the law are appropriate places to expect direction about and delivery of decisions reflecting goals of inclusion and accommodation of individuals and groups. As I argue in the last section of this chapter, judges should have a role in ensuring inclusion and accommodation of homosexuals and that which is distinctive about them (namely, their homosexuality) in the public life of the nation, including education. Homosexuals are members of a group that ought legitimately to expect to enjoy this inclusion and accommodation. This should be a self-evident proposition but it has been the subject of considerable controversy, to some positive legal resolution. The interpretation of section 15 of the Charter so as to prohibit discrimination on the basis of sexual orientation is one manifestation of the legitimacy of the expectation of inclusion and accommodation. In the education context itself, courts have held that colleges, schools, school boards, and school officials are subject to Charter scrutiny.[28] The Supreme Court of Canada has, it is true, curiously held (1990) that the Charter does not apply to universities, which seems a very narrow view of the public role of these institutions.[29] In any event, however, the underlying values of the Charter should be taken into account in judicial decisions generally and in most jurisdictions similar protections will exist by virtue of human rights legislation.

What can the courts do to ensure fairness in education? Their role will be primarily to review decisions by educational institutions that run counter to the inclusive-accommodative ideal. The courts can ensure protection for teachers and students who are homosexual or are suspected of being so. Judges can ensure that the silencing of homosexuals and the silence about homosexuality is not accepted as the norm or as inevitable. To this end, the courts can help break the scholastic and collegiate silence by speaking themselves, by engaging in fair discussion about homosexuality, and by facilitating such expression by others. So far, however, the judicial record to this end has not been good.

Vriend: Judicial Inaction and Imaginings

The Albertan case of *Vriend*, and in particular the reasons given by McClung JA in the Court of Appeal (1996), exemplify the disinclination of the judiciary to interfere with the status quo in educational matters, a status quo that embodies religious values and preserves a special place for (at least some) religious views in educational matters.[30] The majority of the Court of Appeal did nothing to alleviate a situation whereby a person with an excellent record was fired because he was gay. Quite the contrary. A religious-based institution's explicit homophobic prejudices were allowed to triumph. McClung JA even added salt to the wound of the court's inaction by justifying the action of the college with thinly veiled references to distaste for homosexuality and homosexuals. He chose to ignore precedent from other jurisdictions[31] about the Charter's effect on human rights legislation and insulated his role by saying that the question was one for the legislature to decide. In other words, he said that a situation involving the firing of an instructor because of his sexual orientation was not a problem that the court could recognize or remedy.[32]

Vriend was a laboratory coordinator who, we are told, 'in terms of competence and service, was quite satisfactory.'[33] He was employed at King's College, Edmonton, a 'Christian' institution of higher education. In response to an inquiry by the president of the college, Vriend 'admitted' he was a homosexual. Thereupon his employment was terminated. The sole reason given for his termination was his noncompliance with the policy of the college on homosexual practice. At the Queen's Bench level (1994), Russell J ruled that the termination violated antidiscrimination protections of the Individual Rights Protection Act ['IRPA'], which she interpreted to include protection from discrimination on the basis of sexual orientation. The IRPA did not specifically prohibit such discrimination but Russell J read it in in order to enable the legislation to comply with section 15 of the Charter.[34]

The majority of the Court of Appeal overturned this decision and for our purposes the reasons given by McClung JA are particularly germane. It was he who enunciated general views on homosexuals and homosexuality and the education system as well as on the role of the law and the courts in that relationship. It is his position of obstructing the facilitation of equal participation in the education system that in fact has, as I will develop, strong roots in Canadian law. The first thing he did was to make clear that these sorts of issues are not ones the courts should be called upon to decide. McClung JA in effect declared judicial incompetence to make such decisions because the legislature, not the courts, has 'the tools annealed by centuries of constitutional, political and military conflict, tradition and pragmatism, backed by

popular loyalty and confidence, to make laws of general application.'
He said Canadian judges enjoyed 'only 13 years' experience in the process of invalidating legislation under infringements of the legal and
societal rights declared within the Charter.'[35] How long judges must
wait beyond thirteen years before carrying out fully their constitutional duty as mandated in the Charter (and in fact by centuries of the
law's striving for equity) was not made clear. Perhaps never, for
McClung JA went on to say: '"It makes more sense to trust a dog with
my dinner than trust the Supreme Court with the slavery question!"
Horace Greeley's 1855 war cry during the *Dred Scott* case was over-
done, but his point was clear. He was remembering that the people
must have judges, but that by being made judges our prejudices cannot always be suppressed and our intelligence certainly is not
increased.'[36]

American society would look strange indeed today if the Supreme
Court of that country had left it to the legislatures to decide rights
issues.[37] Intolerable it would be for the courts to have remained idle if
the legislature of the United States had not acted on 'the slavery question,' just as it is intolerable for judges of any regime to hide behind
pleas of 'my hands are tied' when reaching unjust decisions.[38] The
whole point of the U.S. constitution and the Canadian Charter is not to
leave these questions to politicians, but to have the courts protect
minorities who cannot be a majority in the legislature for numerical or
historical reasons.[39] McClung JA said that because judges have prejudices they can be excused from doing justice. Judges ought, however,
to explore just what these prejudices are and then suppress them if
they are inconsistent with the expectations of judicial decision making.
McClung JA's view of his role is tantamount to saying, 'I might, as a
judge, have preconceived ideas about what the result of this case
should be, based on negative stereotypes, and therefore, rather than
confronting those stereotypes (or taking myself off the case) I choose to
opt for the status quo, whatever that might be.' Further, it is not as
though the judge thought there was a better place an aggrieved person
such as Mr Vriend might go to expect a fair resolution. McClung JA not
only excused himself from having to resolve on principles the issue of
homosexuality in the school system, he also thought the legislature
had no duty to solve these issues in a principled way.

If the judiciary and the legislature cannot be expected to get
involved in such issues, then where does the instrument of change lie?
It must be in some other social element that is now set against extend-

ing equality protections to gays and lesbians. This element, namely religious doctrine, is hinted at by McClung JA who set up the case before him as embodying a conflict between minority rights and religious forbiddence. McClung JA's decision, because it decides against giving rights to homosexuals, is a bow to 'religious and familial forbiddence.' His deference to religious views on such issues is reinforced by his reliance on U.S. authority that explicitly decided homosexual rights issues by reference to religious values. He said: 'I am unable to conclude that it was a forbidden, let alone a reversible, legislative response for the province of Alberta to step back from the validation of homosexual relations, including sodomy, as a protected and fundamental right, thereby, "... rebutting a millenium of moral teaching". Bowers v. Hardwick ...'[40] The 'moral teaching' in *Bowers* was clearly 'rooted in Judeao-Christian moral and ethical standards.'[41]

The statute the Alberta Court of Appeal was dealing with, namely the IRPA, does not deal with sexual relations – i.e. sodomy – at all, of course. But, as I noted in the previous chapter, McClung JA assumed homosexuality is all about sodomy.[42] As Shannon O'Byrne and James McGinnis say: '... why is Mr. Justice McClung referring to sodomy at all? Mr. Vriend was not fired because he was found engaging in sodomy or any other sexual activity at work – he was fired for being a homosexual. He lost his job because the imaginations of his employers were distasteful to the imaginers.'[43] The immediate association of homosexuality with sodomy is of course biblically based and echoes religious objections to homosexuality that extend from objections to sodomy which is what fundamentalist religionists believe the Bible is getting at when attacking men lying with men.[44] Despite the complete absence of any indication that Mr Vriend was somehow actively 'promoting' homosexuality or physically thrusting himself on the male students (we do not even know if Mr Vriend *did* anything sexual – including engaging in sodomy – that is assumed by the court from its knowledge of Vriend's homosexuality), he must represent some sort of threat to the students. His job as laboratory coordinator was not one where his outside sexual life or views would be raised among the students. But still homosexuality was seen as so powerful, so contagious, and of course so abhorrent, that his very existence was a threat to the impressionable young. To this fear, McClung JA effectively lent his support by refusing to enter the 'controversy' and apply a principled, Charter-based resolution, as had been done in other jurisdictions and by the lower court.

The existence of Mr Vriend's homosexuality was brought to light and made an issue by the college, not Vriend himself. Any controversy that might have coloured Mr Vriend's abilities to carry on normal duties was caused by the college, not Vriend. There is a similar U.S. decision in which a teacher was fired on grounds of 'immorality' because he was a 'known homosexual.'[45] The court thought that his effectiveness as a teacher would be impaired when it was known (having been announced by the school) that he was a homosexual. His teaching ability had not been questioned when it was not known that he was a homosexual; it was the school's own actions in creating the issue that caused him to become (arguably) an ineffective teacher. The fact that he had taught for years without any adverse effect on students demonstrates the unfairness of the dismissal and the idea that homosexuals are unfit teachers.[46] The courts in such cases as this and *Vriend* worry about the negative reaction to the existence of homosexuals in the schools. No concern is shown, however, for how homosexual students, teachers, and members of the public are affected by the hugely symbolic dismissal of the teacher. Which is more detrimental to the people involved?

Homosexuality and Youth: Seduction and Contagion

Mr Vriend's students would probably have been young adults, and the law, in effect, I suggest, accepted the college's right to 'shield' them from his homosexuality. How much more in need of protection must children be when faced with a homosexual or homosexuality. The courts have indicated on numerous occasions that they consider it to be of utmost importance to protect children's interests. Some of these situations were discussed in the previous chapter as part of the study of judicial attitudes of censoriousness towards homosexuality. The protection of children involves separating them from exposure to homosexuality or homosexuals. In fact, of course, this separation probably does more harm than good. At least one judge has pointed out that recognition of homosexual rights and equality promotes the interests of children. In a case (1993) that dealt with whether section 15 of the Charter was infringed when a same-sex couple was denied a marriage licence, Greer J, dissenting, said: 'Any stigma created for these children by their parent's homosexual union would be lessened if the relationship was one of marriage sanctified by the state.'[47] Such judicial attitudes are, however, exceedingly rare. More common is the notion that children and homosexuality do not mix. Children are not even thought a natural part of any situation involving homosexuals. Thus, the majority in the case just referred to said the denial of a marriage licence to a same-sex couple did not infringe the Charter because: 'One of the principal purposes of the institution of marriage is the founding and maintenance of families in which children will be produced and cared for, a procedure which is necessary for the continuance of the species ...'[48] Marriage is thus for procreation, for making children. Marriage and children are constructed as exclusively heterosexual. Homosexuality is kept out of the institution of marriage because homosexuality has nothing to do with children. The two, children and homosexuality, are not even symbolically to mix by admitting homosexuals to marriage, which retains its religious connotations.

Not only is it thought improbable that children and homosexuals should be associated but such association is positively discouraged. *Vriend* is an example of the jurisprudence that supports or condones the cleansing of youth by keeping homosexuality and homosexuals away. As I have said, homosexuality is thought to operate somehow by contagion. For a phenomenon that is supposed to be 'unnatural,' those who seek to prevent or eliminate homosexuality appear to believe that it spreads with amazing ease. Even the mention of homosexuality or the presence of a homosexual might engender converts to homosexuality and a decay of society (which amounts to the same thing). Some laws have had this fear of contagion as their basis. Reed J, in *Halm v. Canada* (1995), said of section 159 of the Criminal Code that: 'A reading of the debates of the legislative history, including the Wolfenden Report, makes it clear that a distinction was made between the age of consent under what is now section 159 and the age of consent for other types of consensual sexual activity because (1) homosexual practices were considered immoral and (2) there was a concern that homosexuality was a learned behaviour or a disease such that de-criminalizing the activity in question could lead to youth being corrupted.'[49]

The assumption of homosexuality by infection in the academic setting was the basis of the School Commission's submissions in *L'Association A.D.G.Q. v. Catholic School Commission of Montreal* (1979). The Catholic School Commission of Montreal denied to a gay organization the right to use a school building to hold a weekend conference. The court said that: 'In fact the real problem is this: respondent refuses to rent to the petitioner because it apprehends the deleterious effect which the rental of a building to a homosexual association would have on its

Catholic students, it being accepted that homosexuality is a practice condemned by the Catholic Church.'[50] The meetings were to have been held on weekends, when the students were not there, and would not involve homosexual acts. Still, their very existence could somehow hurt the children. The ability of homosexuality to corrupt the young must be very potent if it is possible to corrupt students who are not even present. As the court made clear, it could not have been the real concern of the school board that allowing a homosexual organization to use the building would have amounted to a contradiction of the teachings of the church. Other groups with views antithetical to those of the church were permitted to use the school building. The school board's concern was not with self-contradiction but with homosexuality.

The flip side of the coin of the susceptibility of young people to homosexuality is the perceived propensity of homosexuals to prey on children. The linking of homosexuals and homosexuality to a desire to have sex with children is sometimes not entirely a conscious connection on the part of the court, it is more of an automatic association. Thus in a custody case (1980), where the mother alleged that the father had had sex with the young son, Labrosse J said: 'The psychological assessment of the father made by Mr Brooks on March 28, 1980, revealed no evidence of homosexual tendencies and now, suddenly, he is accused of having had sex with his son.'[51] The assumption the judge made is that sex with children (especially boys) is something only a homosexual would do. It is difficult to imagine that if the child had been a girl, there would have been tests to establish 'heterosexual tendencies.' A father having sex with his little boy is constructed as having a 'homosexual tendency' rather than a 'paedophile tendency.' In a Nova Scotian case (1995), a Provincial Court judge ordered a man to stay away from boys 'unless accompanied by a heterosexual adult.'[52] Being accompanied by a homosexual adult would not protect boys from being preyed upon.

While it is rare for a court to make an explicit connection among children, homosexuals, contagion, and paedophilia, it is not thought unusual that witnesses in a court case might jump to such conclusions. Thus, in *R. v. Pink Triangle Press* (1979), a case about whether an article entitled 'Men Loving Boys Loving Men' in *The Body Politic* was indecent, immoral, or scurrilous within the meaning of section 164 of the Criminal Code, the court set out the views of many of the Crown witnesses who made clear their contempt for homosexuality, their espousal of religious ideals in the school context, and their belief in homosexual desire to proselytize. One Crown witness was an evangelical Baptist minister. According to Harris Prov. Ct J 'In his view homosexuality frustrated divine intent and homosexuals should not be allowed even to talk in the schools.'[53] Another Crown witness was Claire Hoy, a newspaper columnist, who, according to the judge, 'describes homosexuals as "creatures" ... He believes homosexuals want to get into the schools to proselytise.'[54] The judge quite rightly thought this evidence of little use, but it is still noteworthy that the Crown called these people to give evidence, supposedly to establish the standards of the community. The fact that these arguments can even be put before the court gives them a certain legitimacy. The same is true when intervenor status is given to groups that oppose equal treatment for homosexuals.[55] The equivalent would be allowing intervenor status to a group opposed to equal rights for people of Chinese or First Nation origin in a case involving racial discrimination. If that is unthinkable, then the question appropriately arises as to why analogous arguments are allowed in cases where homosexuality is in issue.[56]

The fear of conversion/infection of children by homosexuals and homosexuality often appears in the context of a sexual assault by an adult on a child of the same sex. This is evident in a B.C. case (1986) in which a male teacher was charged with sexual assault on a boy. The judge said one of the concerns was about children becoming homosexual by virtue of the assault.[57] There was no judicial consciousness of any double standard, no thought given to the fact that the logical consequence of such a belief is that boys become heterosexual by patterning – perhaps at the hands of a rapacious adult female. Such a position is too absurd to be even considered. But its analogy in the homosexual situation was quite acceptable. So, too, in another case (1987) in which a school principal was convicted of sexual assault on boys, Marshall J, in a lengthy discussion of paedophilia, said: 'Serious problems of sexual adjustment and sexual orientation in life often also follow. All show a sharp loss in self-esteem and confusion in their own sexual orientation. Some go on to develop frank homosexuality and paedophilia itself.'[58] Both homosexuality and paedophilia, closely linked in this formulation, are at the end of a tragic descent.

In cases of sexual assault by one adult on a child of the same sex, the individuality of the accused and the victim are sometimes lost as the whole concept of homosexuality and the whole class of homosexuals are brought into the picture. The case can become something of a paradigm, in the court's view, of the nature of homosexuals and homosexuality generally. This process is part of the tendency to generalize and 'two-dimensionalize' the two I discussed in the previous chapter. This transformation occurred in McClung JA's mind in *Vriend*, where Mr Vriend was imagined to be engaging in sodomy because that is the stereotype of a male homosexual. The individual people in the case before the court become mere types in a tragic morality play. Thus, in a British Columbian case (1987) in which a man was convicted of sexual assault and gross indecency on a boy, the court characterized the act as that of a homosexual attempting to lead a boy into homosexuality. It was not, as it would be in the case of a man sexually assaulting a girl, simply a particular case of sexual assault. The class of homosexuals was brought into the judicial imagination and the idea of conversion was central. Selbie Co. Ct J said:

> This fatherless boy was vulnerable and you took full advantage of that. You deliberately and carefully gained the trust of the boy and his mother with the intention of abusing it and if you believe that leading a youth into homosexuality is not an abuse, then this Court disagrees with you.
>
> We have here then the sordid scenario of an aging homosexual on the hunt for a young vulnerable youth with little or no concern for the long term effect on the youth himself.[59]

The 'aging homosexual,' the 'fatherless boy,' the 'young vulnerable youth,' and 'his mother' are all part of a 'hunt' that is a 'sordid scenario.' One cannot imagine language like 'an aging heterosexual' or 'leading a girl into heterosexuality' being used if the victim had been a girl.

Paradoxically, the current level of public concern with sexual abuse and the way it is reported only increase homophobia because of the magnification such attention can give to latent views equating homosexuals and paedophilia. The attention given to cases of priests molesting boys or hockey coaches and officials luring or forcing youth into sexual activity, particularly when they are identified as 'homosexual,' only serves to exascerbate the perception that such instances of sexual assault are 'only' more examples of the common and stock character of the 'aging homosexual' and the 'vulnerable youth.' One would rarely see today, for example, a statement such as that found in the Wolfenden Report: '... among those who work with notable success in occupations which call for services to others, there are some in whom a latent homosexuality provides the motivation for activities of the greatest value to society. Examples of this are to be found among teachers, clergy, nurses and those who are interested in youth movements and the care of the aged.'[60] Today a homosexual man in such circumstances involved in a youth movement would probably be assumed to be a paedophile. Many homosexuals, men and women, are terrified of having any contact with children at all because of the suspicion that might be engendered.

As I discussed in the previous chapter, the most usual context for the expression about the contagion or corruption of children by homosexuality is in custody disputes. Custody cases provide the most fertile ground for ascertaining judicial attitudes about homosexuality and youth. These cases are strongly analogous to the gay teacher cases because they can be argued as presenting a choice between a homosexual role model (or future) for a young person and a 'normal' role model (or future). In *Saunders v. Saunders* (1989), an access case in which the father was in a homosexual relationship, the judge was very concerned by the fact that the father and his partner did not keep their relationship a secret from the child. Wetmore Co. Ct J did not want to change the situation where 'This child [a boy] has a normal, stable home in which there are only the normal environmental circumstances for maturity to develop.'[61] Throughout the judgment in *Saunders*, 'normal' could hardly have been used more than it was as a synonym for heterosexual. The child was again portrayed as a vulnerable youth who would be deliberately 'exposed' to unnaturalness. The child needed protection from such 'environmental influences,' which could infect him.[62] As in *Vriend*, the court washed its hands of the equality concerns the case raised. Equality for homosexuals was subordinated to more important goals. Wetmore Co. Ct J went on to say: 'I am not convinced, and neither was the Provincial Judge, that the exposure of a child of tender years to an unnatural relationship of a parent to any degree is in the best interests of the development and natural attainment of maturity of that child. That is the issue, not the rights of homosexuals.'[63]

Even where the courts are more accepting of homosexual and homosexuality in deciding cases involving children and homosexuality in some way, a note of concern can creep in that would not in an equivalent heterosexual situation. In *Templeman v. Templeman* (1986), for example, there was a custody/access dispute between a divorced mother and father over two children. The father realized during the marriage that he was gay and the marriage broke down. The court acknowledged that homosexuality in a parent would not prevent custody or access from that parent and gave access to the father, but added: 'In the event that the respondent [father] exposes his children to a promiscuous lifestyle or to harmful influences, the petitioner of course, has the right to vary these access provisions.'[64] There was no factual basis of any sort for a concern about the father's tendency towards promiscuity. He was, however, homosexual, so the concern 'naturally' arose. Nothing was said about whether the mother might cause such exposure. She was heterosexual, so promiscuity was not to be contemplated.[65]

Homosexuality and Education: No More Teachers, No More Books

The generalized fear of infection or corruption or conversion of children by homosexuals or to homosexuality is easily transplanted into the academic setting, where the whole point of instruction is to instil ideas and values in young people. Society, and the courts too, expect great things from schools (and, to a somewhat lesser extent, universities) and those who teach in them. Judges, like others, are apt to become somewhat overwrought in their description of the teacher's place in society. One judge said (1991) that teachers 'occupy a very special place in our society ... As members of this profession, they are welcomed into our communities; into our homes; into our organizations.'[66] The teacher, in such a description, becomes a sort of family member. Because teachers are caught up in notions of family they become subject to the same sort of concerns that arise in custody cases. The teacher should live up to the (heterosexual) family expectations of (heterosexual) decency and (heterosexual) morality. The daily reality of teachers and professors – a routine involving little special contact with 'our homes' – is forgotten.[67] Teachers are often perceived as they were in the past, as 'second-class citizens' whose 'private and school lives were constantly open to public scrutiny and moralistic requirements.'[68]

The courts have acceded at times to the idea that homosexuality has no place in educational institutions, or is appropriate only as a subject for negative or scientific study. This is a reflection of the all-too-common view in society generally that homosexuals and the schools should not mix.[69] This attitude can sometimes reach extremes. In one Nova Scotian case (1994), for example, a man was convicted of the attempted murder of his wife and her adopted daughter. The mother had wanted to take the girl to religion classes, which he objected to because he did not want her taught by 'lesbians.'[70] 'Homosexual' teachers here are the cause of the ruin of family life.

The idea of the inappropriateness of homosexuality for the schools is usually manifested in two forms: exclusion of homosexuals from teaching positions and exclusion of material portraying homosexuality and homosexuals as positive or even neutral. One U.S. study in the 1980s showed that most principals would not fire a teacher simply for being gay, but might give him or her a warning.[71] This sort of view led some to conclude, pre-*Vriend*, that a school in Canada would be unlikely to let a gay teacher go but might be reluctant to hire a known homosexual.[72] *Vriend* illustrates the contrary and a judicial willingness to acquiesce in the purification process. McClung JA refused to 'validate' 'homosexual relations' and rebut 'a millenium of moral teaching.' This 'moral teaching' includes an assumption of homosexual intent to corrupt the young.

Vriend is not a unique case. Logic similar to that of McClung JA appears to have been behind the facts in the *Wilson* case (1976), in which the University of Saskatchewan sought an order from the Saskatchewan Queen's Bench directed to the Saskatchewan Human Rights Commission prohibiting it from proceeding with a formal inquiry under the province's Human Rights Commission Act. A graduate student ('Wilson') in the College of Education at the university was employed as a sessional lecturer. We are told: 'In an advertisement which appeared in an issue of The Sheaf, the campus newspaper, Mr. Wilson publicly associated himself with the "Gay Liberation Movement" and apparently sought to promote an "Academic Gay Association". Mr. Wilson is an admitted homosexual. He also admits his male gender.'[73] After the ad appeared Wilson was informed that he would not be allowed to supervise practice teaching to be carried out by students of the College of Education in the public schools. He complained to the Human Rights Commission and the university was sent a notice of formal inquiry, alleging that it had discriminated against Mr Wilson 'in regard to his employment or any term or condition of his employment by refusing to allow him to supervise practice teachers because of his sex, and in particular because he is a homosexual, contrary to Section 3 of The Fair Employment Practices Act.' Section 3 of the Fair Employment Practices Act forbade discrimination on the basis of 'sex.' The court held that 'sex' did not, however, include sexual orientation.[74] Like other judges in other cases, Johnson J left it up to the legislature to act. It was not for the courts to 'validate' homosexuality or to engage in

issues of social controversy. The court also immediately jumped to conclusions about sexual activity when homosexuality was raised as an
issue. Johnson J said: 'It is also noteworthy that in recent years the public attitude to homosexuality and lesbianism has undergone a marked
change. It is a far cry from the days of Oscar Wilde. The *Criminal Code*
has been amended to permit homosexual activities between consenting adults. If the Legislature had intended the word "sex" as it appears
in s. 3 of the *Fair Employment Practices Act* to cover homosexuality or
lesbianism, it ought to have said so in express language, and its failure
so to do confirms my view that it did not so intend.'[75] Imagery of Oscar
Wilde and Criminal Code offences were thought appropriate references in the course of deciding that there was nothing the court could
do to prevent this deliberate exclusion of a homosexual from the
schools. [76]

A court can see it as unproblematic that a school or school board
would want to buy off a teacher thought to be homosexual. In *Valiquette v. The Gazette* (1991)[77] a teacher with AIDS employed by the
Catholic School Board in Montreal was not allowed to return to work.
A reporter learned of this and wrote a story, without naming the plaintiff and without having spoken to him, saying that a teacher with AIDS
at a particular school who had been on sick leave the previous year
was offered full salary provided he agreed not to return to work. The
plaintiff was the only teacher at that school who had been absent during that period and was thus easily identified. The court used the guarantee of privacy in section 5 of the Quebec Charter of Human Rights
and Freedoms and concluded that the plaintiff's right to anonymity
and solitude had been breached. It accepted that the newspaper report
was 'une véritable "bombe intérieure"' for Mr Valiquette.[78] While the
report said nothing about the plaintiff's sexual orientation, the court
accepted that 'Son orientation sexuelle était soudainement discuté par
plusieurs personnes qui, jusque-là, l'ignorait totalement.'[79] In setting
out the facts, the court acknowledged evidence of discrimination
against the teacher 'based solely on an irrational fear that he would be
injurious to the children or the school,' but it did not pause to consider
that its decision carries the implication that a teacher's homosexuality
ought to be kept hidden and that it is unproblematic to try to get rid of
such a teacher.[80]

Of course there are cases in which some homosexuals should be kept
away from children. Some teachers do sexually assault students, sometimes students of the same sex.[81] But it is inappropriate for the court, as

in *Noyes* (1986), one of the British Columbian cases mentioned earlier, to confuse homosexuality generally with child molestation.[82] At times, in cases of sexual assault by teachers on students of the same sex, the courts are more vexed by the homosexual issue than by the sexual assault issue. Thus, in *R. v. Pilgrim* (1981), a school principal was convicted of indecent assault on male students. The principal was married. In reviewing the sentence given by the trial judge, Mifflin CJN said: 'He [the trial judge] said he was not concerned with the homosexual aspect of the case, but simply the indecent assaults themselves. In my view, if what he says is the case, he should not have considered these assaults to be as grave as he did. I am satisfied that, if it were not the homosexual propensity of the offender, no assault would have taken place, and that, therefore, rehabilitation is a factor to be considered.'[83] It is not altogether clear what the court meant here, but the 'homosexual' aspect of the case was obviously considered significant. Does the court's concern for rehabilitation mean rehabilitation from being a homosexual? If the assaults had been heterosexual in nature, would there have been a need for rehabilitation?

As for the legality or acceptability of excluding (positive) material about homosexuality from the curriculum, there is very little case law directly on point. With no judicial guidance over book banning in school libraries, it is left to parents' groups. Teachers, students, and even politicians have little say in such matters. MacKay comments: 'Such matters do not go beyond debates at school-board meetings and reports in the press.'[84] An instance of a book banning situation in Prince George appears in the case law (1987).[85] A parents' group succeeded in getting a book called *Boys and Sex* banned from the senior secondary school library; it was considered 'inappropriate because it discussed homosexuality, masturbation, premarital sex, sex games among pre-pubescent children, and sex with animals.'[86] The parents feared that the book would 'undermine children's faith in both their parents and in religion.'[87] How easy it appears to be to undermine such things. The decision of course affects all children, not just those of the parents involved.[88] Such deliberate exclusion is quite common.[89] To the extent that homosexuality or homosexuals are mentioned in academic material, it happens outside socialization and cultural courses like literature or history.

Homosexuality, given its association with disease,[90] contagiousness, and infection, is not considered appropriate for inclusion as part of the social and cultural norm of an academic institution, but it is seen fit for scientific and medical examination. Homosexual is something foreign to the scholastic community that can be poked at, theorized, treated even, and thereby denaturalized and deeroticized. In such a context, homosexuality is not a present social threat but an abstract phenomenon for clinical study. Homosexuality (and homosexual imagery) is 'safe' in this context. Again, there is little judicial record of review of such matters, but there is the curious case of *Re University of Manitoba and Deputy Minister, Revenue Canada, Customs & Excise* (1983), where Customs seized a film called 'Male Masturbation' for being 'of an immoral or indecent character.' Films about male masturbation are, of course, thought to be homoerotic and therefore beyond the pale of acceptability. The film was destined for the University of Manitoba Faculty of Medicine, intended to be used in a seminar called 'Sexual Attitudes Reassessment.' The court found that the film was not immoral or obscene in such circumstances, in part because 'while very explicit and realistic in its portrayal, [the film] is done without voice, or embellishment, or any of the usual trappings of the pornographic film maker. It simply portrays the act as it is. And it is used by the faculty as a teaching tool, to illustrate what occurs to the male species during and immediately after that act.'[91] While it is admittedly speculative, one can only assume that without this clinical approach, the film might have been determined to have homosexual pornographic or erotic aspects and therefore to be obscene. Here, however, it was clinical not normative and thus acceptable, given that its audience was medical. The judge distinguished other cases on the basis that this was 'a unique case ... for the education of future doctors of this province.'[92] If a film displaying other overt homosexual sexuality were to be imported for, say art, history, or literature courses, the result would undoubtedly have been different.

This compulsion to eradicate homosexuals, homosexuality, and homosexual material from schools (and other education institutions) makes life difficult or impossible for both teachers and students. Teachers in public schools (and particularly in religious schools or colleges, as in *Vriend*) are likely to find locating or keeping a job difficult if it is known that they are gay or lesbian.[93] It is not simply a question of getting and keeping a teaching job that is an issue. Given the general hostility to homosexuality and the perceived acceptability of that hostility, maintaining the respect of the students or controlling the class that may be very difficult if the children know of the homosexuality of the teacher.[94] By making sexual orientation an issue, as the college did in

Vriend, the educational institution creates a 'problem' that may justify dismissing the teacher. Didi Khayatt quotes one teacher as saying, in response to a question about how a sexual orientation protection clause might affect her life: 'I would be protected from firing. I would not be protected from ostracism, or harassment, or from students, or from colleagues.'[95]

Canadian cases dealing with issues of equality for homosexuals in the education system involve teachers. How much more isolated are homosexual students, who do not even get their day in court? No one would seriously argue that homosexual students do not face discrimination from teachers, schools, counsellors, and other students. In the United States, the courts have been fairly good at protecting the speech and association rights of gay and lesbian students.[96] In one case, *Fricke v. Lynch* (1980),[97] the court held that taking a person of the same sex to a high school prom was an action with 'significant expressive content' and was therefore protected speech under the U.S. First Amendment. As the *Harvard Law Review* editors note, there is a concern that, although this decision makes an advance in protecting the rights of homosexual students, it does so by requiring that the speech be political in some way.[98] It will be extremely uncomfortable, especially for high school students, if all their expressions relating to their sexuality must be politicized in order to be protected.[99] Early feelings of sexuality are difficult enough to cope with without this additional burden.

Judicial inaction to protect interests of sexual orientation equality in the education context is to a large extent part of the judiciary's larger problem when faced with issues involving homosexuality, as discussed throughout this book.[100] Judges often appear disinclined to reach conclusions that would grant homosexuals and homosexuality real protection in *any* situation. There is a tendency for judges to protect homosexual status from discrimination but they are disinclined to treat as equal activities that are homosexual in character. If a judge chooses, he might assume homosexual activities, such as sodomy – as McClung JA did in *Vriend* – so that status automatically becomes activity and protection becomes vulnerability. Bruce Ryder has noted the propensity for judicial *laissez-faire* with regard to homosexuality at the Supreme Court of Canada level: '... when one examines *Gay Alliance* as well as the Supreme Court criminal law decisions touching upon the rights of gay men, it appears that the *Mossop* majority is continuing a Supreme Court tradition of failing to condemn, or even comment upon, heterosexism in laws and social practices.'[101] La Forest J's views in *Egan v. Canada* (1995)[102] are in this tradition, so that he, along with the majority of the Supreme Court of Canada, denied the availability of benefits to a same-sex couple that were available to an opposite-sex couple. The group of judges whose views were represented by La Forest J said that sexual orientation is included in section 15 of the Charter but were not prepared to exert themselves to see that the protection had much practical meaning. La Forest J was disinclined to view family or marriage or spouses in any way other than the traditional, which prevented benefits from going to the partner of the same sex.

In the context of homosexual issues, courts can say things to justify nonaction that would be unthinkable if the rights of another group were in issue. Equal rights for homosexuals are still treated as a debatable proposition. Thus, in *Nielsen v. Canada* (1992), where the court considered an application for recognition of same-sex couples as being entitled to benefits, Muldoon J said, in denying such a right, that Canadian society is 'deeply riven' over the 'question' of homosexual behaviour: 'Firmly held views of some consider such sexual orientation to be a sinful abomination and an irredeemable perversity, while to others' attitudes it is morally neutral and normal. To some, it should not be accorded recognition or status by law because that seems to legitimate a foul example for the impressionable young: it is still regarded as one of the obscene seeds of social decadence, even although only decriminalized only about two decades ago.'[103] The views of McClung JA in *Vriend* fall directly within this tradition of noninvolvement. It is not for judges to ensure that the equality guarantees of the Charter are respected, at least when it comes to issues involving homosexuality and homosexuals. The court cannot decide as between the advocates of equal rights and those who regard homosexuality as 'a sinful abomination,' 'an irredeemable perversity,' 'a foul example for the impressionable young,' or 'one of the obscene seeds of social decadence.' By respecting these views as even arguably correct, the court legitimates them. Given the concern for the 'impressionable young,' even in a case like *Nielsen*, which had nothing to do with young people, it should not be surprising that decisions such as that of McClung JA in *Vriend*, where young people were indirectly involved, continue to exist. Why should such potential monstrosities as homosexuals be allowed near children?[104] Post-1997 jurisprudence, such as the Supreme Court of Canada decision in *Vriend*,[105] on which I will comment in the final chapter, will surely signal a change in this attitude of nonintervention in homosexual cases.

The Religious Underpinnings of Judicial Ideas
about Homosexuality

The decisions of the courts to deny equal treatment to homosexuals in the educational context (as well as many others) are not made in a vacuum. They are made because of the existence of a set of societal values that demands inferior treatment for homosexuals and homosexuality. This value system is entrenched in that it has long existed and is intricately (according to some judges, inextricably) woven into the fabric of society.[106] It is based on particular conservative religious notions. Judicial decisions based on or that take into account this value system are in effect religiously based or tinged decisions.[107] Since judges themselves are never so bold as to identify a specific theology or creed that sustains their view of society, I shall not be any more specific. Judges appear to have a generalized sense of 'religious values' that is probably best described as traditional or conservative Christian, but I will leave the specific identity to some other writer.[108]

The law is not alone in having, for the most part,[109] warmly and (to an extent) unconsciously adopted conservative Christian religious ideas as determinative of standards.[110] Education, science, and business have similarly adopted these traditional 'norms.'[111] In the *Little Sisters* trial, Carole Vance, a U.S. anthropologist and epidemiologist, testified: 'In many ways, this [new] biomedical discourse mapped over the [old] theological discourse and it was not surprising that many of the acts that religious authorities thought were immoral were then described by the biomedical authorities as pathological.'[112] There is a reflexive assumption that religious standards are 'natural.' While religious standards and norms are not automatically inappropriate for use in modern Canadian courts, they are if they are solely dictates of irrational religiosity or other superstition and contrary to ideals of equality and inclusion.[113]

The interest of conservative religion is not difficult to find in the cases that represent a negative view of homosexuals and homosexuality in education. Sometimes the references are lightly encoded. *Vriend v. Alberta* is a good example. McClung JA characterized the case as set in the context of 'religious and familial forbiddence.'[114] He saw the issue as a conflict between religious interests and homosexual rights and he had to decide 'between the platforms of the divinely-driven right and the rights-euphoric, cost-scoffing left.'[115] The judge adopted the views of religion by characterizing the issue in a way that the vested religious interests would have it characterized: as a moral issue rather than as an equality issue. This allowed McClung JA to support legislative and judicial restraint in dealing with it. He said: 'Legislatures ... need not, and do not enter every morally-eruptive social controversy and attempt to resolve it by statutory remedy.'[116] According to this characterization, the dismissal of Vriend for being a homosexual in the school system is not like dismissal of persons for being Jews or blacks, which would hardly be characterized as an issue of morality. But equality for gays and lesbians is only a 'moral' issue because the established religions make it so, by virtue of making homosexuals and homosexuality immoral. If the court accepts that characterization the issue is fought on the terms and territory and using the language established by religion, and of course religion will win. If you invite the door-to-door religious proselytizer in to have a discussion with her (more likely him) about what he or she wants to talk about, you will never win the argument. The proselytizer has set the terms and the ground rules and knows well what the result must be. If you have a discussion with that person about 'whether homosexuality is moral,' you have conceded that homosexuality is an issue in which morality (probably defined by his or her religion) has something to say. By adopting the perspective of religion on a 'homosexual' issue, McClung JA brought into the case all the other religious teachings that attach to homosexuality, such as its condemnation of sodomy, even though they were completely extraneous to the case. Reaching the decision it did, the court thereby preferred the 'millenium of moral teaching' – that is, the antihomosexual Christian view (as portrayed by the religions involved in appealing the decision), which insists on discussing sodomy and morality in a case that is about equality. At least in *Vriend*, the students at the college were probably old enough to decide for themselves whether they accepted the dictates of a homophobic religion. In most contexts, the religious interest protected in educational situations is that of the parents, although the argument is masked as being about the 'best interests' of the young people involved. As Wayne MacKay says: 'To the extent that religious rights are respected in schools, they are the rights of the parents, not the child. Although it is uncommon for children to have a different religion from their parents, it is the parents, not the students, who insist that religious beliefs not be violated.'[117]

This ousting of the interests of homosexuals and homosexuality by reference to religious values that are supposed to permeate society (rather than being confined to the members of a particular religion) is certainly not found in the *Vriend* case alone. It is evident in cases from all periods and at all levels of courts.[118] The displacement of equality arguments by morality arguments when homosexuality and homosexuals are implicated in a case is common. Thus it is not unusual for a judge, in the course of deciding a criminal case (1987) in which a school principal was charged with sexual assault on boys, to say: 'The commandments of Judaism, Christianity, and the basic tenets of virtually every society, repress unacceptable appetites and desires.'[119]

The influence of religious perception of homosexuals and homosexuality on legal outcomes is seen most commonly in the context of same-sex relationships. On the marriage issue courts have appealed to values and traditions that can only be religiously based. The first Canadian case on same-sex marriages was explicit in its reliance on religion. In *Re North and Matheson* (1974), the court had to decide whether two men could marry. The statute involved did not say that the two people had to be of the opposite sex but the court found that two people of the same sex could not marry each other. Philp Co. Ct J relied in part on the case of *Hyde v. Hyde and Woodmansee*, where Lord Penzance said: *'I conceive that marriage, as understood in Christendom, may for this purpose be defined as the voluntary union for life of one man and one woman, to the exclusion of all others.'*[120] In the case (1993) where the majority of the court held proper the refusal to grant a same-sex couple a marriage licence because marriage was for procreation, the argument that some opposite-sex couples (with licences) are childless was met with the response: 'Despite these circumstances in which a marriage will be childless, the institution of marriage is intended by the state, by religion and by society to encourage the procreation of children.'[121] Southey J, as we have seen, expressed an extraordinary view, a view no doubt acceptable to traditional religious ideology, of how a homosexual should cope. It was Southey J who said, in an amazing feat of logic, that: 'The law does not prohibit marriage by homosexuals, provided it takes place between people of the opposite sex. Some homosexuals do marry. The fact that many homosexuals do not choose to marry, because they do not want unions with persons of the opposite sex, is the result of their own preferences, not a requirement of the law.'[122]

Religious views of one of the parties to litigation before the court, where those views touch on a matter relating to homosexuality, are accorded much respect, even when it results in diminishing the value of the party who is homosexual or rendering him or her nothing more than 'a homosexual.' For example, we saw in *Partland v. Partland* (1960) judicial concern for the wife's view that marital life was 'a relationship of profound religious significance,'[123] which prevented her from seeking a divorce even though she knew her husband was homosexual when she married him. The court accepted the wife's (and her religion's) construction of marriage. The husband (and his boyfriend) ought to have conformed to it.

In child custody cases involving a homosexual parent, religion can become an issue when the straight parent's religion denigrates homosexuals and homosexuality. In *P.-B. (D.) v. P.-B. (T.)* (1988), for example, in which a gay father sought access to his children, we are told: 'At the start of her testimony Mrs. B raised the issue of her religious beliefs and what she is attempting to teach her children. Homosexual behaviour, she indicated, is "against my religion."'[124] The judge quite rightly responded that '... her religious beliefs cannot be used to bar [the father's] or [the father's same-sex partner's] access rights where those rights are in the best interests of the children.' However, that judge also said: 'There is no evidence before me that [the father] is doing anything deliberately for the purpose of undermining the children's religious training.' Such behaviour would be unacceptable, but it is apparently acceptable for the straight parent to use her religion to teach hateful ideas about the gay parent's 'lifestyle' and for the gay parent to be forbidden from 'undermining' this teaching.

The use of religious ideas is not confined to the educational or family law contexts. The courts will listen to evidence of religious figures to determine whether something is indecent.[125] Religion was used in *Re Marzan and The Queen* (1981) to justify the fact that section 156 of the Criminal Code (indecent assault by a male on a male) provided for a greater maximum penalty (ten years) than that provided by section 149 in the case of indecent assault by a male on a female or by a female on another female (five years). The court heard and rejected the argument that this was contrary to the Canadian Bill of Rights. O'Sullivan JA, for the court, said: 'It is true that both sections prohibit indecent assaults but, according to the age-old traditions of Judaeo-Christian morality, the types of indecent assault are quite different.'[126] The distinction was based on religion, which judges homosexual sex more harshly. The court accepted that treatment.

The judicial privileging of religious sensibilities in cases involving homosexual issues can take more unusual forms. One example of this occurs in the case of *R. v. Jolicoeur* (1997),[127] in which the accused was charged with assaulting a man in a restaurant in the West End of Vancouver, the city's biggest gay neighbourhood. The man was sitting in the restaurant in a nun's habit and rosary and his religious attire apparently upset the accused. W.J. Kitchen Prov. Ct J, said: '... it's clear that Mr. Johnson, in wearing a nun's robe, upset Mr. Jolicoeur, and wearing the rosary particularly, which is something I didn't understand until Mr. Jolicoeur gave evidence. It apparently has some particular significance. I'm sure Mr. Johnson never intended to upset anyone in that way. It was merely a way of getting attention for something else Mr. Johnson was involved in and that was distributing condoms in the clubs in the West End.' The judge continued: 'Well, if I had to determine the matter on probablilities, I would say that probably what happened here is Mr. Jolicoeur behaved in a way that most people don't behave. He went and initiated a conversation with a stranger because Mr. Johnson was behaving in a way most people don't behave. He was sitting there in the early morning hours as a male wearing a nun's habit.'

Despite the fact that the accused appears to have begun the verbal abuse and physical aggression because his religious sensibilities were offended, the judge in effect found both equally responsible and therefore dismissed the charge. The judge blamed the target for triggering religiously inspired invective from the accused. The target should not have responded; he ought to have put up with religious invective. He ought not to have offended the religious sensibilities of the accused. The target, the judge said, was probably hypersensitive about homophobia and gay bashing.

The invocation of generalized religious terminology and thought processes about homosexuality has appeared in the highest court and recently. It was used by La Forest J in his decision in *Egan v. Canada* (1995), in which he said: 'The legal institution of marriage has long been viewed as the fundamental instrument to promote the underlying values I have referred to.'[128] But he never indicated exactly what these are, talking only of 'long-standing philosophical and religious traditions.' There is little in the way of a 'philosophical tradition' about marriage outside the religious context. La Forest J spoke in code, a common enough characteristic of judges using religious ideology in the context of an equality case. For example, he used the word 'values' in connection with marriage, family, heterosexuality, and children.[129] In fact, there is no religiously neutral philosophy that demands nonrecognition of same-sex unions. Proponents of certain religious ideologies have succeeded in turning the issue into a question of morality, which suits their purposes in ensuring the adoption of their standards and values by society as a whole.

La Forest J's views in *Egan* fit quite comfortably with those of the Catholic jurisprude, John Finnis, who, in his writing against homosexuality, maintains: 'Now, as I have said before, "homosexual orientation," in one of the two main senses of that highly equivocal term, is precisely the deliberate willingness to promote and engage in homosexual acts – the state of mind, will, and character whose self-interpretation came to be expressed in the deplorable but helpfully revealing[130] name "gay." So this willingness and the whole "gay" ideology, treats human sexual capacities in a way which is deeply hostile to the self-understanding of those members of the community who are willing to commit themselves to real marriage.'[131] This statement is of course a self-fulfilling prophesy about marriage. Homosexual unions are not 'real.' There is no discussion beyond that; same-sex couples are simply defined out of marriage.[132] Another Catholic jurisprude responded to Finnis's view that homosexual conduct is wrong with the statement: 'If Finnis cannot construct a sound nonreligious argument in support of the position he wants to defend there is reason to doubt that such an argument exists.'[133] Perry, the writer of this response, examined Finnis's argument in detail and concluded:

> Finnis' nonreligious argument is not sound. It is not an argument we should accept. Nor is it an argument that a person logically *can* accept – even a person who *wants* to accept it, who *wants* to believe that the position that homosexual conduct is always wrong can be rationally vindicated – *if* that person rejects Finnis's argument that 'deliberately contracepted' sexual conduct is always morally bad: The [Germain] Grisez-Finnis argument that 'deliberately contracepted' sexual conduct is always morally bad and the Grisez-Finnis argument that homosexual conduct is always morally bad are essentially *the same argument*. They are the same argument that any sexual conduct between two persons is always morally illicit if it cannot or does not 'actualize' and 'allow them to experience' their relationship as (at least in part) a *procreative* union.[134]

Perry goes on to say that even religious arguments against homosexual conduct 'are deeply problematic, *even for those who count themselves religious.*'[135] Basing decisions in modern situations on traditional religious views is problematic in contexts other than the homosexual. Perry notes, for example, that the official Catholic position once held that slavery was permissible.[136]

Curiously, issues involving homosexuality are some of the few for which the courts still deliberately turn to religious values to help them reach a decision. Cases of gender, race, and even religious rights would be much differently decided if generalized, traditional religious values were allowed to determine their outcome. In his dissenting reasons in *Egan v. Canada*, Linden JA noted that: '... the fact that similar benefits may be available to gay and lesbian partners under a different scheme – a provincial rather than a federal scheme in this case – cannot remedy the discriminatory impact of denying benefits to gay and lesbian partners on the same footing as heterosexual partners ... Such a compromise is reminiscent of the now-discredited 'separate but equal doctrine,' developed by the United States Supreme Court in *Plessey v. Ferguson*, 163 U.S. 537 (1896), which supported discrimination against African-Americans and other people of colour ...'[137] Such a discriminatory regime was also religiously based. Traditional religious notions turned race into an issue of morality. One can imagine how women's equality issues would be decided if the courts turned to the writings of St Paul. It is only by detaching the religious characterization of such issues that a court can achieve an equality analysis of it. Once the religious characterization is removed from an issue of racial or gender discrimination, the issue becomes much more straightforward.[138] So it should be with homosexuality.

Inclusion and Accommodation

The casualness of the judicial acceptance of the influence of generalized, traditional religious input in issues relating to homosexuality is what is most astonishing. What the judges are searching for is a standard to use to test cases involving homosexual issues. Traditional religious values provide the most convenient standard, in part because of their age and in part because of their (negative) clarity. Convenience because of tradition and familiarity is not, however, perceived as acceptable in other cases in which equality issues arise and it should be equally unacceptable in cases involving homosexuality. The judiciary must not automatically rely on 'moral and ethical' or 'religious' values that may well have changed or no longer be appropriate. What then ought the judge to use? By what standards should a modern Canadian court make decisions involving (dis)entitlements and (lack of) access based on a (homosexual) person's characteristics?

There are numerous works that explore Canadian approaches to equality issues.[139] There are also numerous works that examine the

Canadian identity.[140] An elaboration on those general issues is outside the scope of the present study; here I want simply to apply what I see as the essence from the existing learning to the context of legal cases involving homosexuals. For very few other[141] equality issues are traditional religious attitudes seen as appropriate standards or even starting points from which to work. There is a general consensus that an appropriate Canadian approach in human rights cases is to be as inclusive and as accommodative as possible. An inclusive approach is one that is receptive to those who are different from the majority. An inclusive approach accepts difference; it does not have a single model person as the ideal but is open to including as many different backgrounds or characteristics as possible. An accommodative approach resolves disputes by preferring compromise and accommodation instead of resorting to conflict, which will result in a winner and a loser. It comprehends all individuals and groups and does not engage in the practice of having a dominant group make concessions to a minority group. If such approaches are available, whatever their flaws, when minority groups other than homosexuals or when equality issues other than homosexuality are being considered in either a legal or a political context, there is no reason for a regression to traditional religious standards or prejudices when homosexuals or homosexuality are being considered.

An inclusive-accommodative approach in a society is characterized by less certainty than other approaches. The inclusive ideal demands an acceptance of members of different groups.[142] No single historical cultural group is perceived as having a permanent superior position. Resolution of issues can take some time because of the need to accommodate various people and groups.[143] In the Canadian context, important manifestations of this sort of ideal include the multicultural principle and the equality provisions of the Canadian Charter of Rights and Freedoms.[144]

This is not to say by any means that Canada's history is one of social tolerance or that Canada is a utopia for members of different groups.[145] Quite the contrary; Canadian history is the story of the struggle of members of different groups for a place. However, there does exist the idea that a place, an accommodation, can and should be found.[146] Entitlement to such a place is not just a concession from the dominant group. Sheelagh Day and Gwen Brodsky have dealt with the dangers of this formal equality view of accommodation.[147] The equation of accommodation with concessions 'allows,' according to Day and Brodsky, 'those who consider themselves "normal" to continue to construct institutions and relations in their image, as long as others, when they challenge the construction are "accommodated".'[148] This facile view of accommodation only allows the status quo to remain privileged: 'Accommodation conceived of in this way does not challenge deep-seated beliefs about the intrinsic superiority of such characteristics as mobility and sightedness. In short, accommodation is assimilist.'[149] That is why the ideal is and must be inclusive as well as accommodative. The ideal should not be related to any dominant paradigm, but is, instead, an aspiration of inclusiveness and an accommodation that is not a concession but a comprehension. The Charter can be seen as an important document in assisting with this inclusiveness-accommodation. Section 15 of the Charter, in particular the open-ended way in which it has been interpreted, is witness to the nature of the society from which it derived. That it is more 'Canadian' to resolve issues by accommodation and inclusion rather than by conflict and the exclusion of 'losers' is something evidenced in case law. In *Dagenais v. CBC* (1994), for example, Lamer CJC said that in Canada it is appropriate to reject the 'clash model' of competing rights as 'more suited to American than to Canadian jurisprudence.'[150]

It is important that the legal system and agents in Canada address issues relating to gays and lesbians, including issues of homosexuals and homosexuality in the educational system, with a regard to the ideals of the political and legal structures of this state.[151] The inclusiveness and accommodation that characterize the Canadian ideal must apply to homosexuals just as they do to individuals of various religious, ethnic, or racial groups. The Canadian state and Canadian society are far from achieving a perfect inclusiveness and accommodation. Inclusion and accommodation have still to be attained in many areas while existing inclusion and accommodation may, in practice, achieve much less than real equality for some members of some minority groups. Still, homosexuals are entitled to expect to be part of that working through or process towards achievement of inclusion and accommodation and not be sidelined as an exception because some traditional attitude demands such an exception. An inclusive and accommodative approach to homosexuals and homosexuality by the courts, whatever faults such an approach might have in terms of actually delivering equality to minorities, ought not to be avoided because of traditional religious prejudices. Gays and lesbians have yet to be truly accepted into the fabric of this society. Examples of homophobic remarks from our politicians, for example, are not hard to find.[152] To their credit, many Canadian courts have begun to recognize the place of homosexuals in the social fabric of Canadian society. The problem for present purposes is that inclusion and accommodation have had little impact in the context of judicial attitudes towards homosexuality and education.[153] What is needed at schools and on campus is expression about homosexuality, in terms of teaching and of material and in terms of comfortably homosexual-identified teachers, students, and staff. Positive expression about homosexuality will help counter the overwhelming negativity of existing speech about homosexuality, which, for the most part, consists of name calling on the playground, in locker rooms, and in school board meetings.[154] Decisions such as that of McClung JA in *Vriend* do not help in the process of inclusion and accommodation.

In the context of the inclusive-accommodative ideal, what is a court to do when faced with a situation in which respecting religious views generates a different resolution from that which would result from respect accorded to the right to freedom from discrimination on the basis of sexual orientation? The answer is clear: that which includes and accommodates must prevail. When a religious organization or a person with strong, proselytizing religious views enters into a public arena, including education, in any way, that organization or person must expect to operate in that arena by respecting the social ideals of inclusion and accommodation – just as a gay business person, whatever his or her personal beliefs, must not discriminate on the basis of race, sex, religion, and so on. Human rights legislation mandates such an approach in some cases, but where it does not cover the situation, as perhaps in the case of a clash between religious freedom and sexual orientation liberty, a court should adopt a resolution that avoids exclusion. This approach has certainly been used in cases where a right or value other than freedom from discrimination on the basis of sexual orientation has competed with religious interests. In *Jones v. The Queen* (1986), for example, the Supreme Court of Canada found that a provincial law requiring attendance at public school except in specified situations was not an unconstitutional violation of the freedom of religion guaranteed under section 2(a) of the Charter.[155] According to Wilson J: 'In my view, the *School Act* does not offend religious freedom; it accommodates it. It envisages the education of pupils at public schools, private schools, at home or elsewhere. The legislation permits the existence of schools such as the appellant's which have a religious orientation.'[156] In *Zylberberg v. Sudbury (Board of Education)* (1988), the court said that the requirement of reading scripture or having prayers at the beginning or end of each day for those students who were not excused was unconstitutional as infringing the Charter. The majority said: 'It can no longer be assumed that Christian principles are acceptable to the whole community.'[157] The availability of an exemption did not save the situation. The majority said: 'On the contrary, the exemption provision imposes a penalty on pupils from religious minorities who utilize it by stigmatizing them as non-conformists and setting them apart from their fellow students who are members of the dominant religion.'[158] The same arguments ought to impress the court when homosexuality is excluded from or marginalized in the educational institution. The arguments against religiously inspired teaching on an issue such as homosexuality are perhaps even greater than those against instituting religious ceremonies such as prayers, as in *Zylberberg*. Overt religious activities in schools can be easily identified as religious indoctrination and compartmentalized and dismissed as such. More invidious is religious-based instruction on topics such as homosexuality, which is not specifically identified as religious and is consequently accepted as a 'truth.'

The requirement for inclusion and accommodation, even in the context of protecting sexual orientation rights that upset certain religious sensibilities, does not set up a hierarchy of bases of discrimination, one triumphing over another. In fact, it is meant to have quite the opposite effect. The requirement is consistent with what Lamer CJC has said in *Dagenais v. CBC*: 'A hierarchical approach to rights, which places some over others, must be avoided, both when interpreting the *Charter* and when developing the common law. When the protected rights of two individuals come into conflict, as can occur in the case of publication bans, *Charter* principles require a balance to be achieved that fully respects the importance of both sets of rights.[159]

Inclusion and accommodation for homosexuals does not mean that religion is being excluded and refused accommodation. Religious ideology simply should not be used to determine what people who are not of that religion can do or how they should lead their lives or what they should teach or be taught.[160] Religious freedom should not prevail over freedom of sexual orientation merely because religious freedom has been recognized for a longer period of time and because religious ideas have infused the common law. Recognizing true equality for homosexuality does not impair religious freedom. Nobody can seriously argue that religious freedom is precariously positioned in this country in the way that freedom of sexual orientation is. Religion has an entrenched place in society.[161] For example, as we have seen in the education cases, religious values are automatically raised as relevant to the issues at hand. A court that raised sexual orientation issues in the context of deciding a case on religious discrimination in the educational context, in contrast, would be perceived as acting in a most unorthodox fashion. Some religions have their own educational institutions, which are often privileged by constitutional protection.[162] Such guarantees of privilege for some sectarian schools should not mean, however, that they are free to discriminate as they please. It would be intolerable if the guarantee for sectarian schools provided permission for racism (which has been for centuries religiously justified and practised until quite recently in sectarian schools for First Nations students). Likewise, the constitutional permission to establish sectarian schools should not be construed as granting permission for sexist or homophobic policies.

The courts should not draw on religious values to decide issues such as the place homosexuals and homosexuality should occupy in the education system without an awareness of the legacy of this intrusion of religious values on homosexuals and homosexuality in the past. McClung JA, in *Vriend* (1996), purported to equate 'discrimination arising from sexual orientation ... [and discrimination arising from] religion' in that some but not all provincial human rights laws include these heads of discrimination.[163] He thus dismissed the claims to protection of both religion and sexual orientation.[164] Religion and sexual orientation cannot, however, be lumped together as subject to the same treatment by the law, as McClung JA would have us believe. This 'formal' equality is far from meaning that there is equality in practice. A formal equality inevitability means that the interests of religion prevail, given the entrenched position religious interests have had in Canadian (legal) history. Religious tradition has not been kind to (what we now call) homosexuals or to homosexual activity. The role that religion has played in the legal plight of homosexuals was discussed by Timothy Reinig, whose views, while developed in the U.S. context, resonate in the Canadian experience. Reinig says:

> The West's religiously-based moral heritage with respect to lesbians and gay men is, at best, disingenuous and, at worst, corrupt. It represents and perpetuates a legacy of intolerance, oppression and hatred which cannot legitimately be invoked against gay people with any consistency and still

be characterized as moral. The extent to which our constitutional democracy allows certain elements to establish this tradition as the official state morality, with the imprimatur of the government and courts, is to seriously call into question whether or not a violation of the First Amendment's establishment clause is taking place. Its continuing and pervasive influence over law's policy and politics in this nation subjugates millions to a hegemonic system of religiously-based morality while disenfranchising them from democratic entitlements which others take for granted.[165]

Conservative religious leaders and thinkers (as well as judges) are quick to defend human rights documents and doctrines that protect religious freedom, including influence over education. They are also, however, among the first to prevent any attempt to protect homosexuals from discrimination, in particular any attempt to allow expression with respect to homosexuals and homosexuality in the education system. Judges and religious apologists seem curiously unaware of or unbothered by the double standard.[166] It is difficult to know why some conservative religionists are so determined to impose their own views on others even if it means destroying any (positive) sense of identity of another group. Whatever the reason, it is not the job of the courts in Canada to further this goal. Freedom of religion has no superior claim to protection over freedom of sexual orientation, particularly if the former means an annulment of the latter.

Issues of education ought to be decided on the basis of principles such as inclusion and accommodation and not 'traditional religious values.' A judge is allowed any religious belief but he or she is not permitted to exercise that belief on the bench. *As a judge*, he or she has no freedom of religion, just as a judge has no freedom of speech. A judge has no jurisdiction to import religious values into human rights and equality decisions, particularly in the education context, where society's values are being instilled. While no judge can stop the name calling on the playground or the hostility to homosexuality some parents preach, judges do have the tools to prohibit the silencing of homosexuality and the dismissal of homosexuals from the education system. It is just conceivable that over time such actions will help reduce the name calling and hostility.

4

Homophobic Expression

The Symbolism of Homophobic Expression and Judicial Response

This chapter examines instances of hateful, hurtful, or hostile expression directed against homosexuals, focusing on the judicial response to it and thus concentrating on instances that have found their way into the court. Homophobic expression can take many forms, which are often thought of as unrelated. One of the problems in assessing the judicial response to this expression is the disinclination of the judiciary (and others) to recognize that the various forms are somehow linked and – with the possible exception of physical attacks on homosexuals – to treat them primarily as expressions of homophobia. The homophobic character of hate speech, provocation, abuse, robbery, and so on that unites these various expressions is downplayed, so that no linkage is made. But they are united by common popular assumptions, which take the form of negative stereotypes about homosexuals and homosexuality. In this chapter I assess judicial response to homophobic expression as a whole, as well as to its component parts.

The principal point of the exercise is thus to study the range of forms of hostile expression towards homosexuality – some physical, some verbal, some both. The exception here will be outing, which is discussed separately in the next chapter. While hurtful in some cases to the individual identified, outing should not be deemed 'negative' and is often not intended to be homophobic. Moreover, outing is often expression by a homosexually identified person. The types of expression in this chapter, in contrast, in addition to being homophobic are made by people who, with a very few exceptions, do not identify as homosexual – although some people believe that they have and fear homosexual feelings.[1] The intensity and pervasiveness of homophobic expression is sadly all too obvious; the 'naturalness' and unremarkableness of the hostility expressed are also undeniable. The equation of homosexual with victim and homosexuality as symbolic of negativity underly and unite the various instances of homophobic expression. By bringing all of these forms together in this chapter, I want to emphasize the scope of the problem as well as the connectedness of the various forms. This expression often arises as a sort of 'logical' addendum to hostile expression that is not otherwise homophobic, such as, for example, a homophobic remark made to an assault victim who is not actually believed to be homosexual. At other times, the expression is deliberately homophobic and intended to do violence to a person who is thought to be homosexual or to demean that individual by categorizing him or her with homosexuals.

The second point of the exercise of setting out these various types of homophobic expression is to examine critically the response of the judiciary when (negative) expression about homosexuality is involved. The way in which the judiciary treats the homophobic expression of those it judges sets a standard as to what is acceptable in society and what is not. The treatment can also be used to gauge both the judiciary's awareness of the problems and potency of expression and the success of the homophobic expression in trivializing homophobia. If homophobia continues to be rendered commonplace, the struggle for equality still has much work to do. If, however, hateful, hurtful, and hostile expression towards homosexuals is remarkable and seen as requiring deliberate and chastening judicial response, then it is no longer usual and its marginalization is in itself an indication of progress towards true equality. If judges ignore homophobic expression as an unremarkable phenomenon, the judiciary is in a sense condoning that expression. Judicial response constitutes the ultimate, formal societal commentary on any particular activity.

Judicial response in and of itself in any particular case may accomplish rather little, of course. But judges condemn something, there is at least some generalized pressure to refrain from doing the thing condemned. Judges have a choice. They can make narrow statements of law in their reasons for decision or they can make broad statements. They can editorialize or refrain from doing so, comment generally on the individuals and the subject matter before them or not. The appropriate response will vary, depending on what the judge says and whether a particular situation calls for generalized condemnation.

The response of a court to homophobic expression could take several forms. The court could ignore the homophobic aspect and treat the incident in question as just another example of assault or abuse. Such a response closets the homosexual aspect of the situation and hides the homophobia in society, witnessed in the case before the court. The whole motive or ideology of the *homophobic* expression is obscured or denied and justice has at least partially failed. The court might, however, acknowledge the homophobia in the case but respond only with a superficial sympathy for the 'homosexual' target, by using expressions of double standards and failing to condemn the perpetrator's hatred of homosexuals. Worse, the judge might even blame the target for his or her homosexuality, which incited a 'natural' reaction from a 'normal' person. A judge might express sympathy for the target and recognize the homophobic symbolism of the wrong done, but yet feel that nothing can be done, at least not by a mere judge. Such fatalism in the judiciary ought to be compared to judicial reaction in similar situations involving a racial or ethnic minority. Would the court wring its hands in helplessness if the target of the hateful, hurtful, or hostile expression had been black, Chinese, a woman, or disabled? Superficial empathy and sympathy without substantive help is arguably the worst of the possible responses because it communicates a message of the inevitability of homophobia and also of its unimportance: 'We recognise there is a problem but cannot be bothered to do anything about it. Poor you.'

The final response is one in which the judge recognizes the individual and group aspect of the homophobic expression and the impact that expression in a particular instance can have in a more generalized way. An individual is being forced to bear the brunt of a deep-rooted historical hostility and violence towards this group of people. As will be seen, more and more judicial reaction is taking this form. This response and its increasing frequency is encouraging and proves that judicial attitudes can change. The admitted knowledge on the part of some judges of the implications and problematic nature of instances of homophobic expression makes the situation graver, however, when other judges pretend not to know or make statements that indicate their indifference about the situation.

Of course, part of the task of ensuring judicial awareness falls to lawyers. Lawyers often do a poor job of educating judges or convincing them to take notice of social circumstances. Sometimes such judicial education might be perceived by the lawyer to conflict with the narrower interests of the client. The tension between individual versus group interests is difficult to reconcile. In some cases, the target of homophobic expression does not want to be identified with homosexuals and homosexuality in any way and would be absolutely averse to any use of his or her situation to advance the interests of homosexual equality. In some cases, part of the problem as related by the victim might be that the trauma suffered would only be relived by the court's public identification of him or her with homosexuals as a group. The target (homosexual or not) can help to perpetuate homophobia by endeavouring not to belong to such a group.

Instances of Homophobic Expression and Judicial Treatment

The instances of homophobic expression go well beyond negative statements about homosexuals. They involve physical acts, instances of exclusion, and insults. They are both overt and covert, official and 'private.' Homophobic expression is as common between or among people who know each other as it is among strangers. It occurs in urban and in rural areas, in gay ghettos and in Bible belts. People of any age, social circumstance, or gender can be the perpetrator or the target. Most of the perpetrators and targets discussed below are men, as lesbians are infrequently identified in cases. This, as I noted elsewhere, is part of the invisibility of lesbians. I treat instances of homophobic expression in the following order:

1 'homosexual' as a term of abuse;
2 allegations of homosexuality to hurt a person;
3 hate propaganda;
4 association of homosexuality with violence;
5 homosexual panic defence;
6 gay bashing;
7 police harassment;
8 official homophobia; and
9 negativity in the community.

These categories, while they do not constitute an exhaustive treatment of instances of homophobic expression, have some reasonable representation in court decisions. One or two are simply major examples of larger issues – for example, police officers are not the only officials to harass homosexuals. The nine divisions are convenient but they should not be read as distinct or discrete compartments. My purpose in this exercise is to show how they are connected – how looking at schoolground name calling informs the random beating of a homosexual, which in turn informs official reluctance to grant a licence to a homosexual business establishment, and so on.

Homosexual as a Term of Abuse

The best-recognized forms of homophobic expression are such things as gay bashing and hate lines. But they are much less a presence than the persistent day-to-day disparagement of homosexuality. This form of homophobic expression is abuse directed at a person which, taken literally, means the person is a homosexual. Judges are usually unaware of the homophobic implications of such expression and sometimes treat it flippantly, failing to realize that it could have any impact on homosexuals as a group. Perhaps this is so because the targets of such invective are in fact often not homosexuals. The words are rendered in some cases as endearing epithets. Even when they are directed at a person who is gay or lesbian and are intended to insult that person, the courts are not necessarily responsive. They are after all 'just words.' Sticks and stones might break someone's bones but names will never hurt him, or her. A lack of response is, however, to a certain extent at least, an implication in the name calling.

That calling a person a 'homosexual' can cause hurt is recognized by the law in defamation cases. This point is developed in the next chapter. In *Culhane v. Rawlings* (1987), for example, there was an action for defamation by one Ford employee against another. The defendant 'referred to the plaintiff as a son of a bitch and as a male person who performed homosexual acts.'[2] Given the other allegations, made the court thought there could be the basis of a successful defamation action. In the defamation cases, the courts distinguish between using 'homosexual' as a term of abuse, which is possibly defamatory *if you really mean it*, and using it as a term of endearment (so that you do not really mean it), where it is not. Using terms for homosexual as pet names and using them as insults are of course related. One might call somebody, affectionately, an Indian giver or say that the person had 'jewed' you, but those terms might also be used as hurtful epithets. Such words are meant to inferiorize, if not the direct recipient, then the members of the group whose name is used. And if they are heard on a regular basis and without negative comment, they succeed in doing just that. The use of such words should not, except in very exceptional cases, be the subject of a special legal action, but if they come up in the context of a case before the courts the court should not necessarily ignore them.

Attempts to humiliate people by calling them homosexual start early in life. *R. v. Homma* (1989) illustrates the fear of homosexual identification that affects children in schools. In that case, two boys who were being sexually abused by their male teacher did not report the incidents. As Taggart JA says: 'The two boys did not make complaints of the conduct of the appellant because they were embarrassed. They intimated that they might be considered by their peers to be homosexuals.'[3] The denigration of homosexuality first met with in the schoolyard undoubtedly leads to the self-esteem problems homosexuals experience later in life, which is exascerbated by continuing inferiorization from religious bodies, politicians, and even the courts. A child's fear and ridicule of and comtempt for homosexuality is learned from adults, usually in the family context. In one case (1990) of sex abuse within a family, for example, there are several examples of how an expression such as 'cocksucker' was used as a term of abuse.[4] In another case (1994), a mother and father were in a dispute over access by the father to the children. The father was abusive and alcoholic and had previously sexually assaulted a teenage boy, but when the mother wanted to collect the children from the father and 'in front of her sons and the accompanying police, he said "Go play with your homosexual boyfriend."' The father did not perceive himself as homosexual. He had little to be proud of but he could still elevate himself above the mother's 'boyfriend' by diminishing him as 'homosexual.'[5]

Adults can use terms for homosexuals around children in a deliberate attempt to hurt them. They play on the humiliation they know the child has been taught to feel by being associated with homosexuality. In *R. v. Hawkins* (1986), the accused was convicted of sexual assault of a fourteen-year old girl.[6] He used lesbians as fantasy objects. As part of the girl's harrowing experience: 'There was a conversation with her as to whether her friends were lesbians. He appeared to get angry when she denied that.'[7] Here, the adult, apart from the violence he committed, passed on the notion of the lesbian as both a fantasy object for men and a term of abuse. In another case the boyfriend of a mother 'was verbally abusive, calling the girls sluts, tramps and lazy and calling the boys lazy and queer.'[8]

Among adults, examples of the use of the description 'homosexual' as a means of belittling a person are numerous. It might be part of a pattern of harassment in the workplace on the basis of sexual orientation, where the homosexual is the subject of 'fun' and contempt.[9] In one case (1992), a military officer had allegations of sexual harrassment lodged against him.[10] He complained about the process. In his review of what had happened, Cullen J said: 'It is ... clear that there were serious allegations that Hinshaw never divulged to Lee [the officer]. Most damaging of all from the report: "Lee is referred to as a 'fudge packer' which apparently is a term denoting homosexual buggery".'[11] Whether the person who is the subject of such name calling is or is not actually thought to be a homosexual, the impact in the workplace on people who *are* homosexual will be serious. It is not surprising that homosexuals traditionally have been ghettoized in 'safe' professions where there is less chance of such 'casual' verbal abuse.

Using 'homosexual' as a term of abuse is certainly not confined to situations in which the parties know each other. In *Morgentaler v. Wiche* (1989), the Morgentaler clinic in Toronto sought an injunction to prevent the defendants from obstructing the operation of the clinic.[12] Evidence was adduced of various techniques used by the defendants, including shouting at people who entered the clinic, that 'they are "babykillers" and "murderers"; that they are not "Real Women"; and that all the staff of the Clinic are homosexuals and accusing them of doing such things as gagging women and forcing them to have abortions.' One of the defendants 'heard people say some of the staff at the Clinic are lesbians and homosexuals.'[13]

In light of these instances it is perhaps not surprising that when someone deliberately wants to injure a person who is actually thought to be homosexual verbal abuse is at least one of the tools used.[14] Perhaps, too, it is not surprising that a person might react violently to being designated a homosexual. In *R. v. Luxton* (1990), the accused was charged with the murder of a cab driver.[15] The cab driver picked the accused up outside a gay bar. Part of the case against the accused was that he had made an incriminatory statement to another prisoner while in custody awaiting trial, to the effect that he had stabbed the victim inside the cab and again outside the cab because she called him a 'faggot.'[16] Whatever happened in the case, clearly the accused thought that being called a homosexual name was a possible excuse to violence.[17]

It is not feasible to initiate legal action in cases where one person calls another 'homosexual' as a term of abuse, nor is it desirable.[18] Among other problems, such a response would only exascerbate the problem of 'homosexual' being thought a negative term and thing. But that is not to say that the words ought to pass without judicial comment: a court can encourage by its silence. It should certainly not join in the laughter and it should avoid participation in the verbal denigration of homosexuals. In *Culhane v. Rawlings* (1987), where the plaintiff alleged that the defendant, in the presence of a number of other fellow Ford Motor employees, defamed him, McCart DCJ said: 'If I had one dollar for every time I heard either of those expressions during some three years in the armed forces and at summer jobs while attending university and law school, I would have been financially independent by the time I was 25 years old.'[19] The judge thought that in a 'perverse way' they seem to be used as 'expressions of friendship.' Such comments are inappropriate.

Allegations of Homosexuality to Hurt a Person

Related to the use of 'homosexual' as a term of abuse is the situation in which a person is identified as homosexual in a deliberate attempt to hurt him or her in a direct economic, social, or financial way rather than merely to insult that person. Some instances of outing, particularly where it is done deliberately to hurt the outed person's social position, could fall within this type of homophobic expression. Many cases of outing can, however, be differentiated from the instances of expression I include here because the instances of outing cannot be called homophobic. In fact, the outer is often (probably) homosexual and takes issue with the shame and internalized homophobia of the outed person. The purpose of the expression that amounts to outing is (eventually) to achieve equality for homosexuals and homosexuality. In the cases here, on the other hand, such a goal is the last thing the speaker has in mind. The speaker could care less about the status of homosexuals except that it provides a way in which to injure the object of his or her expression. The speaker has in a sense a vested interest in keeping homosexuality inferiorized or the expression loses its sting.

The most common occasion on which allegations of homosexuality intended to hurt are made is in child custody cases, when one parent tells the children or the court of his or her suspicions that the other parent (who wants custody) is a homosexual. The allegation is always meant to poison the perception of the parent so labelled. There are many examples of such homophobic expression. In one case (1986), in a custody battle, the father alleged that the mother had 'lesbian tendencies,' which she denied.[20] In another custody case (1987), it was said that the mother was vindictive and tried to discredit the father. According to Hamilton LJSC, 'The most damaging reference is that by her to her own son, in which she described his father as a "faggot".' She knew it was not true. It apparently started with a 'facetious remark' of the husband, who, when she asked him jokingly if he was a homosexual, said, in an equally facetious manner, 'that if he did have an affair with a man would she forgive him.' According to the judge, 'She has now in her mind built that into a characterization of her former husband as a homosexual. What is important is that she has discredited the father in this manner to the boy himself.'[21] Custody went to the father. However, according to the court, the attempt to discredit the father in the eyes of the boy had worked. Homosexuality was a bad thing; the boy had learnt that even before the parental custody dispute. That custody battle only reinforced the boy's perception of homosexuality as evil.

Re O and O (1980) is another custody case in which the mother raised the issue of the father possibly being homosexual. Labrosse J said: 'According to the father, K reported that he had been told by his mother that it was wrong to sleep in his father's bed and that if he did so he would become homosexual.'[22] The judge rightly found this unusual behaviour on the part of the mother. But the fact that the mother raised the possibility of homosexuality in the father, despite its baselessness, caused the court to examine all the evidence to show that there was in fact no truth to the allegations. Such allegations, easily made, can have very damaging consequences.[23] As in *Re O and O*,[24] in *Whyte v. Whyte* (1991), the mother sought to get custody from the father by alleging that he was homosexual and had sexually abused the child.[25] The court rightly said that his sexual orientation would not necessarily be relevant. As in *Re O and O*, however, homosexuality easily became an issue in court simply because it was raised. Tests were thought necessary to deal with the issue of homosexuality although the court purported to say that it was not 'relevant.'

Whether or not they are true, the court should react carefully to allegations of homosexuality. The court should not contribute to the homophobia evident in the allegation by being sympathetic about the 'hurt' a parent must feel when accused of being homosexual. The court shows that it considers such allegations 'serious' when it hears evidence to decide whether or not they are true. This action only reinforces the view that something legally turns on the homosexuality of one of the parents, a view which, of course, inspired the allegation in the first place. In one case (1986) where a husband petitioned for divorce from his wife on the basis of mental cruelty,[26] among the many

instances alleged was: 'She has an obsession about lesbians and in cor-
recting the children, she tells them they don't want to grow up to be
lesbians ... She has carried on a one sided hate against the husband's
parents because they "drink beer" and because the grandmother is a
"lesbian".' According to the judge, Guerette J: 'There is not one iota of
evidence to support these terrible accusations and the husband has satisfied me that all these manifestations of the wife's personality arise
out of a disoriented and distraught mind.' An accusation of lesbianism
was used to hurt somebody. Lesbian was treated as a hate word, but
not just by the mother. It was the judge who said that calling somebody
is a lesbian is 'terrible' and thought it appropriate to look for evidence
as to whether it were true.[27]

Allegations of homosexuality are intended by the one parent to contribute to an atmosphere of horror. The court ought not to allow homosexuality to become a relevant issue in these cases. It should, however,
question the fitness of a parent who would make such an allegation in
a contemptuous way. How fit is a parent like the husband who threatened to use the fact that his wife had had a brief lesbian relationship to
force her to sign a separation agreement (1996)? He told her that 'if she
did not sign the agreement, she would never see her kids again. He
threatened to drag her through the court system, and to expose, publicly, her lesbian relationship.'[28] What values would such a parent instil
in a child? A court ought not to respond to an allegation of homosexuality on the part of a parent as did the court in *D. v. D.* (1978), discussed
in Chapter 2, in which the court found, somewhat grudgingly, that the
father was probably in a homosexual relationship.[29] It awarded custody to the father, but only after finding that 'It has not been established that Mr D's sexual preferences exclude members of the opposite
sex. He describes himself as bisexual. He is discreet,' and that 'His sexual orientation is not known outside his immediate circle; he does not
flaunt it. Visitors to his house include married couples, mainly.'[30] The
court approved of his self-censorship of homosexual activity and
encouraged the interest in the opposite sex. In light of such judicial
pronouncements it is not really surprising that allegations of homosexuality are made in an effort to hurt the other parent in custody cases.

Hate Propaganda

Verbal denigration of homosexuals and homosexuality takes on an
organized form with homophobic hate advocacy: hate pamphlets, hate

phone lines, and hate pages on the Internet. Here, as compared to the instances of homophobic expression discussed in the previous two sections, it is easier for agencies of the state, such as courts, to identify the need to act to restrict such expression. Fortunately, in Canada the government does act and homosexuals are often thought fit to be included in protection from hate advocacy, although they are not usually the primary recipients of government action. The Criminal Code provisions dealing with hate propaganda do not, however, explicitly deal with sexual orientation.[31]

The courts have been fairly good at recognizing that rights of free expression are not so unlimited as to prevent regulation of hate expression. In *Irwin Toy* (1989), the Supreme Court of Canada excluded violent forms of expression from the scope of Charter protection of freedom of expression.[32] In *R. v. Keegstra* (1990),[33] the majority of the Supreme Court of Canada held that while the hate expression laws were a restriction on freedom of expression, the criminal prohibition was a justiciable restriction under section 1 of the Charter.[34] Dickson CJC said that hate propaganda can cause two types of injury. First, there is the harm done to members of the target group: 'It is indisputable that the emotional damage caused by words may be of grave psychological and social consequence ...'[35] The second harmful effect of hate propaganda is its influence upon society at large.

There have not been many successful criminal actions on the basis of hate propaganda,[36] and certainly not for hate propaganda directed against homosexuals. Perhaps it is the criminal nature of such actions that makes them difficult to win. Richard Moon argues that the responsibility for hate propaganda should be civil rather than criminal, in the form of a group defamation action or a human rights code complaint.[37] The focus would then be on the harm done to the group members rather than on the wrongful intention of the speaker. I share the concern that the law have some regard to the group dynamic of homophobic expression rather than isolating each instance but that must be left to legislative action, not covered in this book, because it is extremely unlikely that a court would embark on this course of its own accord. I am also concerned that such 'group' actions may be counterproductive and in fact amount to 'special' treatment for particular groups, or at least for individual members of particular groups, even though they have not been personally or directly affected. Moon envisages remedies of monetary compensation and impositions to prevent repetition in the context of group defamation. But there are problems with such an approach in the homosexual context (or in any group context). To whom is compensation to be paid? Prior restraints in the form of injunctions to prevent speech are troubling because they can exoticize and thereby potentially privilege the speech that is sought to be restrained, which acquires the allure of the forbidden. Such action might serve only to increase tension in a community, as people become watchful of what they say and see their neighbours get monetary advantage in a way that is unavailable to them. Also, could one homosexual person defame members of his or her own group? And what test would we use for establishing whether a person is homosexual?

There are other ways to tackle homophobic hate propaganda besides the criminal law and possible actions for group defamation. In *McAleer v. Canada (Canadian Human Rights Commission)* (1996), an application was made for a review of a Canadian Human Rights Tribunal decision wherein the tribunal ordered the applicants to cease operating a telephone hate hotline, because it was likely to expose homosexual persons to hatred or contempt.[38] The applicants challenged the ruling on the basis that it infringed their freedom of expression guaranteed under the Charter. The respondent had complained to the Human Rights Tribunal saying that the applicants had discriminated against him on the grounds of his sexual orientation in messages on their hotline. The message on the line began by talking about the North American Man Boy Love Association ['NAMBLA']. Then it went on to say: 'I think the [NAMBLA] newsletter should be allowed in Canada but that child molesters, homo or otherwise, should be executed. This should decrease the possession or circulation within Canada of the newsletter. Hell, the ancient Celts used to take their queers and trample them into the peat bogs. It's not such a bad idea, maybe. Perhaps we have finally stumbled across the argument which will save Burns bog in Delta from development because it is the only bog big enough to service the needs of the progressive city of Vancouver.'[39] The court appropriately denied the application for judicial review.

Hate propaganda can be addressed in a more indirect way than by imposing a sanction on its maker. It is also appropriate to condemn another person for acting in accordance with the dictates of the hate propaganda, however much there are protestations of reluctance by that person to do so. Thus the court acted responsibly in *Korn v. Potter* (1996), in which a physician had refused to artificially inseminate a lesbian because after performing such inseminations in the past, he had 'received telephone calls from persons who criticised him for providing artificial insemination to lesbians.'[40] The court found that the Human Rights Commission did not act unreasonably in finding a violation of section 3 of the Human Rights Act on the basis of sexual orientation. This is a difficult issue, of course, since it places the physician in a potentially dangerous situation. Unless, however, there is a threat of immediate physical harm to the physician, the court's response is rightly not to support the goal of the hatemonger. Inaction could only encourage such threats. The courts should, however, carry this idea into other situations so that the homophobic message of the hatemonger is not allowed to influence the decisions of governments, school boards, customs agents, or any other person in a position to deny equal treatment to homosexuals on the basis that the hatemonger will not like it. There is no clear demarcation, in my opinion, between a direct phone message of hate and 'the platforms of the divinely-driven right' that McClung JA gave so much deference to in the *Vriend* decision (1996).[41] It is important for the courts to acknowledge that homophobia is pervasive and that homophobic hate expression is just an extreme manifestation of a larger social problem. It cannot be treated effectively in isolation.[42]

Association of Homosexuality with Violence

While the other types of homophobic expression I look at in this chapter cause violence, either physical or emotional, to homosexuals and people associated (rightly or not) with homosexuality, the type of homophobic expression discussed in this section is of a different sort. Here the homophobic expression is that which associates homosexuality with violence. This expression is hateful and hurtful in its own right, but its injury is compounded by its leading 'logically' to violence against homosexuals. The association of homosexuality with violence is part of the construction of homosexuality as a negative and infectious thing, which I have dealt with elsewhere,[43] and is linked to other aspects of a censorious attitude, such as the association of homosexuality with child molestation, corruption, contagion, untrustworthiness, and instability. All these imagined attributes are part of the justification for attacks on homosexuality and its inferiorization. Sometimes this automatic association of homosexuality with violence is made by judges. Given the amount of violence that is directed against homosexuals, the courts ought to be careful not to make sweeping statements linking homosexuality, in a general way, with violence.

The association of homosexuality and violence is made in any number of ways. Instances drawn from court cases demonstrate the variety, some of which we have already seen in the previous section. In the *Morgentaler v. Wiche* case (1989), for example, as we saw, anti-abortion activists called people entering an abortion clinic 'babykillers' and 'murderers' and the staff of the clinic homosexuals who gagged women and forced them to have abortions.'[44] If homosexuals are perceived as babykillers and murderers, then it is not surprising that homosexuals are bashed and killed.

Children are sometimes taught that homosexuals ought to be brutalized. In one case (1995), the accused was charged with murder.[45] He claimed, among other defences, that of provocation. The accused provided many versions of what happened. On one occasion he told the police that he was taking drugs with the victim, Mason, and went into a deep sleep from which he was awakened by Mason, who was stroking his penis and inviting him to engage in a homosexual act. This incident 'offended and disgusted him, and he verbally chastised Mason, who retreated to his bedroom.'[46] The accused went for a drive but decided to excuse Mason and came back. The incident bothered him and he decided to go back home. The judge related that: 'As he was about to leave, Mason told him that "man to man" sex was alright [sic], at which point Stewart said he "lost it." He had a strong aversion to homosexuality, stemming from his childhood, during which his father had repeatedly cautioned him and his brothers against such practices and urged them to do violence to any man who attempted to seduce them. He grabbed a knife from the workbench in the woodshed and stabbed Mason first in the back and then several times in the chest.'[47]

Given such early instruction, it is not perhaps surprising that a person who fears he is homosexual will lash out against reminders of his own feelings. Homosexuality is associated with violence in his mind. Some studies show that homophobic violence can stem from fears about the assailant's own homosexuality,[48] and some cases show evidence of this fear as a cause for violence. In *R. v. Moore* (1987), the accused was charged with robbery of a bank.[49] One medical expert testified that the accused 'has developmental and character problems stemming from attempts to cope with life generally and the stigma associated with his homosexual lifestyle ...' Similarly, in another case (1989), in which a fifteen-year-old was charged with the murder of a woman, the psychiatric assessment said that his anxiety was 'mainly fueled by a strong fear of homosexuality (sexual identity not finalized) and more specifically by his fear of homosexual attack (by projection of his own lack of control).'[50]

Apart from these instances in which violence and homosexuality are linked in troubling and personal way in the mind of the perpetrator of violence, the cases show that violence is associated with homosexuality generally in at least three broad areas. First, there is an assumption that homosexual sex is violent. Second, homosexuals are assumed to rule prisons and to force prisoners to engage in homosexual sex. Finally, it is sometimes assumed that homosexual parents must be watched so that they cannot force their sexual orientation on children.

In Chapter 2, I elaborated on the judicial construction of homosexual sex as negative and I will not repeat the content here. The courts sometimes demonstrate an unquestioning acceptance of violent or at least hurtful practices assumed to be typical of homosexual sex whereas it is difficult to imagine that they would accept such practices in the context of generalized statements about heterosexual sex. In *R. v. Valley* (1986), for example, the accused was charged with murder.[51] His defence was provocation. Both the accused and the deceased were described as 'homosexuals.' The accused was discovered in the deceased's room after neighbours heard a lot of noise inside and kicked in the door. He was shaking and he claimed that the deceased had tried to sexually assault him. The police found some LSD on the premises, sex hormones in the fridge, and a suitcase containing some S&M gay magazines, as well as handcuffs. The accused said the deceased tried to rape him and he killed him to stop him. The trial court admitted much evidence about sado-masochism. One witness was 'allowed to testify as to the use and the purpose for which nitrates were used by male homosexuals.'[52] All 'male homosexuals' were in effect treated as using nitrates for sex. The evidence the court admitted about S&M and homosexual sex linked the two in a generalized way that would seem unnatural if 'male heterosexuals' were replaced for 'male homosexuals.'[53]

Some lawyers play on the association the public might make between homosexuals and violence and the propensity of homosexuals, therefore, to do anything violent they might be accused of. *R. v. Charest* (1990) provides an example of Crown counsel using homosexuality to try to prejudice a jury against an accused. In that case, a coach strangled to death an eleven-year-old boy on the team he coached. As Fish JA said on appeal: 'There was no evidence that appellant had sexually assaulted the victim. Crown counsel nonetheless insinuated a sexual motive, resorting to speculation and innuendo ...' Among the things counsel said were: 'C'est pas moi qui a employé le mot homosexuel, c'est le docteur Lapointe dans son rapport, à plusieurs endroits. Monsieur a eu des relations homosexuelles, il se promène avec des gens qui sont d'un acabit particulier, des prostituées, et le reste, et le reste. Je trouve qu'il a pour le moins une vie sexuelle scabreuse, et je vous le prétends, et ceci ne vient que confirmer ce que la défense elle-même a établi devant vous, et ça devient dans le cas qui nous intéresse, ça peut jeter un éclairage qui nous aide à apprécier les motifs lesquels tout ça est arrivé.' Far from reproving the counsel for such an address, the trial judge said: '... je n'ai que des félicitations à adresser aux procureurs.' The Court of Appeal rightly took the trial judge as well as the Crown counsel to task. A new trial was ordered.[54]

There are countless cases in which courts have accepted without question the prevalence of dangerous 'homosexuality' in prison. Richard Posner makes the distinction in his often alarmingly stereotype-laden book, *Sex and Reason*, between 'real' homosexuals and 'opportunistic' homosexuals.[55] The latter sort of homosexual – who would appear to merit the designation because of some odd constructionist approach – only has sex with a person of the same sex because there is nobody convenient of the opposite sex, for example in the navy, prison, seminaries, or boarding school. Posner goes on to say that modern society only really reviles 'real' homosexuals.[56] A better distinction of course is sex which is consensual and that which is not, whether 'homosexual' or otherwise. The courts, however, usually do not make Posner's distinction in situations involving sex in prison, nor do they fail to label the sex as 'homosexual.' It is easier and apparently more natural to generalize it all as 'homosexual' sex. Thus, in *R. v. Cavanagh and Donaldson* (1976), a prisoner killed in prison was described as 'an aggressive, belligerent homosexual who on occasions intimidated younger and weaker inmates.'[57] He was identified as a 'homosexual' in a way that people would not be identified as 'heterosexual' and the association with violence was thereby made self-explanatory.

By far the most usual situation in which a court shows concern about the inevitability of 'homosexual violence' in prison is where it is considering whether a young accused should be moved to ordinary court and therefore potentially into an adult jail if found guilty. In one case (1991), the accused was fourteen when he allegedly committed the first degree murder of a fifty-six-year-old child molester. He had lived with the victim for two years and the man provided him with food, clothing, shelter, and pets. He also permitted him drugs and alcohol and sexually abused the accused. According to the evidence, the victim had had as many as forty boys living with him over the years, all of whom he had supported and sexually abused. The accused, not surprisingly perhaps, developed what the experts called 'intense homophobia.' There was a fear that if he was put in an adult facility he would perhaps be forced into homosexual activity. As the report says, '... he would easily be the target of regular and frequent, sometimes forced homosexual activity that occurs in these [adult] institutions. This includes gang rape and a great deal more.' Violence in institutions is identified as homosexual. The court explained that: 'Aggressive homosexual inmates are not automatically placed in segregation.'[58]

In another young offender case (1992),[59] in setting out why there were problems in moving the person to an adult facility, Murray J said: 'A young offender who is not sufficiently tough will be abused physically, sexually and used to carry out the wishes of the other inmates, such as being a drug courier. If he refuses the protection and homosexual advances from a tougher, older inmate, then he will be raped and abused until he accepts that protection.'[60] The advances are not sexual; they are homosexual.[61]

The attitude that prisoners, homosexuality, and violence are suited for or deserving of each other can cause a court to assume the combination to be inevitable. The cases I have just discussed provide examples of this attitude. Another is found in *R. v. Hennessey, Williams and Kumka* (1968), in which the court dealt with a situation where the accused prisoners conducted a mock trial on the 'hapless complainant' and purported to sentence him to commit acts of sexual indecency. They used physical violence on the complainant to compel him to carry out the acts. The trial judge thought that because the offences occurred while the accused were in prison custody and 'because, as he thought, in such an environment grossly indecent acts from time to time occur,' the accused should receive a lesser sentence than would otherwise be handed down. The Court of Appeal fortunately disagreed, but the trial judge at least thought homosexual acts are what a prisoner deserves and that they are inevitable among prisoners.[62] This attitude of the inevitability of 'homosexual' violence in prison is perpetuated by other officials for their own purposes. In *R. v. Smith* (1989), for example, one witness in a case said that two police officers came to see him and 'He was told that if he didn't provide a statement, he would be locked up for two weeks and that he would be locked up with homosexuals who would rape him while the guards turned a blind eye.'[63]

Of course there are instances of 'real' homosexual activity in prison. There are also many instances of sexual assault, and certainly not only at the hands of 'homosexual' prisoners or indeed of the prisoners at all. In one case (1990), for example, a corrections worker was convicted of sexually assaulting two male inmates by means of intimidating them.[64] Judges should be careful, however, not to make generalizations about such conditions by using the vocabulary of 'homosexuality.' They should be more concerned about why sexual attacks continue to occur so easily in prisons rather than accepting them as the inevitable consequence of not segregating 'aggressive homosexuals.' Judges should also use care not to define rapes and assaults as 'homosexual' when they are simply 'sexual.' The word 'homosexual' adds nothing except another instance of negative stereotyping of the term.

The other area in which there is, occasionally, judicial acceptance of the propensity for violence or at least aggressiveness by homosexuals is in the context of child custody cases. The courts, as I have discussed in Chapters 2 and 3, are often concerned that the homosexual parent with custody not flaunt his or her homosexuality and therefore convert the child. This consideration betrays a fear of interference by homosexuals with the 'normal' heterosexual development of the child. Similar fears are never expressed about heterosexuality, which appears not to be contagious.

A judge should guard against automatically accepting the equation of homosexuality and violence. There is no doubt but that these equations are made in society, but that is no reason for judicial participation in the exercise. Homosexual people can be violent, but there is never a proper occasion to identify a person or a person's activities in legal proceedings as homosexual (any more than they would be characterized as 'heterosexual,' 'Asian,' or 'buddhist') unless it is in the context of a human rights case. Homosexual parents or any other homosexual person ought not to be subject to close scrutiny for violent potential merely because of his or her homosexuality. A sexual assault is a sexual assault; intimidation is intimidation; an aggressive person is an aggressive person. Adding 'homosexual' to the characterization simply feeds the association of homosexuality with violence, as does making generalized statements about homosexuals in the context of a case about a particular violent homosexual person or act.

Homosexual Panic Defence

Closely connected with the association of homosexuality and violence is the idea that it is 'all right' or even proper to react with violence, even extreme violence resulting in death, when threatened with a situation interpreted as involving homosexuality. The law's implication in this equation of violence with homosexuality and the need to take extreme defensive measures against it appears in the 'homosexual panic defence.'[65] In cases when this defence is used, the accused is asking the court to (partially) excuse his or her violence (usually involving the killing of another person) because of the justified alarm the accused felt in a situation involving perceived homosexuality, usually involving fear of homosexual attack. In Canada there is no such thing as a homosexual panic defence, per se. It is an American legal term; in this country, such a defence is subsumed under the guise of provocation or sometimes the defence of automatism, where it can be used to reduce a charge of murder to a conviction for manslaughter. The defence will be attempted in situations such as that in *R. v. Fournier*, a 1982 case in which the defence of automatism was raised to a charge of murder.[66] The accused had been drinking with the victim, with whom he had drunk on several occasions. He knew the victim was a homosexual and he was also aware that he was trying to break down the accused's inhibitions with drink. The accused claimed that he lay down to rest but awoke suddenly and saw the victim standing next to him in the nude. He ran to the kitchen and grabbed a knife and stabbed the victim to death. He then stole two rings from the victim. The trial judge said in these circumstances the defence of automatism was not available but the majority of the Quebec Court of Appeal overturned that decision and said the circumstances could lead to a state of dissociation, which was a disease of the mind. The defence should, therefore, have been left to the jury. Even though the accused was aware of what we are told were attempts at seduction from an early point, the court contemplated that he might still have been in a state of automatism when he committed the crime.[67]

I use the American term in my discussion here, instead of the legally correct Canadian terminology, because it so wonderfully encapsulates the homophobia that lies at the heart of the defence. It does not disguise it in a generalized term such as 'provocation.' The merger of the 'defence' with broad terms like 'provocation' and 'automatism' obscures the frequency of its use in situations where homosexual sex is allegedly feared, while its use in comparable heterosexual situations is non-existent. It is arguable that there might well be situations where a defence of provocation or automatism could arise when a person is threatened by a homosexual person or by a situation involving homosexual sex. However, the absence of such a defence where a 'heterosexual' person or 'heterosexual' sex is involved tends towards the conclusion that 'homosexual' is more important than 'panic' in the Canadian provocation/automatism cases that are equivalent to the homosexual panic cases in the United States. The parallel is whether a woman would be allowed a similar defence in a situation involving a heterosexual assault by a man. These sorts of attacks on women are much more common than 'homosexual' attacks of one man on another. But one would be hard pressed to find cases of heterosexual panic being used by women to defend their killing of a male attacker. Thus, in *R. v. Magliaro*,[68] a 1981 case to be compared with the *Fournier* case, a woman killed a man after he forced her to perform fellatio. The court took into account that the fellatio was over when she killed him. Sullivan CCJ said: 'If the accused was offended by performing the act of fellatio, after having done so she should have left the premises and taken proper action. To take his life was an unreasonable and unwarranted act.'[69] There was no consideration of provocation, automatism, or 'heterosexual' panic.

Donald Casswell, in his examination of the homosexual panic defence, says that former judicial receptiveness to stories of homosexual panic has changed and the courts 'now assess more critically the particular circumstances of the alleged sexual advance.'[70] It is true, as the cases discussed in this section will show, that courts have recently become sceptical of such a defence. For example, the court found homosexual panic implausible, even in a case such as *R. v. Hoyt* (1991), where the facts, if true, engender considerable sympathy for the accused.[71] There, the deceased invited the respondent to walk home with him after a drinking party. On the way through the bushes, the deceased made sexual overtures to the accused, who turned them down. The deceased then overpowered the accused and forcefully had anal intercourse with him. The accused became sufficiently enraged that he struck the deceased so violently in his head and chest that he died immediately. The court considered whether the accused had a defence of provocation but decided in the negative: while the evidence suggested trauma from the sexual assault, there was little to justify characterizing the accused's reaction as what the court called 'heterosexual panic.'[72] As the court pointed out, the men were of the same size, the accused had physical and martial training, and he did not seem to resist much at first. The court did not deny, however, that if the circumstances had been different a homosexual panic defence might have been available.[73] Judicial disbelief that such a panic could justify or partly justify killing another person gives cause for hope. Judges have, on the whole, accepted that violence is never an appropriate response to a homosexual situation. The defence is, however, still commonly attempted. The message appears to be taking its time in filtering down to society as a whole that such violence is never excusable and that no fear of homosexuality could be so grave as to justify violence. Perhaps that is because, although the courts tend not to accept such a defence, they have not eliminated it as a possibility.

Rejection of the homosexual panic defence is usually made on the basis of the illogic that would be involved in its use, rather than as a result of the court's identification of the homophobia that lies behind its availability. In one case (1988) in which the Alberta Court of Appeal thought the jury's rejection of the defence was reasonable,[74] Laycraft CJA agreed that: 'It would, of course, have been extremely difficult for the jury to reconcile any sudden loss of reason flowing from the deceased touching the appellant on the knee with the savage and repetitive nature of the appellant's response by hammer and knife.'[75] In another recent case (1995), the accused was charged with assault of a man whom he said made sexual advances to him while they were in a washroom.[76] A sound track revealed that at least thirty-two blows were struck. The victim was left in a coma and on life support systems. The court said that: 'Exactly what transpired in that washroom may never be fully known but the particulars establish the accused followed the victim into the washroom and what then occurred represented a grossly excessive use of force for whatever was done by the victim.'[77] The courts did not doubt the 'homosexual attack' or the 'homosexual panic.' It was the degree of violence of the response that was condemned and formed the basis for the rejection of the defence, not the idea that the defence was anachronistic and discriminatory.

In assessing the availabilty of the defence, the court will use the standard of the reasonable or ordinary person. How would an 'ordinary person' have reacted to this situation? Just who this ordinary person is is unclear. In one case (1982),[78] a sixteen-year-old accused was charged with first degree murder and he raised as a defence provocation on the basis of a homosexual attack. The Ontario Court of Appeal ordered a new trial because the trial judge should have made it clear that an 'ordinary person' was one of the age and sex of the accused. On appeal (1986), the Supreme Court of Canada restored the conviction and said that while the ordinary person has a sex, race and so on, there was no justification for the trial judge to tell the jury that the ordinary person, for the purposes of the objective test of provocation, had the same age and sex as the accused.[79] Wilson J dissented, however, and would have gone further than the Court of Appeal and made the reasonable person even more accused-specific. She said: '... the appropriate formulation of the objective standard against which the respondent's reaction to the wrongful act must be measured in this case is the standard of the ordinary 16-year-old male subjected to a homosexual assault.'[80] The ordinary person on Wilson J's formulation appears not to be homosexual but was somebody who is subject to homosexual attacks.[81]

The fact that the 'ordinary person' is not 'homosexual' can help an accused in a case such as *R. v. Valley* (1986), where the accused was charged with murder.[82] His defence was provocation. The accused was discovered in the deceased's room after neighbours heard a lot of noise inside. He was shaking and said the deceased had tried to sexually assault him. Both the accused and the deceased were described as 'homosexuals.' The accused said the deceased tried to rape him and he had killed him to stop him. The Court of Appeal held that it was not wrong for the trial judge not to have indicated that the ordinary person was a homosexual. Martin JA, for the court, said: 'I do not think the fact that the appellant was a homosexual would affect the gravity of the provocation to him. Indeed, if anything, I think that the jury might conclude that the reverse would be the case.'[83]

The courts have to be careful, however, with this standard of the 'ordinary person.' A court should not allow double standards, that is, it should not allow defences and 'normal' reactions in a homosexual context that would be unthinkable in a heterosexual context. The court must to avoid inviting an equation of heterosexism (and homosexual panic) with normalcy in the ordinary person. Why cannot the ordinary person be homosexual? By making the ordinary person sexual-orientation free, the court is in fact making him heterosexual. One of the most egregious associations of the ordinary person with heterosexuality was made in *R. v. Lupien* (1968), where the accused was charged with committing an act of gross indecency with 'a man masquerading as a woman.'[84] The accused could not have been charged with the offence of gross indecency if that man, Boisvert, had been a woman. Even though the two were naked and the accused's head 'was lying a very short distance from the female impersonator's genital organs,'[85] the accused said that he 'did not appreciate the obvious fact that Boisvert was a man until the police burst into the room.'[86] The specific question the court was dealing with was the admissibility of expert evidence. As Davey CJBC, dissenting in the result, said: 'Put in simple English the doctors were being invited to say that Lupien was a normal man, and as a normal man he would be instinctively repelled by and recoil from a homosexual act.'[87] The Supreme Court of Canada took a similar approach on the appeal (1969). Martland J characterized the expert evidence as follows: 'Its purpose was to establish (partly on the basis of what the respondent had told the witness) that because the respondent normally reacted violently to homosexual practices he must have been telling the truth when, in the proved situation in which he was discovered, he said he thought his companion was a woman.'[88] Ritchie J said in the same vein: 'Lupien had a certain type of defence mechanism which made him react violently against any homosexual activity.'[89] The court was open to this equation of normalcy with violence against homosexuals and homosexuality. An 'ordinary person' could not be homosexual if he could 'normally' react violently against any homosexual activity.

Even in cases such as *R. v. Hansford* (1987), where the court was sceptical of a defence of homosexual panic, it was comfortable using the language of 'ordinary person' and 'normal' to assess the reaction of a person to a homosexual situation.[90] The court set out the test for provocation, in part, as follows: 'The purpose behind the objective test of the ordinary person is to limit provocation to those persons who respond to events in a normal manner. The requirement for normalcy applies to both the perception of the circumstances relating to the provocation and to the reaction to them.'[91] Does the reaction of a youth merely following parental teaching that homosexuals should be treated with violence[92] constitute a 'normal reaction'? Does a person whose religion teaches that men who lie with men shall surely be put to death[93] react as an 'ordinary person' when he puts a person to death whom he fears wants to commit such a deed with him? By leaving open provocation in the homosexual panic situations, homosexual treated as other. 'Normal,' 'ordinary' persons are not homosexual. Perhaps homosexuals do not deserve to die, but they are beyond the realm of ordinary and normal.[94]

Few people want to be abnormal. The equation the law makes between heterosexuality and normalcy does nothing to discourage situations in which people 'prove' their normalcy by justifying their attack on a homosexual person on the grounds of 'homosexual panic.' As I have said, often there is an element of repressed homosexuality or homoeroticism in the background of the accused in homosexual panic cases, as in many instances of homophobic expression.[95] In *R. v. Kluke* (1987), for example, the accused was convicted at trial of first degree murder.[96] The Court of Appeal substituted a conviction for second degree murder. The appellant, Darrel Kluke, alleged provocation; the Crown argued that the victim's death was the result of a planned and deliberate murder committed by the appellant, who had an obsessive hatred of homosexuals coupled with a preoccupation with being labelled 'gay' himself. On the evening of 20 December 1984, he had attempted a reconciliation with an old girlfriend and had been rebuffed. He came home, cleaned, reassembled, and loaded his rifle, and proceeded to Victoria Park for the purpose of finding and killing a homosexual. The Crown contended, by way of inference, that on confronting his victim, the appellant forced him to disrobe and then shot him. The appellant said he had been drinking heavily that day. According to Lacourcière JA: 'The appellant claimed to have had a number of brief homosexual encounters in the previous year, and that although he had ceased such activity, he had been repeatedly harassed by homosexuals while going through the park on his way home from work. He said that his only purpose when he went to Victoria Park that evening with his rifle was to scare any men present and to convince them to leave him alone. After walking around the park for a short time, he noticed that the victim was following him. He confronted him and, after a brief exchange, the deceased began to disrobe, making sexual suggestions.' The appellant said an altercation ensued and the gun went off accidentally. The victim continued to advance and the remaining shots were fired in self defence. It seems more likely that Kluke, having given up his own homosexual activity, wanted to rid the park of homosexuals. In a recent Ontario case (1996),[97] concerns were expressed because the accused had been referred to by the deceased as a queer several days before the deceased's death. Were the accused in these cases acting as 'normal' persons – or at least trying to establish their normalcy?

Self-loathing stemming from a fear of homosexuality was allegedly a factor in another case (1975) involving a charge of murder, where the defence was non-insane automatism.[98] The accused, who lived in Victoria, tried to make contact with a woman he liked. He failed to do so and got depressed, drank, smoke dope, and went to a park. In the first story he told to the police he said he came upon a body, found a wallet and keys, took the car the keys belonged to, then used the credit card and tried to draw money from the bank account of the deceased. However, he later claimed that the man had tried to do 'homosexual things' to him in the car. The deceased, he said, opened his pants and touched him, then started to give him a blow job. The accused said he felt hate, more for himself than the deceased and so he lashed out and hit the deceased and stabbed him, after which he took the wallet and keys. How ought the court to treat such a reaction, using the language of 'ordinary' and 'normal'? Suppression of homosexual feelings is a source of homophobic acts. Was the accused's reaction not the reaction of a normal person?[99] Whatever the ordinary or normal person might feel, surely it is always unacceptable to kill another person because of a feeling of self-hatred. A court should not even bother to consider such a rationalization of a violent act.

The inferiorizing of homosexuality that is inherent in a homosexual panic defence has been discussed by Eve Kosofsky Sedgwick, who says that the homosexual panic defence 'performs a double act of minoritizing taxonomy.' There are two categories, both minorities: gay people and a population of 'latent' homosexuals whose insecurity about their masculinity permits a plea based on 'diminution of normal moral responsibility.' Sedgwick argues: '... the efficacy of the plea depends on its universalizing force, on whether, as Wertheimer says, it can 'create a climate in which the jurors are able to identify with the perpetrator by saying, "My goodness, maybe *I* would have reacted the same way".' The reliance of the homosexual panic plea on the fact that this male definitional crisis is systemic and endemic is enabled only, and precisely, by its denial of the same fact.'[100]

Even if courts do not today tend to accept a homosexual panic defence, its continued potential availability and its baggage of the ordinary (heterosexual) person perpetuates the minoritization identified by Sedgwick. Homosexuals, or people perceived to be homosexuals, are asked to carry the burden of others' masculine insecurity, of their attempts to be 'normal.' Defendants depend on this sense of heterosexual normalcy when the homosexual panic defence is used in murder charges. In cases where it is unlikely that there was a sexual advance at all, the allegation of an attack is obviously designed in part to solicit the sympathy of the court. The defence is also an assertion of the perpetrator's heterosexuality. The perpetrator escapes the inferiorization of homosexuality and manages to turn himself into the (heterosexual) victim/target.

The courts must not respond sympathetically to this homophobic plea for understanding. Some judges appear to have willingly acknowledged the anger and alarm a man might feel in response to a homosexual advance. In *R. v. Fraser* (1980),[101] for example, the accused was charged with second degree murder and raised provocation as a defence, saying that he went into a homosexual panic. The accused was a taxi driver who picked up the deceased as a ride. They went gambling and then the accused drove the deceased home, where he gave the accused $35 for a $26.50 fare. He asked the accused into his apartment and there supposedly made two separate homosexual advances to the accused. The defence and two psychiatrists called by the defence argued that 'the respondent lapsed into what was described in psychiatric terms as homosexual panic.'[102] The accused beat the deceased nearly senseless, striking him at least fifteen or twenty times with a brass-headed cane. He then robbed him. The target died in hospital. The trial judge rejected the view that the accused's purpose in entering the apartment was to rob the deceased and that the beating happened because of the difficulty he ran into in executing the robbery. The trial judge accepted that a homosexual advance had been made and then said: 'I am of opinion that the accused perceived this as a real threat and as a danger to him, both physically and emotionally, in his perceived image of himself as a male person.'[103] According to the trial judge, the accused would perceive the advance as an insult and it would cause him to act in self-defence. He said nothing about why the accused robbed the victim or why his masculinity was so easily threatened. The trial judge reduced the conviction to manslaughter.

At the Court of Appeal, the 'ordinary person' featured large. McDermid JA was in a minority in his opinion that a defence of provocation should not have been allowed. He said, after reading the evidence of the doctors: 'The respondent panicked; the ordinary man would not.'[104] The majority dealt with the matter differently, however, and refused to find that the trial judge had committed an error, raising the spectre of the 'ordinary person' yet again. Moir JA for the majority said: 'For the defence of provocation to succeed and so reduce murder to manslaughter the learned trial Judge had first to decide objectively whether what occurred could reasonably deprive an ordinary person of the power of self-control.'[105] Moir JA refused to hold that any homosexual assault in this case could not have been the basis of a homosexual panic and therefore the basis of a successful plea of provocation to reduce the murder to manslaughter. The majority of the court thought it conceivable that such an advance, if it took place, could lead an ordinary person to such a panic that killing would ensue.[106]

With the possibility of such sympathetic judges, it is not at all surprising that accused people continue to raise provocation based on homosexual panic or that there is a perception that it is acceptable to kill homosexuals when they make unwelcome sexual advances. More recent cases, however, give some cause to hope that the reputation of the courts for excusing killings on the basis of homosexual panic is diminishing. *R. v. Guy S* (1991) provides an example of the court refusing to believe easily concocted stories of homosexual panic.[107] This was another case of a young man charged with first degree murder of another man, followed by a robbery. In the process of the proceedings to decide whether the accused should be tried in adult court, the accused presented fresh evidence that the victim had made sexual advances to him and that he was therefore 'suffering from a panic attack, perhaps even a homosexual panic' during commission of the crime.[108] The majority of the court did not think much of this new evidence. Goodman JA said: 'The young person had been incarcerated for a substantial period of time. He had ample time to think about a scenario which might be more favourable to him. The homosexual assault, as outlined in Dr. Meen's report, was of a relatively insignificant nature. It seems somewhat incredible that he would have been too embarrassed to tell anyone, even his brothers, where the assault was so minor and the result so serious.'[109]

The double standard problem arises not only by virtue of the absence of heterosexual panic, but also in the sense that while sexual panic is available to a person who claims to be heterosexual it may not be available to a person who identifies himself as or is 'proven' to be homosexual. Such individuals are on somewhat shaky ground in raising a defence of provocation due to a homosexual assault. Having entered the world of the homosexual they have entered a place of abnormality and violence and can be taken to accept as usual any unwelcome advances made to them.

This problem arose in *R. v. Dubois* (1987).[110] In that case the accused went to another man's hotel room after drinking. He claimed that when the deceased started making sexual advances he 'flipped' and grabbed him by the throat, because 'that's what I usually go for.' The accused had had sex with the deceased before, when he (the accused) had been a male prostitute, but he said he did not want to have sex that night and claimed provocation as a defence to murder. The Court of

Appeal rejected the argument that the trial judge had erred in failing to direct the jury with respect to the defence of provocation. Hetherington JA for the court said: 'In our view the advances of the victim in this case are given colour and meaning by events which preceded them. In the statement which he gave to the police from which passages are quoted above, the appellant said that he had "been with guys before," that he "used to be a male prostitute" and that he had previously had sex with the victim. In these circumstances surely no reasonable jury acting judicially could have found that an ordinary person with this background would have been deprived of the power of self-control by the advances of the victim.'[111] The accused, in fact, was not 'ordinary.' Ordinary people might have been justifiably provoked to kill but male prostitutes had no such provocation. They are in fact tainted both by their homosexuality and by their trade and should perhaps expect such advances.[112] Homosexual panic is a very dubious basis for a claim of provocation and the message sent is made worse when it is not available to a homosexual person or to anyone who has had and not repented of a homosexual encounter.

Not all courts have disallowed to homosexuals the defence of provocation, although there are unusual restrictions on its availability. In *R. v. Gauthier* (1975), the accused was charged with murder;[113] he said he killed the deceased when the latter made a homosexual advance. The accused said that he and the deceased were having beer and talking about things when the deceased grabbed his penis and would not stop. The accused kept hitting him until he died. After the accused had caught his breath, he took the deceased's wallet. The Crown wanted to admit evidence that the accused had been seen in a previous homosexual situation. To this Bélanger JA said: '... I fail to see how the evidence of a homosexual act can constitute evidence of similar acts in the circumstances of the present accusation.'[114] This cause for hope must be tempered, however, by what the judge went on to say. Such evidence could only be admitted 'after a defence by the appellant to the effect that at no time before had he committed homosexual acts.'[115] Evidence of previous homosexual acts thus might defeat a claim of homosexual panic. A 'practising' homosexual is in a different position, therefore, from other people with respect to the availability of such a defence.

The inferiorization of homosexuals and homosexuality that underlies the existence of a homosexual panic defence often results in ritualistic humiliation of the (purportedly) homosexual target of the killing. Accompanying the killing of homosexuals, in cases where provocation is claimed as a defence, is a curious pattern of theft. The theft appears to be a sign of final humiliation, since in many cases what is stolen is a very insignificant amount or item. The killing of the homosexual is meant to be a humiliation as well, of course, but theft is a final blow after a mortal wound. It is rather amazing how, in cases in which the court accepts the possibility of homosexual panic, such as R. v. Fraser (1980),[116] the accused had the composure to find and take the property of the deceased. In R. v. Fournier (1982), where the court thought that the defence of automatism would be open to a person who killed a homosexual person, it apparently also found it unproblematic that an automaton had the self-possession to take two rings from the victim.[117]

The frequency of a connection between killing a homosexual (supposedly out of panic) and robbing that person is striking. For example, in R. v. Cribbin (1994), a person was convicted of manslaughter by the lower court for being involved in the killing of a man.[118] This man had offered the accused cocaine in a bar washroom and when it was refused the deceased grabbed him in the genital area. The accused apparently pushed the man's hand away and said he was not a homosexual. They made up their quarrel outside and the deceased and the accused and two others left together in a car. The car stopped on a deserted road; everyone got out and had some beer. The accused said that the deceased touched him on the shoulder and asked him if he wanted to go for a walk alone in the woods. The appellant, apparently 'as a reflex to this unwarranted proposition,' punched the deceased and kicked him. The others got involved and the deceased was beaten to death. After this, the three men, including the accused, went shopping with the deceased's credit cards.[119]

Theft also made an appearance in the Dubois (1987) case, mentioned above, where there was a charge of murder. The accused initially attempted to raise a homosexual panic defence but subsequently revised his story. In the revised version of events, the accused, who had been a male prostitute, met the victim in a bar and remembered him as a former client, for whom he had performed a homosexual act a couple of years earlier. During the evening the victim got drunk and the accused noticed the money roll and the ring that he was flaunting. The victim and the accused arranged for another homosexual act to take place for $50; the payment would be reduced to $25 if the accused was unable to obtain an erection. When he could not get it up the accused wanted to be paid the $25 and leave. The deceased, he said, wanted him to stay; the accused then took the ring as payment and attempted to leave. When the victim tried to stop him the accused picked him up by the testicles, threw him to the floor, beat him repeatedly, and strangled him. He then took the victim's watch, ring, and money. This is a rather more plausible sounding story than that contained in the accused's original statement, in which he claimed that he had simply 'flipped out' when, after going to the hotel room of the victim for a drink, the victim made homosexual advances to him.

The (heterosexual) courts, fortunately, are usually able to recognize the attempt to gain sympathy and thus to resist the defence. For example, the court was able to resist succumbing to stereotypes in *R. v. Hansford* (1987), where, to a charge of murder, the accused relied on the defence of provocation.[120] The deceased was a taxi driver who drove the accused home after he had been drinking. The accused realized he had no money. When the driver reached over to him the accused thought he was 'reaching for my balls' and 'freaked out.' The accused said he had just been subject to another homosexual come on in the bar where he had been drinking, so he stabbed the driver. Here Hutchinson JA said: 'It seems to me that it would have been impossible for the jury in this case to conclude that an ordinary man's sensitivity to a second homosexual approach would lead to anything more than annoyance.'[121] The court thought what had happened was probably just a drunken attempt at robbery that led to the death.[122] It is troubling, however, that the judge said that a more violent reaction to a first 'homosexual approach' might have been more justifiable violence. By the second instance, the person has in a sense become corrupted and therefore co-opted by homosexuality.

The courts, of course, cannot singlehandedly change the perceived need to humiliate homosexuals by beating, killing, and robbing them. They can, however, attempt to recognize the systemic nature of this activity and take it into account in considering particular instances. Just because theft from homosexuals who have been killed is common there is no reason to allow it to pass without comment. Similarly, that many feel it appropriate to kill a person of the same sex who appears to be making a sexual advance is no reason for the court to accept 'homosexual panic' as a defence.

Gay Bashing

Gay bashing is probably the best-known example of homophobic expression. To the personal knowledge of many gay man and lesbians, it is all too common. Cynthia Petersen argues: 'It is not hyperbole to assert that queer-bashing is a social phenomenon of epidemic proportions.'[123] Surprisingly, it is not frequently an issue in the courts. Because gay bashing is perhaps the most extreme form of homophobic violence, with the exception of killing in cases where the homosexual panic defence is used, and because the cause of the violence is hatred of homosexuality, the courts usually have little difficulty identifying the homophobic aspect of bashing. The rarity of such cases in the courts may be due to the homosexual element not being made public and such cases, if reported, are consequently treated as simple assault cases.[124] The target might be loath to have the case identified as gay bashing for fear that he will be outed as a result. Where this is true the perpetrator has the satisfaction not only of physical violence against the target but also emotional violence in the form of the target's fear and shame. This may well be the case as well where the target is not in fact homosexual but is perceived as such by the perpetrator.

Undoubtedly judicial attitudes play a role in homosexuals' perception of whether they are welcome in the legal system and whether they will be treated equitably. For example, would Hugessen ACJQ's comment in *Re Priape* (1979)[125] encourage a gay person to resort to legal redress if he had been beaten up as a result of showing affection in public? As I noted in Chapter 2, Hugessen thought that 'the community standard' of contemporary Canada was less tolerant with regard to overt homosexual acts than with regard to similar acts committed between people of opposite sexes. By way of simple example, he said that a young man and a woman lying on the grass in a sunny city park, at lunch hour, kissing and embracing one another, would 'draw hardly a passing glance' whereas the same conduct in the same place by two men 'would almost certainly lead to a disturbance and to the police being called.'[126] The 'disturbance' might well have been that the two men would be physically attacked. Hugessen ACJQ would seem to blame the target, at least partially, for such an attack.

Gay bashing is often expressed in what might be known as gay areas and is common in gay ghettos.[127] The attacks represent not so much a fear of invasion or conversion by homosexuals as an attempt to suppress and repress homosexuals in their 'own' areas. Sometimes they are unplanned, as in *R. v. Jolicoeur* (1997),[128] mentioned in the last chapter, in which the accused was charged with assaulting a man in a restaurant in the West End of Vancouver because he was wearing a nun's habit and a rosary. In dismissing the charge the court said, in effect, that both parties were to blame. The target was 'hypersensitive' about homophobic bias while the religious sensibilities of the accused had been offended. Kitchen Prov. Ct J said: 'I think sometimes, unfortunately, if you have this expectation, it can become self-fulfilling ... That there was an expectation that there was going to be trouble and because of that expectation, it just moved toward that and it finally happened.'

Physical attacks against homosexuals are only sometimes spontaneous. They often involve both planning and deliberate effort and judicial treatment of such attacks should reflect any premeditation. Even where there is premeditation, however, the attacks are random and their randomness serves to put the whole community on notice of danger. Thus cases of gay bashing do not involve just the target. They are meant to be and are attacks on the entire gay and lesbian community. The courts should therefore take into account not only the impact of the attack on the target but its effect on the homosexual community as a whole.

Judges have at times demonstrated an awareness of the community abuse that comes from cases of gay bashing. A remarkable example of judicial sensitivity is found in R. v. Wilson (1991), in which the accused was charged with assault.[129] I have chosen to reproduce rather long extracts from this case because it provides an unusually detailed description of a typical gay bashing as well as judicial sensitivity. The Crown apparently neglected in its opening recital of the facts to mention the motive for the attack. This came from the witness, who said: 'My concern about this is that it was assault motivated by hatred of homosexuality.' The witness continued:

> I was attracted to the scene, in the first place, because the accused and another man were scuffling down the road ... I heard: 'You fucking faggot. You fucking freak of nature.' And when a gay man, as I am, hears that, you immediately think of gay bashing, which has become imminent in the community. So I went to see what the problem was. It was all over but the shouting by the time I got there. Some woman intervened on the victim's behalf, to say: 'We saw what you did. Leave him alone.' And he called them 'fucking dykes.' And then, he saw me. We exchanged words, calling me the same things – 'fucking dyke' and 'fucking freak of nature.' I, I am sure, told him to 'fuck off' myself, at some point and to get out of the neighbourhood.

The accused was a twenty-year-old student at Ryerson who, the court said, 'enjoys a somewhat privileged and positive background.' According to the report, the accused was celebrating the end of his school term and the stress in relation thereto by attending a party at the residence of his girlfriend. He was 'a bit drunk.' The party had run out of beer and the accused, together with a male companion, left the party to purchase some more. The nearest beer store was located in the Church and Wellesley Street area, Toronto's 'gay ghetto.' On the way to the store, an unknown person apparently brushed by the accused and touched or pinched his 'bottom.' This incident provoked the accused who turned to the person nearest to him and blew up. According to the report, 'He insulted Mr. Russell, the complainant, and his sexual orientation.' As a result, a fight commenced and the accused eventually ran away. Although counsel for the accused described the incident as an assault and not premeditated 'gay bashing,' the police identified it as 'clearly an act of gay bashing.' The accused obviously, if one can use the words of a different judge in a divorce case, felt his self-image as a male to be threatened. The frustration of trying to deal with the attitudes that underlie such violent incidents was apparent in both the presentence report and in the reasons of the judge. The presentence report said in the 'Assessment' portion: 'Due to the conflicting stories provided by the offender and the police, it does not appear that the offender has assumed any responsibility for this offence nor for the fact that such apparent homophobic behaviour, as with all forms of prejudice, will likely re-surface throughout his life until he is prepared to face the motivating factors behind them.' The court said there were a number of aggravating factors, including the fact that the accused was not alone and never 'unrealistically outnumbered.' The court also recognized that 'The victim was assaulted because he appeared to belong, or was sympathetic to, a minority community, or both. That community is also known in popular terms as the "gay community."' The judge also thought it significant that: 'The language employed by the accused throughout was threatening, intimidating, vulgar, obscene, and stereotypically referrable to the gay community.' The judge, Harris Prov. Div. J, asked the victim (whom the judge himself called as a witness) the following: 'Tell me something and this is where you can assist me. It's easy for a Judge to impose different kinds of sentences on people. In this case, a custodial sentence, a monetary penalty, probation, or a combination of those things. There is another issue here. What do you do ... to try and educate someone? How do you change a person's thinking?' The witness responded: 'If I knew the answer to that, I'd be a rich man. But in this case, my feelings would be community service within the gay community, preferably at the community centre at 519, would probably be the best way to do that.'

The judge then embarked on a consideration of the wider issues that were represented in this case. He expressed exasperation that: 'A trend appears to be growing, at least in the community where this offence [gay-bashing] occurred, which is indeed the largest city in Ontario, where it appears it is becoming fashionable and acceptable, but only to a despicable minority, and to use the common street terminology, "to have a few beers and beat up on a queer."' The judge drew analogies with cases in which there were racially or religiously inspired attacks. He said it was appropriate to take into account the group menace posed by the perpetrator in such cases in deciding on sentence. As Dubin JA noted in *R. v. Ingram and Grimsdale* (1970), 'Such assaults, unfortunately, invite imitation and repetition by others and incite retaliation. The danger is even greater in a multicultural, pluralistic urban society. The sentence imposed must be one which expresses the public abhorrence for such conduct and their refusal to countenance it.' The judge in this case cited such authority and continued: 'Accordingly, the sentence I ultimately tailor for this accused is not specifically meant to strike a blow for the gay community, although if in fact it does, so be it. More important, however, the sentence is meant to strike a blow for justice and humanity, and for all the "little people" who strive to live their lives in and around the laws of our country, but for whatever reason may appear to others as being "different," either in body or speech or belief, or in any multitude of ways.'[130]

The judge made clear he was not sentencing the person for holding particular beliefs. But he said the sentence called for a more severe penalty than ordinary assaultive conduct and ordered the accused to spend two months in custody. There was apparently no sentence involving community service, perhaps because the judge had concluded that this particular perpetrator was beyond redemption. The case appears to be unique in the reports in the extent of the care taken by the judge in considering the effect not merely on the immediate target of the violence but also on the gay and lesbian communities. Perhaps part of the reason for the court's sensitivity in this case was the fortuity of a witness/victim who could speak so eloquently to the issue of community impact.

There are other cases in which the court has shown some awareness of the wider impact of a gay bashing. Thus, in *R. v. M. (D.)* (1990), the

Ontario Court of Appeal said that the lower court was correct to order the transfer of the accused to adult court in a case where the offences involved brutality and violence and terrorization of homosexuals. The accused was just short of his eighteenth birthday and had worked in this incident with several adults. As Labrosse JA said: '... the cumulative effect of the extraordinary brutality and violence alleged, society's concern that a class of persons, homosexuals, was being preyed upon and terrorized and the perception of injustice resulting from the possibility of wider disparate sentences to accused persons only a few months apart in age'[131] far outweighed any advantage in keeping the accused out of adult court.[132]

In many cases the perpetrator of the violence does not think he has done anything wrong. In his eyes, homosexuals deserve what they get. This is true in some of the cases I have discussed so far: the homosexual targets are thought to be worthless or at best figures of fun. In *R. v. McDonald* (1995), a case in which the accused was described as 'a violent con man,'[133] Hamilton J said that the accused used violence on 'weaker people': 'He threatens the weaker person, as he did in this particular case, and he takes pride in it and justifies his criminal activities by his reply to Detective Earl when he says the victim is just a fag. So anything that is done to him is justifiable.' The accused indicated that he met people of 'that persuasion' by answering ads in papers and making friends with them and then, as he called it, 'ripping them off.' A similar situation was described in *Duval v. The Queen* (1970), where the accused appealed from a five-year imprisonment sentence for robbery.[134] He and his companions had forced three men, whom they had met at a night club, to get into their car. They drove them to a deserted area and forced them with threats of beatings with an iron bar to give over their jewellery and money. They then forced their victims to undress and abandoned them in the night. The accused tried to argue that it was a joke played on three 'well-known homosexuals.' The court dismissed this coloration of the actions, but the story as told by the accused demonstrates that homosexuals are thought fit to be humiliated and laughed at.

The treatment of homosexuals as figures of fun who invite violent behaviour is not necessarily limited to homosexuals, but can encompass those who 'look' like homosexuals. In *R. v. Benner* (1989), three men were charged with the murder of Ronald Egan in the small town of Aurora, Ontario.[135] Lampkin Prov. Ct J set out some of the tragic facts as follows:

Ronald Egan was a quiet man. He was wont to go to the Four Shields Tavern in Aurora two or three nights a week between Thursday and Saturday. He would sit quietly at a small table by himself drinking beer. On occasion a friend would join him at his table and have a drink with him, or he would go to a friend's table. Throughout the night he would drink four, maybe five, glasses of beer – coasting slowly.

It appears that Egan had had surgery on his throat. He developed the peculiar habit of drinking beer with a straw. It may well have been more comfortable for him to do so. In addition, his voice had a strange texture. Because of these peculiarities some people regarded him as a queer and a faggot – names which in common parlance mean 'homosexual.' It is the theory of the Crown that because of these peculiarities he paid the ultimate penalty – with his life.

One night the three accused men and another (who knew Egan and lived across the road from him) were at the tavern at closing time. Egan asked them for a ride home. The driver said 'no,' but another of the accused said to the third, 'He's a faggot John. We'll give him a ride he won't forget.' Egan apparently did not hear this, as he got in the van. The three men started kicking him with their steel-toed work boots. One of the accused called Egan a 'faggot.' Those not kicking did nothing to stop it. Egan died. The men threw his body out of the van and when it was found: 'The upper part of the body, identified as that of Ronald Egan, was naked. His pants were pulled down around his knees. His head was battered and bloody.'

In the previous section on the homosexual panic defence, I noticed how that form of homophobic expression, in cases where such a defence is used, is often accompanied by theft from the target. So too with cases of gay bashing. The violence is often part of the perpetration of another crime, usually robbery. Gay people are perceived as suitable targets. In *R. v. A.J.-R.* (1991), for example, the Crown applied to have the young person tried as an adult on a charge of first degree murder of a forty-one-year-old male homosexual who had previously paid for sex with the accused.[136] It was alleged that the accused and two other young residents of a treatment centre planned to go AWOL from the centre and the accused said he knew of a man, the target, who had various material possessions. One of the other two, a female, said it might be necessary to kill him and she and the co-accused play acted a stabbing. The accused and the male co-accused went to the victim's residence, where they were given food and shelter. They made arrangements to return and the victim gave them money, which they used in part to buy two knives. They went back to the victim's apartment and stabbed him to death. Afterwards they robbed the victim of several items.[137]

In yet another case (1990) involving the question of whether the accused should be tried in adult court,[138] the accused was charged just before his eighteenth birthday with offences including attempted murder, kidnapping, break and enter, robbery, and so on. The Crown alleged that the accused 'Mr M.' had left his parents' home and become involved in various criminal activities with other individuals. These allegations were described by Linahres de Sousa Prov. Ct J as follows:

> One of these activities was to attack and rob homosexual men at Major's Hill Park, an area of Ottawa apparently known for its homosexual activity. The alleged reasons for the attack were: firstly that they were easy victims tending to be small in stature. They didn't complain and therefore made for successful financial crimes; secondly, an intense dislike for homosexuals among certain members of the group; Mr M. is alleged to have expressed some anti-homosexual sentiments. The Crown alleges that one such attack which forms the basis of one of the three counts of attempt to murder with which Mr M. has been charged was against a Mr Thomas Lindens, an admitted homosexual. Mr. Linden was approached in Major's Hill Park by four male persons. He fled through the park and was pursued by one male who knocked him to the ground and stabbed him three times, twice in the back and once in the arm with a knife

The accused clearly accepted all the stereotypes that inferiorize homosexuality. Homosexuals are timid, small, contemptible, and deserving of violence.

Cases of justification of robbery by the belittlement of homosexuals as 'natural' targets are legion.[139] Homosexuals are perceived to make easy victims because they are in fact less likely to complain. Fear of how they will be treated by the police, the courts, and society in general if it 'gets out' that they are homosexuals is sufficiently intimidating to cause them to suffer in silence in many instances. The bashers are not making assumptions of 'timidity' that have no foundation in truth.

Although many cases of gay bashing involve robbery, not all do. Robbery in fact is just an additional aspect of the most important goal, which is humiliation. Sometimes homosexuals are targets of violence simply because they are homosexual. A most gruesome example is found in *Rose v. Société de transport de la Communauté urbaine de Montréal* (1996).[140] There, the parents of a man killed on a bus operated by Montreal Transport, the defendant, sought damages arising from the death of their son. The son and a friend were coming back from a party in the early hours of the morning and got on a bus. They had been drinking very little. A group of fifteen young people got on the bus. 'Dès le départ de l'autobus, ils commencent à chahuter sérieusement Rose et Dutil. Entre autres choses, ils enlèvent la casquette en cuir de Rose et se la renvoient de l'un à l'autre, en bousculant Rose, qui tente de reprendre possession de sa casquette. La situation devient chaotique et dangereuse. Il est certain que l'agressivité est causée par l'homosexualité apparente de Rose et Dutil.'[141] The targets abandoned the cap and went up to sit behind the bus driver. But the aggression of the gang only got worse. The targets tried to get off the bus at one stop and actually did but when some of the gang got off too, they got back on. The driver failed to use properly a button that would have flashed a message on the exterior of the bus that the police should be called because of a danger on the bus. At the terminus: 'Le groupe d'adolescents devait quitter puisqu'il s'agissait du terminus. Au moins quatre d'entre eux se dirigèrent vers l'avant. Ils s'attaquèrent sauvagement Dutil et Rose. Rose fut battu, poignardé au coeur et rebattu. Dutil, assez serieusement blessé à la tête, a pu en réchapper.'[142]

Unfortunately, unlike in the *Wilson* case and some of the others, the judges in many of these cases do not acknowledge the homophobic expression aspect of the case as having any special significance in considering the appropriate legal response to the crime. It is 'just' another robbery or assault. Unlike in *Wilson*, some judges, in fact, seem to think that homophobia is something that can easily be overcome. Thus in the case of 'Mr. M' in Ottawa (1990),[143] the accused was treated leniently. He supposedly came from a 'good' home, which was a military family. We are apparently meant to believe that his hostility and violence towards homosexuals arose in his one-and-a-half month period when the court said that 'Mr. M was exposed to and participated in a variety of street crime activities such as robberies or what is known in the vernacular as "rolling queers," break and enter and "smash and grabs."'' The court found that he had good chances for rehabilitation and treatment. The profundity of the homophobia was ignored.

Likewise, in *R. v. Gallant* (1994), a man was sentenced by the trial court to two years' imprisonment and two years' probation after he pleaded guilty to a charge of assault causing bodily harm when he and two other young men beat up a person they thought to be a homosexual.[144] The Court of Appeal reduced the sentence to seven months of imprisonment followed by one year of probation. Huband JA said: '[The accused] and two other young men, with nothing to do to amuse themselves in the early morning, decided to attack a man who they perceived to be a homosexual. Unknown to this accused one of his co-accused had a club which was used in the assault. The victim was beaten up, but after treatment as an outpatient at the hospital, he was released.'[145] But the court said that: 'The accused professes to have changed his attitude and to disassociate from those who shaped his previous views. He expresses regret for his actions.' This is the school of quick-change-of-heart-on-homosexuality-come-time-for-sentencing. It would be surprising if the judge were to say the same thing if the victim had been a woman or a Jew, but it appears that homophobia is something uncomplicated enough that it can be probably forgotten.

There is an assumption on the part of the perpetrator that appears below the surface in many of the gay bashing cases that what he did was not in fact wrong in the way that other crimes are wrong. In *R. v. MacFarlane* (1989), for example, the accused was convicted of arson.[146] He was involved with what were described as 'a group of rather unsavoury characters.'[147] We are told about a couple of them – the Levasseurs. 'Bill Levasseur brought home some money that he claimed he had obtained by robbing homosexuals on the Legislative building grounds at night. Dawn Levasseur seemed to think that was a reasonable way to earn a living.'[148] It turned out, however, that 'the earnings came not from robbing homosexuals, but rather by having sex with them for a fee.'[149] Ms Levasseur kicked him out when she discovered the truth. Evidently having sex with homosexuals was more reprehensible than robbery.

The case would be amusing if it were not so tragic. Some perpetrators appear to believe that by physically assaulting homosexuals they are in fact acting as heros for the community, vigilantes who keep society safe for its respectable, normal members. This makes such perpetrators unlike other assaulters and most other criminals, who have no illusions about heroism. There was an element of the self-appointed hero in the explanation given by the accused in *R. v. Kluke* (1987), for instance, discussed above in the homosexual panic defence section.[150] In that case, the accused, who was convicted at trial of first degree murder, combined an obsessive hatred of homosexuals with a fear of being labelled 'gay' himself. This is the man who went to Victoria Park with a loaded rifle, intending to find and kill a homosexual. The accused made himself out as a sort of park hero, taking matters into his own hands to rid the place of homosexuals.

Judges have a duty to set the record straight on self-appointed hero- ism, in which assault is rationalized as the performance of some sort of civic function. The courts have had no difficulty putting vigilantes in their place when the positions are reversed. Thus, in *R. v. Rutledge* (1996), where there was an appeal from conviction and sentence for assault,[151] the trial judge summed up the Crown's theory, found to be proven, as follows:

> The Crown's case is that on the night in question the complainant was obnoxiously drunk and insulted a couple of young men because he thought they behaved in a manner consistent with being homosexuals. The Crown says that the accused and his friend saw the behaviour and acting in the manner of self-righteous bullies, took it upon themselves to punish the complainant. The began by approaching the complainant arm in arm, acting as if they were gay, and challenging the complainant to take issue with their behaviour. The Crown says the complainant, knowing he was in trouble, tried to back out of his problems, but the accused, with the assistance of his friend, beat the complainant up in quite a savage fashion.[152]

The judge said that he would not grant a discharge because: 'It is clear to me that the Court must send a message to the community, and in particular to people who might be tempted to act like the offender, that the Court of Appeal will not tolerate such behaviour. Our streets must be kept safe, even for obnoxious drunks.' There is no comfort in this reversal of roles, in part because homosexuals know that such instances will always be the exception rather than the rule. In any event, vigilantism is never acceptable. Judges must ensure that the same high principles are invoked when homosexuals rather than heterosexuals are the targets.

It will be obvious that all the immediate targets and perpetrators of physical violence in the cases mentioned in this section so far have been men. Lesbians are the subject of violence, directly homophobic in nature, as the verbal abuse in *R. v. Wilson*, makes clear. However, it is difficult to find cases in which the victim of physical violence is specifically identified as a lesbian.[153] Women are the subject of violence generally. It is not a problem peculiar to lesbians, so the lesbian element is often not 'necessary' to explain why the lesbian woman was attacked. As Cynthia Petersen says: 'It is difficult for lesbian victims to determine whether their assailants are motivated specifically by anti-lesbian sentiments rather than by simple misogyny. Accustomed to the daily harassment and violence to which all women are subjected, lesbian victims may have a tendency to identify their target status with their sex rather than their sexuality.'[154] It is difficult, therefore, to say much specifically about lesbian bashing. The cases that are available show that the violence is often perpetrated by somebody the lesbian knows, often a family member, as opposed to bashing of gay men, which is often anonymous and random. This, again, is typical of violence directed towards women in general.

In *R. v. Richard* (1982), the accused was convicted of attempted murder of his wife and her lesbian friend.[155] The accused's wife and the other woman began to wrestle with each other on the floor and the accused asked what was going on. He was told that there had been sexual encounters between the two women. Freedman CJM said that these circumstances 'might have been a mitigating factor on sentence.' He continued, however, 'Unfortunately at least some of the strength of that plea in mitigation was lost when the accused requested that the encounter be enlarged to a threesome, a request which was not granted.'[156] The man attacked the two women with a knife. The brutality lasted for up to one and a half hours. It is hard to see how there could be any 'mitigating' circumstances at all in such a case, whatever the sexual dynamics.

Another lesbian bashing involving family elements is found in *R. v. Longpre* (1993), where the accused pleaded guilty to attempted murder.[157] The complainant victim was the female lover of the accused's twenty-one-year-old married stepdaughter. The stepdaughter's family was 'vehemently opposed' to the lesbian relationship and the two women were forced to flee to Winnipeg from Sudbury. The family found her and the accused and at least two male members of the party set upon the complainant, dragging her into a waiting vehicle. She was then dragged into a residence and on the back porch of that residence the accused threatened her again at knife point to end the relationship; if she refused he would kill her. When the complainant indicated that she was not going to end the relationship, the accused stabbed her while she was being held by persons whom she was unable to identify.

The complainant was repeatedly stabbed in the area of her heart. The fingers of one hand were sliced off and her arm was penetrated. In defending the accused in sentencing, his lawyer 'stressed the unsavoury character of the 30 year old complainant in the view of the step-daughter, Marlene's, family and the effect of the relationship on Marlene's mother and husband and children left behind in Sudbury ...'[158] Here the accused sought to justify his actions by blaming his victim's homosexuality. The solution to a homosexual situation perceived by him as wrong and contrary to the interests of society was to resort to violence.[159] The accused was in a sense only doing what he thought was socially expected of him.

At the end of the day we are left with the problem raised by Harris Prov. Ct J in *R. v. Wilson*. What is the appropriate legal response to these crimes? Perhaps it is community service. Perhaps it is harsh sentences. What is certainly appropriate is a response that situates the crime in the larger context of homophobic expression and homophobia in society. These are not just cases of assault. An entire community is targeted in these attacks and it is actually possible that the perpetrator thinks he is doing the appropriate thing. The victims are often afraid to reach out for the help of legal institutions. The courts ought to make the effort to welcome such people, not just in a specific case, but in general, by attempting to understand the magnitude of the hostility such people face because of their (perceived) sexual orientation. It is to be hoped that changes to the Criminal Code specifically directing courts to take hate motivation into account in sentencing will effect positive change in the reporting of instances of gay bashing.[160] None of the cases discussed here was affected by the hate-motivation provisions.

Police Harassment

People targeted by perpetrators of homophobic violence are often afraid to seek help from the institutions of the state because of the reputation such institutions have for, at best, contempt of homosexuals and homosexuality. The police forces in the majority of Canadian cities are becoming better at public relations with gays and lesbians.[161] But there are serious lapses in the improved record, in the form of instances such as bathhouse raids or verbal abuse. The problems usually arise in smaller centres, where police engage in expensive and time-consuming campaigns to root out homosexual sex. Much of the problem of homosexual mistrust of the police arises from a lingering sense that the police will not take a homosexual complaint seriously. Time and continued police efforts to work on this problem are required.

One of the peculiarities of cases involving homosexuality is the game that appears to be played as between the police and the judges. The role of the police appears to be to find homosexuals engaging in sordid sexual practices as much as possible while the role of courts, as I explained in Chapter 2, is to desexualize what might be regarded as homosexual situations in order to make them 'safe.' Judges try hard not to find homosexuality and give very few details when they do; the police go to elaborate lengths to find homosexual activity to prosecute.[162] Sometimes they are the only people present in the given situation who object to homosexuality. Thus, in *R. v. Goguen* (1977),[163] men were caught by police having sex in a darkened corner of a public washroom facility at 11:40 p.m. It was accepted that 'those frequenting the area at that time were primarily consenting homosexuals and police.'[164] In *R. v. White* (1975),[165] the Ontario Court of Appeal substituted a conditional discharge in place of a fine of $200 for a man who was charged with gross indecency for giving fellatio to another man in a parking lot in Hamilton at 11:30 p.m. The court took into account that there was no public present to be offended except for the police officer. In fact, the court said there was nobody in the vicinity.[166]

Sometimes it is the police who set up the circumstances in which a homosexual act can take place. An example of this is *R. v. Mailhot* (1996). Chamberland J tells us that after meeting casually in a public area and striking up a conversation, the accused and the police officer on patrol ('dressed in Bermuda shorts and a tee shirt') went for a walk in a trail, talking about their common interest in biking. Then:

> At some point, the appellant said to officer Bolduc: 'Do you want to see me?'; the officer, surprised, did not answer. The appellant repeated: 'Do you want to see me?' The officer remained silent, all the while continuing to look at him. The appellant then went to a big tree, which was near by, where he took off his glasses and his tee shirt, and then pulled his shorts down to his knees. He then began to touch himself, to caress his penis and then began to masturbate. When he had an erection, the officer, still quite uncomfortable, asked him 'if he was going to come.' The appellant answered in the negative. The officer then got up, went over to the appellant, identified himself and proceeded to put him under arrest.[167]

Not surprisingly, the judge found that the accused had no criminal intent. He said: 'The meeting with the officer, the friendly conversation they had, their stroll to the spring, the officer's silence when the appellant, twice, revealed his plans, all these elements contributed to leading the appellant to believe that the officer was interested in giving a sexual twist to their meeting.'[168]

Police exercises to root out homosexual acts in such cases take on somewhat comical aspects as the police on the one hand try hard to maintain a macho image (itself of course homoerotic) and on the other hand become involved in situations that involve gay sex in order to arrest people. Of course, it is never admitted that situations of entrapment create an erotic atmosphere for some gay men, which leads to the sex that is supposed to be controlled. Absent the element of danger, the turn-on disappears for many of the men involved. There is, in a sense, a symbiotic relationship between the police and some gay men. The charges are made, the fines paid, and publicity is kept to a minimum.

Police zealousness to detect homosexual activity might not be quite so ardent when one of their own is discovered to be possibly involved. I discussed the case of *Re L. (R.)* (1981),[169] in Chapter 2. There, an off-duty police officer was charged with discreditable conduct for allegedly picking up a male hustler and giving him a blow job in a car in Ottawa. The accused was observed picking up 'O' on a well-known street for male hustlers; 'O' admitted he was a male prostitute and he said they were engaging in sex. The court chose to disbelieve him.

The courts can undertake to monitor overzealous police efforts to deter (and create) homosexual incidents, and they should be careful not to make statements or give decisions that encourage such a sexual cleansing of society. The prime example of a situation in which police tactics went completely without challenge is *R. v. Lupien* (1968), in which the accused was charged with committing an act of gross indecency.[170] Experts were called to show that the accused as a normal person would have reacted violently if he had known that the person he was with was a man in drag. Though the court said a great deal about expert evidence and proving normalcy, at no point was it ever concerned with the nature of the police efforts to control homosexual activity. They were considered unremarkable.

Police expression of homophobia comes up in other situations as well. Earlier in the chapter, I mentioned the case of *R. v. Smith* (1989), in which one witness said that two police officers told him that unless he provided a statement he 'would be locked up with homosexuals who would rape him while the guards turned a blind eye.'[171] In another case

(1992), it was alleged that the police acted wrongly in arresting the accused at a rock concert. Batiot Prov. Ct J said: 'The defendant recalls that after having been pinned to the ground there was an allegation that he was gay, there was an offer by an officer for a "blow job." He was offended by the way he was being treated without knowing the reasons why he was being arrested and he spat on an officer as the only means available to him to retaliate. He recalls being pushed to the ground, being kneed in the back, being accused of being gay and set down so that he could not spit again, of being told he was a nuisance and being taken downtown and being booked and lodged in a cell ...'[172]

Where such allegations are true, of course, they call out for judicial comment and condemnation. Other instances of homophobic expression will not be reported to the police and therefore fail to reach the courts if these attitudes are implicitly accepted. Such expression ought not to be seen simply as part of the job of policing.

Official Homophobia

Police homophobia (and judicial homophobia, for that matter) is part of a larger issue of 'official homophobia.' In this category I include the innumerable ways in which homosexuals and homosexuality are marginalized, trivialized, and inferiorized by the state or state agencies. Official homophobia is very prevalent but often difficult to identify. It usually takes the form of recognizing or benefitting heterosexuality and refusing similar recognition to homosexuals and homosexuality. The most common examples of this treatment involve benefits issues. I will not examine the law on same-sex benefits in any detail, although the courts' treatment of benefits cases are mentioned throughout this book.[173] The courts are getting better at detecting and providing remedies for situations that involve heterosexism by the state. But, as is evident from the *Egan* case, some of them appear at times to find it impossible to throw out a tradition of censorious attitudes about homosexuality. Courts frequently refuse to recognize official homophobia or to do anything about it: official homophobia is often seen as a policy matter which, for some reason, is beyond judicial jurisdiction.

The types of official homophobia not directly benefits related are myriad. They can take the form of special days to celebrate events (heterosexual 'Family Day' in Alberta), recognition of married or unmarried (in its heterosexual form) status only on documents; assumptions in schools that heterosexuality is the only sexual orientation; having a 'king' and 'queen' in community or school events; or creating separate boys' and girls' teams on the basis that a girl might distract a boy but another boy could never do so. These instances are intentionally symbolic. They send the message that heterosexuality is normal and homosexuality is not. These various forms of official homophobia are powerful devices for inclusion or exclusion. The fact that such actions have a long history makes them no more tolerable than instances of deep-rooted and traditional racism or sexism.

As I have said, the most obvious form of official homophobia is the refusal to give benefits to same-sex couples in the way that opposite-sex couples receive them. Same-sex couples are unable to have marriages recognized and may encounter extreme difficulty in getting a same-sex partner into the country; medical coverage is often denied to a same-sex partner, who may also experience difficulty in obtaining visitation rights in prisons or hospitals. For a long time, homosexuals, along with other 'misfits,' could be excluded from Canada. There was little litigation on these points because the government deliberately tried to keep immigration matters out of court.[174] The courts participate in official homophobia when they refuse to use their constitutionally vested power under the Charter to annul such laws. They participate in official homophobia by finding it 'demonstrably justifiable in a free and democratic society' under section 1.

Officialdom does not exclude homosexuals only from benefits for or from a same-sex partner. Exclusion of homosexuals is common in many official decisions, decisions all too often acquiesced in by the judiciary. Thus, for example, as discussed in the previous chapter, homosexuals are kept out of schools, either as teachers or as members of homosexual organizations. Historically, homosexuals were excluded from police and military positions.[175] Homosexual literature and art are treated with greater scrutiny by Customs and the police.[176] Today the exclusion is apt to be from the immigration processes, either as a same-sex spouse or as a refugee.[177]

Fortunately in many recent cases there has been a positive reaction from the courts to complaints of inequality, but they do not appear to impress the governments and bureaucracies with the seriousness of the issues, nor have they convinced officialdom that homophobic policies are unacceptable. Instances of official homophobia have constantly to be litigated. The courts have not been categorical enough in their condemnation of official homophobia to convey the message that it is never acceptable. For instance, in a 1990 case against the city of Toronto,[178] the municipal authorities had refused to issue a permit for a commercial bathhouse that would cater to men only, even though such use was within the zoning controls for the area. The court ruled that there was an improper motive in refusing to issue the permit. Herold DCJ said: 'It is quite clear from the material that a series of incidents in Toronto history, some ten years ago, known as the "bath house" raids is at least lurking just beneath the surface, if not the reason for the refusal of the building commissioner to issue a permit.'[179] Even with that clear view of the history of the issue, the judge said that it was 'not inappropriate' for the building department to have 'a predisposition against the proliferation of establishments which might appear to encourage and permit an alternate, if not unhealthy and perhaps downright dangerous, lifestyle.' In the court's opinion that was something for city council to decide, not the building commissioner. 'Lifestyle' is a loaded concept in the context of homosexual issues. Homosexual sexual orientation is often called a 'lifestyle,' implying it is a choice on par with decor. The court said it was improper for the commissioner to make a decision based on a negative view of this 'life-style,' but apparently it would be acceptable for city council to do so.

The unwillingness of the judiciary to stand fast and consistent on its decisions relating to official homophobia is illustrated as well by *Haig v. Durrell* (1990).[180] There, Ottawa city council proclaimed 17 June 1990 as Lesbian and Gay Pride Day. The council reconsidered the matter, changed the date to 10 June, and then cancelled the whole event. An application made to quash the resolution cancelling the event was granted on the basis of the urgency of the subject matter. In making his original order, Austin J found evidence of discrimination against Ottawa's lesbian and gay community and the Lesbian and Gay Pride Day was the only day that the city had refused to proclaim in the previous four years. The judge in this case also showed an understanding of history when he said: 'There is evidence in the material from the applicants to the effect that Lesbian and Gay Pride Day is recognized as a form of acknowledgement and redress to help balance the historical scale after years of ridicule, oppression and denial of the rights of lesbians and gays.' But then the court heard of an identical application in Toronto, which was not granted because it was not 'urgent.' The judge, on his own initiative, consequently changed his mind, decided the issue was not 'urgent' and transferred the matter to Divisional Court. The Toronto court's view that such matters were not urgent was assumed to be correct.[181] Thus homosexuals in Ottawa suffered from changes of mind from both governmental and judicial institutions on an important symbolic issue. The importance accorded to their equality concerns was fleeting at best.

The problem of official homophobia is thus twofold. The homophobic policies of officials and governments constitute one aspect of the problem. The symbolism of heterosexist official practices is often not even recognized, nor is there any indication of an awareness that a homophobic policy in one area necessarily colours the ways in which homosexuals are treated generally and how they are perceived, by themselves and others. The second problem is a hesitant judiciary that sometimes corrects official homophobia but too often does not. Sometimes, in fact, as we have seen, the courts are the speakers in this most invidious form of homophobic expression.

Negativity in the Community

Parallel with forms of official homophobic expression are the countless instances of homophobia in society in general. Instances of the negative perception of homosexuality in the community come up in court cases all the time. In this section I attempt merely to provide some illustrations of the variety of ways in which homosexuals and homosexuality can be targeted for inferiorization. The examples selected serve to demonstrate the enormity of the task of social reform and education that is required. Judicial silence on or accommodation of social expressions of hostility does nothing to encourage reform.

One frequent method of social expression of homophobia is the exclusion of homosexuals from the mainstream of community events. The forms of exclusion are as numerous as there are social activities.[182] In a case (1994) that came before the Quebec Human Rights Tribunal, for example, two women were refused entry to a campground.[183] According to S. Brossard J: 'Un préposé de la défenderesse leur a alors refusé l'accès au motif que la réglementation interne interdisait l'accès de deux ou de plusieurs femmes, sauf dans un contexte familial. La défenderesse, qui se définit comme un camping "familial," n'accepte précisément qu'une famille ou qu'un couple hétérosexuel.' The tribunal found this to be discrimination contrary to the Quebec Charter on the basis of sex, civil status, and sexual orientation. The decision is interesting because it is one of the few that has made the obvious connection between sex discrimination and sexual orientation discrimination that seems so difficult for courts generally to grasp.[184]

Exclusion can also occur in commercial situations. In an Alberta case, a tenant decided to improve the income from its restaurant lounge by turning the lounge into a private gay night club.[185] The other tenants and the neighbours complained and the landlord refused to consent to the use of the lounge for that purpose. The tenant went ahead and the landlord locked the doors of the premises. The court granted an interlocutory injunction against the landlord.

Fear of hostility from the community was also a factor in *R. v. Humphrey* (1984),[186] where there was an application to change the venue of a first degree murder trial. The trial was in a rural part of Ontario and the accused said there would be an inherent bias against him because he was a homosexual. Henry J refused the application. The judge placed his trust in legal safeguards 'to eliminate as far as one can do so in such proceedings a bias based upon a prejudice that might exist on the part of some persons in any community with respect to sexual orientation.' The judge said that an accused should be tried in the community in which the alleged offence occurred. While he recognized that there was a potential problem. Henry was confident that proper instruction of the jury would be sufficient to protect the accused. An accused might well, however, be concerned that all the jury instruction in the world might not persuade a hostile community to leave its homophobia at the courtroom door.

A decade later, in the *Parks* case (1993),[187] the Ontario Court of Appeal made it much easier to challenge for cause in jury selection based on allegations of racial bias. A couple years after that, however, in *R. v. Alli* (1996),[188] the court refused to extend the *ratio* of *Parks* to situations in which the accused would be identified as homosexual. According to the Court of Appeal any extension of *Parks* should be 'approached with caution.'[189] Evidence offered at trial to support the proposed extension would be required. In other words, the court would not automatically assume hostility to homosexuals. This may not be problematic if all courts take the attitude found in a judgment made only three days after *Alli*, by a lower court evidently unaware of the Court of Appeal's restrictive judgment. In *R. v. Musson* (1996),[190] Clarke J said: 'Despite flaws and gaps in the research however, I am persuaded that there is a realistic possibility of bias in the case at bar and that a Challenge for Cause based on homophobia and homosexual conduct is appropriate.'[191] Clarke J was willing to make this finding even though the accused took the position that he was not homosexual. Clarke J found 'that a substantial number of people called to jury duty may harbour deep rooted negative feelings about homosexual acts that potentially would affect their impartiality in deciding the charges against him.'[192]

Community hostility to homosexuals can metamorphose into community 'action' against homosexuals. The many cases of gay bashing fall in this category. As I mentioned earlier, the target does not necessarily have to 'be' homosexual: Ronald Egan was murdered by neighbours who 'regarded him as a queer and a faggot' because of his speech impediment.[193] Instances of verbal abuse likewise illustrate negativity towards homosexuality in the community. Sometimes the abuse can take a much more sinister form, in which people are forced into physically abusive situations regarded as homosexual as part of a process of humiliation. In *R. v. Chaisson* (1995), two men and a woman assaulted and humiliated three men in their rooming house.[194] The woman and one of the men began by 'calling virtually everyone in the household, queers, fagots [sic], gays.' Then:

Sarah MacMillan continued calling them queers and said she would like to see the queers [suck] each other's penis. She ordered them all to pull down their pants, which they did out of fear of the continued beatings.

Mr. André Boudreau was ordered to suck the penis of Steven Gordon and then Steven Gordon was ordered to suck the penis of André Boudreau. And then Sarah MacMillan ordered Steven Gordon to [suck] on Alvin Mellish's penis while André Boudreau was licking his rectum ...

Sarah MacMillan was saying 'that's what you cocksuckers deserve.' She then went into the kitchen to fetch her curling iron and returned into the bedroom. She had Mr. Chaisson and Mr. Bindas hold down André Boudreau and inserted the curling iron in his rectum it would appear for a few seconds. The curling iron was then inserted in the rectums of Mr. Steven Gordon and Alvin Mellish in the same fashion.[195]

This humiliation was seen as the ultimate in degradation because of its homosexual connotations.

While judges should be alive to homophobic expression, this is not to say that a judge should see homophobia under every rock or accept that it exists merely because it is alleged. *Mercedes Homes Inc. v. Grace* (1993) provides an example of the importance of not assuming that every negative thing that is said to a homosexual indicates homophobia.[196] In that case there was a dispute between a landlord and two gay male tenants. After they started an action for abatement of rent, the tenants claimed harassment and discrimination because of sexual orientation. The judge did adopt a rather condescending attitude to the situation but was probably right in saying that the tenants were too sensitive. The judge noted that the building in question was in the gay ghetto and said that it would obviously hurt any landlord in this area to be described as homophobic. Sutherland J said: 'There was reflected in the actions and in the testimony of Grace and Belford [the tenants] a conviction that any opposition or resistance to them, as openly gay persons, must necessarily be a manifestation of a homophobic attitude. The trouble with that proposition is not far to seek. Pushed to an extreme it would mean that any conduct on their part, however invasive of the rights of others, if it fell short of crime, would have to be countenanced or excused if its victim was to avoid stigmatization as a homophobe.'

Judges have a duty to be alive to instances of homophobic expression and how they might be addressed by the court, but there is no duty to assume homophobia. It is perhaps understandable, given the many instances of actual homophobic expression that a gay or lesbian might be supersensitive to what is said to them by an apparently heterosexual person. Fighting phantoms, however, is not a helpful exercise either for the individual involved or for the communities to which he or she belong.

Judicial Awareness of the Symbolic Importance of Expression

Expression in many of the instances described above is symbolic. It is not directed solely at the immediate target, but aimed instead at homosexuals as a group and homosexuality as a concept. It is important for the courts to recognize the symbolic aspect of homophobic expression. This is what gives homosexuals as a group a stake in the cases involved, and in what judges say. What the courts say in response to these situations has likewise a symbolic value. The courts rarely link instances of homophobia into a unity. They do not see a theme of homophobia, which is odd, since the perpetrators of the acts of homophobic expression involved would themselves probably link many of the types of acts together as legitimate and proper expression of the inferiority of homosexuals. If the judiciary fails to see the link when others use such expression, they are unlikely to recognize a link in any homophobic assumptions made in their own expression. They might be careful to avoid homophobia in one particular instance but fail to see that in another they have lapsed into a use of stereotypical and inferiorizing language.

There are judges, of course, who see larger symbolic issues in the cases they are deciding. For example, in *Layland v. Ontario (Minister of Consumer and Commercial Relations)* (1993), in which the court dealt with whether section 15 of the Charter was infringed when a same-sex couple was denied a marriage licence,[197] the majority said it did not infringe the Charter because: 'One of the principal purposes of the institution of marriage is the founding and maintenance of families in which children will be produced and cared for, a procedure which is necessary for the continuance of the species ...'[198] Greer J, however, dissented. She saw the symbolism that was at stake and the hysteria provoked in some, including the majority of the court, when faced with the prospect of change. She said that because of the restriction: 'The message [the applicants and others who wish to marry a person of the same sex] receive must surely give them the perception that they are inferior persons in our society.'[199] Likewise in *Egan v. Canada*, Mahoney JA in the majority at the appeal level (1993) compared same-sex couples to 'cohabitation by siblings.'[200] Linden JA, however, addressed the more symbolic issue: 'To treat lesbian and gay relationships like all other non-spousal relationships is to rely on and perpetuate the prejudiced view of the legitimacy and worth of those relationships.'[201] The division was seen again at the Supreme Court of Canada (1995), where some judges recognized the greater symbolism of the decision and others did not. La Forest J relied on 'long-standing philosophical and religious traditions' to conclude that 'marriage is by nature heterosexual.'[202] L'Heureux-Dubé J, however, addressed the symbolic message sent: 'Given the marginalized position of homosexuals in society, the metamessage that flows almost inevitably from excluding same-sex couples from such an important institution is essentially that society considers such relationships to be less worthy of respect, concern and consideration than relationships involving members of the opposite sex.'[203]

That a judge recognizes the symbolism of a wrong does not guarantee that the court will take any action to remedy the negative symbolism. In *Brown v. British Columbia (Minister of Health)* (1990) there was a Charter challenge to the B.C. government's decision not to fund the experimental drug AZT to treat HIV when other provinces were doing so.[204] Coultas J recognized discrimination against homosexuals and the ways in which it can be espressed: 'The history of western civilization records that from biblical times to our own, homosexuals have been subjected to discrimination because of their sexual orientation. As with other forms of discrimination, it is unjust for it fails to take into account individual merit, character or accomplishment.'[205] The judge accepted the existence of discrimination against those who were HIV positive or had AIDS. The plaintiffs gave as examples of direct discrimination a comment of the minister of health of British Columbia who said: 'I know there are people who are innocent, they did not go out and wilfully or very carelessly through their lifestyle, contract that disease.'[206] The judge said: 'That comment was unnecessary, inflammatory and reflected a regrettable ignorance of the disease that one would not expect from a Minister of Health.'[207] But he continued: '... while comments of that kind are unwise and regrettable, they fall short of proving deliberate discrimination.'[208]

It is encouraging that the courts occasionally make analogies with other situations in which groups are the subject of hateful, hurtful, and hostile expression. This removes homosexuals from the position of strangeness and allows them to occupy 'friendly' ground. *R. v. Wilson* (1991)[209] provides an example. In the context of a gay bashing, Harris Prov. Div. J said: '... I could not help but think that permitting repulsive conduct of this nature to fester without going unchecked is reminiscent of what history says took place in Europe as recently as during the 1930's and 1940's.' Without giving homosexuals 'special' treatment he recognized the symbolism of the act and situated it in the context of discrimination generally. Such an approach avoids the use of double standards and the impression that homosexuals are being 'favoured' or treated as particularly 'other,' depending on the person's point of view.

Because one of the purposes of the attacks on homosexuals and homosexuality is to trivialize or marginalize, it is important that in hearing a case involving homophobic expression the court not trivialize or dismiss homosexuals and homosexuality or the homosexual component of the case at hand. The trivialization of homosexuals, through verbally and physically abusive expression, often has its seeds in imitative behaviour. Thus children imitate adults, adults imitate officials, officials imitate judges, and judges imitate clerics. There is a chain of trivialization of homosexuals and their lives, a constant marginalization and inferiorization. At the legal level, homosexual relations have long been trivialized. Behind some of the violence directed at homosexuals is surely an imitation of what goes on at a more official level, where homosexuals are linked to violence. The two situations feed off each other. Contempt among children for homosexuals and homosexuality is learned from their elders, who see variants in homophobic expression all around them, including at official levels. Such contempt cannot be unlearned so long as the courts (and other officials) continue to inferiorize homosexuals and what homosexuals do. In *R. v. Smith* (1989), where the witness was threatened with being locked up 'with homosexuals who would rape him,'[210] homosexuals were linked with violence by a public official. Why should a member of the public not do the same? If judges and others involved in legal institutions lump all homosexuals together, why should not other members of the public?

One of the challenges before a court in confronting homophobic expression is assessing whether the traditional categories for dealing with illegal or antisocial behaviour are adequate to respond to what is really at issue. Only sometimes do judges emphasize the homophobic expression contained in various cases. To the judge these cases are primarily domestic disputes, robbery, provocation, assault, and so on. This attitude decontextualizes the antisocial activity that has taken place. The downplaying of homophobic expression means that judges are less aware of its prevalence than they ought to be. Perhaps this explains how, in *Andrews v. Law Society of British Columbia* (1989),[211] McIntyre J was able to say: 'The enumerated grounds [in s. 15(1)] ... reflect the most common and probably the most socially destructive and historically practised bases of discrimination ...'[212] Sexual orientation was not listed by McIntyre J. It is not unusual for a judge simply to overlook it, as he almost certainly would not do for race or religion, for example.

In this survey of the various types of homophobic expression the common thread running through most of them should be obvious. They are ways in which hostility for homosexuals and homosexuality is expressed, ways in which homosexuals can be physically or emotionally hurt. These various expressions are linked by an assumption on the part of the person who makes them that it is socially acceptable to participate in that type of expression. They are linked by assumptions of the inferiority of homosexuals and homosexuality and the assumption that society would be better off without homosexuals and homosexuality; at the very least, 'those people' should be put in their (inferior) place. All of these forms of expression assume that homophobia is the way of the world, that homosexuals are, have been, and will be unnatural. Furthermore, all the forms of expression are imitative; they have long traditions. It is true that the various manifestations of homophobic expression are very different. Killing a homosexual or beating her is a much more severe expression than insulting one's ex-wife by calling her a 'dyke.' The message sent, however, if not identical, is at least similar. Homosexuals and homosexuality are bad, evil, disgusting things. Homosexuals deserve to be ostracized, by force if necessary. However bad a person or a person's acts might be, the homosexual and the homosexual act is always worse. They are beyond the pale; they are outlaw.

If a court ignores the homophobic message implicated in these various forms of expression it ignores the social and historical context of what has taken place. It ignores the fact that what has occurred affects not just the immediate participants but a homosexual community that has to deal with a constant barrage of such expression directed against its members. On an individual and community level, the homophobic expression can have the impact Dickson CJC spoke of in *Keegstra* (1990), in the context of hate propaganda: 'The derision, hostility and abuse encouraged by hate propaganda therefore have a severely negative impact on the individual's sense of self-worth and acceptance. This impact may cause target group members to take drastic measures in reaction, perhaps avoiding activities which bring them into contact with non-group members or adopting attitudes and postures directed towards blending in with the majority.'[213]

The impact of the homophobic expression on society generally has the effect Dickson CJC identified as the second harmful effect of hate propaganda: 'It is thus not inconceivable that the active dissemination of hate propaganda can attract individuals to its cause, and in the process create serious discord between various cultural groups in society. Moreover, the alteration of views held by the recipients of hate propaganda may occur subtly, and is not always attendant upon conscious acceptance of the communicated ideas. Even if the message of hate propaganda is outwardly rejected, there is evidence that its premise of racial or religious inferiority may persist in a recipient's mind as an idea that holds some truth ...'[214]

It is not just homophobic hate propaganda that can have this effect in the homosexual context, but all homophobic expression. In fact, the 'milder' forms of homophobic expression are more invidious in that they are not 'obviously' irrational and extreme but so commonplace as to be perceived as 'normal.' If a judge at least takes time to notice the problem, that is, to situate the issue he or she is dealing with in the context of the larger problem, at least the matter has become remarkable. It is no longer ordinary. That is a large step in confronting the pervasive discrimination against homosexuals.

It is thus refreshing when a judge situates, say, an assault in the context of homophobia, as Harris Prov. Div. J did in the *Wilson* case.[215] The judge clearly identified why the assault took place. '[T]he accused concluded, for whatever reason or standard, that he was gay and the accused possessed an obvious dislike for gay persons.' He then situated the particular incident within a larger social problem, namely, gay bashing. More usually, however, the homosexual aspect of the case, if mentioned at all, is rendered as a reasonably minor background element. If the judiciary cannot see the common threads and the importance of the homophobic expression in cases before them, it is unlikely to recognize those same matters in its own words and actions. If judges cannot see their own homophobia who are they to judge cases of homophobic expression by others?

5

Outing

Introduction

Among the most talked about subjects is sex. Whether in an explicit
form or in the indirect way of discourse about weddings, babies, and
'boyfriends,' we are obsessed by the subject. Much of this discussion
centres on the sex lives and proclivities of others and occurs without
their consent. Michel Foucault has studied how, over the past three
centuries, westerners have been drawn to the task of telling everything
about their sex.[1] He argues: 'What is peculiar to modern societies, in
fact, is not that they consigned sex to a shadow existence, but that they
dedicated themselves to speaking of it *ad infinitum*, while exploiting it
as *the* secret.'[2]

According to Foucault, we are 'a singularly confessing society.'[3] That
is not to say that all sexuality has become accepted. Sexuality and
speech about it has become regularized. Not all sexuality (or speech
about it) is condoned. Homosexuality is traditionally condemned, as is
speech about it. As we have seen, the law is deeply implicated in this
development. Outing – revealing another's purported homosexuality
without that person's permission – fosters discussion of homosexuality.
To the extent that it represents pride in homosexuality it is a challenge to
the accepted norms of regularized sex speech. This development is consistent with Foucault's idea that condemnation in discourse can produce a 'reverse' discourse. The condemned, homosexuality, can speak
on its own behalf to demand legitimacy or regularization.[4]

The discussion of outing in this chapter is structured around the
ideas of privacy and freedom of expression. The significance of outing,
however, is much broader. Outing is mainly about the place of homo-

sexuals in this society. It is about legal attitudes that foster inferiorization and make it seem 'natural,' even to those (that is, homosexuals) who are assigned the inferior position.[5] Outing is about the recognition of inequality and the correction of its legal manifestations and in this sense, it is part of the struggle for equal rights.[6] As I have argued elsewhere, the law cannot (at least by itself) change attitudes and create actual equality, but it can refrain from perpetuating and legitimizing inequality. Because sexual orientation is such an emotive, highly politicized issue, it might be helpful to bear in mind that analogies exist with other types of outing. Outing, of one form or another, is the stuff of literature and film. The film *Europa, Europa* portrays the story of a boy who passes as 'German' and fears that he will be discovered as a Jew. In the book and TV series *Tales of the City*, by Armistead Maupin, a character passing as African-American fears the economic and social consequences of being exposed as a sham. Use of analogies can help to reveal the double standards of the law. However, care must be used to choose the 'right' analogies. The law now often associates homosexuality with criminality and diseases. It is not equated with Jewishness or with belonging to a visible minority, and it is certainly not equated with heterosexuality.

Homosexuality and speech about it must be accepted, at least legally, as ordinary and normal. John Boswell noted that it is now 'normal' to be Jewish in the United States but it is not yet 'normal' to be gay.[7] Jews have not always been 'normal.' Boswell distinguishes three categories of minorities: 'distinguishable insider,' 'inferior insider,' and 'outsider.' Gays and Jews have at various points in western history occupied all three of these categories.[8] In modern Canadian society, homosexuals are arguably 'inferior insiders.' The goal is to move to the category of the distinguishable insider, as Jews have done. Canada, an inclusive-accommodative society, is a society of distinguishable insiders.

Outing is generally thought of as a political act by 'gay activists' to expose 'traitors' to the gay cause.[9] I will redefine the term to mean simply the revelation of a person's sexuality (in particular that person's homosexuality) without that person's consent and contrary to his or her wishes.[10] Outing is a real concern in Canada. The relative absence of legal cases on the issue is due to the invisibility of homosexuals. Few people can honestly say they have not received or given information about another's (supposed) homosexuality contrary to that person's wishes. For the most part, however, the media in this country, unlike its citizens, are unwilling to identify anybody as gay or lesbian. Those

who publicly or widely spread information about another's homosexuality are treated harshly. A few years ago, a University of
Saskatchewan art student, Christopher Lefler, was expelled for dis-
obeying the university's order to remove his potentially 'defamatory'
art work from a gallery on campus. His art identified a prominent
Saskatchewan woman as a lesbian.[11] The university said that it wanted
the display taken down because it could result in a lawsuit being taken
against the university. The student union president agreed with the
university and was quoted as saying: 'As a personal view, the right of
academic freedom does not supersede the right to privacy. To publicly
state one's sexual preference is a personal matter.' Following the university's decision to expel Lefler, the Saskatchewan Arts Board
revoked the grant that would have allowed him to continue his work
exploring the gay identity. An artist loses his education and his funding because he called somebody a lesbian. How does the law react to
outing? How ought it to react?

I argue that there should be no special legal response to any outing
of homosexuality. Whether the person outed is homosexual or not
should be irrelevant. Homosexuality ought to be treated just as heterosexuality (or any other positive characteristic) is treated. A different
response, whether it is on the basis of an invasion of privacy or defamation, contributes to and approves of the inferiorization of homosexuality and homosexuals. Such a situation is unacceptable in a society
such as Canada, which claims to forbid discrimination on the basis of
sexual orientation. I examine the problems of a legal response to outing
in three ways: by looking at the complexity of defining outing and by
examining two legal concepts used to respond to it: privacy and free
expression.

Outing: Definitions and Impact

The term 'outing' comes from the practice adopted by some gay activists of exposing a particular public figure, usually a person who is perceived to be working against the political interests of homosexuals, as
gay. It has been promoted by certain groups, such as Queer Nation,
and by certain British and American publications. Previously heterosexuals outed homosexuals for their own purposes, when they wished
to harm gay people. Now gays out other gays. I use the term to include
not just political outing, but any speech about a person's homosexuality that reveals what was hidden (or maybe even what is not true). I

begin this chapter by discussing the (negative) impact outing can have on an individual and the problems of defining outing.

The process of coming out involves identifying and coming to terms with one's sexual orientation and overcoming and learning to live with the hostility of the world, including, historically, the law. The process is usually slow and full of pitfalls. It is characterized by stops and starts, the person often retreating to the closet to lick his or her wounds. Someone who suddenly wakes up and proclaims to the world, 'I'm queer and happy' may exist but I have yet to meet or hear of that person. The person coming out will carefully plan and time the revelation to friends, family, and colleagues.[12] Everyone values the ability to decide what others see of him or her.[13] Outing someone, rather than allowing that person to come out, removes some of his or her control over the process of self-revelation. The person loses control over the order in which people are told and over what, specifically, they are told. He or she has no way to prepare them or to gauge their reactions and is not present to answer their questions and concerns.

Outing can without doubt have a negative impact on the outed individual, whether or not the information revealed is 'true.' Families might disown the outed individual or treat him or her as a pariah. People once considered friends may disappear. Invitations to parties and dinners dry up. To the extent that socializing with friends and families continues to take place, it will often be strained and certain topics will cause awkwardness. People may not leave their children with the outed person. In fact, contact with children at all might become difficult. The outed person might lose custody of a child,[14] since there is a firm view that lesbians and even more, gay men, are not fit parents.

Another form of prejudice will be professional or economic. Outing can cause a person to lose his or her job or prevent that person from being hired in the first place.[15] In a B.C. case (1995), the court ordered a publication ban on the names of three male witnesses in a trial. The witnesses were homosexual and the judge accepted as valid their concerns about being revealed as gay. Low J said: 'Each is concerned with how the public revelation of his sexual orientation would likely affect him in the work place and with respect to his goals for professional achievement and advancement. There is no question that there is a high degree of homophobia in our society and that the concern of the witnesses are realistic.'[16]

The outed person might not find the same collegiality at work.[17] Promotions may be ruled out,[18] and the person might become ghettoized in his or her job.[19] Certain people are more likely to suffer than others in their jobs if they are outed. Until very recently, a RCMP officer could be forced to resign if he had homosexual experiences (1986).[20] When I was interviewed by a federal psychiatrist for security clearance for a position with the foreign service (in 1990), I was explicitly asked whether I was a 'homosexual.' I sidestepped the question by answering, truthfully, that I had a girlfriend. I was given security clearance, but I do not know what would have happened if I had answered, again truthfully, that I was gay. Teachers in public schools (and particularly in religious schools) are likely to find locating or keeping a job (not to mention maintaining the respect of the students) difficult if they are known to be lesbian or gay.[21] Even writers in the gay studies area are sometimes careful to preserve their self-image of heterosexuality.[22] Such an approach shows sympathy for the homosexual predicament but also a desire to be perceived as straight.

One of the by-products of the secrecy of the closet and the hostility to homosexuality is the historical vulnerability of homosexuals to blackmail. This situation has given rise to the idea in this century that homosexuals are a security threat and ought not to be placed in positions involving spying, diplomacy, or the military.[23] It is not homosexuality, but the state, of course, that gives rise to the circumstances that allow blackmail. Laws that restrict or deny benefits to gays – or, worse, punish them – encourage blackmail because they create a situation in which the homosexual cannot win.[24] He or she could just pay the blackmailer. If a decision is made not to, the blackmailer's victim will be revealed as a homosexual and the legal implications of this situation will then await him or her. The laws that excluded homosexuals from certain government positions or the military in fact encouraged blackmail, as the Boyer Report on Equality recognized.[25] In response to arguments from the armed forces and the RCMP that allowing homosexuals into those bodies would hurt morale and invite blackmail, the committee disagreed, saying: 'The arguments do not justify the present policies. They are based on the stereotypical view of homosexuals that assumes them to be dangerous people imposing their sexual preference on others. They also give undue weight to the sensitivities of others. Finally, the blackmail argument is a circular one – if sexual orientation were not a factor in employment, the main reason for any such vulnerability of homosexuals would disappear. If a foreign power, or anyone else, wants to subvert a Canadian, they would use whatever blandishments would be most compelling to that particular individual, in this regard, heterosexuals are as vulnerable as homosexuals.'[26]

Another prejudice that could be suffered is to the person's physical and emotional security. Gays get beaten up. The outed person will probably be subject to insults and other verbal abuse.[27] An outed woman will assume that people are ridiculing her behind her back. An outed male will be afraid that others will draw conclusions about him which, however unjustifiable, carry stigma and the threat of insecurity: that he is a sexual monster, that he has AIDS, that he is a paedophile, that he is weak, that he is a misogynist, that he is pitiable. The threat to security exists not only for the outed individual but also for that person's friends and family.[28] A related argument was made in a 1964 Ontario case, where one man was accused of murdering another. They were both described as 'homosexually oriented.' The accused sought unsuccessfully to have his trial moved on the basis that, according to the judge, 'it will be difficult in a small community, perhaps I should say a small rural community, to obtain a jury who will not be biased against the accused because of his sexual orientation.'[29] The validity of this insecurity was recognized by Wilson J in *Re Canadian AIDS Society and Ontario* (1995), in which the nonvoluntary disclosure of the identity of blood donors carrying the HIV was challenged. Wilson J said: 'It would be difficult to conclude that the disclosure of the donors' names to the public health authorities would not cause psychological stress to some donors, and in particular gay donors.'[30]

The threat to security exists not only for the outed individual but also for his or her friends and family. The outed person might have a same-sex partner who has been known as 'just a friend' or 'just a room-mate.' The outed individual might be married or have children or both. These family members might suffer all the social, economic, and security threats of the outed person. Friends who stick with the outed person might be avoided as being 'tainted' by homosexuality themselves. Women who remain friends with an outed man might be called 'fag-hags.' Erving Goffman writes: 'In general, the tendency for a stigma to spread from the stigmatized individual to his close connections provides a reason why such relations tend either to be avoided or to be terminated, where existing.'[31]

As a result of this potential prejudice, it is not surprising that outing has caused a hostile reaction. Austen and Wellington have criticized Richard Mohr's underestimation of the need some people feel for the closet: '... many people feel a responsibility to attempt to protect women from the effects of violence. It is not seen as complicity with the forces that make social life less safe for women generally. Mohr's argument is analogous to saying that women, in order to protest violence against them, should be forced to walk the streets alone at all hours of the night, leaving themselves open to sexual assault.'[32]

Austen and Wellington would probably say that providing no legal remedy to a person who has been outed is akin to allowing a person to force a woman to walk the streets alone in a dangerous area without providing a legal remedy against the person who so forces her. Most homosexual people have been closeted at some point in their lives and it might be thought that those who are out should demonstrate greater sympathy for those who remain in the closet. Outing is using the tactics of the straight gutter press. It has been argued: 'The problem with outing is that it claims an unjustifiable right to sacrifice the lives of others as well, whether they agree or not.'[33]

Despite these negative consequences, it can be said that the law itself has an interest in outing in at least two situations: (1) where the law punishes a particular sexual orientation; and (2) where the law is silent on the status of one particular sexual orientation but rewards another. If the law punishes somebody for being lesbian or gay then there should (logically) be no legal consequences for revealing another's sexual orientation. In fact relatively few laws deal so nakedly with sexual orientation. One notorious example was Nazi Germany's Paragraph 175, which was modified and interpreted so as to make any act remotely homosexual a crime.[34] More commonly it will be a particular act connected to a person's sexual orientation that will be prohibited, especially sodomy between men. Outing someone for sodomy with another man in contravention of one of these statutes could surely attract no legal repercussions; legally, it is tantamount to revealing a murderer or a thief. Such an outing would of course inferentially tell the world that the person is homosexual (even if that were not true).

In the second class of situations, where the law is silent on being gay or lesbian but rewards those who are not, Canadian law provides more examples. A gay man or a lesbian cannot in many situations gain the benefits for a spouse available to a straight person.[35] A lesbian cannot marry another woman.[36] A person cannot sponsor a partner of the same sex for immigration purposes.[37] The law in these cases does not specifically punish lesbians and gays; rather, it rewards those who are straight. The consequences of an 'outing,' say, in the case of an arranged marriage for immigration purposes, could be severe but are invited by the law itself.

What, then, actually constitutes the process of outing? What does one have to say or do to 'out' another individual? An explicit statement to the effect that Adam is gay or a 'pansy'[38] or that Mary is lesbian is probably sufficient.[39] However, those statements are known to most children as simple insults devoid of actual meaning. What if it is said that Adam 'likes boys' or Mary is a 'confirmed spinster'? There are any number of euphemisms to describe the state of being homosexual. Such expressions, which, on their face, might seem neutral, can be used against those in a group (as an insult) or by members of a group (as a term of inclusion).[40] Often the words or expressions pass from the former to the latter category. 'Queer,' 'fag,' and 'dyke' originated as derogatory euphemisms; they are often now used by homosexuals as terms of identities and endearment and inclusion.

The words used to out someone need not be as explicit as those just mentioned but may simply describe a stereotype associated with lesbians and gays. Do we 'out' Adam by saying that he 'minces' or is 'limp-wristed,' or Mary by saying that she is 'into leather' or bikes or diesel? In *Thompson v. The King* (1918),[41] the accused was charged with acts of gross indecency with boys. The court admitted evidence that the accused was carrying powder puffs and had indecent photos of boys. To the court, the presence of powder puffs was sufficient to indicate that an individual engaged in homosexual activities. Former New Brunswick premier Richard Hatfield was reported as having given licorice underwear to a teenage boy.[42] Was he outed? In some instances the circumlocution might relate more to the identity of the person involved in sexual activity rather than to homosexuality itself. The Atlantic Canada *Frank* magazine reported that police in Scotia Square (Mall) in Halifax 'Jumped out of a washroom ceiling to arrest a number of men engaged in various sexual acts. One, a deputy minister in the PEI Government, subsequently committed suicide over the affair.'[43] In this case the person has not actually been named, but it would probably not take too much investigation to identify him. In *Franck v. Webster* (1994), it was argued that a priest had outed his parishioner by giving him a gift of a male pornographic calendar in a public gathering.[44]

The outing could be entirely unintentional. In the United States, at least one court found (1991) an 'outing' in the case of a woman who wished to be named the guardian of her lover who was left brain damaged and paralysed after a serious car accident. The blood relatives of the hospitalized woman denied access to the lover, who began a series of actions both legal and political to restore her to her place beside her partner. Eventually, these actions were successful.[45] However, along the road to that result, one judge who decided against the lover's request to be named guardian took into account that the lover had revealed the lesbian relationship. The judge said that the lover had committed an 'invasion of privacy' by 'outing' the injured person to her family and the world by revealing that the two were lesbian lovers. This, according to the judge, showed that the lover seeking guardianship was acting in her own interest rather than in the interest of the injured woman.[46]

One revelation that has consistently been perceived to be tantamount to outing a person as gay is the revelation that the person is HIV-positive or living with AIDS.[47] The combination of outing as homosexual by identification with AIDS is illustrated by the case of *Valiquette v. The Gazette* (1991),[48] discussed in Chapter 3. This was the case in which a teacher with AIDS employed by the Catholic School Board was not allowed to return to work and a reporter wrote a story about the incident. Although the teacher in question was not named, as the only teacher at that school who had been absent during that period he was easily identified. The court concluded that his right to anonymity and right to solitude had been breached and accepted that the newspaper report constituted 'une véritable "bombe intérieure"' for Mr Valiquette.[49] Although the report said nothing about the plaintiff's sexual orientation, the court also accepted that his sexual orientation had become the subject of discussion.

The expression that could constitute outing might relate to a particular incident rather than take the form of a general statement about a person's status. What if Adam is reported to have been seen coming from a gay bar or a gay bathhouse? What if we report simply that Adam once had sex with a man?[51] What if Brenda claims that Mary has a picture of herself kissing another woman, or simply reports that Mary has a picture of another woman on her desk? Are these remarks sufficient to be deemed to 'out' the individual? One writer has said that 'Newspaper stories about a person being seen in a gay bar are different than stories commenting on that person's sexuality.'[52] It is not clear why this is so. Adam's having sex with another man or going to a 'gay' film might not be sufficient to give Adam a 'gay identity.' Surely, however, the message to the public is the same. In the eyes of most people, the report that a 'prominent PEI politician' had sex in a public washroom with another man makes that politician homosexual.

Some of these terminological difficulties arise because the terms used can be understood only by a particular audience. There are two essential elements of outing relating to the listening audience. First, the audience must understand the words used to mean that the subject of discussion is homosexual. Second, the audience must not already be aware of the subject's homosexuality. Adam cannot be outed to people who already know that he is homosexual, nor can he be outed if the audience thinks the description of him as being a regular at Lees Trail in Stanley Park relates to a fondness he has for nature walks.

A person comes out (that is, identifies himself or herself as a homosexual) in stages, in many ways, and in different aspects and at different times. Coming out is a long-term process and is never really finished. Most people have the luxury of coming out to themselves first and then in slow stages revealing their sexual preference to others. Can I be said to be outed if I am out to most people but not to all?[53] In an article about the UBC Law School in the newspaper *Xtra! West*, I was named as one of the 'openly gay' faculty members.[54] The fact is that almost everyone who knows me – especially at the law school – knows that I am gay. But the newspaper did not check with me before publishing the information. Was I 'outed' because (assuming there is a readership for such an article) more people knew after publication of that information?

People may know that Adam identifies himself as gay but be unaware of the actual nature of his homosexual identity. Despite Adam's efforts to conceal details of his sexuality from others, it is likely that at least some people are aware of them. These people could include his sex partners, certain friends, people in a gay bar, or the person who sells him a pornographic video. Humans being what they are, it is likely that some of these people have told others. Can Adam be outed if people know he is 'gay' but are struck by the news that he likes to be the dominant partner in a situation involving bondage? Is revealing that information outing Adam? People may know that Mary dates other women but be unaware of her preference for older, academic 'types.' Is public disclosure of that information outing Mary?

What people are willing to reveal to the world is often slightly different from what they reveal to themselves. Sometimes a person wants certain things to be kept hidden. At the office, for instance, a given person's bookshelves might hold learned texts on homosexuality. Her library at home might contain such tomes as *Desert of the Heart* or *The Swimming Pool Library*, while collections of erotic stories might be found on the bedside table. Copies of *Lezzie Smut* or *Torso* might be hidden under the bed.[55] What is on display and where it is located tells a great deal about how 'out' that person thinks she is. A known lesbian may not want to reveal that she has a copy of erotic short stories in the bedroom. The same person might at one time have kept the learned book on homosexuality under the bed too. Eventually it made its way to her office shelf, as the short stories may do, given time. But anybody who figuratively places those books there before she has decided to move them 'outs' that individual.

Outing need not be of a specific individual. It could be of a whole group or it could be done *en masse*. The prosecutions, in the past decade or so, against Roman Catholic priests and teaching brothers as child molesters can be interpreted so as to taint all clerics, especially Catholic ones, as paedophiles and often as homosexuals. In 1991, a British group called FROCS (Faggots Rooting Out Closeted Sexuality) threatened to out a large group of political, legal, religious, entertainment, and other individuals. They did not carry out their project, saying that they were satisfied with the publicity that showed the negative way in which being gay was regarded.[56]

Any legal solution to outing must take into account the complexity of the process as well as the complexity inherent terms such as 'homosexual,' and 'gay,' and 'lesbian,' which I discussed in Chapter 1. The complexity of outing, however, does not lend itself to the certainty on which a legal response should be based. Outing has too many definitional grey areas to lend itself to satisfactory legal response. Nonetheless, the law does respond to speech about homosexuality. I turn now to the two concepts employed by the law to deal with outing: privacy and freedom of expression.

Privacy

Rights to Privacy in Law

One argument in favour of judicial action in response to outing is that outing invades the right of the outed individual to privacy. The argument is that an individual should be able to control information about his or her sexuality. A person's sexual activities or preferences or identity, it will be said, are sacrosanct and should not be revealed without that individual's consent. Unlike a defamation claim, the right to privacy would not depend on the truth or falseness of the assertion that

Mary is homosexual. In fact, it might be argued that Mary needs the 'protection' of the law of defamation where she is straight and the right to privacy when she is homosexual. The outing issue is unusual in that those who defend the right to out others usually also argue that they have a right to privacy that requires the state to stay out of their personal (sexual) affairs. If the law respects that privacy, should it not also respect (and enhance) privacy in the sense of preventing those affairs from being exposed to the public?[57] I argue that, whatever the law on privacy might be, it is inappropriate to apply it differently in the context of homosexuality than in that of heterosexuality. To conclude that homosexuality or homosexuals are more in need of privacy protection is to undermine the argument of equality. At present, however, Canadian law probably arrives at a different conclusion.

Privacy or related concepts mean different things in different cultures at different times. Arthur Schafer notes that 'there are cultures, Hutterite colonies, for example, in which to describe an action as having been done "in private" could involve an accusation of impropriety rather than a claim to immunity from interference.'[58] The term 'privacy,' it has even been said, is unique to the English language and has no exact counterpart in the Continental languages.[59] Our idea of privacy is culture specific. It can also be argued that the development of ideas of privacy are part of the secularization of our society.[60] For some religious people, who feel God always watches them, there is no absolute privacy.

What we have to decide is whether, given our notions of privacy and about sexual orientation, the existence of a right to privacy that prevents disclosure about a person's homosexuality is appropriate today. Legal protection of privacy is the result of the increasing emphasis on individual development and happiness, the weakening of social norms and community homogeneity, and the increasing ease of monitoring and surveillance made possible by technology.[61] It has been argued that concern about privacy flows from the expansion of population and the loss of a frontier.[62] Privacy law is a relatively recent phenomenon and the right to privacy has been protected in some international human rights documents.[63] Domestically, privacy law can be divided into two areas: a torts area and a constitutional law area. The constitutional law area of privacy in the context of homosexuality is concerned with whether the state should be able to interfere in homosexual relations. In Canada, although there are some unsettling lapses in the idea of state noninterference, in theory both homosexuals and heterosexuals are protected by the Charter against state interference in their sex lives.[64] This aspect of privacy is distinct from the private law aspect, which deals with the ability of others to know or recount facts or information about a person.

In the torts area, much is owed, particularly in the United States but also in Canada, to an article written in 1890 by Samuel Warren and Louis Brandeis.[65] In the United States the idea of a 'public disclosure tort' or a 'private facts tort' has grown from their views.[66] The 'private facts tort' is described in the Restatement (Second) of Torts [1977] as follows: 'One who gives publicity to a matter concerning the private life of another is subject to liability to the other for invasion of his privacy, if the matter publicized is of a kind that (a) would be highly offensive to a reasonable person, and (b) is not of a legitimate concern to the public.'[67] In this area, William Prosser has developed a well-accepted fourfold categorization of a private facts tort:

1 Intrusion upon the plaintiff's seclusion or solitude, or into his private affairs.
2 Public disclosure of embarrassing facts about the plaintiff.
3 Publicity that places the plaintiff in a false light in the public eye.
4 Appropriation, for the defendant's advantage, of the plaintiff's name or likeness.[68]

The items of most relevance to outing are, of course, the second and third.[69]

The common law outside the United States has traditionally been sceptical about recognizing a general right to privacy.[70] The appearance of the Wolfenden Report in Britain in 1957 did much to foster the idea that the state should have only limited involvement in 'private' sexual relations between consenting adults. This report began the slow movement in most Commonwealth countries to eject the state from the bedroom.[71] Still, there has been a reluctance to develop a generalized approach to a right to privacy. Until very recently, the only way to bring a claim for invasion of privacy was to do it indirectly, by means of causes of action that indirectly protected privacy interests. These included defamation, injurious falsehood, and wilful infliction of mental distress.[72] The tort of breach of confidence is well established.[73] In Canada, the recognition of a tort of invasion of privacy has developed slowly.[74] In light of the reluctance of the common law to act, several jurisdictions have legislated on the matter of privacy.[75] There is some jurisprudence under the provincial Privacy Acts, especially that of British Columbia. The jurisprudence under this legislation deals mainly with the legality of techniques used to monitor or spy on people.[76] It does not usually deal with an issue such as outing.

Valiquette, discussed above, provides an exception to the jurisprudential vacuum on outing as a privacy issue. There, the court found a breach of the right to privacy guaranteed in the Quebec Charter of Human Rights and Freedoms. Some support for an action for breach of privacy is found in *Franck v. Webster* (1994), in which an action for breach of confidence was brought by Wendell Franck and his mother Gloria Franck against a defendant priest and his church. It was claimed the Mr Franck made disclosures about his homosexuality and HIV status to the priest in the course of counselling. At a public gathering the priest was alleged to have given Wendell Franck a male pornographic calendar, 'which had the effect of outing Wendell to many friends and members of his family who, it is alleged, were not aware that he was gay.' The plaintiffs claimed damages for 'loss of enjoyment of [Wendell's] remaining life, mental depression, traumatic neurosis, loss of religion and spiritual guidance, shunning by the gay community of Winnipeg, and loss of opportunity for a death with dignity.' The mother claimed damages for 'mental depression, traumatic neurosis and loss of religious faith.' The court allowed a number of allegations in the statement of claim to be struck out on the basis that they did not constitute proper pleadings. But Master Lee said: 'I am persuaded that the allegations remaining, after the deletion of portions of the statement of claim indicated above, contain the essential elements for an action for breach of confidence.'[77]

Privacy and Sexual Orientation

Why is privacy relevant to a consideration of a person's sexual orientation? It has been said that privacy is important because we are all concerned about how we appear before others.[78] It might be argued that privacy is necessary to develop feelings like love and trust and friendship and respect.[79] But often we convey such emotions to total strangers.[80] The argument for privacy is usually framed in terms of personal autonomy and individual development, which are seen as important to participation in a democracy. J.S. Mill argued that there is a close relationship between privacy and an individual's ability to develop his or her individuality and creativity.[81] For Vincent J. Samar, the right to privacy is closely linked, though not equivalent to, the right to autonomy.[82] According to one U.S. writer, the private facts tort should cover cases of outing or at least be modified so that it can. Ronald F. Wick has written: 'Surely no publicity can be more offensive to its subject than a public disclosure of his homosexuality, given the private nature of sexual relations and the stigma many attach to homosexuality.'[83] Wick advocates a private facts tort that is slightly modified from that set out in the Restatement. According to Wick, the problem with the tort as now stated is that if a person is at all open about his or her homosexuality then it cannot really be said to be a private aspect of that person's life and so would not be caught by the tort. Wick writes: 'Under the current approach, when a gay person attempts to tackle the stigma attached to homosexuality by living a normal life and interacting in public – without going so far as to become openly gay [!][84] – he thereby decreases his chances of winning a potential private facts lawsuit, because he has strengthened the potential media defendant's assertion that his homosexuality was not a private life.'[85] Wick thinks that the tort should be based on information about which a plaintiff has a 'reasonable expectation of privacy.'[86] He would also put an onus on the defendant, once the plaintiff has established a *prima facie* case for privacy, to show that the community mores would not be shocked or offended by the disclosure of the matter in question and that the public has a legitimate interest in the matter.

Such a call for privacy to attach to the revelation of a person's homosexuality is based on a negative vision of homosexuality and an acceptance, however reluctant, of homophobia. It represents a justification for a broad scope for privacy that would simply not be thought acceptable in the heterosexual context. The law, and the courts in particular, ought to eschew a double standard in privacy. In fact, privacy per se has no justification but can only be rationalized in the context of the subject matter for privacy. Justifications for privacy take on a whole different complexion when they are discussed in the context of heterosexuality rather than homosexuality. Homosexuals deserve as much protection from the state as do heterosexuals in their sexual activity. But homosexuals do not require more delicate legal treatment than heterosexuals when it comes to speech about their sexual orientation, however well intended it is. Such an approach endorses the inferiorization of homosexuality.

Richard Mohr criticizes privacy arguments in the outing context because they amount to an approval of keeping homosexuality a secret. There is an unwritten code in the homosexual community that one does not talk to nonhomosexuals about who is and is not gay (although within the community there is much such conversation). For Mohr this convention is part of the secrecy about homosexuality that he applauds outing as designed to break down: '[W]hat a strange convention The Secret is. That which binds the community together is a commitment to a belief in the community's worthlessness.'[87] One of the problems with this position in the legal context is that, at least in the United States, the courts have never differentiated secrecy from privacy.[88] Mohr distinguishes between a person's sexual orientation and that person's behaviour, including his or her sexual practices. He says that it is sexual acts, and derivatively talk of them, not sexual orientations, that are protected by privacy.[89] It is difficult in practice, however, to draw the line between the two in many cases. Expression about a person's sexual orientation will be construed by most recipients of the information as at least an implication that the person does or wants to do a particular sexual deed. The distinction drawn by Mohr is another of the invidious being/doing distinctions so often made in the context of homosexuality. It is fine to be homosexual so long as you do not do anything about it. One is socially acceptable and the other is not. I can talk about another's thoughts but not about another's deeds. But the line cannot be drawn so finely. If I say that somebody goes to a gay bar or that somebody is gay, there is not much to distinguish between the two statements in terms of one being about privacy and the other about secrecy. In the end the information they convey is much the same.[90] This is particularly so in a society where the construction of homosexuals and homosexuality means that people assume that nasty things (like going to bars and being promiscuous) flow 'naturally' from being homosexual. Even judges make these assumptions, as I discussed in Chapter 2.

Our society, and thus our legal system, is awkward when it comes to dealing with issues relating to sex. Sex is considered the most private of acts and yet its exploitation is one of the most lucrative elements in our economy. The courts do not want to hear certain cases, where the hearing would cause the court to be sullied,[91] although the most sordid cases of rape and sexual assault come before them all the time. The problem is establishing what is acceptable to be spoken of publicly and what should be repressed by the state. Which of the following statements are acceptable as not intruding on the private:

Adam is gay? Adam has sex with men? Adam goes to the beach to have sex with men? Last night Adam went to the beach and had sex with Barry? Rather than have a court attempt to determine what is tolerable and what is not, it is much simpler just to say that none of these revelations is acceptable unless Adam (and even Barry) consents to having the details revealed. An advocate of a legal sanction for outing would draw the line at the very beginning of this series of statements. Such an approach – all or nothing – might actually be the most severely logical, given the difficulty of distinguishing orientation from deed. However, the law does draw lines. In an equivalent set of statements for a heterosexual male, the line would probably be drawn after 'Adam has sex with women,' or perhaps after 'Adam is straight.' If it were alleged that Adam was straight or had girlfriends, such allegations would not be equated with the unmentionable, the taboo, or the pornographic.

The problem, then, arises when the law and society draw the line at a different place for homosexuals than for heterosexuals, and it is exacerbated when assumptions are made about homosexuals and homosexuality (for example, all homosexuals are promiscuous) that are not made about heterosexuals, heterosexuality, or heterosexual practices. This double standard is not uncommon. Society often becomes indignant when confronted with homosexual affection. It is assumed that homosexuals want to make their sex public and equally assumed that straights do not do this. Take the remarks of George Brookes, a member of the Tasmanian State Legislative Council, reacting to news that Tasmania's antigay laws were the subject of a complaint made directly to the UN Human Rights Committee in Geneva: 'The homosexual community want to publicly display their affection, as they do in New South Wales. They'll tell all the lies under the sun purely and simply so they can get the laws changed and display their affection in public. Why should they be allowed to do that?'[92]

Homosexual affection and sex should at best be kept strictly private and never be evidenced in public.[93] By imposing a sanction on outing in the case of a gay or lesbian where no such sanction would apply in the case of a straight person, the law condones the idea that homosexuality is inferior and something to be ashamed of. Bruce Ryder has said that: 'The legal denial of lesbian and gay personhood has a number of effects. At an ideological level: it naturalizes heterosexuality and renders all other sexualities suspect.'[94] The courts cannot overcome their historic hostility to homosexuals – or at least to homosexual acts – so long as they treat them differently from heterosexuals or heterosexual acts. Britain's Wolfenden Report[95] made the important distinction of private and public. It advocated a legal vacuum when homosexual acts were done in private but not when they were done in public. What outing does is force homosexuality into the public and challenge the law's view (post-Wolfenden) that public homosexuality is taboo. If expression about homosexuality is impermissible where expression about hetero-sexuality is acceptable, and 'homosexual' carries negative assumptions that 'heterosexual' (or 'married,' 'parent,' 'his girlfriend,' etc.) do not, then the courts have retained the dichotomy (the double standard) of public/private. This is unacceptable if homosexuals are to be treated as legal equals to heterosexuals.

The goal should be to eradicate, to the extent that courts are capable of doing so, the conditions that cause gays and lesbians trauma in the first place. So long as judges react to expression about homosexuality differently than they do to expression about heterosexuality, gay and lesbian children and adults will feel abnormal and be traumatized by their sexuality. Media 'shock' stories about homosexuality and outing flourish because of the atmosphere of secrecy and shame that is culti-vated, at least in part because of legal reactions to outing.[96] The courts' concern ought to be discrimination against homosexuals and homo-sexuality, not discriminating themselves against homosexuals and homosexuality. Wholehearted protection against discrimination on the basis of sexual orientation in the arts, on television, in school books, hiring, and so on would make those who are homosexual feel less excluded.

That, it might be argued, is a grand design for a perfect world or a utopian future but it does not address the trauma suffered by homo-sexuals today. This would seem to be the point made by Austen and Wellington, cited earlier, who liken outing to forcing a woman to walk alone in an area of high risk of sexual assault. It is difficult, however, to see how imposing a legal sanction on outing would ameliorate the trauma suffered. Outing, as we have seen, can take many forms and lit-igation would be essential to decide whether or not outing had actu-ally taken place. Evidence could be called on whether or not people already knew. Few people who suffer such trauma are likely to go to court to prolong the ordeal. The damage would already be done. Per-haps, however, one or two successful cases[97] involving a penalty on an 'outer' would impose such a chill that no one would out anyone else. In this way people would be spared the trauma of outing. Homosexuality, however, is not the only thing that could cause a person trauma or economic disadvantage such as job loss. Mary might be traumatized because she has a Japanese grandfather; Adam might be fired if he is known to be a Moslem or a Mason. It might be difficult to find an argument that these actions are 'morally justified,' to use Austen and Wellington's term.[98] These are more apt comparisons than that of forcing a woman to walk alone in a dangerous area. Does the law demand that such characteristics not be mentioned, or that the person involved be consulted before they are discussed, to assess whether they are traumatic for that person? It does not, because the law does not consider these characteristics to be 'bad.' One can imagine the justifiable uproar if legal sanctions were imposed on those who discussed another person's Jewishness or African heritage on the basis that the person's right to privacy had been infringed.[99] Even where the person who is outed is not homosexual or does not identify as homosexual, no different standard of privacy should apply than if the person was 'outed' as straight when she identifies as a lesbian. A different approach equates homosexuality with a characteristic such as criminality, being a rape victim,[100] or being a leper – all conditions that society might (not always logically) characterize as 'shameful,' 'bad,' or 'pitiable.'[101] If a court imposes a sanction on outing it forbids a person from being identified as gay in a casual or positive sense but allows to pass the frequent juxtaposition of 'homosexual' and 'paedophile,' thus encouraging the association of those terms. Homosexuality can be mentioned only in a negative context, otherwise it is an invasion of privacy. This approach belies the true status of homosexuality as viewed by the judiciary, despite its rhetorical equality. Homosexuality is at best something to be pitied; one should feel sorry for homosexuals. Bruce Ryder has developed this idea of the 'compassion/condonation dichotomy' in approaching homosexuality: 'The compassion/condonation dichotomy provides the discursive framework through which the social and legal construction of heterosexual privilege is placed beyond critical examination ... For many years, homosexuality was treated as a pathology of the soul, leading to criminalization; later, as a pathology of the body or mind, leading to medicalization. The criminal and medical models have been discredited, but the tendency to believe that biology or nature has somehow failed the homosexual remains. She or he deserves our compassion for this trick of fate.'[102]

The fact that society continues to associate homosexuality with negative concepts of criminality and illness does not justify judicial condonation of this discrimination. Society in general may also equate some races with criminality and some religions with illness, and it might therefore be morally dubious to assert that people are members of these groups, but that is quite different from saying that the court ought to impose a penalty on the person who makes the identification. In its concern to show that justice is done, the courts ought not to give sustenance to unjust negative stereotypes.

The notion that outing is an invasion of a person's privacy rings a little hollow when it is remembered that society invades personal privacy in any event with the expectation that the person is or will at least pretend to be straight. All of the laws passed that condemn homosexuality or discriminate against homosexuals are based on the idea that an individual's sexual preferences and practices are not a private matter but are open for scrutiny by the state. In matters such as marriage, divorce, child custody, and adoption the state has always been prepared to assert that it is its business to monitor the sexuality of its members. Moreover, as I discussed in the previous chapter, the state often creates events and distinctions and asks questions that assume that heterosexuality is the norm. For example, people are asked on official documents whether they are 'single, married, separated, or divorced.' These questions assume that all relationships are heterosexual. Institutions with considerable influence – churches, the schools, and the media – constantly bombard all members of society, including (especially) homosexuals, with the message that being straight is the norm and the only truly acceptable sexual identity. This message seems particularly important for the most homosocial of organizations: the military, the police, the Roman Catholic Church, sports teams, Boy Scouts, 'service' clubs, and so on. The security and privacy of the individual and real choice is denied.

Being forced to remain in the closet is an invasion of privacy. The person is only there because society has forbidden that person the right to privacy to express his or her sexuality. There is no privacy when it comes to conformity.[103] The closet has been described as an 'epistemological' space where threatening, subversive knowledge and discourse is kept. The more it challenges established norms and truths, the deeper it is put in the closet.[104] The 'privacy' of the closet, secrets and hidden lives, is only part of a desire to protect the status quo concerning what is 'good' and what is 'bad,' what is male and what is female, and what the power dynamic between them should be.[105] Refusal to accept a closet imposed by society is the only real privacy.

Privacy and Who Is Outed: The Public Figure Issue

Should a right to privacy depend on who is being outed? That is, should the legal response to outing vary depending on whether the person outed is a member of Parliament as opposed to a teacher as opposed to a shoe seller? Should we adopt the U.S. idea that some people are 'public figures' and therefore 'fair game,' while others are not? Making a distinction between public and private figures leads to problems, the most basic of which is defining who is a public figure and who is not. While it might be easy to decide in the case of the Prime Minister or a postal worker, many other decisions will be more difficult. What of the teacher, a member of a political party, the writer of a letter to the editor, an athlete? In a certain sense these individuals are held up as role models or seek to influence public opinion, but it would be surprising if it were concluded that they had less of a right to privacy than other individuals. Furthermore, making the distinction has the unfortunate effect of having the law accept a situation in which some people are more 'important' than others.

How a public figure distinction would be used in the context of outing is problematic. Proponents of such a distinction might well argue that respected people who were homosexual could be used as role models to change public opinion about homosexuality.[106] However, as John F. Hernandez says: 'Outing of this nature appears to do little to alter the deeply held positions of the outee and other affected parties.'[107] The fact is, in any event, in our society, people deliberately held up as role models are usually turned into ridiculous figures as a result. Those who are purposely portrayed as saintly or who have certain aspects of their character emphasized in a propagandistic way end up making that characteristic seem absurd. Society, especially its young people, is much too worldly to believe that certain things that can be said in the context of public figures and not others must make those things acceptable. The public figures are made to look silly by being dressed up as role models and the public will pick up on the double standard. Why do we never read in the description of a hockey coach that he is gay (instead of 'married') or in the news of a pedestrian hit by a car that she has adopted her lover's children (instead of being 'married with three children')? Allowing a separate standard for public figures as opposed to private ones in the context of outing can only make homosexuality seem exotic and other worldly – and probably decadent. Homosexuality already suffers from a certain tarnish by being associated with decadent classes – such as German industrialists, Roman Catholic priests, British aristocrats, Hollywood movie moguls, Italian fashion designers. Sir Edward Coke attributed the origin of sodomy to 'pride, excesse of diet, idlenesse and contempt of the poor.'[108] This has usually been the cause of further public revulsion towards homosexuality rather than an acceptance of it. It would be much more useful if the woman down the street, the star on the screen, or the lieutenant-governor could equally be indentified as lesbians.[109]

Outing might be designed to show that a public figure is homosexual and therefore homosexual is good, but is more likely to be designed to show that the public figure identified as homosexual is therefore not to be respected after all. Setting up role models does not sell newspapers or air time, cutting down tall poppies does. Public figures are usually outed to reveal them as 'other' and therefore not worthy of respect. There is still the idea that outing is only acceptable in the case of blatant hypocrisy.[110] This is in fact the context in which people are now usually thought to be outed. *Frank* magazine outed four Ontario MPPs who voted against the legislation that would have given legal recognition to same-sex couples.[111] The names of these individuals were supplied by 'sources in Toronto's gay and lesbian community.' While this rationale for outing might be legitimate, it can give a very negative impression of homosexuality. Forcing people out of the closet may give the impression that being homosexual is something shameful and only for hypocrites. However, a court can compound this negativity by imposing a sanction on the outer: the court is certainly saying that the person should have stayed in the closet. Where a court only allows outing of public figures and does not treat heterosexuality as private, it is saying that homosexuals who are not public figures should stay in the closet. Restricting outing to public figures makes homosexuality appear abnormal and the sign of a hypocrite. Only when ordinary people can be called homosexual will homosexuality be called ordinary. The public/private person distinction is, therefore, of no help in addressing the issue of outing and attitudes to homosexuality.

I do not deny that there is or ought to be a right to privacy and that lines must be drawn. No distinction should be made, however, between homosexuality and heterosexuality when it comes to a right to privacy. There should be no special category of people for whom discussion of homosexuality is legally acceptable and another category in which it is not acceptable.[112] An argument might even be made that given the widespread repression of references to homosexuality, bisexuality, or other manifestations of queerness, a person should have a greater freedom of expression to deal with homosexuality generally in order to redress the balance. However, all that is necessary is equality. No right of privacy prevents a reference to a person's heterosexuality. The same should extend to homosexuality; there should be a real equivalency between the two. A true heterosexual equivalent to a homosexual issue should be sought when the law decides whether a privacy right should prevail over a freedom of expression. The code words for heterosexuality might differ from those for homosexuality. People are commonly identified as heterosexual by use of words such as 'wife,' 'family,' 'marriage,' 'boyfriend,' 'engaged,' 'fiancé,' and so on. Homosexual code words differ; for men they might be 'partner,' 'special friend,' 'relationship,' or even 'fuck buddy.' Because some of these words might not be used in the heterosexual context does not mean that equality prevents them from being protected words in the homosexual context. Privacy ought not to be the legal tool of inferiorization.

Free Speech

Arguments for Freedom of Expression

Usually contrasted with the interest of privacy is the interest of freedom of expression. The discussions about freedom of expression, in general, are legion and little can be added here that would not cover territory already better discussed by others.[113] There are various arguments as to why, in the outing context, a freedom of expression should trump an argument based on the right to privacy.[114] These include a political interest in addressing the cause of homosexual rights and of achieving equality for gays and lesbians; a social interest in terms of identifying members of the community and communicating with each other; a social interest in terms of communicating with the non-homosexual (or dominant) community to show the pervasiveness of homosexuality and the vibrancy of the homosexual community or communities; and an expression interest that is inward looking and simply allows one individual to express his or her thoughts for purely personal reasons and purposes.

Political Interest in Free Speech

The first interest of free expression can be characterized as political.

This is probably the most accepted of the justifications for freedom of expression, especially in the context of outing. The idea is that speech or expression allows an individual to participate in the processes of power in this country. It allows the individual's views to be heard and it allows the individual to hear the views of others. Participation cannot be achieved if an individual cannot be heard or hear. In the outing context the political argument for free expression takes the form of saying that homosexuals must be permitted to be full participants as gays or lesbians or bisexuals in the political processes.[115] They must be allowed to express their identity just as heterosexuals are allowed to express theirs. Other participants in the political process are not denied the ability to talk of other members of their group. This enhances their political cause and promotes their interests. Exposing the hypocrisy of those who would deny equality to homosexuals can also have this effect. Homosexuals should not be precluded from using other homosexuals for their political purposes.

Freedom of expression is a means for enabling all individuals to be involved and to feel like full participants in society. How can permitting outing achieve this? When the legal system allows a person to identify in another a characteristic of his or her own, it treats the person with that characteristic as a full member of the community. Imposing a legal sanction on the outing would be to say that that characteristic is to be kept hidden, that it is shameful. Shameless people might choose to reveal it, but others should not be shamed by having it exposed without their consent. This approach serves to render those with that characteristic second-class citizens. And second-class citizens cannot be full participants in the political process.

Social Interest: Identification as a Member of a Group

A second speech interest that can be advanced by the ability to out another is the social interest of homosexuals in identifying others who are (or might be or even should be) homosexual. This interest is related to the political interest just discussed. To identify as homosexual is to identify as part of a homosexual culture or one of the many homosexual cultures.[116] A culture is simply a group of people who share distinctive traditions, literature, language, and attitudes.[117] Such a group has a sense of community and a habit of passing on their distinctive traits to subsequent generations. All of these characteristics are found within the gay and lesbian community or communities.[118]

Homosexuals, like other members of nonvisible minorities, are particularly in need of a liberty to communicate in order to define their group and to be identified as having a collectivity or collective interests. Homosexuals do not grow up in homosexual surroundings. I need no particular freedom of expression in order to identify other members of my white community. People with certain physical disabilities do not need such a freedom of expression in order to identify others who are part of their group. The same is true of members of age groups, some religious groups, and many economic groups. Heterosexuals have no equivalent need for such a freedom of expression because of the assumption that everybody is heterosexual unless proven otherwise. Homosexuals, however, can only identify other members of their group and break the sense of isolation if there is communication as to the existence of other homosexuals. Homosexuals need to know that others exist. Like all humans, they need to feel the safety of not being alone, the comfort of companionship.[119] There are many ways of indicating that I have a homosexual identity, some of them non-verbal. I could dress in a certain way or behave in a stereotypical manner. I could wear an identifying pin or T-shirt.[120] For purposes of sexual activity I could go to a place known to be a meeting place for gays or lesbians or I could use eye contact in cruising.[121] Most homosexuals are aware of the endless time that is spent discussing who is and who is not homosexual. This is part of belonging. All groups do this, minority or majority. Oxford men try to identify other Oxford men. Baptists discuss other Baptists. Canadians have a fascination for identifying those in U.S. and British society who are in fact Canadian.[122] Homosexuals should not be made to feel different by having their expression about who is and who is not a member of their group limited by legal sanctions if they identify someone as a member of their group without that person's consent. Expression that labels a person as homosexual should not be equated with hate speech, which attracts a legal sanction.[123] Homosexuality is not shameful; it is not criminal. Adam, a homosexual, should therefore have the freedom to claim Barry as a fellow homosexual. That process is part of outing.

Social Interest in Communicating with the Outside World

The freedom of expression interest in outing can also be cast in terms of the social interest in demonstrating to the nonhomosexual (or dominant) community the reality of homosexuality and the true character of the homosexual community or communities. Because of the closeted nature of so many homosexuals, society as a whole has no idea of the true nature of homosexuality and the characteristics of individual homosexuals. Their view of homosexuals (and the view of homosexuals who have not been able to establish relations or communications with their community) is of exotic, laughable creatures, incompetent fairies or threatening lesbians, child molesters, or sex fiends who seek to 'convert' children to their 'cause' or 'lifestyle.' A homosexual needs to be able to enlighten this group of people as to the truth of the situation. Freedom of expression is especially important here because of the media's insistent message that only heterosexuality is normal.[124]

To combat the distortion that results from this view of the world, homosexuals need the liberty to point to other homosexuals to prove to society that we exist and have always existed everywhere. Reference to historical figures is important, but identification as homosexual cannot be restricted to them. I should be able to point to living people as well. It is important to demonstrate that highly regarded people are homosexual and that homosexuals are capable of achieving great results in politics, theatre, sports, and so on. To do this with pride it must be possible to identify these people without having to seek their permission to be named. It must also be possible to identify 'ordinary' people, to show that homosexuality is in fact not freakishness or the preserve of special achievers. It must be possible to show that homosexuality is ordinary, ordinary in the sense of being omnipresent. Communication with society generally cannot be limited to certain types of 'acceptable' homosexuals. Outing activists tend to reveal their internalized homophobia by outing only 'respectable' homosexuals. Sympathetic films tend to portray homosexuals who are 'acceptable' to the mainstream, where films historically portrayed them as ominous.[125] Neither approach makes homosexuality normal. The true scope and depth of the homosexual community should be made evident. Legal acceptance of selective outing only, whether it is of conservative politicians, drag queens, or child molesters, can never achieve this equality goal.

Interest in Self-Expression

The final freedom of expression interest in outing is the interest an individual has simply in expressing himself or herself by means of identifying the homosexuality of another. This may be done for no particular political or social reason at all, or those reasons may be secondary. An artist may, for example, purely or mainly for self-expression depict somebody and identify that person as homosexual. Is this expression to be penalized by the law? It should be penalized only to the extent that the law would penalize someone for painting a picture of a person identified as heterosexual, or as a Mohawk, a Jew, or a Catholic. Expression about a person's (supposed) homosexuality should not have to be made in the service of a 'cause' in order for it to be protected.

Take the example of the artist Lefler from Saskatchewan, discussed above, who included in his work an identification of a woman as a lesbian. He suffered withdrawal of financial support for his work of art and as well as expulsion, which probably involves the deprivation of his education and injury to his future. For what similar artistic expression would one face expulsion from a Canadian university? Perhaps for stirring up hatred towards people or threatening them with physical harm or perhaps for wrongly identifying someone as a murderer or a thief. Does identifying another person as a homosexual justify the most drastic punishment an educational institution can mete out? Expulsion is the academic equivalent of exile. The message sent by the University of Saskatchewan is that it is unacceptable to be homosexual because anybody who identifies you as such warrants banishment for the (obvious) pain the label will cause you. Mr Lefler should not have to prove that his art was for a 'cause' in order for it to be valued.

Expression by lesbians and gays about homosexuality and homosexuals is important given the repression that homosexuals almost invariably experience in their early years. When a person comes out, it often seems that all that person can talk about is his or her homosexuality and the other gays he or she knows. Sometimes this is annoying, even to liberal, heterosexual people, who wish that person would simply shut up and accept it. What such people fail to realize is that after years of being silenced, the uncloseted person wants to be able to proclaim his or her homosexual identity with pride. This may involve celebrating the homosexuality of others, as well. The law should accept this as reason enough on its own to protect such expression. There ought to be no requirement of any lofty political or social motive in order for expression about homosexuality to be protected.[126]

Interests Affected by Expression about Homosexuality

What interests will be affected by the acceptance of all or some of these freedom of expression justifications for protecting outing? The main interest of course, will be the right to privacy. As I argued above, no distinction should be made between homosexuality and heterosexuality when it comes to a right to privacy.

Aside from possible infringement of a person's privacy right (and the security that goes with it), protection of the expression interest in outing could curtail the expression interests of the outed person. An outed person will be characterized as a liar or fraud by those who believe the speech about his or her homosexuality. The trauma suffered by an outed person may make him or her less inclined to speak. The wrong done to the outed person will be perceived by many to be even more egregious if that person is not in fact 'homosexual.' While the expression interests of the outer may be enhanced by protecting his or her speech, the equivalent interests of the outed person may be threatened. How is this conflict to be resolved?

One resolution is in favour of the outed person. There are two claims (that of the outer and that of the outed) based on freedom of expression. The subject of the expression of both claims is the outed person and perhaps the claim of that person should prevail. The outer can choose another person or subject to talk about, whereas the outed person cannot change who he or she is. Furthermore, any impairment to the free expression interests of the outer is temporary. It is rarely vital that the outed person be the only one talked about. The harm done to the outed person, in contrast, will be permanent. Anything he or she talks about after being outed could be affected, limiting that person's expression. If we take a pragmatic approach to the issue of conflicting expression interests, the balance of convenience in terms of actual harm to the two individuals involved would tip in favour of the outed person.[127]

Should this issue be resolved, however, in terms of actual harm to the individuals involved? The question is one of rights, liberties, and symbolism, and such questions should be answered first in a principled way. Pragmatism is usually an excuse for rationalizing discrimination. Suppose Enoch is a member of a church that dislikes First Nations people and discourages its members from associating with them. Enoch owns a store that sells goods primarily to church members. Faye, a First Nations person, drives by the store and drops in to buy a few items. Enoch refuses to serve Faye on the basis that Faye is First Nations and Enoch will lose business if he allows her patronage. Enoch will also lose his social connections and could be expelled from the church. Faye will claim a right not to be discriminated against;

Enoch will claim freedom of religion and freedom of association. The consequences for Enoch are much more direct. If Enoch serves Faye he will be in breach of his religious beliefs and his social and economic position could collapse. Faye could easily go to the next store (say just down the block) to get the same items. However, the issue would undoubtedly be settled in favour of Faye, because it is a fundamental principle of our society that tolerance and acceptance, inclusion and accommodation, be promoted. Enoch is arguing for the right to exclude; Faye is arguing for the right to be included. The latter will triumph over the former. Pragmatism and rationalization have no place in this matter.

To take another example, suppose Gerald is a Jew but his colleagues do not know. Gerald is an editor at a newspaper known for its attacks on minorities, including Jews. Hannah, also a Jew, wants to reveal that Gerald is Jewish, perhaps to demonstrate his (and, indirectly, the newspaper's) hypocrisy. Hannah could choose to 'out' someone else as a Jew or simply not to identify anyone as Jewish who did not want to be so identified. In either case she would very likely get on with her life quite nicely and Gerald would not be outed. However, despite the probably dire consequences for Gerald, especially where his expression interests rights, are concerned the problem would be resolved in favour of Hannah if she chose to out him. Gerald's argument is in favour of excluding his membership in a group, thereby excluding the group as a legitimate part of society. Hannah's argument will win even though on balance Gerald's expression interest (and other interests) will be more directly affected. Hannah, it will be decided, has said nothing 'bad' about Gerald; it would be inappropriate to 'protect' people from being called (rightly or wrongly) Jewish. In some places and at some times, even in Canada, being labelled Jewish has or has had very negative consequences for the person so labelled. To 'protect' a person from such consequences in Canada today by applying special sanctions in the event of the use of the label Jewish would be to participate in the exclusionary exercise of those who would advocate the negative consequences.

The same principled approach should operate in the outing situation in which the information revealed is the homosexuality of Adam. Karl could out someone else but would be met each time with a pragmatic argument that he should choose a different subject of speech. Karl's interest is to reveal homosexuality in society. He will never be able to do this if the pragmatic approach is used in each case. At the end of the process, Karl's expression interests may well be as adversely affected on a pragmatic basis as are the interests of each Adam who comes along in turn in the process. If a court truly seeks to include and accommodate homosexuals as a legitimate part of society then it must accept the expression interest of the outer rather than the outed. As discussed in the section on privacy, the only limits that should be placed on this expression interest are those that would be put on the expression if it were about straights, whites, blacks, Jews, Scots, and so on.

Outing affects more than the interests of the outed individual; the interests of the status quo in not seeing the boat rocked may also be affected. If a priest is outed the interest of the church in general as well as the personal interest of the priest, is affected. The church may be thought to be hypocritical and less reliable on other matters as well. Outing of an individual could affect the interests of any group or organization to which he or she belongs, particularly where that group or organization has taken intolerant views or prides itself in espousing 'traditional' values. That outing is perceived as a threat to the status quo is borne out by the involvement of institutions when an outing occurs. One of the peculiarities of outing is that for the outed person to obtain legal redress for any wrong committed, he or she must go to court and risk a greater invasion of privacy in order to defend against the earlier invasion of privacy. To avoid this situation, third parties seem willing to get involved. For example, in the Lefler case, the action against the artist involved was not taken by the woman outed but by the University of Saskatchewan. The university seemed to see the outing as a threat to its own security and took on the combined role of plaintiff and prosecutor in the matter.

Outing can also affect more frivolous interests of society in preserving the status quo. Especially where the outed person is famous, outing can undermine people's well-being by shattering their illusions about their heroes. Outing can be iconoclasm in an idolatrous society. Thus, the vehemence of the negative reaction when it is argued that a person of Schubert's stature was what we would now call gay. For example, in an article entitled 'Was Schubert gay and does it really matter?'[128] American composer Ned Rorem[129] is quoted as saying he 'had to laugh when reading about the way Schubert's homosexuality was discussed in a recent symposium. Apparently someone in the audience got up and said, "Nobody has mentioned the fact that Schubert was short, fat and ugly." That has certainly as much to do with his music as being homosexual.' The inference was that he was not homo-sexual and that even if he had been it was not relevant and should not be mentioned.[130] Nobody seems to think it odd, however, when stories are made up about Schubert that imply that he was heterosexual and that women somehow inspired his work. For example, in the notes to the Deutsche Grammophon recording of Schubert's 'Trout' Quintet,[131] William Mann attributes the quality of the quintet to the fact that it 'belongs to this delicious world of sublime entertainment.' One place where Schubert was 'happy' was Steyr 'what with "unimaginably beautiful scenery", agreeable friends, plenty of pretty girls to flirt with, and opportunities for music; his pleasure is to be detected in this piano quintet ...' Sexuality is thus obviously relevant to a discussion of a great musician so long as it is heterosexuality.[132] A somewhat more recent example was well described by Richard Meyer in an incident with reference to actor Rock Hudson: '... sex-therapist Ruth Westhe-imer told *Playboy* magazine, 'I feel sad for all the thousands of women who fantasized about being in [Rock Hudson's] arms, who now have to realize that he never really cared about them.' Because he has been revealed as a homo through a spectacle of illness, Hudson is said to betray the projective fantasies of his heterosexual spectator, here a female one. Rather than scrutinizing the extreme over-investment of these spectators in Rock Hudson's starbody, Westheimer blames Hud-son for not reciprocating their desire.'[133]

The horror with which some people react to outing is uncannily sim-ilar to society's reaction to someone who is 'obviously' gay or lesbian. So long as a person passes as heterosexual, it really does not matter a great deal to many people if that person is actually gay or lesbian or bisexual. Even if his or her sexual orientation is known, it does not upset society so long as that person 'fits' in. This is the acceptable face of homosexuality.[134] However, if the person makes it clear by his or her dress, walk, speech, demeanour, or otherwise that he or she is homo-sexual the equanimity of society is shattered. Outing does something similar. A closeted homosexual person is trying to fit in. Despite suspi-cions that others might entertain, any 'peculiarities' are tolerated so long as they are very subtle. Outing the individual shatters that illu-sion or self-deception. It forces society to face the person for what he or she is (or might be). The façade of uniformity falls and difference is exposed.[135]

Homosexuality as a negative and shameful state has been necessary to straight society in terms of defining itself. In order for there to be an 'us,' there must be a 'them.'[136] In patriarchal, masculine society 'them' includes homosexuals and women (lesbians are particularly excluded). Gay men challenge the assumptions and certainties about groups of men.[137] Thus, in a masculinist society like Nazi Germany or even the United States, there can be a particularly negative reaction to homosexuality. Similarly in homosocial organizations like the Roman Catholic Church or the Boy Scouts gay men are feared and loathed as a logical conclusion to their own homosocial principles. In article in the *Globe and Mail*,[138] Toronto Maple Leafs coach Pat Burns said 'An avowed homosexual, that would never be accepted in hockey – never.'[139] The 'concern' of people like Burns echoes that voiced by many in the U.S. military, who feared the effect on morale if a soldier had to shower beside a gay man who might, it seems, cast amorous glances his way or, worse, thrust himself upon the poor heterosexual soldier. The equanimity of the male athlete and warrior appears to be shattered if they can be thought of as sex objects by other men. In their minds, this places them in the role relegated to women. It is in the interests of gay men – as well as women – to challenge these patriarchal, masculinist social structures. Concerns in preserving the status quo, if such preservation means perpetuating the identification of a legitimate group like homosexuals as deviants and inferior, do not warrant reflection in the legal system. The same principles ought to apply where the outed person is a member of a particular ethnic, cultural, geographical, or religious community where the reaction to the outing may be more than usually negative to the outed person and those around her.[140] There is a myth in many cultures that homosexuality is a 'white man's disease.'[141] This can make homosexuality especially difficult or dangerous for members of non-white groups.[142] The courts ought not to accept different levels of tolerance for homosexuals in different parts of the country or in different segments of it. The law does not have different levels of acceptability for heterosexuality in such circumstances. A court would have the same (non) reaction, whatever the surrounding circumstances, if the outing were of a person's African heritage or Jewish heritage.[143] So it ought to be for speech about homosexuality.

Defamation

The civil action most often used to limit or curtail a freedom of expression interest is defamation.[144] The requirements of defamation are well established, as are the defences.[145] The actionability of a defamation claim was set out by Lord Sumner in *Jones v. Jones*,[146] where he said: 'Defamation, spoken or written, is always actionable if damage is proved, and, even if it is not, the law will infer the damage needed to found the action (1.) when the words are written or printed; (2.) when the words spoken impute a crime punishable with imprisonment; (3.) when they impute certain diseases naturally excluding the patient from social intercourse; (4.) when words are spoken of a person following a calling, and spoken of him in that calling, which impute to him unfitness for or misconduct in that calling.'[147]

The question is whether statements about a person's homosexuality should be fitted into any of these categories. The very idea of sex outside marriage is central to homosexual sex, given the present exclusion of homosexuals from the institution of marriage. Thus an allegation of homosexuality could often be an allegation of unchastity. Some homosexual acts are crimes and many gay men live with AIDS, which would probably be called by the law a 'loathsome disease.' In deciding questions relating to defamation the courts frequently resort to the character known as the 'right-thinking member of society.'[148] As I discussed in the previous chapter, it is not clear who exactly this person is or what values he or she represents, but the 'right-thinking member of society' is probably not homosexual. Given the history of the law's attitudes to homosexuality to date, there is every good reason for homosexuals to fear this person.

There is some authority (not all of it dated) for the view that simply making a statement that a person is homosexual is defamatory.[149] In *Kerr v. Kennedy* (1942),[150] it was held that an allegation that a woman is a lesbian is an imputation of unchastity within section 1 of the Slander of Women Act 1891. Asquith J said: 'Can any distinction be drawn on this basis between adultery and fornication, on the one hand, and unnatural relations with other women on the other, except that the imputation of the latter is, if anything, more wounding, more likely to excite abhorrence on the part of the average reasonable person, more likely to spoil the victim's prospects of marriage?'[151]

In *R. v. Bishop* (1974),[152] the defendant was tried on a charge involving theft from a bedroom. In evidence he explained the presence of his fingerprints in the room by saying he had had a homosexual relationship with a prosecution witness. The witness denied this and the prosecution sought leave to ask the defendant questions tending to show that he had been convicted of offences other than that charged because the nature and conduct of the defence was such as to involve imputations on the character of the witness for the prosecution. The defendant objected on the basis that, because of the Sexual Offences Act 1967, an allegation that a man was a homosexual or practised homosexuality was not an imputation on his character. This objection was rejected and the appeal dismissed. Stephenson LJ said: 'If Mr. Price were to sue the defendant in respect of his allegation if repeated outside a court of law, we venture to think that a submission that the words were incapable of a defamatory meaning would be bound to fail and a jury would generally be likely to find them defamatory.'[153]

He also said: '... [W]e read the Act of 1967 as saying that even though homosexual acts between consenting adults in private may be corrupting, if people choose to corrupt themselves in this way, that is their affair and the law will not interfere.'[154]

In a 1974 case, the Ontario Court of Appeal said that there was rightly held to be libel where a plaintiff '... alleged that the defendants were academically and professionally unqualified, referred to their doctoral degrees as "phony" and in addition referred to them in terms which were *prima facie* defamatory suggesting that they were in charge of a "goon squad" or "armed band," that they were blackmailers, "political homosexuals" and suffering from an incurable mental condition, among other charges.'[155]

In *A.M.N. v. O'Halpin* (1996),[156] a patient at a treatment centre launched an action for defamation based on a statement made to him to the following effect: 'Al, being gay is okay ... many gay people have access to children ... just because you're gay doesn't mean that you're a paedophile.' The plaintiff said this was an attack on him personally. The court found against the plaintiff but only because the words did not constitute an accusation about the plaintiff and because they were made in good faith and nobody who heard them felt that they had sullied the plaintiff's reputation. The court was impliedly of the view that being called gay in other circumstances might amount to defamation.

Of cause for some concern, given the copious slang used by and against homosexuals and homosexuality, is that defamation law allows a person to allege that even if the words used do not have primarily a defamatory meaning, then they have a secondary meaning that the court should consider.[157] On the other hand, some words, which might be defamatory, are not actionable because they are 'mere terms of abuse.' In *Lever v. George* (1950),[158] the words 'cheap bastard' were found to be mere terms of abuse and not actionable without proof of special damage.[159] Words relating to homosexuality could also fall within this principle. In the previous chapter I mentioned the case of *Culhane v. Rawlings* (1987), in which the plaintiff alleged that the defendant, in the presence of a number of fellow Ford Motor employees, defamed him. The defendant apparently called the plaintiff a son of a bitch and 'a male person who performed homosexual acts.' McCart DCJ, you will remember, said that these words on their own disclosed 'no reasonable cause of action.' Their use was 'so commonplace as to be virtually incapable of constituting defamation. In some perverse way they seem to be used as expressions of friendship.'[160] Thus, 'fag' is not apparently actionable when a term of abuse. The bizarre result is that calling somebody a homosexual if it is meant to be a term of abuse is not actionable, but if you mean it to be true, it is defamatory. No clearer example of the law's homophobia is necessary. Q.E.D.

If the law worked with the precision and accuracy for which courts strive then it might be said that the right to privacy would be the resort of 'true homosexuals' in the event of outing, whereas defamation would be the action of choice for heterosexuals wrongly 'accused' of being gay. Allegations about homosexuality are often true.[161] The defence of truth should prevent 'real' homosexuals from succeeding in a defamation action. The statement need not be exactly true so long as it is substantially true.[162] Given society's longing for there to be no homosexuality, it is not surprising that the defence of truth has not succeeded even in so clear a case as that of Liberace, who won a defamation case when he was called 'fruit-flavoured.'[163] If it could not be shown that Liberace was in fact homosexual, it will be difficult to prove it of anybody who has not publicly said so.

The whole concept of homosexuality as defamatory is of course ridiculous and offensive.[164] Its continued existence demonstrates that the law and the courts, in particular, have not truly accepted homosexuality as equal to heterosexuality. Why should an assertion of a person's homosexuality be defamatory in *any* circumstances? Given the difficulty of defining homosexuality, there are arguably legions of people who could fit within the term 'homosexual' or 'queer' or some such related term. But even if there were only one person who was homosexual or who identified as a homosexual, the idea that the term is defamatory is offensive. To label a certain characteristic as defamatory is to relegate it to exclusion, to otherness, to inferiority. I can defame people by calling them 'child molester,' 'thief,' or 'perjurer,' absent the defence of truth. Inclusion of 'homosexual,' 'queer,' or similar term in that same category equates homosexuals with those individuals. I cannot defame people by calling them straight, Jew, First Nations, or black,[165] even if those terms are not true. The law does not get to the 'truth' stage. Those terms would never be considered defamatory.

The resort to any community standards to judge the 'acceptability' of the term homosexual fits uncomfortably in the inclusive-accommo-dative society that Canada strives to be. While it is true that the bulk of Canadian society might find the description of a person or themselves as homosexual to be injurious, it does not mean that the courts should accept that bigoted view and promote it through laws on defamation. Judges should reflect the principles, ideals, and aspirations of a society and not its lowest common denominator, especially in a context such as defamation. For some characteristics which are certainly not now defamatory – such as ethnicity, religion, race – there is no resort to community tests of acceptability, even though a poll of Canadians might find that they would think less of a person if told she were First Nations or a Jew or black. Canadian courts cannot protect individuals from discrimination on the basis of a particular characteristic (for example, sexual orientation) in a Charter of Rights or in a human rights context but accept in civil law the views of a majority of society (without even being polled) that a person with that characteristic is objectionable and being labelled as such is an 'injurious' thing.

Conclusion

There may well be times when a court should impose a sanction on someone who calls other people homosexual, but that should not be because homosexual is bad (versus heterosexual being good). The call-ing of names in any situation can amount to harassment. For example, in *Brotherhood of Maintenance of Way Employees v. Canadian Pacific Ltd.* (1997)[166] there was a challenge to an arbitrator's award. A man was discharged for sexual harassment of his fellow employees by falsely accusing them of being in a homosexual relationship. The dismissal was upheld by the arbitrator and the union challenged this decision on the basis that the arbitrator contravened the Canadian Human Rights Act and the Quebec Charter of Human Rights and Freedoms in affirm-ing that it is humiliating for a heterosexual person to be represented as homosexual. Duval Hesler J rejected this characterization, saying it turned 'the issue on its head.' As the judge said: 'The fact is, however, that Mr. Parker made a declarative statement that his victims were homosexuals and then attacked them, and all homosexuals, for it. It does not matter that his victims were not, in fact, homosexuals. What matters is that he made the statements in the way that he made them, with the evident intent of shaming and demeaning them, as well as all homosexuals.' The result would have been the same if the accusation was that the persons were in a heterosexual relationship and the person intended to shame and demean them (as well as all heterosexuals) by such an accusation. I do not argue that accusations of homosexuality can never be the subject of something like an harassment complaint. But it should be subject to no special considerations that serve to inferiorize homosexuality.

Sometimes names can hurt just as sticks and stones can. But forcing someone to be ashamed of his or her identity and regulating expression about it will certainly hurt that individual when his or her neighbour is allowed to be proud of an equivalent identity. Sometimes, perhaps, the harm done is tolerable, where it flows from an identity that is acceptably negative, such as murderer or rapist. Homosexuality, however, cannot keep such company and the courts ought not to force it to do so. Expression is essential to the well-being of homosexuals and to positive attitudes about homosexuality. Judges should foster, not hinder it.

The judicial system must do what is right and what is principled. Its workings should reflect the ideals and aspirations of its host society. Homosexuality has historically been inferiorized by society and by the law and this inferiorization is undoubtedly wrong. Canadian law and society now recognize, at least in theory, the principle of nondiscrimination on the basis of sexual orientation. Vestiges of the old attitudes, such as actions for defamation or invasion of privacy in response to outing, prevent real legal implementation of this principle. They also send out messages of the acceptability of the inferior status of homosexuals and double standards. In any given instance, the lack of a legal response to outing might possibly hurt the outed individual. But so too might the lack of a legal response to the revelation of a person's First Nations heritage. The principled judicial response to discrimination against homosexuality is action; to expression about homosexuality, it is silence.

Conclusion

Judicial attitudes are tenacious but they can change. The biggest obstacle to change in attitudes is the failure to recognize the presence of the attitudes in the first place. The problems discussed in this book have largely consisted of the unintentional application by judges of negative or inferiorizing stereotypes to homosexuals or to situations involving homosexuality. Judges ought to be made aware that the situation exists. This book has shown a remarkable persistence of judicial attitudes and assumptions over approximately forty years. Some evidence of the judicial ability to change in this respect is apparent in recent cases, making recent examples of old attitudes and assumptions even more striking and egregious. The onus is on lawyers to educate judges and on judges to educate themselves. There is also an onus on people who go to court not to be afraid to have an issue involving homosexuality raised and explored in a way other than the adoption of stereotypes. When an issue involving homosexuality comes before a court, there is an obligation on all involved, but particularly on the judge, to consider the impact of the case not just on the immediate participants but on others who might somehow fall within the scope of the language and categories involved in the case.

This study has been rooted in an examination of cases from Canadian courts from 1960 to mid-1997. In this final chapter, I reflect on some of the cases heard in the year since. Just possibly, it is now fair to say that in recent cases more often than not judicial expression about homosexuals and homosexuality no longer betrays assumptions of uniformity, inferiority, and contagion.

One of the challenges faced by the judiciary is to recognize that when an issue or fact of homosexuality comes before the court, there are parallels with cases involving different types of minority factors, especially racial and gender. Attitudes about homosexuality are part of a general pattern of attitudes towards minorities, although where homosexuality is concerned they have often been at their most extreme and the expression most shrill. If judges are now more aware of and concerned about homosexual issues in a positive way, it is largely by virtue of a more general judicial phenomenon of awareness of and concern about expression by and about members of other groups that have traditionally been marginalized. Clearly, however, it is thought still appropriate by some judges and in some contexts to say things about homosexuals and homosexuality that could not be said in other contexts with respect to other minorities. The problem often stems from a failure to recognize that homosexuals are analogous to other groups. The problem is often, too, one of the use of a double standard, in which homosexuality is seen as different, in the sense of being 'other' so that parallels with heterosexuality that would allow homosexuality equivalent treatment are not thought to be appropriate. We have seen this happening in all sorts of contexts, from outing to school curriculum issues to custody cases.

There are still instances in which homosexuality is identified as 'other' by virtue of being singled out when heterosexuality is not. For example, in R. v. J.A.F.,[1] Paradis Prov. Ct J, briefly set out the facts of three joined cases as follows: 'In J.A.F., a case of homosexual assaults on two brothers between 1961 and 1974, the Crown seeks a penitentiary term of two to four years; In A.C.H., again a case of homosexual assaults on two brothers between 1962 and 1965, the Crown seeks a prison term of one to two years. Finally, in R.T., a case of a sexual assault upon the twelve-year-old daughter of a woman with whom the accused was living, such assaults taking place over a three-month period in early 1996, the Crown seeks a prison term of one to two years.' It is immediately apparent that the boys were subject to 'homosexual' assaults whereas the girl was subject to 'sexual' – not 'heterosexual' – assaults. The fact that the assaults were 'homosexual' is about as relevant as the fact that they might have been 'interracial' or 'interreligious' assaults, at least where there is no allegation of a hate aspect involved.

If analogies are to be made with members of other minority groups, it is important that homosexuals not be thought of as the most recent 'kids on the block' and that it is therefore appropriate to consider homosexual rights last where they are thought to conflict somehow with other rights. There ought not to be a hierarchy of protections, with sexual orientation at the bottom. Protection should not be based on longevity of legal recognition and protection such that religion comes before race, which comes before gender, which comes before sexual orientation, and so on. This attitude really only surfaces now in the context of cases in which a conflict between protecting from discrimination on the basis of sexual orientation versus on the basis of religion is perceived. In such cases, religious rights are privileged.

The B.C. Supreme Court recently dealt with the tension between protection of religious views and the protection of sexual orientation in *Trinity Western University v. College of Teachers (BC)*.[2] The college refused to accredit the teacher education program of the university because the proposed program was discriminatory and contrary to public policy and the public interest in that its graduates were likely to be biased when dealing with homosexual students. The basis for the college's view was that students at the university were required to agree on admission to a code of conduct that included an obligation to refrain from homosexual behaviour. This requirement was found in a paragraph entitled: 'REFRAIN FROM PRACTICES THAT ARE BIBLICALLY CONDEMNED.' The decision of the college was upheld on appeal to the college's council. Davies J, however, allowed the application for *certiorari* on the basis that the council had no evidence that the graduates of the university were intolerant. Davies J stated that he should treat religious freedom and sexual orientation freedom equally: 'Further, we should look at the fundamental values of our society. Freedom of religion means that society must take a neutral stance with respect to religions. This requirement of neutrality does not mean that the members of society may not have differing religious beliefs for this would obliterate the freedom. Instead, members of society are required to be tolerant – to respect others and their views. Also, our society prohibits discrimination on the basis of sexual orientation. This means that each member of society must be tolerant of another person's sexual orientation and respectful of that other person regardless of the beliefs held.'[3]

This is very much in line with what I identified in Chapter 3 as the inclusive/accommodative Canadian ideal. Davies J asked himself whether 'if an applicant has met all the standards set by the BCCT in the public interest in regard to education, professional responsibility, and competence,' the BCCT could nevertheless refuse to certify the teacher on the basis of certain beliefs held by that teacher. 'That is to say,' asked Davies J, 'can the BCCT refuse to allow a qualified teacher to teach in British Columbia because of a religious belief that homosexual behaviour is a sin?'[4] He thought the answer to that question was no.

Nobody doubted that the college was an appropriate judge of the ability of graduates to teach effectively in a multicultural and pluralistic society, which meant an assessment of the graduates' tolerance for others. In concluding that there was no evidence of intolerance on the part of the graduates of the university, the judge overlooked the fact that all the graduates will have agreed with the idea that homosexual activities are 'BIBLICALLY CONDEMNED.' The institution seeking certification required all of its students to adhere to such a belief. Such views were somehow privileged and insulated from being labelled intolerant on the basis that they are religious convictions. The court appeared to accede to the view that it is acceptable to hate homosexual activities but to love homosexual persons, which is the action/status distinction with respect to homosexuality, itself a religious device for repression and inferiorization. One wonders whether if, say, graduates of an educational institution specifically agreed on admission that all Sikh practices are evil and to be avoided at all costs and that those who engage in them are eternally condemned would not be taken as evidence of intolerance. Would such an institution and its graduates be judged fit to instruct teachers or to teach in the public schools when the schools contained students, a large number of whom (or any of whom) were Sikh? Discrimination when dressed in the context of religious beliefs is still accorded privilege, however much the court protests that religion and sexual orientation are being given equal treatment.

Aside from instances in which religious values are offered as a rationalization for homophobia, judicial acceptance of the idea of inclusion and accommodation has meant that concern has been shown about homosexuality that would not necessarily have been shown in past years. Improvement in the Canadian judicial record becomes even more apparent when the situation for homosexuals in other countries is examined. The courts have been open to arguments based on the idea that Canadian society seeks to include and accommodate its gay and lesbian citizens. Even the *Trinity Western* case itself, as we have just seen, contains such statements of aspiration. These concerns have arisen recently in the context of extradition cases, where the fear is that a homosexual person will not be treated fairly in a foreign country because of his sexual orientation. In *United States of Mexico v. Hurley,*[5] McMurtry CJO said:

The nature of the persecution in question in the present case 'sufficiently shocks the conscience' and is 'fundamentally unacceptable' to Canadian society. The material submitted to the minister, and accepted by him, documents very serious human rights abuses (including torture and murder) committed in Mexico against individuals based solely on their sexual orientation. Persecution of gays and lesbians is unacceptable by Canadian standards and it is against these very types of abuses that Canadian citizens must be protected.

If it is established, in accordance with the applicable onus of proof, that a Canadian citizen will be subjected to this type of persecution, protection against such abuse must be afforded to the fugitive.[6]

The courts also appear more willing to acknowledge that including and accommodating homosexuals does not mean that heterosexuals or other groups (except possibly religions) are somehow less accommodated or included. For example, in *Rosenberg v. Canada (Attorney General)*,[7] Abella JA said: 'Extending survivor benefits to persons who are not heterosexual does not diminish the importance of protecting the economic rights of women in traditional relationships.'[8]

In order for judges to decide cases with a homosexual aspect sensitively and equitably they need to strive not just for formal equality but equivalency. Homosexual terminology and homosexual relationships have not developed exactly as heterosexual ones have and so a fair legal standard will encompass equivalents rather than being satisfied with formal equality in all cases. An equivalency approach is now evident in some custody cases, where judges recognize same-sex couples and their families while accepting that they are not necessarily identical to traditional families in a formal way. It is not now unusual for a court to recognize that homosexuality should be irrelevant in deciding custody disputes. In *Buist v. Greaves*,[9] where two lesbians who had been a couple were disputing custody of a child, Benotto J said: 'The sexual orientation of the parties is not relevant to my decision. Families exist in a variety of forms.' Of course, in that case, the court had little option but to award custody to a homosexual person, as both claimants were lesbian.

The idea that the law should look for equivalents between homosexuality and heterosexuality, rather than merely formal equality, was also recognized in *R. v. Roy*,[10] where the court found that section 159 of the Criminal Code, making anal intercourse an offence in certain situations where vaginal intercourse would not be, was unconstitutional because of its disproportionate effect on homosexuals as opposed to heterosexuals. LeBel J, giving the opinion of the court, said:

> Bien que l'on puisse argumenter que ce régime législatif s'applique à tous les adolescents non mariés, l'effet de la loi est beaucoup plus préjudiciable aux homosexuels, pour qui les relations sexuelles anales représentent une pratique sexuelle courante. Pour les mineurs hétérosexuels, la pratique la plus courante demeure évidemment celle de la relation sexuelle vaginale, qui peut être pratiquée de consentement dès l'âge de quatorze ans. En d'autres termes, à partir d'une discrimination fondée sur l'âge, l'article 159 C. cr. nie aux mineurs homosexuels la liberté de choix et d'expression de leur sexualité.
>
> En conséquence, cette disposition impose un fardeau plus lourd au groupe des homosexuels et perpétue les stéréotypes et les désavantages historiques subis par le groupe, en violation des principes de liberté et de dignité humaine qui sous-tendent l'article 15 de la Charte.

What LeBel J says is significant in its acknowledgment of the symbolic role of certain laws for homosexuals, laws that do not have the same symbolism for heterosexuals. This symbolism can apply even if not all homosexuals actually engage in the activity that is the subject of the law and even if, on its face, the law does not distinguish between heterosexuals and homosexuals.

As I discussed in Chapter 2, homosexuality is rendered as 'other' just as much by treating it with kid gloves as by adopting negative stereotypes. Judges should not suddenly take the opposite of their historical approach so as to be overly protective of homosexuality, whether it be in terms of censorship or outing or heterosexism in violence. A judge need not overcompensate; this is simply another form of double standard. It may seem churlish to be critical of judges who have gone out of their way to be generous to homosexuals and homosexuality, but such an approach can simply move homosexuals as a group from inclusion with the criminal and the dangerous to inclusion with the childlike and the irresponsible. Judges may well despair that they are damned if they do and damned if they don't, but what is important is that they attempt to achieve equal, that is equivalent, treatment.

An example of judges striving to achieve such a result is found the B.C. Court of Appeal decision in *Little Sisters* in 1998.[11] The majority of the court dismissed the bookstore's appeal that the Customs legislation, at least as it applies to homosexual material, is unconstitutional. While the court's lack of criticism for a censorship system of prior restraints is disappointing, it is heartening that both the majority and the minority were clear in their opinion that homosexual material should be treated no differently from heterosexual material. The disagreement arose as to how to assess difference of treatment. Macfarlane JA, for the majority, opted for a test of formal equality: 'If the appellants' argument is that Parliament had no reasoned basis for apprehending harm because no harm results from the receipt and use by the gay/lesbian community of obscene material, then I must reject it. Harm is not to be determined by the standard of the gay/lesbian community but by application of a general community standard. The question is not whether harm will be caused to the gay/lesbian community by the importation of obscene material, but whether harm to society generally may be caused by importation and proliferation of such material'. Finch JA, dissenting, was receptive to arguments that homosexual material should not necessarily be subject to the same obscenity tests as heterosexual material. In particular, he doubted whether it was appropriate to apply the *Butler* decision. He said: 'There is, in my view, therefore an open question as to whether homosexual pornography would meet the "reasoned apprehension of harm" test discussed by Mr. Justice Sopinka.' Finch JA also said that the Crown had not proven the point that there is a risk of harm from homosexual pornography and that expert evidence produced by the Crown to that end was inconclusive. What is remarkable about both the minority and majority decisions is the effort made in each to achieve equality. Macfarlane JA arguably made the test much too formally equal and overlooked the differences between homosexual and heterosexual pornography, especially in light of the *Butler* case. Finch JA may have been too solicitous of the argument that while heterosexual pornography is bad, homosexual pornography is good. He did not, however, make conclusions on this point. Furthermore, he did not make the sweeping statements about homosexuals and their need for pornography made by Smith J in the trial decision. Finch JA's point was simply that the Crown did not make out the case it needed to justify a breach of a Charter guarantee under section 1. Finch JA certainly raised a valid point about the heterosexual-centredness of *Butler* and the need to look for equivalence between heterosexual and homosexual pornography rather than formal equality.

One of the surest signs of judicial acceptance of homosexuality as 'normal' is the willingness to recognize that homosexuals do not form one monolithic group, that one homosexual person cannot represent the views or the practices of all homosexuals. In *Kane v. Ontario (Attorney General)*,[12] the Ontario Court of Justice was asked to decide whether the definition of spouse in the Ontario Insurance Act was unconstitutional in excluding a same-sex person as spouse. Coo J alluded to disagreement within the homosexual community as to whether homosexuals ought to adopt heterosexual models such as marriage and spouses: 'Whether or not there are factions in any notional homosexual community that do or do not support the concept of a spousal or family atmosphere for couples is irrelevant. Undoubtedly some in the heterosexual community see things differently, and that too is irrelevant. Such social issues have nothing to do with legislative choice and judicial deference in regard thereto, or with any argument based on an incremental approach to the legislative process.'

Judicial recognition of diversity within the homosexual community is welcome so long as it does not mean judicial acceptance of and protection for only those homosexuals who resemble heterosexuals or heterosexual ideals in everything but the gender of their partners. Protection should not be reserved for mainstream sexual orientation in the sense of gay men who are 'straight-looking, straight-acting' or lesbians who look like the girl next door. It should also be extended to others, who are probably even more isolated.

Judges occupy an enhanced position, which accords them a responsibility to set and respect standards that govern society, as recent statements from a very senior level recognize. It is encumbent on all judges to be the leaders they are expected to be by virtue of their enhanced role under the Charter. This was strongly asserted by the Supreme Court of Canada when it overturned the Alberta Court of Appeal decision in *Vriend*.[13] With the exception of the lone dissenting judge, the judges emphatically disagreed with McClung JA's view that the case was inappropriate for a court to decide. They made it clear that, far from being inappropriate for a court to engage in such controversies, this role is in fact central to the Canadian concept of the judicial. Cory J, typically, made a forceful statement that members of different groups, including sexual orientation groups, need not be excluded:

It is easy to say that everybody who is just like 'us' is entitled to equality. Everyone finds it more difficult to say that those who are 'different' from us in some way should have the same equality rights that we enjoy. Yet so soon as we say any enumerated or analogous group is less deserving and unworthy of equal protection and benefit of the law all minorities and all of Canadian society are demeaned. It is so deceptively simple and so devastatingly injurious to say that those who are handicapped or of a different race, or religion, or colour or sexual orientation are less worthy. Yet, if any enumerated or analogous group is denied the equality provided by s. 15 then the equality of every other minority group is threatened. That equality is guaranteed by our Constitution. If equality rights for minorities had been recognized, the all too frequent tragedies of history might have ben avoided. It can never be forgotten that discrimination is the antithesis of equality and that it is the recognition of equality which will foster the dignity of every individual.[14]

With respect to the specific legislation impugned in *Vriend*, Cory J thought that the omission of sexual orientation as a protected ground in the IRPA created a distinction on the basis of sexual orientation. The 'silence' of the act with respect to discrimination on the ground of sexual orientation was not, therefore, 'neutral.' Gay men and lesbians were treated differently from other disadvantaged groups and from heterosexuals, who unlike gays and lesbians, received protection from discrimination on the grounds that are likely to be relevant to them.[15] Cory J said:

The exclusion sends a message to all Albertans that it is permissible, and perhaps even acceptable, to discriminate against individuals on the basis of their sexual orientation. The effect of that message on gays and lesbians is one whose significance cannot be underestimated. As a practical matter, it tells them that they have no protection from discrimination on the basis of their sexual orientation. Deprived of any legal redress they must accept and live in constant fear of discrimination. These are burdens which are not imposed on heterosexuals.

Perhaps most important is the psychological harm which may ensue from this state of affairs. Fear of discrimination will logically lead to concealment of true identity and this must be harmful to personal confidence and self-esteem. Compounding that effect is the implicit message conveyed by the exclusion, that gays and lesbians, unlike other individuals, are not worthy of protection. This is clearly an example of a distinction which demeans the individual and strengthens and perpetuates the view that gays and lesbians are less worthy of protection as individuals in Canada's society. The potential harm to the dignity and perceived worth of gay and lesbian individuals constitutes a particularly cruel form of discrimination.[16]

Expression is important for homosexuals and homosexuality. What homosexuality is, what a homosexual is, while impossible to define precisely, is certainly defined through expression. Certain resoundingly negative attitudes have long been expressed about homosexuals. It is through expression that such attitudes will be changed. Judicial expression plays a role in this process, as do judicial attitudes towards the expression of others – homosexuals and nonhomosexuals. Judges are probably now more aware of homosexuals and homosexuality and less likely to make an off-the-cuff remark. There are few instances now in which it is probable that a judge intends to insult homosexuals or homosexuality. Deliberate negative expression by a judge ought not to pass without comment by other judges. Judges have not been particularly good at taking their brethren to task. In *Vriend*, both Cory and Iacobucci JJ indirectly and gently criticized McClung JA's language and attitudes about homosexuals. For example, Iacobucci J said: 'In his reasons for judgment, McClung J.A. alludes to "moral" considerations that likely informed the Legislature's choice. However, even if such considerations could be said to amount to a pressing and substantial objective (a position which I find difficult to accept in this case) ...'[17] But no judge went out of his or her way to disapprove emphatically of such judicial language. In deciding that a government acts inappropriately in drafting laws that exclude groups like homosexuals, the court weakens its point by not taking a judge to task for using language that does exactly that.

While many recent cases demonstrate a change in the pattern of the past four decades, some concerns still exist. Judges should recognize the impediments to attitudinal change in the legal system in which they work. They should be conscious of the role a precedent-based legal system plays in perpetuating stereotypes. The common law has proven remarkably resilient and reliable largely because of the stability the precedent-based approach encourages. It does, however, also encourage a stability of other ideas and attitudes, such as the appropriate role and nature of the members of various groups, including homosexuals. Furthermore, the isolation of each particular case from others factually like it acts as a brake on change. Judges, like lawyers, generally group cases together in specific ways that have been developed over the generations: tort cases, theft cases, mortgage foreclosure cases. Often lost are groupings based on the nature of the parties before the court. Sometimes, of course, this is of no significance. But often the existing legal groupings tend to obscure what is at play in the way the law affects or is affected by the members of a particular group. Recognition of a problematic issue or attitude is the first step in addressing it. Related is the vexed issue of how to deal with a problem of general, traditionally negative treatment of the members of a group in the context of a single case that comes before the court. But the problems cannot even begin to be solved unless the courts take their respective turns in addressing the issues. Maybe one set of judicial reasons cannot do much on its own, but a number like it, particularly if they become 'normal,' can effect a great deal of change. Finally, it is essential that the judicial norms of equality and inclusion and accommodation are applied across the country and not limited to one or two provinces or urban areas. Enlightened judges are especially needed in some of the areas in which societal attitudes towards homosexuality have been less progressive.

Before closing I should note that there are qualifications and limitations to a study such as this. First, any critique of judicial expression and reaction to expression should not be interpreted as a first step in a form of thought/expression policing for the general public. Homosexuals have legitimately complained about censorship of homosexual expression in the past (and present). Great care has to be taken that censorship not be resurrected in an opposite form in situations that do not seriously threaten anybody. The expressive awareness and constraint I urge for the judiciary I do not advocate for the general public in any legally normative way. Furthermore, I emphasize again that judicial expression and attitudes alone do not tell the whole story. Judicial attitudes are an extension of more general legal and social attitudes. It is impossible to change judicial attitudes and expression completely without changing those more general legal and social attitudes. However, I think it is impossible to alter those more general attitudes without also changing judicial attitudes.

This study has at times made generalizations about judges. It is of course unfair to overgeneralize about judges, just as I have argued that judges should not make generalizations about homosexuals. Not all judges have engaged in generalization and the other practices I have detailed and commented on in this study. But it is fair to say that judges have often done so and to the extent that they have, they are rightly taken to task. All judges have an ongoing obligation to consider the ramifications of what they say and of what they do not say. Judges, while on the bench, do not have freedom of expression. They have an obligation to reflect and enhance the ideals of inclusion, accommodation, equality, and tolerance, particularly for those who, like homosexuals, can never have the numbers to be confident of legislative protection for and who have historically been deprived of the fruits of those ideals.

Notes

Introduction

1 *Egan v. Canada* (1995), 124 DLR (4th) 609 (SCC). See also *M. v. H.* (1996), 27
 OR (3d) 593 (Gen. Div.); *Veysey v. Canada (Correctional Service)*, [1990] 1 FC
 321 (TD), varied (1990), 43 Admin. LR 316 (FCA); *Brown v. British Columbia
 (Minister of Health)* (1990), 66 DLR (4th) 444 (BCSC); *Knodel v. British Columbia (Medical Services Commission)* (1991), 58 BCLR (2d) 356 (SC). For critiques
 of Canadian legal attitudes to homosexuality, see Mary Eaton, 'Lesbians,
 Gays and the Struggle for Equality: Reversing the Progressive Hypothesis,'
 Dalhousie Law Journal 17 (1994), 130; Carl F. Stychin, 'A Postmodern Constitutionalism: Equality Rights, Identity Politics and the Canadian National
 Imagination' *Dalhousie Law Journal* 17 (1994), 61. Human rights codes give
 similar protection, either expressly or by virtue of having such protection
 read in. See Donald G. Casswell, *Lesbians, Gay Men, and Canadian Law*
 (Toronto: Emond Montgomery 1996), chap. 3.
2 See Lorenne M.G. Clark, 'Liberalism and the Living-Tree: Women, Equality,
 and the Charter,' *Alberta Law Review* 2 (1990), 384 at 393.
3 Robert Martin, 'Criticising the Judges,' *McGill Law Journal* 28 (1982) 1, 22.
4 For a broader-based examination, see Gary Kinsman, *The Regulation of Desire:
 Homo and Hetero Sexualities*, rev. ed. (Montreal: Black Rose Books 1996).
5 Les Moran considers the issue of how the law has defined homosexuality
 and homosexuals in 'Sexual fix, Sexual Surveillance: Homosexual in Law,'
 chapter 10 of Simon Shepherd and Mick Wallis, eds., *Coming on Strong:
 Gay Politics and Culture* (London: Unwin Hyman 1989). Moran says: 'The
 law produces homosexuality through a curious collage of languages,
 medieval and modern' (188). The medieval is Christianity and the modern
 is medicine.

6 John Bell, 'The Judge as Bureaucrat,' in John Eekelaar and John Bell, eds., *Oxford Essays in Jurisprudence*, 3rd Series (Oxford: Oxford University Press 1987), 46.

7 See the excellent collection of essays in Sheilah L. Martin and Kathleen E. Mahoney, eds., *Equality and Judicial Neutrality* (Scarborough, Ont: Carswell 1987).

8 Robert Wintemute, *Sexual Orientation and Human Rights: The United States Constitution, the European Convention, and the Canadian Charter* (Oxford: Oxford University Press 1995), 15–16.

9 Montesquieu, *De l'esprit des lois*, 1748, quoted and translated by John Bell in *Policy Arguments in Judicial Decisions* (Oxford: Oxford University Press 1983), 1.

10 Many writers have commented on this judicial role in fostering change. See, for example, Ronald Dworkin, *Taking Rights Seriously* (London: Duckworth 1977); Lon L. Fuller, *The Morality of Law* (New Haven: Yale University Press 1964); Julius Stone, *Precedent and Law: Dynamics of Common Law Growth* (Sydney: Butterworths 1985). A Dworkinian interpretation of human rights is found in Richard Nordahl, 'Ronald Dworkin and the Defense of Human Rights,' *Canadian Journal of Law and jurisprudence* 8 (1995), 19.

11 For another consideration of judicial activism, see Mark R. MacGuigan, 'Sources of Judicial Decision Making and Judicial Activism,' in Martin and Mahoney, eds., *Equality and Judicial Neutrality*, 30–40.

12 See *Re Haig and the Queen* (1992), 94 DLR (4th) 1 (Ont. CA) (where the court read protection on the basis of sexual orientation into the Canadian Human Rights Act, RSC 1985, c. H-6); *Vriend v. Alberta*, [1994] 6 WWR 414 (Alta. QB) (where the court read protection on the basis of sexual orientation into the Individual's Rights Protection Act, RSA 1980, c. I-2); and *Newfoundland and Labrador (Human Rights Commission) v. Newfoundland and Labrador (Minister of Employment and Labour Relations)* (1995), 127 DLR (4th) 694 (Nfld SCTD). See also Shirish Chotalia, 'The *Vriend* Decision: A Case Study in Constitutional Remedies in the Human Rights Context,' *Alberta Law Review* 32 (1994), 825.

13 This is the interpretation given to *Swann v. Charlotte-Mecklenburg Board of Education*, 402 US 1 (1971).

14 In *Re Delius*, [1957] Chap. 299, the court accepted charitable status for an organization that promoted the music of Delius. Roxburgh J said: '... if it is charitable to promote music in general it must be charitable to promote the music of a particular composer, presupposing (as in this case I can assume) that the composer is one whose music is worth appreciating' (307). We assume the judge could tell if the music was not worth appreciating.

15 Others have commented on the role judges have in labelling and 'judging' things. Leon Trakman says: 'Regardless of the extent to which courts treat negative liberty as the essence of liberal pluralism, they cannot help but mediate among diverse social, economic, and political interests. Regardless of the extent to which judges purport to be neutral towards substantive differences among Canadian people, they cannot discount differences if they are to achieve justice.' Leon Trakman, 'Group Rights: A Canadian Perspective,' *International Law and Politics* 24 (1992), 1579 at 1583–4. Donald Casswell argues: 'To the extent that Canadian law continues to be based on heterosexist assumptions and continues to privilege heterosexuals ahead of lesbians and gay men, it reinforces, perpetuates and legitimizes heterosexual privilege and contributes to homophobia in general and homophobic violence in particular.' Casswell, *Lesbians, Gay Men, and Canadian Law*, 13. A brief analysis of judicial construction of homosexuality in the United States is found in Arthur S. Leonard, 'Homophobia, Heterosexism and Judicial Decision Making,' *Journal of Gay and Lesbian Psychotherapy* 1 (1991), 65.

16 *Thibaudeau v. M.N.R.*, [1994] 2 FC 189 at 211 (CA); appeal allowed (1995), 12 RFL (4th) 1 (SCC).

17 A Quebec judge, Mr Justice Jean Bienvenue, has recently attracted strong criticism for his comments that Jews died in Nazi concentration camps 'without suffering' and that 'when they fall, women reach a level of baseness that the most vile men could not reach.' André Picard, 'Jews Didn't Suffer, Quebec Judge Says,' *Globe and Mail*, 9 December 1995, A4. The judge later apologized. See 'Judge Retracts Remarks,' *Globe and Mail*, national edition, 16 December 1995, A6. In a hearing to investigate his behaviour there was testimony that Bienvenue called the accused in one case a 'Negress' and in the same case said: 'That has to be her lesbian friend. I wonder who plays the man in that relationship.' See Jack Branswell, 'Judge Referred to Accused as 'Negress, Lesbian',' *Vancouver Sun*, 6 March 1996, A3. On the perils of saying mean things about judges, see Jack Watson, 'Badmouthing the Bench: Is There a Clear and Present Danger? To What?' *Saskatchewan Law Review* 56 (1992), 113.

18 Bryan Schwartz argues that judges should not be seen as 'oracles' who know all the answers and that judges should themselves be aware of the limitations of their personal knowledge. A judge should be more like an artist than a performer and possess good communication skills. Bryan Schwartz, 'On Choosing Judges – Oracles and Performers; or Philosophers and Sages?' *Queen's Law Journal* 17 (1992), 479.

19 On judicial conduct, see Canadian Judical Council, *Commentaries on Judicial Conduct* (Cowansville, Que.: Yvon Blais 1991); Martin L. Friedland, *A Place*

Apart: Judicial Independence and Accountability in Canada (Canadian Judicial Council 1995); and Peter H. Russell, *The Judiciary in Canada: The Third Branch of Government* (Toronto: McGraw-Hill Ryerson 1987), Part 3.

20 See generally (and less absolutely), A. Wayne MacKay, 'Judicial Free Speech and Accountability: Should Judges Be Seen But Not Heard?' *National Journal of Constitutional Law* 3 (1993), 159 at 174.

21 There may be different considerations for judicial expression off the bench, which I do not consider here. See Jeremy Webber, 'The Limits to Judges' Free Speech: A Comment on the Report of the Committee of Investigation into the Conduct of the Hon. Mr Justice Berger,' *McGill Law Journal* 29 (1984), 369.

22 William A. Esson, 'The Judiciary and Freedom of Expression' (1985), 23 *University Western Ont. Law Review* 159 at 160.

23 Stone, *Precedent and Law*, 112, emphasis in original.

24 MacKay, 'Judicial Free Speech,' 179.

25 *Re Section 24, B.N.A. Act*, [1930] 1 DLR 98 (PC).

26 In *Egan v. Canada* (1993), 103 DLR (4th) 336 (FCA), Linden JA (dissenting) compared the case before him to the 'persons' case. The Women's Legal Education and Action Fund 'LEAF' organizes 'Person's Day Breakfasts' across Canada in part to mark the Privy Council decision.

27 Its justifications are dealt with elsewhere. See Frederick Schauer, *Free Speech: A Philosophical Enquiry* (Cambridge: Cambridge University Press 1982); Franklyn S. Haiman, *Speech and Law in a Free Society* (Chicago: University of Chicago Press 1982); Eric Barendt, *Freedom of Speech* (Oxford: Clarendon Press 1985); T. Scanlon, 'A Theory of Freedom of Expression,' in R.M. Dworkin, ed., *The Philosophy of Law* (Oxford: Oxford University Press 1977), 153–71. See, among many cases, *Irwin Toy Ltd. v. Quebec (Attorney-General)* (1989), 58 DLR (4th) 577 (SCC); *R. v. Keegstra* (1990), 61 CCC (3d) 1 (SCC); and *R. v. Butler* (1992), 89 DLR (4th) 449 (SCC).

28 For example, a conviction was quashed and a new trial ordered in an Ontario case because of the racist language used by the judge, who showed great hostility towards the accused. In giving his reasons for quashing the trial, Borins DCJ said: 'Such a cross-examination [of the accused by the trial judge] has no place in a Canadian court, nor do the views of the trial judge who, from his questioning of the appellant, appears to believe that the only impropriety in what the arresting officers said to the [Canadian] appellant was that they called him a "Paki" when they should have called him an "Indian".' *R. v. Goel* (1986), 27 CCC (3d) 438 at 447–8 (Dist. Ct).

29 See note 1, above.

30 Justice D.G. Blair, 'The Charter and the Judges: A View from the Bench,'

Manitoba Law Journal 13 (1983), 445 at 453. See also Pamela A. Chapman, 'The Politics of Judging: Section 1 of the *Charter of Rights and Freedoms,'* *Osgoode Hall Law Journal* 24 (1986), 867.

31 *Edwards Books & Art Ltd. v. The Queen*, [1986] 2 SCR 713 at 795.

32 Eaton, 'Lesbians, Gays and the Struggle for Equality Rights: Reversing the Progressive Hypothesis.'

33 With a couple of exceptions, the research for this book stopped on 1 June 1997. The computerized databases, in particular Quicklaw, are invaluable for this type of research. To find cases possibly involving some aspect of homosexuality I searched the following words and their variants: gay, homosexual, lesbian, sexual orientation, sodomy, gross indecency, anal intercourse, masturbation, same-sex, between women, queer, outing, faggot, lezzie, bisexual, heterosexual, HIV, and AIDS. In addition, I researched the indices of all Canadian law reports series, except those such as the *Personal Property Security Act Cases*, which did not seem particularly worthwhile for such purposes. Some reports are found in none of these places and the original court transcript was used; these cases were usually initially identified through news reports.

34 Many of the cases, of course, had little that was useful. Just under one-third are cited in this book.

35 See Casswell, *Lesbians, Gay Men, and Canadian Law.* Casswell is good not just for judicial decisions but provides a thorough treatment of statutory material and useful references to other works. A summary in plain English is John A. Yogis, Randall R. Duplak, and J. Royden Trainor, *Sexual Orientation and Canadian Law: An Assessment in the Law Affecting Lesbian and Gay Persons* (Toronto: Emond Montgomery 1996).

36 *Irwin Toy Ltd. v. Quebec (Attorney-General)*, at 607. See also *R. v. Keegstra*, at 24.

37 On the difficulties of terminology in this area, see Sarah Chinn and Kris Franklin, '"I Am What I Am" (Or Am I?): The Making and Unmaking of Lesbian and Gay Identity in *High Tech Gays,' Discourse* 15.1 (Fall 1992), 11–26; Wintemute, *Sexual Orientation and Human Rights*, 6–18. On 'queer' see Carl Stychin, *Law's Desire* (London: Routledge 1995), 140–7. On the historical development of terminology from a 'sodomite' to a 'queer' see Warren Johansson and William A. Percy, *Outing: Shattering the Conspiracy of Silence* (New York: Harrington Park Press 1994), 10–17.

38 See, e.g., Casswell, *Lesbians, Gay Men, and Canadian Law,* 233 and 408.

39 Ibid., 408.

40 Perhaps it is the word that dares not speak its name.

41 Note, Casswell uses 'heterosexual' as both a noun and an adjective even

though straight people are unlikely ever to use it. See, e.g., Casswell, Lesbians, Gay Men, and Canadian Law 474, for instances of both. I feel some brotherhood with Richard Dyer who uses 'gay' in day-to-day speech but is troubled by it. He comments: 'It's just that to use "gay" is a rather trivial word, too much suggesting only fun-fun-fun, not adequate to the complexities and variedness of being ... gay. No word could ever do all that, but "gay" feels like a delimitation, an insistence on one aspect.' Richard Dyer, 'In a word,' in *The Matter of Images: Essays on Representation* (London: Routledge 1993), 7. This chapter is very good on the problems of nomenclature. Unlike Dyer, who would not use the word 'homosexual,' I do. There may be other reasons for disliking the word 'homosexual.' The character A.E. Housman in Tom Stoppard's play, *The Invention of Love*, calls it a 'barbarity' because, 'It's half Greek and half Latin!' Tom Stoppard, *The Invention of Love* (London: Faber and Faber 1997), 94.

42 Thus, for instance, the *Toronto Star* refused to use the word 'gay' and insisted on 'homosexual' in 1974. See Donald W. McLeod, *Lesbian and Gay Liberation in Canada: A Selected Annotated Chronology, 1964–1975* (Toronto: ECW Press 1996), 168 and 185.

43 On issues involving lesbians and terminology, see Lynne Pearlman, 'Theorizing Lesbian Oppression and the Politics of Outness in the *Case of Waterman v. National Life Assurance*: A Beginning in Lesbian Human Rights/ Equality Jurisprudence,' *Canadian Journal of Women and the Law* 7 (1994), 454 at 455–66.

44 See, for example, Diana Majury, 'Refashioning the Unfashionable: Claiming Lesbian Identities in the Legal Context,' *Canadian Journal of Women and the Law* 7 (1994), 286.

45 Suzanne Pharr, *Homophobia: A Weapon of Sexism* (Inverness, Cal.: Chardon Press 1988), at 18. See also Sylvia A. Law, 'Homosexuality and the Social Meaning of Gender,' *Wisconsin Law Review* [1988], 187.

46 See Jonathan Dollimore, *Sexual Dissidence: Augustine to Wilde, Freud to Foucault* (Oxford: Clarendon Press 1991), 265. The language use by the court in *Boardman v. DPP*, [1974] 3 All ER 887 (HL) is instructive as to judicial attitudes of what is male and what is female. In that case, a schoolmaster sexually assaulted male students. The court said that this case was 'unusual' because 'It was not merely a straight case of a schoolmaster taking advantage of a pupil and indecently assaulting a pupil but that there was the "unusual feature" that a grown man attempted to get an adolescent boy to take the male part to the master's passive part in acts of buggery' (895, Lord Morris summarizing trial judge's findings) See also *R. v. Pinard and Maltais* (1982), 5 CCC (3d) 460 at 461, per Monet JA (Que. CA).

47 Cynthia Petersen, 'Envisioning a Lesbian Equality Jurisprudence,' in Didi Herman and Carl Stychin, eds., *Legal Inversions: Lesbians, Gay Men, and the Politics of Law* (Philadelphia: Temple University Press 1995), 118–37, at 120.
48 Majury, 'Refashioning the Unfashionable,' 315.
49 Ibid., 312.
50 This may be true of other concepts I use, such as 'paedophile.'

Chapter 1: What's in a Name?

1 See, generally, John Gibbons, ed., *Language and the Law* (London: Longman 1994).
2 And the common law system has successfully insinuated itself into many areas of Quebec's law.
3 Note that most western laws against male homosexuality stem from Lev. 20:13, which says: 'If a man also lie with mankind, as he lieth with a woman, both of them have committed an abomination: they shall surely be put to death; their blood *shall be* upon them.' This provision develops an earlier prohibition in Lev. 18:22: 'Thou shalt not lie with mankind, as with womankind; it *is* abomination.' The first abolition of punishment of homosexuality in the western world occurred in 1810, in the French Penal Code. This book cannot trace the history of the legal treatment of homosexuals in Canada. On historical matters, see Gary Kinsman, *The Regulation of Desire: Homo and Hetero Sexualities*, rev. ed. (Montreal: Black Rose Books 1996); Bruce Ryder, 'Straight Talk: Male Heterosexual Privilege,' *Queen's Law Journal* 16 (1991), 287; Alex K. Gigeroff, *Sexual Deviations in the Criminal Law: Homosexual, Exhibitionistic, and Pedophilic Offences in Canada* (Toronto: Clarke Institute of Psychiatry 1968); Terry L. Chapman, 'Male Homosexuality: Legal Restraints and Social Attitudes in Western Canada, 1890–1920' in Louis A. Knafla, *Law and Justice in a New Land: Essays in Western Canadian Legal History* (Toronto: Carswell 1986); T.L. Chapman, 'An Oscar Wilde Type: The "Abominable Crime of Buggery" in Western Canada, 1890–1920,' *Criminal Justice History* 4 (1983), 97–118; Margaret Leopold and Wendy King, 'Compulsory Heterosexuality, Lesbians, and the Law: The Case for Constitutional Protection,' (1985), 1 *Canadian Journal of Woman and the Law* 163; Philip Girard, 'From Subversion to Liberation: Homosexuals and the Immigration Act 1952–1977,' *Canadian Journal of Law and Society* 2 (1987), 1; Philip Girard, 'Sexual Orientation as a Human Rights Issue in Canada 1969–1985,' *Dalhousie Law Journal* 10 (1986), 267; Didi Herman, 'Are We Family? Lesbian Rights and Women's Liberation,' *Osgoode Hall Law Journal* 28 (1990), 789; Sharon Dale Stone, ed., *Lesbians in Canada* (Toronto: Between

the Lines 1990). On the history of sentencing homosexual offenders, see D.E. Saunders [*sic*], Note in *Criminal Law Quarterly* 10 (1967), 25. On the English background to hostility to homosexuality and sodomy, see Wayne C. Bartee and Alice Fleetwood Bartee, *Litigating Morality: American Legal Thought and Its English Roots* (New York: Praeger 1992), chap. 2, 'English Common and Statutury Law and Sodomy in American Law,' 31–55. The classic study of lesbianism over the centuries is Lillian Faderman, *Surpassing the Love of Men: Romantic Friendship and Love between Women from the Renaissance to the Present* (New York: William Morrow 1991). Research shows that lesbians were subject to laws in the Middle Ages and later for their actions. It is somewhat of a myth that the law was never interested in lesbians. See Louis Crompton, 'The Myth of Lesbian Impunity: Capital Laws from 1270 to 1791,' *Journal of Homosexuality* 6 (1980–1), 11. Terminology use over the centuries presents difficulties. On the difficulty of using the same terms – like homosexuality and sodomy – over the course of history, see Arthur N. Gilbert, 'Conceptions of Homosexuality and Sodomy in Western History,' *Journal of Homosexuality* 6 (1980–1), 57. On the possibly centuries-old use of 'gay' or 'gai' to mean homosexual, see John Boswell, *Christianity, Social Tolerance and Homosexuality: Gay People in Western Europe from the Beginning of the Christian Era to the Fourteenth Century* (Chicago: University of Chicago Press 1980), 43, note 6.

4 One notable exception is Jeremy Bentham who said: 'I have been tormenting myself for years to find if possible a sufficient ground for treating them [people we would call homosexuals] with the severity with which they are treated at this time of day by all European nations: but upon the principle of utility I can find none.' 'An Essay on "Paederasty",' (1978), 3 *Journal of Homosexuality* 389.

5 5 Eliz., c. 17.

6 25 Henry VIII, c. 6 (1533).

7 See generally Gigeroff, *Sexual Deviations in the Criminal Law,* 15, note 4.

8 Edward Coke, *Institutes of the Laws of England*, Third Part, chap. 10, 'Of Buggery, or Sodomy' (1658–9; London: Clarke 1823).

9 Gigeroff, *Sexual Deviations in the Criminal Law,* 8.

10 See also Britton, who says the penalty should be burning (Book I, chap. X), and Fleta, who says sodomites should be buried alive (Book I, chap. XXXV). This is also the punishment according to Britton for 'those who have connexion with Jews and Jewesses.' It is interesting to note that these two offences are set out in the same sentence with bestiality. *Britton: An English Translation*, F.M. Nichols, ed., (Washington, D.C.: John Byrne 1901), *Fleta* N.G. Richardson & G.O. Sayles, ed (London: Selden Society 1955).

11 See Wayne R. Dynes, ed., *Encyclopedia of Homosexuality* (Chicago: St James Press 1990), vol. 2, 'Nameless Sin (or Crime),' 873–4.

12 The term 'sodomy' can mean different things. I use it to mean anal sex between men unless the context indicates otherwise.

13 See Dynes, ed., *Encyclopedia of Homosexuality*, vol. 2, 'Nazism,' 882. See also Richard Plant, *The Pink Triangle* (New York: Henry Holt 1986). For a first-hand account of a homosexual prisoner in the Nazi concentration camps, see Heinz Heger, *The Men with the Pink Triangle* (Boston: Alyson 1980).

14 *The Report of the Committee on Homosexual Offences and Prostitution* ('The Wolfenden Report') (London: HMSO, CMND 247 1957).

15 There is a celebrated debate that followed from the Wolfenden Report between Lord Devlin and H.L.A. Hart as to whether the state had a duty to legislate to protect good morals. According to Devlin, since homosexuality is against Christianity and since Christianity is the basis for moral standards which, in turn, provide the basis for our legal system, the legal system can make a claim to take action against homosexual acts, even if done in private by consenting adults. Patrick Devlin, 'Morals and the Criminal Law,' in *The Enforcement of Morals* (London: Oxford University Press 1965). Hart argued: 'Homosexual intercourse between consenting adults in private is immoral according to conventional morality, but not an affront to public decency, though it would be if it took place in public.' H.L.A. Hart, *Law, Liberty and Morality* (Oxford: Oxford University Press 1963,) 45. This view is based on the notions of privacy. Both of these views, while highly contentious at the time, are largely irrelevant to the modern debate on outing. Homosexuality is not immoral; homosexual activity, per se, is not immoral.

16 *OED*, 'bugger.'

17 Robert Wintemute, *Sexual Orientation and Human Rights: The United States Constitution, the European Convention, and the Canadian Charter* (Oxford: Oxford University Press 1995), 251.

18 A general treatment of the effect of labels is found in Martha Minow, *Making all the Difference: Inclusion, Exclusion, and American Law* (Ithaca, N.Y.: Cornell University Press 1990).

19 See David Halperin, et al., *Before Sexuality: The Construction of Erotic Experience in the Ancient Greek World* (Princeton, N.J.: Princeton University Press 1990).

20 As Richard Dyer says: 'But *we* live in this society at this time, where some people do feel that they "are" lesbian or gay, and often enough to wish to make common cause with others who feel the same.' Richard Dyer, 'Introduction,' in *The Matter of Images: Essays on Representations* (London: Routledge 1993), 3.

21 Kinsman, *The Regulation of Desire*, 25.
22 One the problems of using labels is that, as Judith Butler says, 'identity categories tend to be instruments of regulatory regimes, whether as the nor-
malizing categories of oppressive structures or as the rallying points for a
liberatory contestation of that very oppression.' Judith Butler, 'Imitation
and Gender Insubordination,' chap. 1 of Diana Fuss, ed., *Inside/Out: Lesbian
Theories, Gay Theories* (London: Routledge 1991), 13–14.
23 On homophobia, see the articles in *Journal of Homosexuality* 10, nos. 1 and 2
(1984); and Guy Hocquenghem, *Homosexual Desire* (Durham, N.C.: Duke
University Press 1993). Cynthia Petersen has treated the subject of how
friends and relatives prefer to overlook the existence of heterosexism or
homophobia. She notes, for example, that when gay AIDS activist Joe
Rose was murdered on a city bus in 1989, having been taunted with
shouts of 'faggot,' Rose's father refused to accept that it was gay bashing.
Cynthia Petersen, 'A Queer Response to Bashing: Legislating against
Hate,' *Queen's Law Journal* 16 (1991), 237 at 246. 'Homophobia' is perhaps
not the happiest of terms but it is widely used. Gary Kinsman prefers the
word heterosexism to homophobia because 'it ["homophobia"] individu-
alizes and privatizes gay and lesbian oppression and obscures the social
relationships that organize it. It reduces homophobia to a mental illness,
detaching it from its social contexts and reproducing all the problems of
psychological definitions.' Kinsman, *The Regulation of Desire*, 33. The manifestations of homophobia are thus in a sense excused, as we will see in
several contexts in subsequent chapters. For example, 'homosexual panic'
is an excuse at times for killing homosexuals. I will use both 'heterosexism' and 'homophobia' and perhaps force homophobia to have a broader,
less individual psychological meaning than it logically should possess.
On 'homophobia,' Gregory Herek has written: 'Characterizing antihomosexual prejudice as a phobia has been criticized for several reasons,
including the implication that such prejudice is an irrational fear and a
manifestation of individual pathology rather than of cultural norms ...
Care should be taken, therefore, to identify homophobia as a prejudice,
comparable to racism and anti-Semitism, rather than an irrational fear
similar to claustrophobia or agoraphobia.' Dynes, ed., *Encyclopedia of
Homosexuality*, vol. 1, 'Homophobia,' at 552. Even with Kinsman's gloss,
homophobia is in fact often the proper word for my purposes in this book
because, as will become clear, especially in Chapter 4, the courts tend to
see issues involving negativity for homosexuals as in a sense personal
private issues between particular individuals that have no broader social
or state connection.

24 John Finnis, 'Law, Morality, and "Sexual Orientation"' *Notre Dame Journal of Law, Ethics and Public Policy* 9 (1995), 11.
25 Ibid., 14.
26 Gregory M. Herek, 'The Social Psychology of Homophobia: Toward a Practical Theory,' *NYU Review of Law and Social Change* 14 (1986), 923 at 928.
27 The same could be said of the legal profession as a whole. See James B. Stewart, 'Death of a Partner,' *The New Yorker*, 21 June 1993, 54–71.
28 An article in *Xtra West!* Reports that: 'At least two gay male lawyers have been appointed to the bench in Ontario this year. But both judges refused to talk. "It would be absolutely inappropriate for me to discuss this with you," one said. The other said that he wanted to talk about being gay, but that his understanding of the law is that judges are not allowed to discuss anything with the media.' 29 June 1995, 7. Heterosexual judges would be unlikely to think it is 'against the law' to talk about their wives or husbands. There is no study on the sexual orientation of judges in Canada; in fact, there are few studies of judges at all. The characterless façade helps the myth of impartiality. For studies of the Canadian judiciary, see Peter McCormick and Ian Greene, *Judges and Judging* (Toronto: Lorimer 1990); John Hogarth, *Sentencing as a Human Process* (Toronto: University of Toronto Press 1971); Peter McCormick, 'Judicial Career Patterns and the Delivery of Reasons for Judgment in the Supreme Court of Canada, 1949–1993,' *Supreme Court Law Review* 5 (1994), 499. McCormick and Greene note that most judges are married. 'As a result, judges may have some difficulty in understanding the problems of Canadians who are single (whether heterosexual or gay) or divorced' (68).
29 On who judges are, see A. Wayne MacKay, 'Judicial Free Speech and Accountability: Should Judges Be Seen but Not Heard?' *National Journal of Constitutional Law* 3 (1993), 159, at 167–9. On issues of appointing judges, see Claire L'Heureux-Dubé, 'Nomination of Supreme Court Judges: Some Issues for Canada,' *Manitoba Law Journal* 20 (1991), 600.
30 *Knodel v. British Columbia (Medical Services Commission)* (1991), 58 BCLR (2d) 356 (SC).
31 *Re Board of Governors of the University of Saskatchewan and Saskatchewan Human Rights Commission* (1976), 66 DLR (3d) 561 at 563, per Johnson J (Sask. QB).
32 *R. v. Neil* (1957), 26 CR 281 at 293 (SCC), per Cartwright J.
33 See, e.g., *Egan v. Canada* (1995), 124 DLR (4th) 609 (SCC), where L'Heureux-Dubé and McLachlin JJ concurred with Cory J; *Re Attorney General of Canada and Mossop*, (1993), 100 DLR (4th) 658 (SCC), where L'Heureux-Dubé and McLachlin dissented (along with Cory J); Greer J in *Layland v. Ontario*

(Minister of Consumer and Commercial Relations) (1993), 104 DLR (4th) 214 (Ont. Ct Gen. Div.).

34 See Bertha Wilson (Madame Justice), 'Will Women Judges Really Make a Difference?' *Osgoode Hall Law Journal* 28 (1990), 508; Peter McCormick and Twyla Job, 'Do Women Judges Make a Difference? An Analysis by Appeal Court Data,' *Canadian Journal of Law and Society* 8 (1993), 135; Joan Brockman, 'A Difference without a Distinction?' *Canadian Journal of Law and Society* 8 (1993), 149; S.L. Martin, 'Women as Lawmakers,' *Alberta Law Review* 30 (1992), 738.

35 See Jeffrey Weeks, 'Necessary Fictions,' in Jacqueline Murray, ed., *Constructing Sexualities* University of Windsor Working Papers in the Humanities I (1993), 93 at 103; Richard Collier, *Masculinity, Law and the Family* (London: Routledge 1995), 101–5.

36 E.g., Bruce Ryder, 'Straight Talk: Male Heterosexual Privilege,' *Queen's Law Journal* 16 (1991), 287.

37 Eve Kosofsky Sedgwick, *Epistemology of the Closet* (Berkeley: University of California Press 1990), 1.

38 The words 'homosexual' and 'heterosexual' were probably coined by Károly Mária Kertbeny in a letter to Karl Heinrichs Ulrichs 6 May 1868. Manfred Herzer, 'Kertbeny and the Nameless Love,' *Journal of Homosexuality*, 12 (1985), 1. The term 'homosexual,' therefore, was developed by a closeted advocate of homosexual rights. It came to be associated with an imposition by the scientific or medical community as a term of abnormality, but it did not in fact originate as such. The term 'bisexual' is the earliest term and was used in the first decade of the nineteenth century in botany to mean 'having the sexual organs of both sexes.' Dynes, ed., *Encyclopedia of Homosexuality*, 'Homosexual (Term),' 555. On bisexuals, see Loraine Hutchins and Lani Kaahumanu, *Bi Any Other Name: Bisexual People Speak Out* (Boston: Alyson 1991).

39 Diana Fuss writes: 'Heterosexuality can never fully ignore the close psychical proximity of its terrifyingly (homo)sexual other, any more than homosexuality can entirely escape the equally insistent societal pressures of (hetero)sexual conformity.' Fuss, 'Introduction,' *Inside/Out*, 3.

40 Eve Kosofsky Sedgwick is of the view that there is no overarching label that includes both 'homosexual' and 'gay': '"[H]omosexual" and "gay" seem more and more to be terms applicable to distinct, nonoverlapping periods in the history of a phenomenon for which there then remains no overarching label.' Sedgwick, *The Epistemology of the Closet*, 17.

41 See, on contingency in judicial decisions, Donna Greschner, 'Judicial Approaches to Equality and Critical Legal Studies,' in Sheilah L. Martin

and Kathleen E. Mahoney, eds., *Equality and Judicial Neutrality* (Scarborough, Ont.: Carswell 1987), 59–70.

42 'Sex' I use in a very elastic way in this book. Usually I mean an intimate physical act between two (or more) people when at least one of the two persons derives or purports to derive sensual gratification from the act. In some contexts, however, there is no reason why activity such as masturbation or voyeurism cannot be called 'sex.' Sometimes, the word simply means the same as what is often called 'gender.'

43 Jeffrey Weeks, 'Discourse, Desire and Sexual Deviance: Some Problems in a History of Homosexuality,' Kenneth Plummer, ed., *The Making of the Modern Homosexual* (London: Hutchinson 1981), 87.

44 See Leslie J. Moran, *The Homosexual(ity) of Law* (London: Routledge 1996), esp. chap. 5 'The Enigma of "Homosexual Offences."'

45 Richard Posner, *Sex and Reason* (Cambridge, Mass.: Harvard University Press 1992), chap. 11.

46 The Wolfenden Report, *para. 35.*

47 Jeffrey Weeks, *Invented Moralities: Sexual Values in an Age of Uncertainty* (New York: Columbia University Press 1995), 68.

48 The excessive investment in symbolism that accompanies every homosexual act is part of our society's practice of according to all sexual acts enormous significance beyond the act itself. The never-ending debates on depictions of sexual acts is another aspect. The label pornography, for example, bestows a negative connotation on material or expression so labelled. There is a distinction made between erotica and pornography, the former having some artistic value and the latter having none or very little. Pornography serves only to arouse the sexual desire of a person whereas erotica, it would seem, also elevates the mind or spirit. It is questionable why expression that raises or satisfies sexual desire alone is inherently bad. Many forms of expression raise sexual desire but appear to be acceptable because they stimulate consumer desire as well. What is so terrible about sexual desire or sexual function per se that they can be censored out of existence? Some depictions of a sexual nature might be done innovatively or with wit or style, but why should this elevate them from the category of pornography into that of erotica for the purposes of censorship? Some paintings of ships or trees or flora are functional, crude, unimaginative, or cliché but they are still paintings and subject to the same expression considerations and protections as a great masterpiece. Why should paintings, books, or photos of a sexual nature be any different? An attempt to distinguish is simply a retention of guilt feelings about sex: some sex is good, but we must not say that all sex is okay.

49 Wintemute, *Sexual Orientation and Human Rights*, 8. The last category is very subjective and probably means that only the person himself can decide whether it is appropriate to apply the label. Although this seems fair in some ways, it can encourage what might be called 'internal homophobia' and it fosters closeting. The problems inherent in leaving homosexual labelling to the person who is the subject of expression are discussed in Chapter 5, the chapter on 'outing.'

50 Richard Posner opines that a person's sexual preference is given not chosen, but the decision to engage in an particular sex act is a matter of choice. Posner, *Sex and Reason*, 87.

51 In *Newfoundland and Labrador (Human Rights Commission) v. Newfoundland and Labrador (Minister of Employment and Labour Relations)* (1995), 127 DLR (4th) 694 (Nfld TD), Barry J took the very progressive step of reading 'sexual orientation' into the Newfoundland Human Rights Code, but sought (apparently) to soothe ruffled feathers by saying that: 'If there is such a lack [of social support for such a measure], because of the opinion that homosexual activity is immoral, the public can be encouraged to recall the maxim "Hate the sin but love the sinner"' (716).

52 Finnis, 'Law, Morality, and "Sexual Orientation",' 15.

53 Ibid., 16.

54 E.g., Jon E. Grant, 'Note – "Outing" and Freedom of the Press: Sexual Orientation's Challenge to the Supreme Court's Categorical Jurisprudence,' *Cornell Law Review* 77 (1991), 103, at 107.

55 *Gaveronski v. Gaveronski* (1974), 45 DLR (3d) 317 (Sask. QB).

56 As I said in the Introduction, since I write as a gay man, it is possible that some of my generalizations about homosexuality do not really apply to lesbians, and perhaps I do not always realize that.

57 'Gay' had the meaning of a loose woman; 'faggot,' a slatternly woman, and 'queer,' a trollop. See Dynes, ed., *Encyclopedia of Homosexuality*, vol. 1, 'Effeminacy, Historical Semantics of,' 347–9. It is clear that an equation is made between gay men and women, an equation presumed to insult men.

58 Treatment of this 'numbers game' is found in Donald Casswell, *Lesbians, Gay Men, and Canadian Law* (Toronto: Emond-Montgomery 1996), 14–17.

59 The figure of 10 per cent of the population being homosexual to a greater or lesser extent comes from the 'Kinsey Report,' although it oversimplifies the findings of that report. See Alfred Kinsey, et al., *Sexual Behavior in the Human Male* (Philadelphia: W.B. Saunders 1949), esp. at 259–61 and chap. 21 (610–66) and Alfred Kinsey, et al., *Sexual Behavior in the Human Female* (Philadelphia: W.B. Saunders 1953), esp. chap. 11 (446–501). More recent reports suggest that only 1 per cent of men and one-third of 1 per cent of

women reported having only same-sex relations over the past five years. However, roughly 8 to 12 per cent of people experienced homosexual attractions but did not act on them. The figures varied greatly from country to country. *Globe and Mail*, Thursday, 18 August 1994, A1. These figures are useless. They say nothing about what attraction or sex is, nor do they consider the reasons why people would tell the truth or not or whether they used the terms in the same way.

60 But see Collier, *Masculinity, Law and the Family*, chap. 4.

61 See Minow, *Making all the Difference*, 53–60.

62 Jan Schippers, 'Homosexual Identity, Essentialism and Constructionism,' in Dennis Altman et al., eds., *Homosexuality, Which Homosexuality?* (London: GMP 1989), 143.

63 *McAleer v. Canada (Canadian Human Rights Commission)* (1996), 132 DLR (4th) 672 (FCTD).

64 Ibid., 685.

65 *Re Barkley and Barkley* (1980), 28 OR (2d) 136 (Prov. Ct – Fam. Div.), 141.

66 On the essentialist versus social construction debate, see Larry Gross, *Contested Closets: The Politics and Ethics of Outing* (Minneapolis: University of Minnesota Press 1993), 109–10; Richard D. Mohr, *Gays/Justice: A Study of Ethics, Society, and Law* (New York: Columbia University Press 1988); Schippers, 'Homosexual Identity, Essentialism and Constructionism,' 139–48; Weeks, 'Discourse, Desire and Sexual Deviance'; David F. Greenberg, *The Construction of Homosexuality* (Chicago: University Chicago Press 1988); Celia Kitzinger, *The Social Construction of Lesbianism* (London: SAGE Publications 1987); Richard R. Troiden, *Gay and Lesbian Identity: A Sociological Analysis* (Dix Hills, N.Y.: General Hall 1988), chaps. 6 and 7; and *Journal of Homosexuality* 24, nos. 3 and 4 (1993); Edward Stein, ed., *Forms of Desire: Sexual Orientation and the Social Constructionist Controversy* (New York: Garland 1990); Cheshire Calhoun, 'Denaturalizing and Desexualizing Lesbian and Gay Liberation,' *Virginia Law Review* 79 (1993), 1859; Morris B. Kaplan, 'Constructing Lesbian and Gay Rights and Liberation,' *Virginia Law Review* 79 (1993), 1877; Janet E. Halley, 'The Politics of the Closet: Towards Equal Protection for Gay, Lesbian, and Bisexual Identity,' *UCLA Law Review* 36 (1989), 915; and Collier, *Masculinity, Law and the Family*. The debate among lesbians is sometimes between essentialism and anti-essentialism rather than constructionism. See Daniel R. Ortiz, 'Creating Controversy: Essentialism and Constructivism and the Politics of Gay Identity,' *Virginia Law Review* 79 (1993), 1833; Teresa de Lauretis, 'Queer Theory: Lesbian and Gay Sexualities – An Introduction,' *Differences* 3 (1991), 111; and Jody Freeman, 'Defining Family in *Mossop v. DSS*: The Challenge of Anti-Essentialism and

Interactive Discrimination for Human Rights Legislation,' *University of Toronto Law Journal* 44 (1994), 14.

67 Carl Stychin thinks likewise and says that 'the vast majority of subscribers to the immutable/essentialist position within the lesbian and gay community are gay men, while more lesbians consider their sexuality to be socially constructed.' Carl Stychin, 'Essential Rights and Contested Identities: Sexual Orientation and Equality Rights Jurisprudence in Canada,' *Canadian Journal of Law and Jurisprudence* 8 (1995), 49, 58.

68 *R. v. Noyes* (1986), 6 BCLR (2d) 306 at 316 (BCSC); affirmed (1987), 22 BCLR (2d) 45 (CA); leave to appeal to SCC refused 16 May 1988, 27 BCLR (2d) xxxv.

69 *Anderson v. Luoma* (1986), 50 RFL (2d) 127 at 147 (BCSC).

70 *Layland v. Ontario (Minister of Consumer and Commercial Relations)* per Southey J, at 223.

71 For a treatment of how science has dealt with homosexuality as a subject for investigation, see Richard Green, *Sexual Science and the Law* (Cambridge, Mass.: Harvard University Press 1992). On science and psychology and homosexuality, see Michael Ruse, *Homosexuality* (Oxford: Blackwell 1988); Robert H. Hopcke, *Jung, Jungians and Homosexuality* (Boston: Shambhala 1991); Kenneth Lewes, *The Psychoanalytic Theory of Male Homosexuality* (New York: Simon and Schuster 1988); John Money, *Gay, Straight, and In-Between: The Sexology of Erotic Orientation* (New York: Oxford University Press 1988); and C.A. Tripp, *The Homosexual Matrix* (New York: McGraw-Hill 1975). On the origins of homosexuality, see the articles in *Journal of Homosexuality* 6, no. 4 (1981). On the innate nature of sexual orientation and the difficulty of 'sexual reorientation' see Richard Green, 'The Immutability of (Homo)sexual Orientation: Behavioral Science Implications for a Constitutional (Legal) Analysis,' *Journal of Psychiatry and the Law* 16 (1988), 537.

72 *R. v. Neve* (1994), 160 AR 255 (QB).

73 Ibid., 277.

74 See also *Knodel v. British Columbia (Medical Services Commission)*, where a good deal of psychiatric evidence was admitted just to show that homosexuals are capable of 'normal' ralationships.

75 See Morris B. Kaplan, *Sexual Justice: Democratic Citizenship and the Politics of Desire* (New York: Routledge 1997), esp. chap. 2, 'Historicizing Sexuality.'

76 Jeffrey Weeks sees sexual identities as 'simultaneously historical and contingent.' Weeks, 'Necessary Fictions,' 101.

77 *Partland v. Partland* (1960), 24 DLR (2d) 576 (Ont. HC).

78 Mary McIntosh, 'The Homosexual Role,' *Social Problems* 16 (Fall 1968), 182, reprinted as chap. 3 in Stein, ed., *Forms of Desire*, 27.

79 *Guay v. The Queen* (1978), 42 CCC (2d) 536 (SCC).

80 *R. v. Salida* ([1969] 1 OR 203 (Mag. Ct).

81 There is then back formation – the adjective that has become a noun becomes an adjective again. Thus a 'homosexual' act makes a person 'homosexual' and the neighbourhood he lives in becomes a 'homosexual' neighbourhood.

82 In particular, Canadian criminal law dealt with buggery and gross indecency. See Gigeroff, *Sexual Deviations*. On the fate of these crimes, see Bruce Ryder, 'Equality Rights and Sexual Orientation: Confronting Heterosexual Family Privilege,' *Canadian Journal of Family Law* 9 (1990), 39 at 63–4. Andrew Koppelman draws an analogy between sodomy laws and miscegenation laws in 'Note. The Miscegenation Analogy: Sodomy Law as Sex Discrimination,' *Yale Law Journal* 98 (1988), 15. Koppelman says of both types of laws: 'Beyond the immediate harm they inflict upon their victims, their purpose is to support a regime of caste that locks people into inferior social positions at birth' (147). The most famous case is *Klippert v. The Queen*, [1968] 2 CCC 129 (SCC). Of this case, Donald Casswell notes: 'The case of Everett Klippert stirred considerable public support for decriminalization of lesbian and gay sexual activity. In 1965, Klippert, who was a mechanic's helper in Pine Point, Northwest Territories, was questioned by the RCMP concerning an arson. Klippert was not a suspect in connection with the arson. For some reason, Klippert gave information to the police regarding his sexual activity with four other consenting adult males. Klippert was charged with four counts of gross indecency. He pleaded guilty and was sentenced to three years imprisonment.' Casswell, *Lesbians, Gay Men, and Canadian Law*, 108. Klippert was declared a 'dangerous sexual offender.' Justice J.H. Sissons of the NWT Territorial Court, in sentencing him, said of the indefinite period of detention for being a dangerous sexual offender: 'I think the penitentiary term is going to do the accused considerable harm and will not help him and will not help the public.' Quoted in Donald W. McLeod, *Lesbian and Gay Liberation in Canada: A Selected Annotated Chronology, 1964–1975* (Toronto: ECW Press 1996), at 24. See also Cyril Greenland, 'Dangerous Sexual Offenders in Canada,' *Canadian Journal of Criminology and Corrections* 14 (1972) 44.

83 See also Collier, *Masculinity, Law and the Family*, esp. 90–110.

84 See, e.g., L'Heureux-Dubé J in *Egan v. Canada*, Greer J in *Layland v. Ontario (Minister of Consumer and Commercial Relations)*, Harris Prov. Div. J in *R. v. Wilson*, [1991] OJ No. 1746 (QL) (Prov. Div.).

85 Or aborted. See 'Abortion okay if fetus has gay gene, scientist says,' *Vancouver Sun*, 17 February 1997, A9.

86 *R. v. Five Accused Persons*, 12 July 1961, Magistrate Rice, see Criminal Law Quarterly 4 (1961–62), 124.

87 *R. v. Veysey*, [1989] OJ No. 1015 (QL) (CA). Throughout this book where there are citations to electronic data bases, such as Quicklaw 'QL,' there are no page references given.

88 *Partland v. Partland.*

89 Ibid., at 581.

90 *R. v. Lupien*, [1970] 2 CCC 193 at 204 (SCC).

91 See *R. v. Noyes.*

92 *R. v. Roestad* (1971), 19 CR (NS) 190 (Ont. Co. Ct): leave to appeal refused (1971), 19 CR (NS) 235n (Ont. CA).

93 Ibid., 230. There was also adduced evidence to the contrary.

94 *Children's Aid Society of the District of Thunder Bay v. T.T.*, [1992] OJ No. 2975 (QL) (Prov. Div.).

95 *Anderson v. Luoma.*

96 *Egan v. Canada.*

97 Ibid., 626.

98 *Re Board of Governors of the University of Saskatchewan.*

99 Ibid., at 562.

100 In *R. v. Patterson* (1972), 9 CCC (2d) 364 (Ont. Co. Ct), there was a charge of soliciting for the purposes of prostitution. The male accused was dressed up as a female and was caught by the police opening the trousers of a man who did not know (it seems) that the accused was male. Clunis Co. Ct J, after discussing whether a male could be a 'prostitute,' said: 'The conduct of this accused is abhorrent to all but a small fraction of our society. The preponderant majority would feel no doubt that conduct of this kind is too revolting to permit an acquittal based on the fine meaning of words. I incline to that view' (367). So the judge is critical of the (secret) homosexuality involved and not really of the prostitution. But the judge decided that the accused could not be a prostitute because all dictionary definitions of prostitute referred to females. Cf. *R. v. Obey* (1973), 11 CCC (2d) 28 (BCSC), where it was decided that a male can be a prostitute. There are many cases of the old category of the criminal sexual psychopath that deal with homosexuals. An example is *R. v. Neil* (1957), 26 CR 281 (SCC), where Cartwright J said, in summary of the facts, that the accused 'has had a recurring abnormal desire to indulge in homosexual practices' (293).

101 *R. v. Fraser* (1980), 55 CCC (2d) 503 at 514 (Alta. CA).

102 'Homosexual' is already identified as abnormal just by being named. One would never see the word 'heterosexual' when there was a charge of advances made by a man to a woman.

103 *R. v. Fraser.*

104 Michèle L. Caron, 'Variations sur le thème de l'invisibilisation,' *Canadian Journal of Women and Law* 7 (1994), 271, 277.

105 *Morrison v. Morrison* (1972), 2 Nfld & PEIR 465 (PEISC).

106 Ibid., at 471. This was the first Canadian case in which 'engagement in a homosexual act' was used as grounds for divorce. Noted in McLeod, *Lesbian and Gay Liberation in Canada*, 90.

107 This is part of larger gender and gender-identification issues. See Robert Wintemute, 'Recognising New Kinds of Direct Sex Discrimination: Transsexualism, Sexual Orientation and Dress Codes,' *Modern Law Review* 60 (1997), 334; Jean-Louis Baudoin, 'La vérité et le droit des personnes: aspects nouveaux,' Revue générale de droit 18 (1987), 801.

108 *H.I.M. v. W.A.M.*, [1994] BCJ No. 2824 (QL) (Prov. Ct).

109 *R. v. DeBattista* (1986), 26 CCC (3d) 38 (Man. CA).

110 Ibid., at 40. On the history of sentencing homosexual offenders, see D.E. Saunders, 'Note,' in *Criminal Law Quarterly* 10 (1967), 25.

111 *R. v. LeBeau and Lofthouse* (1988), 41 CCC (3d) 163 (Ont. CA), appeal quashed (1990), 149 NR 236 (SCC).

112 Ibid., at 183.

113 Ibid., at 189.

114 *R. v. Silva* (1995), 26 OR (3d) 554 at 558 (Gen. Div.), 558, per Zelinski J.

115 Ibid., 559.

116 *Brand v. College of Physicians and Surgeons of Saskatchewan*, [1989] 5 WWR 516 (Sask. QB); affirmed [1990] 3 WWR 272 (Sask. CA).

117 Ibid., at 525.

118 *R. v. Caskenette* (1993), 80 CCC (3d) 439 (BCCA).

119 Ibid., at 441. See also *R. v. G.B.H.*, [1985] OJ No. 702 (QL) (Prov. Ct – Fam. Div.). For cases associating homosexuality with paedophilia, see also *R. v. Roestad; R. v. Tetley* (1985), 40 Alta. LR (2d) 409 (CA); *Young v. R.* (1980), 27 CR (3d) 85 (BCCA); *R. v. Dubois* (1982), 69 CCC (2d) 494 (Alta. CA).

120 *R. v. Hansford* (1987), 33 CCC (3d) 74 at 85 (Alta. CA); at 85, leave to appeal to SCC refused (1987), 56 CR (3d) xxviii.

121 *R. v. Kluke*, [1987] OJ No. 766 (QL) (CA).

122 *R. v. Ryznar* (1986), 43 Man. R (2d) 143 (CA); leave to appeal to SCC refused (1986), 46 Man. R (2d) 160n.

123 Ibid., at 145, per Philp JA.

124 See also *R. v. Robertson* (1979), 46 CCC (2d) 573 (Ont. CA) – 'homosexual act' at 575 in the context of a charge against a Scout leader of sexually assaulting three boys on a camping trip; *R. v. Pilgrim* (1981), 64 CCC (2d) 523 (Nfld CA) – 'homosexual relations' at 527 in the context of a charge

against a school principal of indecent assault against male students; *R. v. Hill* (1985), 51 CR (3d) 97 (SCC) – 'homosexual lovers' and 'homosexual assault' at 105 and 110 in a case of first degree murder and a defence of provocation; *R. v. Hansford* – 'homosexual approach' at 89 in a charge of murder and defence of provocation.

125 *Re L. (R.),* [1981] OJ No. 382 (QL) (Co. Ct).

126 *C.A. v. Critchley* [1997] BCJ No. 1020 (QL) (SC).

127 *R. v. Ruby,* [1986] NJ No. 154 (QL) (CA).

128 See Chapter 5.

129 In the United States, the legal system acquiesces in inferiorization of gays by allowing them at times to use 'Doe' designations or their initials simply because they are gay. See Robert G. Bagnall, Patrick C. Gallagher, and Joni L. Goldstein, 'Burdens on Gay Litigants and Bias in the Court System: Homosexual Panic, Child Custody, and Anonymous Parties,' *Harvard Civil Rights – Civil Liberties Law Review* 19 (1984), 546–58.

130 Mary Eaton, 'Homosexual Unmodified: Speculations on Law's Discourse, Race, and the Construction of Sexual Identity,' in Didi Herman and Carl Stychin, eds., *Legal Inversions: Lesbians, Gay Men, and the Politics of Law* (Philadelphia: Temple University Press 1995), 51.

131 John Boswell, 'Categories, Experiences and Sexuality,' in Stein, ed., *Forms of Desire*, chap. 7, 143.

132 *Layland v. Ontario (Minister of Consumer and Commercial Relations).*

133 Ibid., at 223, Sirois J in concurrence.

134 *Canada v. Ward,* [1993] 2 SCR 689.

135 *Veysey v. Canada,* [1990] 1 FC 321 at 329 (TD); at 329 varied (1990), 43 Admin. LR 316 (FCA).

136 *Egan v. Canada,* at 619.

137 Ibid.

138 Stychin, 'Essential Rights and Contested Identities,' 59.

139 Sedgwick, *The Epistemology of the Closet*, 41.

140 Ibid., 42.

141 Ibid.

142 Nicole La Violette, 'The Immutable Refugees: Sexual Orientation in *Canada (A.G.) v. Ward,*' *University of Toronto Faculty of Law Review* 55 (1997), 1 at 37.

143 Ibid.

144 Ibid., 41.

145 *Re Inaudi* (unreported), IRB No. T91-04459, 9 April 1992. See Ellen Vagelos, 'The Social Group that Dare Not Speak Its Name: Should Homosexuals Constitute a Particular Social Group for Purposes of Obtaining Refugee

Status? Comment on *Re: Inaudi,' Fordham International Law Journal* 17 (1993), 229.

146 *Veysey v. Canada.*
147 See Vagelos, 'The Social Group That Dare Not Speak Its Name,' 265.
148 Weeks, *Invented Moralities*, 7.
149 On invisibility see Jane Rule, 'Lesbian and Writer: Making the Real Visible,' in Margaret Cruikshank, ed., *New Lesbian Writing* (San Francisco: Grey Fox Press 1984), 96–9, at 97; Suzanne Pharr, *Homophobia: A Weapon of Sexism* (Inverness, Cal.: Chardon Press 1988); Marshall Kirk and Hunter Madsen, *After the Ball: How America Will Conquer Its Fear and Hatred of Gays in the 90s* (New York: Doubleday 1989); Stuart Byron, 'The Closet Syndrome,' in Karla kay and Allen Young, eds., *Out of the Closets: Voices of Gay Liberation* (New York: Douglas 1972), 58–65.
150 See Randall W. Jones and John E. Bates, 'Satisfaction in Male Homosexual Couples,' in John DeCecco, ed., *Gay Relationships* (New York: Haworth 1988); George Weinberg, *Society and the Healthy Homosexual* (New York: St Martin's Press 1972).
151 Dyer, 'Introduction,' *The Matter of Images*, 1.
152 Duncan Kennedy, 'Freedom and Constraint in Adjudication: A Critical Phenomenology,' *Journal of Legal Education* 36 (1986), 518 at 537.
153 On stereotypes, see Dyer, 'The role of stereotypes,' in *The Matter of Images*, 11–18.
154 *R. v. T.D.E.* (1991), 116 AR 382 (Prov. Ct).
155 See the discussion of the association of homosexuality with violence in Chapter 4.
156 See, e.g., *Re Attorney-General of Canada and Mossop* (1990), 71 DLR (4th) 661 (FCA); *Re Attorney-General of Canada and Mossop*, [1993] 1 SCR 554; *Egan v. Canada.*
157 See Catherine MacKinnon, *Feminism Unmodified* (Cambridge, Mass.: Harvard University Press 1987), Part III; *R. v. Butler* (1992), 89 DLR (4th) 449 (SCC).
158 *M. v. H.* (1996), 31 OR (3d) 417 at 451 (CA).
159 On equivalency, see Freeman, 'Defining Family in *Mossop v. DSS.*'
160 Ibid., 435.
161 Ibid., 436–7.
162 Janice Ristock, '"And Justice for All?" ... The Social Context of Legal Responses to Abuse in Lesbian Relationships,' *Canadian Journal of Women and the Law* 7 (1994), 415 at 428.
163 Paul Siegel, 'Second Hand Prejudice, Racial Analogies and Shared Showers: Why "Don't Ask, Don't Tell" Won't Sell,' *Notre Dame Journal of Law,*

Ethics and Public Policy 9 (1995), 185 at 209, quoting Ellis Close, *The Rage of a Privileged Class* (1993), 55–6.

Chapter 2: Censoriousness and Censorship

1 See *R. v. Hicklin* (1868), LR 3 QB 360; *R. v. National News Co. Ltd.*, [1953] OR 533 (CA). This approach to obscenity was ruled superfluous to the Criminal Code test for obscenity in *Brodie, Dansky and Rubin v. The Queen*, [1962] SCR 681 by some judges and by the Ontario Court of Appeal in *R. v. C. Coles Co. Ltd.*, [1966] 2 OR 777.

2 See *R. v. Tremblett* (1975), 8 APR 482 (Nfld Mag. Ct); *R. v. Before and After* (1982) Ltd. (1982), 111 APR 17 (Nfld Dist. Ct); *R. v. Penthouse Int'l Ltd.* (1979), 96 DLR (3d) 735 (Ont. CA), leave to appeal refused (1979), 96 DLR (3d) 735n (SCC); *R. v. Pereira-Vasquez* (1988), 43 CCC (3d) 82 (BCCA); *R. v. Cinema International Canada Ltd.* (1982), 13 Man. R. (2d) 335 (CA).

3 *Little Sisters Book and Art Emporium v. Minister of Justice* (1996), 131 DLR (4th) 486 (BCSC); affirmed [1998] BCJ No. 1507 QL (CA). An account of the trial of this case is contained in Janine Fuller and Stuart Blackley, *Restricted Entry: Censorship on Trial* (Vancouver: Press Gang 1995).

4 See *R. v. Butler* (1992), 89 DLR (4th) 449 at 464–6 (SCC).

5 On censorship, see, e.g., Neil Boyd, 'Censorship and Obscenity: Jurisdiction and the Boundaries of Free Expression,' *Osgoode Hall Law Journal* 23 (1985), 37; Michael Alexander, 'Censorship and the Limits of Liberalism,' *University of Toronto Faculty of Law Review* 47 (1988), 58; Leo Groarke, 'Pornography, Censorship, and Obscenity Law in Canada,' *Windsor Review of Legal and Social Issues* 2 (1990), 25.

6 There are five aspects of this judicial censoriousness, which I explore below.

7 *Re Priape Enrg. and the Deputy Minister of National Revenue* (1979), 52 CCC (2d) 44 (Que. Super. Ct – Crim Div.).

8 Ibid., 48. See also *R. v. Pereira-Vasquez*, where the court said that: 'Many publications which would not have been tolerated in 1962 are now tolerated' (87); and *R. v. K. and H.* (1957), 26 CR 186 (Alta. SC).

9 See also *R. v. L. (G.E.)*, [1988] BCJ No. 860 (QL) (Co. Ct).

10 *Little Sisters.* For a sampling of some of the writings detained in this case, see *Forbidden Passages: Writings Banned in Canada* (Pittsburgh: Cleis 1995).

11 This is not the only case to have dealt with customs seizures. See e.g., *Glad Day Bookshop Inc. v. Canada (Deputy Minister of National Revenue, Customs and Excise – M.N.R.)* (1992), 90 DLR (4th) 527 (Ont. Ct Just. – Gen. Div.) and *Re Priape Enrg.*

12 *Little Sisters*, 492.

13 Ibid., 502.

14 Fuller and Blackley, *Restricted Entry*, 111.

15 *Little Sisters*, 511.

16 Ibid., 512.

17 Ibid., 507.

18 Ibid., 519.

19 Ibid.

20 Ibid.

21 Ibid., 520. Code 9956(a) of the Customs Tariff prohibits the importation of goods described as '9956. Books, printed paper, drawings, paintings, prints, photographs or representations of any kind that (a) are deemed to be obscene under subsection 163(8) of the *Criminal Code*.'

22 Ibid., 515.

23 Ibid., 516.

24 Ibid.

25 Ibid., 517.

26 Ibid., 518.

27 See a discussion of this case in Christopher Nowlin, 'The Relevance of Stereotypes to s. 15 Analysis – *Little Sisters Book and Art Emporium et al. v. The Minister of Justice et al.*,' *UBC Law Review* 30 (1996) 333.

28 For an example of an analysis of a non-Canadian case on 'homosexuality,' see Leslie J. Moran's analysis of *Dudgeon v. UK* (1982), 4 EHRR 149 in *The Homosexual(ity) of Law* (London: Routledge 1996), 174–80.

29 *R. v. Prairie Schooner News Ltd. and Powers* (1970), 1 CCC (2d) 251 at 262 (Man. CA); leave to appeal refused, [1970] SCR x.

30 *Nielsen v. Canada*, [1992] 2 FC 561 (TD).

31 Ibid., 577.

32 *Vriend v. Alberta* (1996), 132 DLR (4th) 595 at 618 (Alta. CA); reversed (1998), 156 DLR (4th) 385 (SCC). See Chapter 3.

33 *Re Priape Enrg.*

34 Ibid., 48, per Hugessen ACJQ.

35 *R. v. L. (G.E.).*

36 There are attempts to sensitize the legal profession to homosexual issues. For example, the Law Society of British Columbia has studied sexual orientation issues in the profession. They have tried to get messages to lawyers. See, e.g., Gail H. Forsythe, 'Sexual orientation – two professional experiences,' in Law Society of BC *Benchers' Bulletin*, April 1997, 6.

37 *R. v. Prairie Schooner News.*

38 Ibid., 256.

39 *R. v. LeBeau; R. v. Lofthouse* (1988), 41 CCC (3d) 163 (Ont. CA); appeal quashed for mootness (because of death) (1990), 149 NR 236 (SCC).

40 The court explored this issue, even though the court said it was not necessary to do so.

41 *Egan v. Canada* (1995), 124 DLR (4th) 609 (SCC). See Dianne Pothier, 'M'Aider, Mayday: Section 15 of the *Charter* in Distress,' *National Journal of Constitutional Law* 6 (1996), 295.

42 Ibid., 625. This was supported by Finlayson JA, dissenting, in *M. v. H.* (1996), 31 OR (3d) 417 at 430. (CA).

43 *Egan v. Canada* 627.

44 *Re Attorney-General of Canada and Mossop* (1990), 71 DLR (4th) 661 (FCA); appeal dismissed (1993), 100 DLR (4th) 658 (SCC). See Jody Freeman, 'Defining Family in *Mossop v. DSS:* The Challenge of Anti-Essentialism and Interactive Discrimination for Human Rights Legislation,' *University of Toronto Law Journal* 44 (1994), 41.

45 *Re Attorney General of Canada and Mossop*, 673–4.

46 *Anderson v. Luoma* (1986), 50 RFL (2d) 127 at 147 (BCSC).

47 *R. v. Duvivier, Kowalchuk and Hollingsworth* (1990), 75 OR (2d) 203 at 211 (HCJ), affirmed (1991), 3 OR (3d) 49 (CA).

48 N. Kathleen ('Sam') Banks discusses this double standard and the increased burden on homosexual plaintiffs in her comment on the *Knodel v. B.C. (Medical Services Commission)* (1991), 58 BCLR (2d) 356 (SC) case in *Canadian Journal of Family Law* 11 (1993), 287. In particular, Banks criticizes the heterosexist approach in a judgment that appears to be sympathetic to homosexuals. For example, Banks points out that the judge's finding in *Knodel* that the two men were 'living together as husband and wife' perpetuates the heterosexist assumptions about relationships.

49 *Egan*, 672.

50 Ibid., 682.

51 *Re Priape Enrg.*

52 Ibid., 49.

53 In a recently reported case, a heterosexual couple was fined $100 for kissing while nude on a public beach in Ontario. They were watched by about a hundred people. See *Globe and Mail* (national edition), 19 February 1997, A4. See also Jeff Moore, 'When gay couples dare to show their hand,' *Globe and Mail* (national edition), 30 July 1993, A16.

54 David Dyzenhaus, 'Regulating Free Speech,' *Ottawa Law Review* 23 (1991), 289 at 304.

55 *Re Priape Enrg.* at 50.

56 *R. v. K. and H.*

57 Ibid., 188.
58 *R. v. Mason* (1981), 59 CCC (2d) 461 (Ont. Prov. Ct – Crim. Div.).
59 Ibid., 469.
60 Ibid., 470.
61 Ibid., 476.
62 Ibid., 479 (emphasis added).
63 *Little Sisters*, at 522.
64 Brenda Cossman and Bruce Ryder, 'Customs Censorship and the *Charter*: The *Little Sisters* Case,' *Constitutional Forum* 7 (1996), 103 at 105.
65 See also Nowlin, 'The Relevance of Stereotypes.'
66 *R. v. Butler.*
67 *Little Sisters.*
68 Ibid., 524.
69 *Vriend v. Alberta.*
70 Ibid.
71 Donald Casswell, having discussed some cases on sex in public places, says: 'It is impossible to leave these cases without comment on why some men go to public washrooms to meet other men for sexual gratification. No doubt there are some who choose the public washroom venue because it adds excitement to their sexual activity. However, it is likely others resort to public washrooms because they are unable to identify themselves as gay, and meeting other men in washrooms is the furthest they can come out of the closet to satisfy their desire for sexual activity with other men. If "caught," they can at least say they were "just using the toilet." The phenomenon of men going to washrooms for sexual contact with other men is, at least in part, another manifestation of homophobia's power in our society.' Donald Casswell, *Lesbians, Gay Men, and Candian Law* (Toronto: Emond Montgomery 1996), 106–7. As for reasons why men go to such places for sex, I suspect the second of Casswell's reasons leads to the first.
72 *R. v. Salida*, [1969] 1 OR 203 at 209 (Mag. Ct). See also *R. v. Cinema International; R. v. Before and After; R. v. Video World Ltd.* (1985), 22 CCC (3d) 331 (Man. CA); affirmed (1987), 35 CCC (3d) 191 (SCC); *R. v. National News Co. Ltd.*, [1953] OR 533 (CA); *R. v. C* (1981), 84 APR 451 (Nfld Dist. Ct Judge's Crim. Ct). Distaste for homosexual activity was expressed in *R. v. Patterson* (1972), 9 CCC (2d) 364 (Ont. Co. Ct). Cf. the case of *R. v. Obey* (1973), 11 CCC (2d) 28 (BCSC). Even the vaguest hint of homosexual interest is disgusting to the court. This appears to have been the cause for comments made in *R. v. Munster* (1960), 129 CCC 277 (NSSC). The accused was charged with the offence of making obscene pictures contrary to s. 150(1)(a) of the Criminal Code. The accused, an amateur painter and sculptor, took photos of his

nude sons. He said the photos were for his art work. The magistrate acquit-
ted him, saying the photos did not come within the definition of obscenity
as having the dominant characteristic of undue exploitation of sex. The
Supreme Court ordered a new trial, noting that some of the pictures 'seem
to give prominence to the sexual organs of the boys' (per Ilsley CJ, 279).
Ilsley CJ noted authority that said that just because paintings of women in a
gallery or textbook are not obscene does not mean that copies of them can
be distributed on the street. The court used the imagery of such pictures
having 'a tendency to deprave and corrupt' (281). Again we have the view
that art is somehow not entirely respectable and might deprave and corrupt
the masses. The courts have an especial horror of the male genitals and the
depravity feared if pictures of naked men were distributed on the street is
no doubt a fear of homosexuality. The concern here was not so much with
the welfare of the boys but with the homosexual association of such activities and the undermining influence on society it could contribute to. Here it
is better to censor art that has some homosexual connotation than to let
such expression flourish. The court ordered a new trial.
73 *R. v. Duthie Books Ltd.*, [1967] 1 CCC 254 (BCCA). See also *Guay v. The Queen*
(1978), 42 CCC (2d) 536 (SCC).
74 *R. v. Duthie Books Ltd.*, 258.
75 *R. v. Pinard and Maltais* (1982), 5 CCC (3d) 460 (Que. CA).
76 Ibid., 461.
77 Ibid.
78 Ibid., 464. The need to associate homosexuality with sex when the identification is really irrelevant to the case at hand is seen again in *R. v. Pisces
Health Spa Ltd.* (1981), 63 CCC (2d) 427 (Alta. CA), where there was a charge
of keeping a common bawdy house. The court thought it necessary to say
that it made no difference whether a bawdy house was homosexual or heterosexual. Nonetheless, it went out of its way to point out that this was a
homosexual bawdy house.
79 The censoriousness of the court in its equation of homosexuality with perverse sex is sometimes less direct. In *R. v. Bishop*, [1970] 5 CCC 387 (Ont.
Prov. Ct), one man left another man a note asking if he wanted to have sex
with him. The court found there was no offence committed because the
accused was seeking to obtain consent and did not want to have sex in a
public place. However, the judge showed his dislike for such activity by
lamenting the decision:

> There is no attempt, in the evidence, to indicate he wanted to do it
> in a public place. In my opinion there is no evidence upon which a
> properly instructed jury could find the accused guilty of the

offence with which he was charged [attempt to commit gross inde-
cency]. I think it is reprehensible.

I think that perhaps for the protection of the public the Parliament should amend the Act so an attempt to persuade someone to
commit such an act itself would be a separate offence (390, per
McMahon Prov. Ct J).

There is of course no equivalent offence for heterosexual acts. This judge
would advocate in effect that gay sex be made a crime. Note that there was
no comment about the police tactics in monitoring this episode. The man
who received the note took it to the police who told him two play along
until they 'caught' the accused.

80 *Saunders v. Saunders* (1989), 20 RFL (3d) 368 (BC Co. Ct).
81 Ibid., 370–1.
82 On same-sex couples see Bruce Ryder, 'Becoming Spouses: The Rights of
    Lesbian and Gay Couples,' [1993] *Special Lectures of the Law Society of Upper
    Canada – Family Law*, 399; Patricia Lefebour, 'Same Sex Spousal Recognition
    in Ontario: Declarations and Denials: A Class Perspective,' *Journal of Law
    and Social Policy* 9 (1993), 272. For a somewhat cool view of same-sex cou-
    ples, see Édith Deleury, 'L'union homosexuelle et le droit de la famille,'
    Cahiers de droit 25 (1984), 751.
83 Good theoretical treatments of gay marriage are: Alice Woolley, 'Excluded
    by Definition: Same-Sex Couples and the Right to Marry,' *University of
    Toronto Law Journal* 45 (1995), 471; Nitya Duclos, 'Some Complicating
    Thoughts on Same-Sex Marriage,' *Law and Sexuality* 1 (1991), 31.
84 *Egan v. Canada* (1991), 87 DLR (4th) 320 at 332–3 (FCTD).
85 Ibid., 333.
86 *Egan v. Canada* (1993), 103 DLR (4th) 336 at 342 (FCA). On the Court of
    Appeal views, see J.P. McEvoy, 'The *Charter* and Spousal Benefits: The Case
    of the Same-Sex Spouses,' *Review of Constitutional Studies* 2 (1994), 39.
87 Ibid., 359.
88 *Egan v. Canada* (1995), 124 DLR (4th) 609 at 624 (SCC).
89 A letter in the B.C. lawyers' magazine, *The Advocate*, made this comparison
    (July 1994).
90 *Re Andrews and Minister of Health for Ontario* (1988), 49 DLR (4th) 584 (Ont.
    HCJ).
91 Ibid., 589.
92 *Layland v. Ontario (Minister of Consumer and Commercial Relations)* (1993), 104
    DLR (4th) 214 (Ont. Ct – Gen. Div.).
93 Ibid., per Southey J at 222.
94 Ibid., 223. Greer J dissented. She said that because of the restriction: 'The

message [the applicants and others who wish to marry a person of the same sex] receive must surely give them the perception that they are inferior persons in our society' (231).

95 Casswell, *Lesbians, Gay Men, and Canadian Law*, 233.

96 On homosexual parents, see Wendy L. Gross, 'Judging the Best Interests of the Child: Child Custody and the Homosexual Parent,' *Canadian Journal of Women and the Law* 1 (1986), 505; Katherine Arnup, '"Mothers Just Like Others": Lesbians, Divorce, and Child Custody in Canada,' *Canadian Journal of Women and the Law* 3 (1989), 18; Mary Eaton, 'Lesbians and the Law,' in Sharon Dale Stone, ed., *Lesbians in Canada*, chap. 8 (Toronto: Between the Lines 1990); Christine Boyle, 'Custody, Adoption and the Homosexual Parent' (1976), 23 *Reports of Family Law* 129; Dian Day, 'Lesbian/Mother,' in Stone, ed., *Lesbians in Canada* chap. 2; Marilyn Riley, 'Note: The Avowed Lesbian Mother and Her Right to Child Custody: A Constitutional Challenge that Can No Longer Be Denied,' *San Diego Law Review* 12 (1975), 799; Frank Bates, 'Child Law and the Homosexual Parent – Recent Developments in the United States,' *Australian Gay and Lesbian Law Journal* 1 (1992), 21; Frank Bates, 'Child Custody and the Homosexual Parent: Some Further Developments in Australia and the United States,' *Australian Gay and Lesbian Law Journal* 1 (1992), 1; Margaret Bateman, 'Lesbians, Gays and Child Custody: An Australian Legal History' (1992), 1 *Australian Gay and Lesbian Law Journal* 47; Jennie Millbank, 'Lesbian Mothers, Gay Fathers: Sameness and Difference,' *Australian Gay and Lesbian Law Journal* 2 (1992), 21.

97 *Elliott v. Elliott*, [1987] BCJ No. 43 (QL) (SC).

98 *Worby v. Worby* (1985), 48 RFL (2d) 369 (Sask. QB).

99 Ibid., 368.

100 Ibid., 371.

101 See also *Bernhardt v. Bernhardt* (1979), 10 RFL (2d) 32 (Man. QB). In *Bezaire v. Bezaire* (1980), 20 RFL (2d) 358 (Ont. CA), Arnup JA made it clear that '... homosexuality, either as a tendency, a proclivity or a practised way of life, is not in itself alone a ground for refusing custody to the parent with respect to whom such evidence is given' (365). But obviously it can come into play in relation to previous factors in a way that heterosexuality would not. In *Robertson v. Geisinger* (1991), 36 RFL (3d) 261 (Sask. QB), there was a custody dispute. Both parents were in homosexual relationships by the time of the action. Not surprisingly 'sexual orientation [was] not ... raised as a parenting issue by either party' (263, per Barclay J). This focus on a homosexual parent overlooks the fact that studies show that the sexual orientation of the parent is a minor factor at best in good parenting.

See, e.g., Jennifer Ditchburn, 'Homosexuality called no barrier to good parenting,' *Globe and Mail* (national edition), 16 July 1997, A7.

102 *K. v. K.*, [1976] 2 WWR 462 (Alta. Prov. Ct).

103 Ibid., 466.

104 *D. v. D.* (1978), 88 DLR (3d) 578 (Ont. Co. Ct).

105 Ibid., 583, per Smith Co. Ct J.

106 See also *Re Barkley and Barkley* (1980), 28 OR (2d) 136 (Prov. Ct – Fam. Div.).

107 *P.-B. (D.) v. P.-B. (T.)*, [1988] OJ No. 2398 (QL) (Prov. Ct – Fam. Div.).

108 *White v. The Queen* (1964), 44 CR 75 (NBSC App. Div.).

109 Ibid., 77–8.

110 But perhaps the court overreacts the other way sometimes. Thus, in *R. v. Mattais*, [1970] 5 CCC 344 (Que. CA), we are told 'At about 3 a.m. respondent and his companion Noel were found in a locked and unlighted office. They had been drinking and were sleeping heavily, but from their positions and state of their clothing it might be inferred that they had performed or were intending to perform some erotic act' (345 per Montgomery JA).

111 *T. v. T. and W.* (1975), 24 RFL 57 (Man. QB).

112 Ibid., 62.

113 Ibid., 63.

114 *Gaveronski v. Gaveronski* (1974), 45 DLR (3d) 317 (Sask. QB).

115 Ibid., 318, per MacPherson J.

116 *Re L. (R.)*, [1981] OJ No. 382 (QL) (Co. Ct).

117 Criminal Code, s. 159.

118 See *The Report of the Committee on Homosexual Offences and Prostitution* ('The Wolfenden Report') (London: HMSO, CMND 247 1957).

119 On the unnaturalness of homosexuality, see Richard Collier, *Masculinity, Law and the Family* (London: Routledge 1995), 97–8.

120 *Saunders v. Saunders.*

121 Ibid., 370–1 (per Wetmore Co. Ct J).

122 *R. v. Noyes* (1986), 6 BCLR (2d) 306 (BCSC); affirmed (1987), 22 BCLR (2d) 45 (CA); leave to appeal to SCC refused 16 May 1988, 27 BCLR (2d) xxxv.

123 Ibid., at 316. In *R. v. Roestad* (1971), 19 CR(NS) 190 (Ont. Co. Ct), leave to appeal refused (1971), 19 CR (NS) 235n (Ont. CA), there was a question of a designation as a dangerous sexual offender where a man faced charges involving sex with boys. The court heard evidence on the subject of whether the boys could become homosexual as a result of the attacks. Several experts were called. The evidence of one of them was summarized by Graburn Co. Ct J as follows: '[H]e is of the view that out of the large number of boys who would be involved, it could be assumed that at least two would be adversely affected either by becoming a homosexual or by suf-

fering psychological disturbances' (229). In reference to another situation, the judge referred to becoming homosexual 'a potential harm' (230). See also *R. v. S. (W.B.); R. v. P. (M.)* (1992), 73 CCC (3d) 530 (Alta. CA).

124 *Valiquette v. The Gazette* (1991), 8 CCLT (2d) 302 (Que. Super. Ct).

125 *R. v. National News Co. Ltd.*, 536.

126 Ibid.

127 Ibid., 542.

128 See section entitled 'Homosexuality as Remarkable' and the final section, both in Chapter 1.

129 *Worby v. Worby.*

130 Ibid., 371 (per McIntyre J).

131 *Partland v. Partland* (1960), 24 DLR (2d) 576 at 577 (Ont. HC).

132 *King v. King*, [1985] OJ No. 432 (QL) (HCJ).

133 *Little Sisters*, 522.

134 Freeman, 'Defining Family in *Mossop v. DSS*,' 74–80. There is a particularly rich U.S. literature on 'intersectionality.' See, esp., Kimberle Crenshaw, 'Mapping the Margins: Intersectionality, Identity Politics, and Violence Against Women of Color,' *Stanford Law Review* 43 (1991), 1241 and the literature cited therein.

135 Freeman, 'Defining Family in *Mossop v. DSS*,' 74–5.

136 Some of the difficulties in litigating a case with a homosexual element are discussed in ibid.

137 See 'Seal-protest ad ruled misleading,' *Vancouver Sun*, 14 February 1996, A1.

138 *Egan v. Canada.*

139 Ibid. See Cory J at 672 and Iacobucci J at 682 (SCC).

140 Shelley A.M. Gavigan, 'A Parent(ly) Knot: Can Heather Have Two Mommies?' in Didi Herman and Carl Stychin, eds., *Legal Inversions: Lesbians, Gay Men, and the Politics of Law* (Philadelphia: Temple University Press 1995), 102–17 at 106. The citation for 'Eagleton' is Terry Eagleton, *Ideology: An Introduction* (London: Verso 1991), 2.

141 Mary Eaton, 'Lesbians, Gays and the Struggle for Equality Rights: Reversing the Progressive Hypothesis,' *Dalhousie Law Journal* 17 (1994), 130 at 173. See also Didi Herman, 'Are We Family? Lesbian Rights and Women's Liberation,' *Osgoode Hall Law Journal* 28 (1990), 789.

142 In *Andrews v. Law Society of BC*, [1989] 1 SCR 143.

143 Eaton, 'Lesbians, Gays and the Struggle for Equality Rights,' 184.

144 Nitya Iyer deals with the problem of suppressing differences and emphasizing similarities in human rights litigation in 'Categorical Denials: Equality Rights and the Shaping of Social Identity,' *Queen's Law Journal* 19 (1993), 179.

145 See Nowlin, 'The Relevance of Stereotypes,' 343. And it did not get us far, as the court found that it was not homosexual erotica that was obscene but the application of the law that has caused the problem. Counsel in *Little Sisters* developed the distinction between hetersexual and homosexual porn to get around the *Butler* decision. See Fuller and Blackley, *Restricted Entry*, 46.

146 Fuller and Blackley, *Restricted Entry*, 43–4.

147 Casswell, *Lesbians, Gay Men, and Canadian Law*, 517–30 on *Butler*. The quotation is from page 518 and the citations have been omitted.

148 A defence of *Butler* (though not of its application) is found in Ann Scales, 'Avoiding Constitutional Depression: Bad Attitudes and the Fate of *Butler*,' *Canadian Journal of Women and the Law* 7 (1994), 349. On the gay pornography debate, see Carl F. Stychin, 'Exploring the Limits: Feminism and the Legal Regulation of Gay Male Pornography,' *Vermont Law Review* 16 (1992), 857; Christopher N. Kendall, '"Real Dominant, Real Fun!": Gay Male Pornography and the Pursuit of Masculinity,' *Saskatchewan Law Review* 57 (1993), 21.

149 *Egan*, 669.

150 *Re Haig and The Queen in right of Canada* (1992), 94 DLR (4th) 1 (Ont. CA).

151 Ibid., 10.

152 See Ijeoma Ross, 'Courts left to shape same-sex policy,' *Globe and Mail* (national edition), 12 October 1996, A5.

Chapter 3: Silence in the Classroom

1 A 1994 study by the American Academy of Pediatrics found that sexually abused children were unlikely to have been molested by identifiably gay or lesbian people. *Globe and Mail*, 1 July 1994. On gay men as not disproportionately prone to molest children, see R. Geiser, *Hidden Victims: The Sexual Abuse of Children* (Boston: Beacon Press 1979).

2 Steve Beery, 'Liz Smith Mon Amour,' *OutWeek*, May 16, 1990, 44–6.

3 This is slowly changing. See Chris Dafoe, 'Prime-time Characters Busting Out of Closets All Over TV,' *Globe and Mail* (national edition), 27 August 1997, A11.

4 See Marcia K. Lieberman, '"Someday My Prince Will Come": Female Acculturation through the Fairy Tale,' *College English* 34 (Urbana, Ill.: National Council of Teachers of English 1972), 383–95; reprinted in Melita Schaum and Connie Flanagan, ed., *Gender Images: Readings for Composition* (Boston: Houghton Mifflin 1992), at 247–61.

5 Cooper Thompson, in 'A New Vision of Masculinity,' which appeared in a

journal called *Changing Men* in 1985 and was extracted in Melita Schaum
and Connie Flanagan, eds., *Gender Images: Readings for Composition* (Boston:
Houghton Mifflin 1992), at 77.

6 *Vriend v. Alberta* (1996), 132 DLR (4th) 595 (Alta. CA); reversed (1998), 156
   DLR (4th) 385 (SCC). All subsequent references to this case in this chapter,
   except at notes 34 and 105, are to the Alberta Court of Appeal's decision.

7 See Sharon Dale Stone, 'Introduction,' in Sharon Dale Stone, ed., *Lesbians in
   Canada* (Toronto: Between the Lines 1990), 10. Stone notes that girls are
   always told that they should marry, although studies show that never-
   married old women lead happy and fulfilling lives. She cites Barbara Levy
   Simon, *Never Married Women* (Philadelphia: Temple University Press 1987).
   See also Jeanette A. Auger, 'Lesbians and Aging: Triple Trouble or Tremendous Thrill,' in Dale Stone, ed., *Lesbians in Canada*, chap. 1.

8 The numbers game is unhelpful in rights cases, but one recent news item
   put the percentage of Calgary school students who are homosexual or
   bisexual at 12.9 per cent. See 'Many students gay, board told,' *Vancouver
   Sun*, 13 June 1996, A3.

9 The effect is tantamount to the situation in some foreign jurisdictions that
   expressly prohibit 'promotion' of homosexuality in schools. See Robert
   Wintemute, *Sexual Orientation and Human Rights: The United States Constitu-
   tion, the European Convention, and the Canadian Charter* (Oxford: Oxford Uni-
   versity Press, 1995), 192, note 86; Carl Stychin, 'Of Prohibitions and
   Promotions,' in *Law's Desire: Sexuality and the Limits of Justice*, chap. 2 (Lon-
   don: Routledge 1995), 38–54; David M. Rayside, 'Homophobia, Class and
   Party in England,' *Canadian Journal of Political Science* 25 (1992) 121; Simon
   Watney, 'School's Out,' in Diana Fuss, ed., *Inside/Out: Lesbian Theories, Gay
   Theories*, chap. 17 (New York: Routledge 1991).

10 See, generally, Karen M. Harbeck, ed., *Coming Out of the Classroom Closet:
   Gay and Lesbian Students, Teachers and Curricula* (New York: Harrington Park
   Press 1992).

11 See, e.g., Shannon Bell, 'Ban Urged on Teaching about Homosexuality,' *Vancouver Sun*, 28 April 1997, B1; and Raj Takhar, 'Queer Lessons,' [Vancouver]
   Angles, May 1997, 1, among many articles dealing with the homophobic
   agitation of a B.C. parents' group.

12 Note, the British Columbia Teachers' Federation and the group Gay and
   Lesbian Educators of BC have been mobilizing to ensure access to material
   on homosexuality in the schools of British Columbia. See, e.g., Pat Johnson,
   'Teaching Mutual Respect,' *Xtra! West*, 9 January 1997, No. 89, 7; and Kim
   Bolan, 'Teachers Move to Tackle Homophobia in Province's Schools,' *Van-
   couver Sun*, 18 March 1997, B1. There is similar activity in Calgary at least –

see Alanna Mitchell, 'School Trustees Create Storm over Gay Rights,' *Globe and Mail* (national edition), 7 March 1997, A2.

13 See Kinsman's summary of the history of attempts and failures in Toronto in Gary Kinsman, *The Regulation of Desire: Homo and Hetero Sexualities*, rev. ed. (Montreal: Black Rose 1996), 326–7, note 115.

14 Some growing up lesbian stories are set out in Carolyn Gammon, et al., 'Organizing Lesbian Studies at Concordia,' in Stone, ed., *Lesbians in Canada*, chap. 15.

15 On the problem of suicide and gays and lesbians, see Eric E. Rofes, *'I Thought People Like That Killed Themselves': Lesbians, Gay Men and Suicide* (San Francisco: Grey Fox 1983). He notes that both homosexuality and suicide are difficult to assess in a population but has no problem saying that suicide is higher among homosexuals. A report of the U.S, Department of Health and Human Services in 1989 said that because gay youth face a hostile and condemning environment, verbal and physical abuse, and rejection and isolation from families and peers, they were two to three times more likely than others to commit suicide. See also Shannon K. O'Byrne and James F. McGinnis, 'Case Comment. *Vriend v. Alberta: Plessy* Revisited: Lesbian and Gay Rights in the Province of Alberta,' *Alberta Law Review* 34 (1996), 892 who cite Ian T. Kroll and Lorne B. Warneke, *The Dynamics of Sexual Orientation and Adolescent Suicide: A Comprehensive Review and Developmental Perspective* (Calgary: University of Calgary and University of Alberta 1995).

16 Cynthia Petersen, 'Living Dangerously: Speaking Lesbian, Teaching Law,' *Canadian Journal of Women and the Law* 7 (1994), 318 at 348.

17 See Michael Manley-Casimir, 'Teaching as a Normative Enterprise,' *Education and the Law Journal* 5 (1993), 1; Stephen Arons, 'Constitutional Litigation and Education Reform: Canada's Opportunity,' in Michael E. Manley-Casimir and Terri A. Sussel, eds., *Courts in the Classroom: Education and the Charter of Rights and Freedoms*, chap. 8 (Calgary: Detselig 1986), 153.

18 Manley-Casimir, 'Teaching as a Normative Enterprise,' 20. Stephen Arons writes that most people see schooling as 'two-edged.' He writes: 'First, schooling is held to be a process of opening minds, liberating the thought process, creating a marketplace of ideas and beliefs in which individual minds move unencumbered by government and political majorities. Second, schooling is seen as a process of transmitting particular values and, indeed, entire sets of cultural assumptions from one generation to the next, a means of legitimizing and inculcating beliefs in the minds of children. These two aspects of schooling are two faces of a single process, the process of communication as it takes place in schools.' Arons, 'Constitutional Litigation and Education Reform,' 153. See also Paul T. Clarke, 'Free Speech

and Canada's Public School Teachers: An Employment Law and Constitutional Law Analysis' (Unpublished PhD dissertation, University of
Saskatchewan 1997).

19 Most religions, except perhaps those that do not allow their members to
procreate, encourage parents to proselytize at least to their children.
20 Historically religions had a great interest in the university system as well,
particularly in the eastern half of Canada. On historical aspects, see C.B.
Sissons, *Church and State in Canadian Education: An Historical Study* (Toronto:
Ryerson 1959).
21 See Didi Herman, *Rights of Passage: Struggles for Lesbian & Gay Legal Equality*
(Toronto: University of Toronto Press 1994); Kenneth L. Karst, *Law's Promise, Law's Expression: Visions of Power in the Politics of Race, Gender, and Religion* (New Haven: Yale University Press 1993).
22 Some provincial education acts specifically authorize teaching of Christian
morality. See Education Act, RSNS 1989, c. 136, s. 54(e) and Education Act,
RSO 1990, c. E.2, s. 264(1)(c).
23 For treatments of education and the law, see Douglas A. Schmeiser and
Roderick J. Wood, 'Student Rights under the Charter,' *Saskatchewan Law
Review* 49 (1984) 49; A. Wayne MacKay, *Education Law in Canada* (Toronto:
Emond-Montgomery 1984). For a treatment of how disputes between teachers and school boards are resolved, see Stuart Piddocke, 'Settling Disputes
between School Boards and Teachers: A Review of Formal Procedures and
Some Provincial Variations,' *Education and the Law Journal* 5 (1993), 23.
24 MacKay, *Education Law in Canada*, 29.
25 See ibid., see also David Givan, 'The Ross Decision and Control in Professional Employment,' *UNB Law Journal* 41 (1992), 333.
26 See A. Wayne MacKay, 'The Canadian Charter of Rights and Freedoms: A
Springboard to Students' Rights,' *Windsor Yearbook of Access to Justice* 4
(1984), 174.
27 Michael Manley-Casimir deals with the parallels and relationships of education and law. He says that law and education 'are concerned with the
maintenance and inculcation, respectively, of the "collective representations" (to borrow the phrase of Durkheim) that model ideal behaviour.'
Manley-Casimir, 'Teaching as a Normative Enterprise,' 4. See also T.A.
Sussel and M.E. Manley-Casimir, 'The Supreme Court of Canada as a
"National School Board": The Charter and Educational Change,' in
Manley-Casimir and Sussel, eds., *Courts in the Classroom*, chap. 11.
28 *Douglas/Kwantlen Faculty Association v. Douglas College* (1990), 77 DLR (4th)
95 (SCC); *Lavigne v. O.P.S.E.U.* (1991), 81 DLR (4th) 545 (SCC); *Re Ontario
English Catholic Teachers Asociation and Essex County Roman Catholic School*

Board (1987), 58 OR (2d) 545 (HCJ – Div. Ct.); leave to appeal to SCC refused (1988), 51 DLR (4th) vii; *R. v. H.* (1985), 43 Alta. LR (2d) 250 (Prov. Ct – Youth Div.); *Jones v. The Queen* (1986), 31 DLR (4th) 569 (SCC); *Zylberberg v. Sudbury Board of Education (Director)* (1988), 52 DLR (4th) 577 (Ont. CA); Banafsheh Sokhansanj, 'Our Father Who Art in the Classroom: Exploring a *Charter* Challenge to Prayer in Public Schools,' *Saskatchewan Law Review* 56 (1992), 47; William J. Smith, 'Rights and Freedoms in Education: The Application of the *Charter* to Public School Boards,' *Education and the Law Journal* 4 (1993), 107.

29 *McKinney v. University of Guelph* (1990), 76 DLR (4th) 545 (SCC); *Harrison v. UBC* (1990), 77 DLR (4th) 55 (SCC).

30 *Vriend*. On *Vriend*, see O'Byrne and McGinnis, 'Case Comment'; Wayne N. Renke, 'Case Comment. *Vriend v. Alberta*: Discrimination, Burden of Proof, and Judicial Notice,' *Alberta Law Review* 34 (1996), 925; F.C. De Coste, 'Case Comment. *Vriend v. Alberta*: Sexual Orientation and Liberal Policy,' *Alberta Law Review* 34 (1996), 950; Kathleen Mahoney, 'Case Comment. *Vriend v. Alberta*: A Victory for Discrimination,' *Canadian Labour and Employment Law Journal* 4 (1996) 389; William Black, '*Vriend*, Rights and Democracy,' *Constitutional Forum* 7 (1996), 126.

31 *Re Haig and the Queen* (1992), 94 DLR (4th) 1 (Ont. CA); *Newfoundland and Labrador (Human Rights Commission) v. Newfoundland and Labrador (Minister of Employment and Labour Relations)* (1995), 127 DLR (4th) 694 (Nfld TD). The latter case, which relied on the trial decision in *Vriend*, does not appear to have been considered by the Alberta Court of Appeal.

32 Others have dealt with McClung JA's main stated argument about laws of general application falling within the legislative realm. See the articles in note 30, above.

33 *Vriend*, at 599 per McClung JA.

34 *Vriend v. Alberta*, [1994] 6 WWR 414 (Alta. QB).

35 *Vriend*, 618. Homosexual groups did in fact try to get sexual orientation included in the IRPA when it was proposed in 1972. The law was passed in 1973 without including protection against discrimination on the basis of sexual orientation. Noted in Donald W. McLeod, *Lesbian and Gay Liberation in Canada: A Selected Annotated Chronology, 1964–1975* (Toronto: ECW Press 1996), 108.

36 *Vriend*, 619.

37 See O'Byrne and McGinnis, 'Case Comment.'

38 H.L.A. Hart, *The Concept of Law* (Oxford: Clarendon Press 1961), esp. chap. 9, 'Laws and Morals.'

39 McClung JA disagreed even with senior courts, which might take a con-

trary view, and would be opposed to reading in sexual orientation in s. 15
of the Charter (617). Apart from Charter or other constitutional protections
of equal treatment, the law has long seen for itself a role in ensuring fairness. That is the basis of the system of equity and the basis for private law
doctrines like restitution and unconscionability.

40 *Vriend*, 609. *Bowers v. Hardwick* 92 L. Ed. 2d 140 (USSC 1986), per Burger CJ
at 150. *Bowers v. Hardwick* may not even be particularly good law in the
United States given the U.S. Supreme Court decision in *Romer v. Evans*, 134
L. Ed. 2d 855 (USSC, 1996). See Wintemute, *Sexual Orientation and Human
Rights*, 'Preface' to the paperback edition (Oxford: Oxford University Press
1997), v–vii.

41 *Bowers v. Hardwick*, at 149, per Burger CJ.

42 That is not even the jurisdiction of the Province of Alberta.

43 O'Byrne and McGinnis, 'Case Comment,' 910. See also De Coste, 'Case
Comment,' 964.

44 The connection between homosexuality and strange and aberrant behaviour (i.e., sodomy) that could undermine society is subsequently reinforced
when McClung JA said: 'I say nothing as well of the respondent's answer to
the appellant's concerns that the term "sexual orientation" is limited to
"traditional" homosexual practices shared by consenting adults, and its
IRPA inclusion would never be raised as a permissive shield sheltering
other practices, both heterosexual and homosexual, commonly regarded as
deviance in both communities. It is pointless to deny that the Dahmer, Bernardo and Clifford Robert Olsen prosecutions have recently heightened
public concern about violently aberrant sexual configurations and how
they find expression against their victims' (*Vriend*, 611). It is perhaps not
coincidental that McClung JA used two religiously charged examples as
parallels with homosexuality. He said: 'That "sexual orientation" is so obviously a divisive issue, like right-to-life or euthanasia (issues which are also
touched by the declarations of the Canadian Charter of Rights and Freedoms), does not, by its gravity alone, force the hand of the legislator' (607).
As to the reference to Dahmer, Bernardo, and Olsen, as Shannon O'Byrne
and James McGinnis say, 'That Mr. Vriend and these individuals should
even be mentioned together on the same page does an outrageous injustice
to Vriend, if only by the proximity of the association.' O'Byrne and McGinnis, 'Case Comment,' 923.

45 *Gaylord v. Tacoma School District No. 10*, 559 P 2d 1340 (Wash. 1977).

46 See Fernand N. Dutile, *Sex, Schools and the Law: A Study of the Legal Implications of Sexual Matters Relating to the Public School Curriculum (With a Separate
Chapter on Sex Education), the Public School Library, the Personal Lives of Teach-*

ers and Students, and the Student Press (Springfield, Ill.: Charles Thomas 1986), 127.

47 *Layland v. Ontario (Minister of Consumer and Commercial Relations)* (1993), 104 DLR (4th) 214 (Ont. Ct – Gen. Div.), 235.

48 Ibid., at 222, per Southey J.

49 *Halm v. Canada (Minister of Employment and Immigration)*, [1995] 2 FC 331 at 358–9 (TD). See also Abella JA in *R. v. M. (C.)* (1995), 41 CR (4th) 134 at 141–2 (Ont. CA).

50 *L'Association A.D.G.Q. v. Catholic School Commission of Montreal* (1979), 112 DLR (3d) 230 at 234 (Que. Super. Ct).

51 *Re O and O* (1980), 30 OR (2d) 588 at 593 (HCJ).

52 See Rick Conrad, 'Apology Not Enough, Says Gay Rights Group,' [Halifax] *Mail-Star*, 16 December 1995, A9.

53 *R. v. Pink Triangle Press* (1979), 45 CCC (2d) 385 at 400–1 (Ont. Prov. Ct); reversed (1980), 51 CCC (2d) 485 (Ont. Co. Ct). Lest these views be thought dated, see the current debate in British Columbia about making gay-positive material available in the schools (see notes 10 and 11, above). It is not always adults who want the books removed. See 'Students Wants [sic] Book Pulled,' *The* [Vancouver] *Province.* 6 June 1991, 20, which contains an article about a student who wanted Timothy Findley's novel *The Wars* removed from her school curriculum because 'it's offensive and pressures readers to accept homosexuality.'

54 *R. v. Pink Triangle Press*, 401.

55 As often occurs. See *Vriend* and *Egan* as examples.

56 Some courts are careful to exclude irrelevant evidence about a person's homosexuality on the basis that it can unfairly prejudice an accused. E.g., *R. v. Wilson* (1990), 59 CCC (3d) 432 (BCCA) and *R. v. Taylor* (1982), 66 CCC (2d) 437 (Ont. CA).

57 *R. v. Noyes* (1986), 6 BCLR (2d) 306 at 316 (SC); appeal dismissed (1987), 22 BCLR (2d) 45 (CA); leave to appeal refused, (1988), 27 BCLR (2d) xxxv.

58 *R. v. H. (E.)*, [1987] NWTJ No. 3 (QL) (SC).

59 *R. v. Paquette*, [1988] BCJ No. 1624 (QL) (Co. Ct).

60 *The Report of the Committee on Homosexual Offences and Prostitution* ('The Wolfenden Report') (London: HMSO, CMND 247 1957), para. 24.

61 *Saunders v. Saunders* (1989), 20 RFL (3d) 368 at 370–1 (BC Co. Ct).

62 See also *Droit de la famille – 31*, [1983] CS 69.

63 *Saunders v. Saunders*, 371.

64 *Templeman v. Templeman*, [1986] BCJ No. 1426 (QL) (SC).

65 See also *Monette v. Sylvestre*, [1981] CS 731, where custody was awarded to

the heterosexual father who could provide 'une cellule familiale complète,' which the homosexual mother could not. And see *Johnston v. Rochette*, [1982] CS 407; *Cloutier v. Trudel*, [1982] CS 951.

66 *R. v. Ledinski* (1991), 95 Sask. R 1 at 4 (QB); affirmed (1995), 134 Sask. R 256 (CA).

67 See Dutile, *Sex, Schools and the Law*, 104.

68 Arons, 'Constitutional Litigation and Education Reform,' 157. Some writers have supported this role model. E.L Hurlbert and M.A. Hurlbert write: 'Parents expect a teacher to serve as an adult model for their child. They would not be willing to have their child taught by a teacher whom they considered immoral. It is this burden which separates the occupation of teaching from other occupations such as engineering or accounting.' E.L. Hurlbert and M.A. Hurlbert, *School Law under the Charter of Rights and Freedoms* (Calgary: University Calgary Press 1992), 185. That is not to say that teachers always lose their status when they speak outside the school. As Lambert JA said in *Cromer v. BC Teachers' Federation*, [1986] 5 WWR 638 at 657–8 (BCCA): 'I do not think people are free to choose which hat they will wear on what occasion. Mrs Cromer does not always speak as a teacher, nor does she always speak as a parent. But she always speaks as Mrs. Cromer. The perception of her by her audience will depend on their knowledge of her training, her skills, her experience and her occupation, among other things. The impact of what she says will depend on the content of what she says and the occasion on which she says it.'

69 On being lesbian and a teacher, see Diane Williams, 'Who's That Teacher? The Problems of Being a Lesbian Teacher of Colour,' in M. Oikawa, D. Falconer and A. Decter, eds., *Resist: Essays against a Homophobic Culture* (Toronto: Women's Press 1994), 65; Didi Khayatt, 'In and Out: Experiences in the Academy,' ibid., 210.

70 *R. v. Gillis* (1994), 134 NSR (2d) 119 at 120 (CA).

71 See Joshua Dressler, 'Survey of School Principals Regarding Alleged Homosexual Teachers in the Classroom: How Likely (Really) Is Discharge?' *University of Dayton Law Review* 10 (1984), 599.

72 Hurlbert and Hurlbert, *School Law*, 187. See also Dutile, *Sex, Schools and the Law*, 111.

73 *Re Board of Governors of the University of Saskatchewan and Saskatchewan Human Rights Commission* (1976), 66 DLR (3d) 561 at 563 (Sask. QB), per Johnson J.

74 Ibid., 564.

75 Ibid., 565.

76 The situation is only worsened when it is realized that the Saskatchewan

Court of Appeal thought the Queen's Bench Division might have got this point wrong. In a later case, where the jurisdiction of the Saskatchewan Human Rights Commission was in issue, Culliton CJS, delivering the judgment of the Court of Appeal said:

> In my respectful view, the learned Chambers Judge, in *Re Board of Governors of the University of Saskatchewan and Saskatchewan Human Rights Com'n* ... did what I have said should not be done. In that case, the issue was not one of jurisdiction. The allegation there was that the complaint, although alleged to be in respect of 'sex,' was not one in respect of sex, and, therefore, the Commission was without jurisdiction. The learned Chambers Judge agreed with this submission and issued the order of prohibition. With all deference, I am satisfied he was wrong in so doing. The issues raised in that case were those which the Commission had the right and obligation to determine and the Court should not, in prohibition proceedings, have usurped the Commission's jurisdiction.

Re CIP Paper Products Ltd. and Saskatchewan Human Rights Commission (1978), 87 DLR (3d) 609 at 612 (Sask. CA), per Culliton CJS. Not all courts are liable to this tacit acceptance of the need to exclude homosexuals from schools. Obviously the lower decisions in *Vriend v. Alberta* and *Re Board of Governors of the University of Saskatchewan and Saskatchewan Human Rights Commission* are examples where the courts or tribunals were otherwise inclined. So too was the case in *L'Association A.D.G.Q.*

77 *Valiquette v. The Gazette* (1991), 8 CCLT (2d) 302 (Que. Super. Ct).

78 Ibid., 309, per Viau J.

79 Ibid., 310.

80 See Bruce MacDougall, 'Outing: The Law Reacts to Speech about Homosexuality,' *Queen's Law Journal* 21 (1995), 79.

81 E.g. *R. v. Ledinski*; *R. v. Waldie*, [1987] BCJ No. 2291 (QL) (Co. Ct). On teacher misconduct, see Michael E. Manley-Casimir and Stuart M. Piddocke, 'Teachers in a Goldfish Bowl: A Case of "Misconduct,"' *Education and the Law Journal* 3 (1991), 115; Elizabeth Grace, 'Professional Misconduct or Moral Pronouncement: A Study of "Contentious" Teacher Behaviour in Quebec,' *Education and the Law Journal* 5 (1993), 99; Romulo Magsino, 'Institutional Responses to Teacher Misconduct in Manitoba,' *Education and the Law Journal* 5 (1993), 71; Romulo Magsino, 'Institutional Responses to Teacher Misconduct in the Atlantic Provinces,' *Education and the Law Journal* 5 (1993), 143.

82 See text accompanying note 57, above.

83 *R. v. Pilgrim* (1981), 64 CCC (2d) 523 at 531 (Nfld CA).

84 MacKay, *Education Law*, 304. A system of prior approval is usually in place. Even in the United States, with its jurisprudence hostile to prior restraint, courts have found such an approach acceptable in the schools context. Hurlbert and Hurlbert, *School Law*, 56.

85 See *Serup v. School District No. 57* (1987), 14 BCLR (2d) 393 (SC). This is discussed and elaborated on in Terri Sussel, *Controversies in School Law: A Handbook for Educational Administrators* (Vancouver: EduServ 1990), 89*ff*.

86 Ibid., 89.

87 Ibid.

88 Later that year, the same group wanted the book *Girls and Sex* banned for similar reasons. This time the book banning was not accepted. Because the woman spearheading the book banning, Mrs Serup, was becoming a nuisance with her monitoring of the library books, the library banned her. This issue went to court. See *Serup*. An appeal was allowed as to whether there was a triable issue (1989), 54 BCLR (2d) 258 (CA).

89 See notes 11 and 12, above.

90 See *Valiquette*, 308.

91 *Re University of Manitoba and Deputy Minister, Revenue Canada, Customs & Excise* (1983), 4 DLR (4th) 658 at 660 (Man. Co. Ct).

92 Ibid., 662.

93 See, e.g., Didi Khayatt, 'Lesbian Teachers: Coping at School,' in Stone, ed., *Lesbians in Canada*, chap. 6, 81–93; Jeri Dawn Wine, 'Outsiders on the Inside: Lesbians in Canadian Academe,' in ibid., 157–70.

94 The other aspect of this issue, however, is the extent to which gays and lesbians have colluded in the silencing. Every gay and lesbian I know could furnish a substantial list of gays and lesbians in the educational system. Everyone knows we are there. Yet there is still this silence. Is there not some good reason for society generally to see homosexuality as sinister if its numbers remain so silent, and if gays and lesbians tacitly accept the inferiorization? Does the shame this silence attests to not generate the fear and the fun directed at homosexuality?.

95 Khayatt, 'Lesbian Teachers: Coping at School,' 83.

96 See *Harvard Law Review* editors, *Sexual Orientation and the Law* (Cambridge, Mass.: Harvard University Press 1989), 76–85.

97 *Fricke v. Lynch*, 491 F Supp. 381 (US Dist Ct, 1980). Note article in *Vancouver Sun*, 2 May 1996, A10, about Toronto high schools having their first gay-and-lesbian prom.

98 *Harvard Law Review* editors, *Sexual Orientation and the Law*, 77.

99 See also *Healy v. James*, 408 US 169 (1972); *Gay Students Organization v. Bonner*, 509 F 2d 652 (1st Circ. 1974).

100 Homosexuality is probably not unique in this area. Judicial inaction in cases involving poverty, race, and certain religions might make useful comparisons.

101 Bruce Ryder, 'Family Status, Sexuality and "The Province of the Judiciary"': The Implications of *Mossop v. Attorney-General Canada*,' *Windsor Yearbook of Access to Justice* 13 (1993), 3, 5.

102 *Egan v. Canada* (1995), 124 DLR (4th) 609 (SCC).

103 *Nielsen v. Canada*, [1992] 2 FC 561 at 577 (TD).

104 Even in cases where the court is obviously more sympathetic to homosexuals, it can be prone to inaction: *Brown v. British Columbia (Minister of Health)* (1990), 66 DLR (4th) 444 at 457 (BCSC). Judges can exert themselves when they want to get a reasonable decision. In *St Paul's Roman Catholic Separate School (District No. 20) v. C.U.P.E, Local 2268*, [1987] SJ No. 209 (QL) (CA) a Roman Catholic school fired a woman who was in a common law relationship with a man because she had indicated that she was 'married' when applying to get the job. Bayda CJS went to elaborate lengths to explain that, today, 'married' could include common law relationships. The majority was thus prepared to enter this morally eruptive controversy. It is interesting to note, though, that judges might shy away from entering these 'heterosexual' cases when they fear the decision might be used by homosexuals. Thus, in the *St Paul's* case, Matheson J came to the opposite conclusion and appeared worried about the extension of such a decision to homosexual and lesbian couples.

105 *Vriend v. Alberta* (1998), 156 DLR (4th) 385 (SCC).

106 The antipathy of Christianity to homosexuality may not be as ancient and enduring as is commonly thought. See John Boswell, *Christianity, Social Tolerance, and Homosexuality: Gay People in Western Europe from the Beginning of the Christian Era to the Fourteenth Century* (Chicago: University of Chicago Press 1980); John Boswell, *Same-Sex Unions in Premodern Europe* (New York: Villard 1994).

107 Note the controversy in British Columbia where the B.C. Teachers' Federation refused to recognize Trinity Western University's teaching program because that religious-based institution requires its students to sign a 'Community Standards' contract promising to avoid 'biblically condemned practices,' including homosexuality. Douglas Todd, 'The Bible Tells Them So,' *Vancouver Sun*, 15 February 1997, G1. The university cried foul, of course, but one wonders what their response would be about the suitability of a student who studied at a university that made its students sign a 'Community Standards' contract promising to avoid 'belief in God' or 'mixed-race events and relationships.' The B.C. Supreme Court ruled

that the BCTF acted wrongly. See 'School's Position on Gays Allowed,' *Globe and Mail* (national edition), 13 September 1997, A6.

108 Some religious groups, it is true, such as the United Church of Canada and Reform Judaism, depart from traditional, conservative religious ideology but this more enlightened religious dogma is not what judges appear to mean when they rely on 'religious values' or 'religion.' On the United Church of Canada's (limited) acceptance of gays and lesbians, see Michael Riordan, *The First Stone* (Toronto: McClelland & Stewart 1990). Even the United Church does not advocate absolute equality in something like same-sex marriages. But see 'Reform Rabbis Expected to Vote in Favour of Gay Marriages,' *Globe and Mail* (national edition), 28 March 1996, A9.

109 It is possible for judges to recognize the religious origin of much homophobia. For example, in *R. v. Musson* (1996), 3 CR (5th) 61 (Ont. Gen. Div.) Clarke J accepted expert evidence that religious teachings about homosexuality are one of the sources of homophobia.

110 A celebrated defence of this connection is Patrick Devlin, *The Enforcement of Morals* (London: Oxford University Press 1965). Devlin says: 'Morals and religion are inextricably joined – the moral standards generally accepted in Western civilization being those belonging to Christianity ... A state which refuses to enforce Christian beliefs has lost the right to enforce Christian morals' (4–5).

111 On the role religious groups seek to play in education, see Terri A. Sussel, 'Schoolrooms of a Lesser God: The Fundamentalist Challenge to Public Education,' *Education Law Journal* 1 (1989) 72.

112 Quoted in Janine Fuller and Stuart Blackley, *Restricted Entry: Censorship on Trial* (Vancouver: Press Gang 1993), 52.

113 The possible coincidence of religious values and Charter guarantees was alluded to in *Canadian Civil Liberties Association v. Ontario (Minister of Education)* (1990), 65 DLR (4th) 1 (Ont. CA).

114 *Vriend*, 602.

115 Ibid., 606–7.

116 Ibid., 605.

117 MacKay, *Education Law in Canada*, 64. See also *Reference Re Child Welfare Act (Nfld)* (1988), 48 CRR 281 (Nfld SC – Unified Family Court).

118 Of course what the judges do only mirrors to a large extent what goes on in society. Another example of discrimination against a homosexual teacher on religious grounds is that of Eric Smith, in the Shelburne County, Nova Scotia, system, discussed by Jack Graham in 'AIDS in Schools: A Model of Enlightenment and Tolerance?' *Education and the Law*

Journal 2 (1990), 299, 312–13. See also Martha MacKinnon, 'Aids and Schools,' William F. Foster, ed., *Education & Law: A Plea for Partnership*, chap. 10 (Welland, Ont.: Soleil 1992), 103. Mr Smith was forced because of public opinion expressed at meetings to stay away from the classroom. Graham says that Smith's homosexuality was an important factor: '... many of the public meetings organized in Shelburne County to oppose Mr. Smith's return to the classroom, featured fundamentalist religious videos that characterized AIDS as a disease sent by God to punish those who engaged in what was felt to be sexually promiscuous behaviour, especially homosexuality.' The situation is perhaps worse elsewhere, particularly in the United States. For example, in the American *Gaylord* case in which a teacher was fired once the vice-principal found out he was gay, the judge writing for the majority cited as authority on the morality (or not) of homosexuality the *New Catholic Encyclopedia. Gaylord v. Tacoma School District No. 10*, 559 P 2d 1340 (Wash. 1977), per Horowitz AJ.

119 *R. v. H. (E.)*, [1987] NWTJ No. 3 (QL) (SC), per Marshall J.

120 *Re North and Matheson* (1974), 52 DLR (3d) 280 (Man. Co. Ct), 284, per Philp Co. Ct J, who added the italics, citing *Hyde v. Hyde and Woodmansee* (1866), LR 1 P&D 130 at 133. This case was applied in *C. (L.) v. C. (C.)* (1992), 10 OR (3d) 254 (Ont. Ct – Gen. Div.).

121 *Layland v. Ontario (Minister of Consumer and Commercial Relations)*, 223.

122 Ibid., 223. See also *Egan v. Canada* (1991), 87 DLR (4th) 320 at 333 (FCTD), where he said: 'Within the non-spousal group into which the plaintiffs fall, they also fall into a sub-group of same-sex partners whose life-style mirrors many of the characteristics or attitudes of the spousal group but that does not, in my view at least, bring them within the traditionally understood meaning of a spousal couple which forms the fundamental building block of any society' (333).

123 *Partland v. Partland* (1960), 24 DLR (2d) 576 at 581 (Ont. HC).

124 *P.-B. (D.) v. P.-B. (T.)*, [1988] OJ No. 2398 (QL) (Prov. Ct – Fam. Div.), per Felstiner Prov. Ct J.

125 See *R. v. Pink Triangle Press*, 400–1.

126 *Re Marzan and The Queen* (1981), 131 DLR (3d) 370 at 371 (Man. CA), appeal allowed (1982), 131 DLR (3d) 370n (SCC).

127 *R. v. Jolicoeur* (unreported), BC Prov. Ct, 7 February 1997.

128 *Egan*, 626.

129 Ibid., for example. There is no real concept in Canadian law of a 'family' as having any collective rights comparable to those of a corporation. See *Reference Re Child Welfare Act (Nfld)*.

130 Finnis does not tell us why.

131 John Finnis, 'Law, Morality, and "Sexual Orientation,"' *Notre Dame Journal of Law, Ethics and Public Policy* 9 (1995), 11 at 32.

132 Finnis also says that there is a 'philosophical and common-sense rejection of extra-marital sex.' Ibid., 28. He sees no basis for protecting or making any sex outside of marriage and any sex that is not reproductive in nature or imitative of reproductive sex. So this is La Forest J's company.

133 Michael J. Perry, 'The Morality of Homosexual Conduct: A Response to John Finnis,' *Notre Dame Journal of Law, Ethics and Public Policy* 9 (1995), 41 at 45–6.

134 Ibid., 64.

135 Ibid., 65 (emphasis added).

136 Ibid., 68.

137 *Egan v. Canada* (1993), 103 DLR (4th) 336 (FCA), appeal dismissed, note 102 above. Shannon O'Byrne and James McGinnis note the startling coincidence of the Alberta Court of Appeal *Vriend* decision and the centenary of *Plessy* [*Plessey v. Ferguson*, 163 US 537 (1896)] and also the similarity in judicial approach between Brown J in *Plessy* and McClung JA in *Vriend*. See O'Byrne and McGinnis, 'Case Comment.'

138 That is not to say that no other social value systems – for example, secular patriarchy – would be an impediment to achievement of equality. But traditional religious ideology presents the most formidable obstacle.

139 See, e.g., Peter Hogg, *Constitutional Law of Canada*, 4th ed. (Scarborough, Ont.: Carswell 1996), esp. Pt III; John R. Sproat, *Equality Rights and Fundamental Freedoms* (Scarborough, Ont.: Carswell 1996); David Stratas, *The Charter of Rights in Litigation: Direction from the Supreme Court of Canada* (Aurora, Ont.: Canada Law Book 1997), esp. chap. 40; Gérald-A. Beaudoin and Errol Mendes, eds., *The Canadian Charter of Rights and Freedoms* (3rd ed. (Scarborough, Ont.: Carswell 1996).

140 See, e.g., W.L. Morton, *Canadian Identity*, 2nd ed. (Toronto: University of Toronto Press 1972); Kieran Keohane, *Symptoms of Canada: An Essay on the Canadian Identity* (Toronto: University of Toronto Press 1997).

141 The few would include such things as incest and polygamy.

142 The importance of the group is argued forcefully in Denise Réaume, 'Individuals, Groups, and Rights to Public Goods,' *University Toronto Law Journal* 38 (1988), 1.

143 I acknowledge the liberal roots of this idea of inclusion-accommodation. It has, however, the 'maximalist' liberal pedigree rather than the 'minimalist' liberal pedigree as discussed by Lorenne M.G. Clark in 'Liberalism and the Living-Tree: Women, Equality, and the Charter,' *Alberta Law Review* 28 (1990), 384.

144 See James E. Jefferson, 'Gay Rights and the *Charter*,' *University Toronto Faculty Law Review* 43 (1985), 43 (1985), 70. This article sets out the drafting history of s. 15 with reference to homosexuality. For pre-Charter analysis, see Philip Girard, 'Sexual Orientation as a Human Rights Issue in Canada 1969–1985,' *Dalhousie Law Journal* 10 (1986), 267.

145 Many have been critical of Canadian approaches to inclusion of members of various groups. See, e.g., Himani Bannerji, *Thinking Through: Essays on Feminism, Marxism and Anti-racism* (Toronto: Women's Press 1995).

146 On the struggle of gays and lesbians, see Kinsman, *The Regulation of Desire*. Carl Stychin calls this Canadian idea 'postmodern nationalism.' Carl Stychin, 'Equality Rights, Identity Politics, and the Canadian National Imagination,' in *Law's Desire*, chap. 6, at 106.

147 See Shelagh Day and Gwen Brodsky, 'The Duty to Accommodate: Who Will Benefit?' *Canadian Bar Review* 75 (1996), 433. The authors study recent court cases that employ at least a partial accommodative view of what is proper in the Canadian context.

148 Ibid., 462.

149 Ibid.

150 *Dagenais v. CBC*, [1994] 3 SCR 835 at 882.

151 This is not to say that other societies will come to a different response to issues relating to gays and lesbians, like outing. They simply get there by different means.

152 A former Liberal MP, Roseanne Skoke embarrassed herself regularly by saying such things as: 'Homosexuality is not natural, it is immoral and it is undermining the inherent rights and values of our Canadian families.' Her colleague, Tom Wappel, pontificated: 'Homosexuality is statistically abnormal, it is physically abnormal and it is morally immoral.' *Globe and Mail*, Wednesday, 28 September 1994, A1. The Prime Minister said Skoke was entitled to her right of free speech. See also some political pearls set out in Becki Ross, 'Sexual Dis/Orientation or Playing House: To Be or Not to Be Coded Human,' in Stone, ed., *Lesbians in Canada*, chap. 9, 133–45.

153 The ideal of inclusion and accommodation cannot be satisfied simply by transferring the homosexual teacher to an administrative position or buying him or her out of the system, as happened in the cases of Eric Smith or *Valiquette*, discussed above.

154 I am not a proponent of deliberately banning such expression on the playground and other places just because it is 'not nice.' Banning expression, especially at the school level, only glamorizes it. Speech codes should be imposed only in extreme cases where life is being made intolerable for a

particular (group of) student(s). Expression that is otherwise controlled, for example hate speech or harassment or defamation, should be controlled at schools or on campuses but it is antithetical to the academic aim of educational institutions to impose greater controls on expression than exist in society at large, in the name of creating welcoming environments. See a variety of views on this matter in Marie-France Major, 'American Campus Speech Codes: Models for Canadian Universities?' *Education and the Law Journal* 7 (1995), 13; Maurice A. Green and Margaret Correia, 'Comment: Freedom of Speech and Teachers' Duties: *Ross* Revisited,' *Education and the Law Journal* 5 (1993), 361; John J. Furedy, 'Academic Freedom, Opinions and Acts: The Voltaire–Mill Perspective Applied to Current Canadian Cases,' *UNB Law Journal* 44 (1995), 131; Svend Robinson, 'The Collision of Rights,' *UNB Law Journal* 44 (1995), 61; Kelly Lamrock, 'Free Speech on Campus: The Principle Beyond the Crucible,' *UNB Law Journal* 44 (1995), 103; Rhonda Hartman, 'Revitalizing Group Defamation as a Remedy for Hate Speech on Campus,' *Oregon Law Review* 71 (1992), 855; Allison Reyes, 'Freedom of Expression and Public School Teachers,' *Dalhousie Journal of Legal Studies* 4 (1995), 35.

155 *Jones v. The Queen.*
156 Ibid., 577.
157 *Zylberberg v. Sudbury Board of Education (Director)*, 589.
158 Ibid., 592. On this case, see Carol A. Stephenson, 'Religious Exercises and Instruction in Ontario Public Schools,' *University of Toronto Faculty Law Review* 49 (1991), 82. See also *Russow v. British Columbia (Attorney-General)* (1989), 62 DLR (4th) 98 (BCSC).
159 *Dagenais v. CBC*, 877. Likewise, in his dissenting judgment in the New Brunswick Ross case, Ryan JA said: 'As contended by the Human Rights Commission, the rights and freedoms specifically guaranteed by the *Charter*, including those of speech and religion, may be measured against the underlying values and principles of a free and democratic society which are their very genesis, and limited where to do so furthers those values and principles. Included in these are the inherent dignity of the human being, commitment to social justice and equality and respect for cultural and group identity. To give free reign to the asserted freedom of speech and religion of Ross would be to trample upon these underlying values and principles, themselves having the status of entrenched rights under the *Charter* and in international law' (*Attis v. Board of Education of District No. 15* (1993), 142 NBR (2d) 1 at 36 (CA).
160 Even children being raised in a particular religious tradition should not be exposed to ideology that excludes and refuses to accommodate homosex-

uality in their education. The state has an interest in all education of the young and state ideals should prevail.

161 On the role religious groups seek to play in education, see Terri A. Sussel, 'Schoolrooms of a Lesser God: The Fundamentalist Challenge to Public Education,' *Education Law Journal* 1 (1989), 72.

162 Section 29 of the Charter says that nothing in the Charter 'abrogates or derogates from any rights or privileges by or under the Constitution of Canada in respect of denominational, separate or dissentient schools.' This, of course, is an enshrinement of privilege for particular sects at the expense of others or at the expense of society at large. It is an unfortunate perpetuation of nineteenth-century historical concerns into twenty-first century Canada. Jurisdictions like Newfoundland and Quebec have consequently to obtain constitutional amendments to modernize their schools systems. The constitutional provision only covers some denominational schools in some provinces, of course. See *Reference re An Act to Amend the Education Act (Ontario)* (1987), 40 DLR (4th) 18 (SCC); *Re Caldwell and Stuart* (1980), 114 DLR (3d) 357 (BCSC); *Re Caldwell and Stuart* (1982), 132 DLR (3d) 79 (BCCA), appeal dismissed; (1984), 15 DLR (4th) 1 (SCC); Romulo Magsino, 'Denominational Rights in Education,' in Manley-Casimir and Sussel, eds., *Courts in the Classroom*, chap. 3, 88; Marie Parker-Jenkins and Judith A. Osborne, 'Rights in Conflict: The Case of Margaret Caldwell,' *Canadian Journal of Education* 10 (1985), 66; *Re Caldwell and Stuart* (1984), 15 DLR (4th) 1 (SCC).

163 McClung JA in *Vriend* set out a list of grounds on which, according to him, there is no Canadawide protection in human rights legislation. He said: 'While there is unanimous condemnation, in all, the statutes to which we were referred, against discrimination on the grounds of race, colour, sex, age, disability, there is no common or general legislative front against discrimination arising from sexual orientation, nationality or ethnic origin, religion, pregnancy, marital status, ancestry, political belief, creed, nationality/citizenship, criminal convictions, family status, place of origin, source of income, alcohol/drug dependency, civil status, language, social origin, or condition and place of residence. All of these are declared heads of discrimination in one or more, but not all, of the legislative regimes I have mentioned' *Vriend*, 603–4.

164 McClung JA equated their situations and left both to fend for themselves. In fact, the two are not equivalent. Among the many possible grounds of discrimination set out by McClung JA in his list, religion, along with 'political belief' is the 'odd man' out. Religion and political belief are arguably not so much individual characteristics (like race, sexual orientation,

nationality, gender, or disability) as contexts of expression. They are contextual circumstances wherein people deliberately act (usually by expression) to alter society to fit their belief of how it should be ordered. To some extent or another, both religion and politics seek to form society in their own image. They fit uncomfortably with bases for nondiscrimination like gender and sexual orientation which (contrary to the construction often imposed in the case of sexual orientation) do not seek to convert society. Religion is even more unusual than political belief, because the latter, in Canada, will itself be constrained in practice by the Charter of Rights. Political beliefs, put in practice, that are contrary to principles of the Charter can be put into effect only with great difficulty, if at all. A politician in Canada could not act constitutionally and deliberately set up educational institutions, like that in *Vriend*, that excluded people because of their characteristics, like homosexuality. If the views of McClung JA are correct, a religion can do so under the guise of religious freedom. In an inclusive-accommodative society, this should not be the case, especially in the discharge of a public function such as education.

165 Timothy W. Reinig, 'Sin, Stigma & Society: A Critique of Morality and Values in Democratic Law and Policy,' *Buffalo Law Review* 38 (1990), 859 at 878.

166 Commenting on the views of John Finnis, which I referred to earlier, Robert Wintemute says: 'If it were suggested that the beliefs of a Roman Catholic (or Jewish) minority were "the pursuit of an illusion" and were "deeply hostile" and "an active threat" to a Protestant (or Roman Catholic) majority, many would respond that it is for Roman Catholics (or Jews) to decide whether their beliefs are "an illusion" and that the fact that Roman Catholics (or Jews) practise their religion does not prevent Protestants (or Roman Catholics) from practising their religion' (Wintemute, *Sexual Orientation and Human Rights*, 252).

Chapter 4: Homophobic Expression

1 See 'Homosexual Panic Defence,' below.
2 *Culhane v. Rawlings*, [1987] OJ No. 1562 (QL) (Dist. Ct.).
3 *R. v. Homma*, [1989] BCJ No. 793 (QL) (CA).
4 *Children's Aid Society of the Regional Municipality of Waterloo v. R. (T.)*, [1990] OJ No. 766 (QL) (Prov. Ct – Fam. Div.).
5 *R.R.T. v. G.T.*, [1994] OJ No. 2453 (QL) (Prov. Div.).
6 *R. v. Hawkins*, [1986] BCJ No. 1115 (QL) (CA).
7 Per Esson JA.

8 *R. v. (R.K.) N.* (1997), 32 OR (3d) 537 at 540 (CA).
9 See, for example, *Bertrand v. Hôpital Général Juif*, [1994] JTDPQ No. 19 (QL) (H.R. Trib. Mtl); *R. v. J.H.* (1996), 15 OTC 380 (Gen. Div.).
10 *Lee v. Canada (Armed Forces, Chief of Defence Staff)* (1992), 51 FTR 136 (TD).
11 Ibid., 148.
12 *Morgentaler v. Wiche*, [1989] OJ No. 2582 (QL) (HCJ).
13 The court granted the interlocutory injunction.
14 See section on gay bashing, below.
15 *R. v. Luxton*, [1990] 2 SCR 711.
16 Ibid., 716.
17 The Supreme Court of Canada dismissed the appeal which was on issues of constitutional questions. See also *Murphy v. Little Memphis Cabaret Inc.* (1996), 20 OTC 313 (Gen. Div.).
18 See note 158 in Chapter 3 for arguments against barring homophobic expression in schools.
19 *Culhane v. Rawlings.*
20 *P.A.P. v. M.B.P.*, [1986] NSJ No. 492 (QL) (Fam. Ct). The court granted custody to the mother.
21 *Martini v. Martini*, [1987] BCJ No. 2757 (QL) (SC).
22 *Re O and O* (1980), 30 OR (2d) 588 (HCJ).
23 *Guerard v. Parent*, [1986] BCJ No. 1836 (QL) (SC) was a custody case where the mother alleged homosexuality on the part of Mr Guerard who was not the father but played a major role in raising the boy. Drost LJSC said: 'During the course of the trial it became apparent that Cynthia Parent was the source of several allegations concerning Mr. Guerard, namely: that he is a homosexual and had at one time a homosexual relationship with the child's father, Georges Parent; that he had unsavoury and dangerous contacts in the underworld who were a threat to Mrs. Parent's safety; and that he might have sexually abused the child. When Mrs. Parent gave evidence concerning these and other matters, I concluded that her testimony was untrue. There was no evidence to support her claim that Mr. Guerard is homosexual.' The court gave custody to Mr Guerard. In *R.R.T. v. G.T.*, a mother and father were in a dispute over access by the father to the children. The father, an abusive alcoholic who had also sexually assaulted a teenage boy, referred to the mother's boyfriend as a 'homosexual' in an attempt to get the children. In *Adams v. Woodbury*, [1986] BCJ No. 2735 (QL) (SC) there was a custody battle between the natural mother and the couple found by the mother's parents to adopt her child when the parents discovered that their daughter was a lesbian. 'They were disturbed by the fact that their daughter was a lesbian and also questioned whether Brandice should

be raised by her' (per Lamperson LJSC). Even the relatives of a lesbian can take steps to try to take a child away.

Those who ought to know better also make allegations of homosexuality in custody cases. In *Hahn v. Stafford*, [1985] OJ No. 595 (QL) (HCJ), a solicitor father alleged lesbianism on the part of his doctor wife in a dispute over custody of the daughter. The court accepted that the allegations of lesbianism were untrue. Callon J said: 'Since, in any event, as stated by Dr. Awad [who did a clinical assessment of the child], that [i.e., lesbianism] would be a non-issue in regards to custody, and that would or should be appreciated by the petitioner as a practising solicitor, I am satisfied that by these unfounded allegations, he introduced into the litigation a reaction of anger and hostility on the part of the respondent for which he is entirely responsible.'

24 *Re O and O.*
25 *Whyte v. Whyte* (1991), 101 NSR (2d) 249 (SC TD).
26 *Austin v. Austin*, [1986] NBJ No. 547 (QL) (QB – Fam. Div.).
27 The divorce was granted and custody of the two girls awarded to the father.
28 *J.E.B. v. R.G.B.*, [1996] BCJ No. 2717 (QL) (SC).
29 *D. v. D.* (1978), 88 DLR (3d) 578 (Ont. Co. Ct).
30 Ibid., 583 per Smith Co Ct J.
31 See Marie-France Major, 'Sexual-Orientation Hate Propaganda: Time to Regroup,' *Canadian Journal of Law and Society* 11 (1996), 221. The Canadian Criminal Code sections of relevance are RSC 1985, c. C-42, ss. 181, 318, and 319. There is a large body of writing on hate expression. See, e.g., the symposium entitled 'Language as Violence *v.* Freedom of Expression in the Canadian and American Perspectives on Group Defamation,' *Buffalo Law Review* 37 (1988), 337; Eddie Taylor, 'Hanging up on Hate: Contempt of Court as a Tool to Shut Down Hatelines,' *National Journal of Constitutional Law* 5 (1995), 163; Evelyn Kalen, 'Never Again: Target Group Responses to the Debate Concerning Anti-Hate Propaganda Legislation,' *Windsor Yearbook of Access to Justice* 11 (1991), 46; Richard Moon, 'The Supreme Court of Canada on the Structure of Freedom of Expression Adjudication,' *University of Toronto Law Journal* 45 (1995), 419; Keith Dubick, 'Freedom to Hate: Do the Criminal Code Proscriptions against Hate Propaganda Infringe the Charter?' *Saskatchewan Law Review* 54 (1990), 149; Martha Shaffer, 'Criminal Responses to Hate-Motivated Violence: Is Bill C-41 Tough Enough?' *McGill Law Journal* 41 (1995), 199; Martine Valois, 'Hate Propaganda, Section 2(b) and Section 1 of the Charter: A Canadian Constitutional Dilemma,' *Revue juridique Thémis* 26 (1992), 373; Mayo Moran, 'Talking about Hate Speech: A Rhetorical Analysis of American and Canadian Approaches to the Regulation of Hate Speech,' *Wisconsin Law Review* [1994] 1424; Ian B. McKenna,

'Canada's Hate Propaganda Laws – A Critique,' *Ottawa Law Review* 26 (1994), 159; Bruce Elman, 'Combatting Racist Speech: The Canadian Experience,' *Alberta Law Review* 32 (1989), 623; Alan R. Regel, 'Hate Propaganda: A Reason to Limit Freedom of Speech,' *Saskatchewan Law Review* 49 (1984), 303.

32 *Irwin Toy Ltd. v. Quebec (Attorney-General)* (1989), 58 DLR (4th) 577 (SCC).

33 *R. v. Keegstra* (1990), 61 CCC (3d) 1 (SCC).

34 See Richard Moon, 'Drawing Lines in a Culture of Prejudice: R. *v.* Keegstra and the Restriction of Hate Propaganda,' *UBC Law Review* 26 (1992), 99; Moon, 'The Supreme Court of Canada.'

35 *R. v. Keegstra*, 36–7.

36 Derek Raymaker and David Kilgour, 'The Freedom to Promote Hate: What We Learned from Jim Keegstra and Malcolm Ross,' *UNB Law Journal* 41 (1992), 327 at 329.

37 Moon, 'Drawing Lines in a Culture of Prejudice,' 139.

38 *McAleer v. Canada (Canadian Human Rights Commission)* (1996), 132 DLR (4th) 672 (FCTD).

39 Ibid., 675.

40 *Korn v. Potter* (1996), 134 DLR (4th) 437 at 440 (BCSC), per Holmes J.

41 *Vriend v. Alberta* (1996), 132 DLR (4th) 595 at 606 (Alta. CA); reversed (1998), 156 DLR (4th) 385 (SCC).

42 Note that McKenna develops this view in the race context in 'Canada's Hate Propaganda Laws.'

43 See Chapter 1.

44 *Morgentaler v. Wiche.*

45 *R. v. Stewart* (1995), 41 CR (4th) 102 (BCCA).

46 Ibid., 106.

47 Ibid., 106–7, per Wood JA.

48 See note 95, below.

49 *R. v. Moore*, [1987] BCJ No. 2734 (QL) (Co. Ct).

50 *R. v. R. (S).*, [1989] OJ No. 1487 (QL) (Youth Ct). Of course homosexuals can do violence to other homosexuals. For one example of a brutal sexual relationship that lead to death, see *R. v. Kendall*, [1987] OJ No. 388 (QL) (CA).

51 *R. v. Valley* (1986), 26 CCC (3d) 207 (Ont. CA); leave to appeal to SCC refused, 22 April 1986.

52 Ibid., 240.

53 The association of (male) homosexuals and violence in S&M situations was made explicit in the English decision of *R. v. Brown*, [1993] 2 All ER 75 (HL). See David McArdle, 'A Few Hard Cases? Sport, Sadomasochism and Public Policy in the English Courts,' *Canadian Journal of Law and Society* 10 (1995),

109; Law Commission (of England), *Consent in the Criminal Law* (consultation paper number 139) (London 1995).

54 *R. v. Charest*, [1990] AQ No. 405 (QL) (CA).

55 Richard Posner, *Sex and Reason* (Cambridge, Mass.: Harvard University Press 1992), 125. There is a similar distinction between a 'real' lesbian and a woman who is simply 'pretending' (out of caprice?). Dian Day says (ironically): 'Real lesbians don't have children. This is proclaimed with equal loudness by both straight women (and men) and 'real' lesbians. Real lesbians have never been fucked (perhaps rape is an exception). Real lesbians have never had sperm inside their bodies ... Real lesbians are not interested in children – especially male children. Real lesbians find children boring and tedious. Real lesbians have much more important work to do.' Dian Day, 'Lesbian/Mother,' in Sharon Dale Stone, ed., *Lesbians in Canada*, chap. 2 (Toronto: Between the Lines 1990), at 36.

56 Posner, *Sex and Reason*, 233.

57 *R. v. Cavanagh and Donaldson* (1976), 15 OR (2d) 173 (CA).

58 *R. v. T.D.E.* (1991), 116 AR 382 (Prov. Ct).

59 *R. v. G.J.M.* (1992), 130 AR 33 (QB), reversed (1993), 135 AR 204 (CA).

60 See also *Collin v. Kaplan*, [1983] 1 FC 496 (TD); *R. v. R.A.H.*, [1989] OJ No. 604 (QL) (Youth Ct); *R. v. S.W.*, [1989] OJ No. 65 (QL) (CA); *R. v. A.J.M.* (1986), 29 CCC (3d) 418 (Alta. QB); *Piche v. Canada (Solicitor General)*, [1984] FCJ No. 1008 (QL) (TD).

61 In *R. v. E.S.*, [1991] AJ No. 873 (QL) (Prov. Ct) the court dealt with such an application to move a case to adult court. The accused was a sixteen-year-old male prostitute charged with attempted murder, unlawful confinement, possession of a weapon, and aggravated assault – not somebody of whom, if the accusation were true, one would immediately have thought incapable of looking after himself. One of the factors the court was asked to take into account was that 'if placed in either the Federal or Provincial corrections systems, unless he chose otherwise, the accused because of his appearance, chosen lifestyle and probable sexual attractiveness to adult predators, for his own well being would likely be placed in a form of protective custody situation.' The court held that it would not be best to transfer the youth because 'this youth is small of stature, of feminine appearance and characteristics, allegedly a male prostitute who cross-dresses.' The inevitability of homosexual violence towards him was of considerable concern to the court.

62 *R. v. Hennessey, Williams and Kumka*, [1969] 2 CCC 372 (Man. CA).

63 *R. v. Smith*, [1989] MJ No. 394 (QL) (Prov. Ct – Crim. Div.).

64 *R. v. White* (1990), 88 Sask. R 54 (QB); appeal dismissed (1991), 91 Sask. R 225 (CA).

65 See Dennis Dahl, '"Homosexual-panic defence" a justification of violence,' *Vancouver Sun*, 28 December 1995, A15.
66 *R. v. Fournier* (1982), 70 CCC (2d) 351 (Que. CA).
67 See also *R. v. Tanner* (1994), 19 OR (3d) 259 (CA), reversed (1995), 97 CCC (3d) 289 (SCC).
68 *R. v. Magliaro* (1981), 45 NSR (2d) 504 (Co. Ct).
69 Ibid., 512.
70 Donald Casswell, *Lesbians, Gay Men, and Canadian Law* (Toronto: Emond Montgomery 1996), 633.
71 *R. v. Hoyt*, [1991] YJ No. 176 (QL) (Terr. Ct).
72 The court referred to Ruby on *Sentencing*, 3rd ed. at (Toronto: Butterworths 1987), 416, where he deals with what is probably an even more accurate label than 'homosexual panic,' namely 'heterosexual panic.'
73 See also *R. v. Ryznar* (1986), 43 Man. R (2d) 143 (CA); leave to appeal to SCC refused (1986), 46 Man. R (2d) 160n; *R. v. Butler* (1995), 104 CCC (3d) 198 (BCCA); leave to appeal to SCC refused, 23 May 1996.
74 *R. v. Carifelle* (1988), 90 AR 316 (CA).
75 Ibid., 319.
76 *R. v. Carolan* (1995), 163 AR 238 at 239 (Prov. Ct).
77 Per McMeekin Prov. Ct J. See also *R. v. Moore* (1996), 81 BCAC 153 (CA).
78 *R. v. Hill* (1982), 32 CR (3d) 88 (Ont. CA); appeal allowed (1985), 51 CR (3d) 97 (SCC).
79 Ibid.
80 Ibid., 218.
81 See also *R. v. Wilson*, [1991] OJ No. 1746 (QL) (Prov. Div.).
82 *R. v. Valley.*
83 Ibid., 218.
84 *R. v. Lupien*, [1969] 1 CCC 32 at 34 (BCCA), per Davey CJBC, dissenting.
85 Ibid., 38.
86 Ibid., 34.
87 Ibid., 36.
88 *R. v. Lupien*, at 196.
89 Ibid., 198.
90 *R. v. Hansford* (1987), 33 CCC (3d) 74 (Alta. CA); leave to appeal to SCC refused (1987), 56 CR (3d) xxviii.
91 Ibid., 82, per Hutchinson JA for the court.
92 See *R. v. Stewart.*
93 Lev. 20:13.
94 Donald Casswell says: 'It is submitted that there should be no reason to prevent a tribunal or court from assessing alleged sexual orientation

discrimination from the victim's perspective – that is, by using a "reasonable lesbian" or "reasonable gay man" test.' He makes this argument in the context of human rights legislation, but perhaps it should apply in the present situations. Casswell, *Lesbians, Gay Men, and Canadian Law,* 43.

95 Henry E. Adams, Lester W. Wright, Jr, and Bethany A. Lohr, 'Is Homophobia Associated with Homosexual Arousal?' *Journal of Abnormal Psychology* 105 (1996), 440. The authors conclude: 'The results of this study indicate that individuals who score in the homophobic range and admit negative affect toward homosexuality demonstrate significant sexual arousal to male homosexual erotic stimuli' (443). There is an excellent reference list for books on homophobia and homophobic behaviour on pages 444–5. See a survey of this issue in Linda Bates, 'Lying in Wait to Pound a "Queer" May Be a Sign of Latent Homosexuality,' *Vancouver Sun,* 24 March 1997, B7. See also the item under 'Lust' in *Globe and Mail* (national edition), 12 September 1996, A20.

96 *R. v. Kluke,* [1987] OJ No. 766 (QL) (CA).

97 *R. v. Dutton* (1996), 6 OTC 371 (Gen. Div.).

98 *R. v. Berger* (1975), 27 CCC (2d) 357 (BCCA), leave to appeal to SCC refused (1975), 27 CCC (2d) 357n.

99 In the Wolfenden Report we are told: 'There are other cases in which the existence of a latent homosexuality may be inferred from an individual's outlook or judgment; for instance, a persistent and indignant preoccupation with the subject of homosexuality has been taken to suggest in some cases the existence of repressed homosexuality.' *The Report of the Committee on Homosexual Offences and Prostitution* ('The Wolfenden Report') (London: HMSO, CMND 247 1957), para. 24.

100 Eve Kosofsky Sedgwick, *The Epistemology of the Closet* (Berkeley: University of California Press 1990), 20.

101 *R. v. Fraser* (1980), 55 CCC (2d) 503 (Alta. CA).

102 Ibid., 507, per McDermid JA.

103 Ibid., quoted at 507.

104 Ibid., 512. McDermid JA cited changes in attitudes to homosexuals: '... in the last decade the attitude of the general public to homosexuality has changed considerably so that even if not approved of by the great majority, it is at least tolerated. We read in the newspapers of conventions by homosexuals, of parades and of clubs being formed for homosexuals. However the best evidence as to their toleration is that the Parliament of Canada has provided that a homosexual act between consenting persons over 21 committed in private is no longer an offence' (513).

105 Ibid., 518.

106 Another case where the court had some sympathy for the homosexual panic defence was *R. v. Lee* (1985), 166 APR 387 (NSCA). In this case, the accused was convicted of robbery of a man whom he said made sexual advances to him. The accused struck the man and stole his stereo, some records, and $140 in cash. The Court of Appeal dismissed an appeal of a sentence of five years' imprisonment. In deciding the case, however, Macdonald JA said: 'Of more relevance perhaps is the fact that on the hearing of this appeal the appellant by way of background and in the absence of a pre-sentence report told the court that he, when quite young, had been sexually assaulted by one of his older brothers and that his violent reaction when sexually approached by Mr. Cushing was in part caused by remembrance of the earlier episode. He also said that his previous robbery conviction was committed as a result of a homosexual advance made to him. He also told the court that his nephew who was with him at Mr. Cushing's is a homosexual but that he was not aware of such fact at that time' (389).

107 *R. v. Guy S.* (1991), 5 OR (3d) 97 (CA), leave to appeal to SCC refused (1992), 6 OR (3d) xiii.

108 Ibid., 101.

109 Ibid., at 111.

110 *R. v. Dubois* (1987), 83 AR 161 (CA).

111 Ibid., 163–4.

112 One judge, albeit a dissenting one, thought that the homosexual panic defence could conceivably be available to a homosexual person. *R. v. Donoghue* (1978), 42 CCC (2d) 40 (Ont. CA) was a case of a man convicted of manslaughter at trial. Both the deceased and the accused were gay and the accused admitted the killing. The accused brought the deceased to his place for sex but he said the deceased refused to engage in a particular encounter and so the accused ordered the deceased out. He did not leave and the accused agreed he could stay overnight. But he said the deceased grabbed a knife, a fight ensued, and the accused stabbed him. The accused was convicted, but Dubin JA on appeal dissented and thought that there might have been a misdirection. He said: 'It was the theory of the defence that the deceased attacked the accused either to rob him or by reason of a homosexual panic. On the latter theory, there was evidence tendered to support it. On the robbery theory, the deceased was obviously destitute. The accused had money, and there was some evidence of a discussion of money. No reference was made to any of the evidence bearing on that theory' (46).

113 *R. v. Gauthier* (1975), 34 CCC (2d) 266 (Que. CA).

114 Ibid., 275.
115 Ibid.
116 *R. v. Fraser.*
117 *R. v. Fournier.* See also *R. v. Gauthier; R. v. Lee.*
118 *R. v. Cribbin* (1994), 17 OR (3d) 548 (CA).
119 See also *R. v. Stewart; R. v. Plato,* [1987] AJ No. 903 (QL) (CA).
120 *R. v. Hansford.*
121 Ibid., 89.
122 See also *R. v. Guy S; R. v. Dubois.* The court appeared to doubt the inciden-
     tal nature of the robbery in a situation where homosexual panic was raised
     in *R. v. L.B.* (1989), 98 AR 259 (Prov. Ct – Youth Div.), in which it was
     argued that a young person charged with second degree murder be
     moved to adult court. The accused had been occasionally employed by the
     deceased in Edmonton. They went on a trip to Calgary together and
     stayed in a hotel. According to the accused ('L.B.'): 'after watching a por-
     nographic movie which the young person described as 'sick,' we show-
     ered, had another drink, and fell asleep on one of the twin beds, clothed in
     his own underwear and G.A.'s [the deceased's] dressing gown. Some time
     in the night he awoke to discover that G.A. was by then occupying the
     same bed and was fondling the young person's genitals. L.B. got out of
     bed and finding himself naked, put on his underwear which he found on
     the floor. L.B. went to the bathroom, had a cigarette and an alcoholic
     drink, and pondered what he believed G.A. had been doing to him. G.A.
     addressed the young person from the bed saying it was too early to get up
     and that L.B. should come back to bed. He returned to the same bed and
     believing that G.A. was feigning sleep, L.B. did likewise. Half an hour
     later G.A. again began to fondle the young person's genitals whereupon
     L.B. again went to the bathroom and smoked another cigarette. He turned
     out the bathroom light, picked up the toilet tank lid, wrapped it in a towel
     and walked to the side of the bed where G.A. was lying on his left side.'
     L.B. struck him several times and then took G.A.'s money, rings, watch,
     alcohol, and briefcase. The court thought it unlikely that a defence of prov-
     ocation would succeed.
123 Cynthia Petersen, 'A Queer Response to Bashing: Legislating Against
     Hate,' *Queen's Law Journal* 16 (1991), 237 at 237. See also Henk van den
     Boogaard, 'Blood Furious Underneath the Skins ...: On Anti-Homosexual
     Violence: Its Nature and the Needs of the Victims,' in *Homosexuality, Which
     Homosexuality?* (London: GMP 1989), 49; Ruthann Robson, *Lesbian
     (Out)Law: Survival under the Rule of Law* (Ithaca, N.Y.: Firebrand 1992), esp.
     chap. 12.

124 The underreporting of hate crimes is mentioned in Julian *v.* Roberts, *Disproportionate Harm: Hate Crimes in Canada – An Analysis of Recent Statistics* (Ottawa: Department of Justice 1995), 23.

125 *Re Priape Enrg. and the Deputy Minister of National Revenue* (1979), 52 CCC (2d) 44 (Que. Super. Ct – Crim. Div.).

126 Ibid., 49.

127 See, e.g., Miro Cernetig, 'Gaybashing in Vancouver Routine,' *Globe and Mail* (national edition), 12 December 1996, A7B.

128 *R. v. Jolicoeur* (unreported), BC Prov. Ct, 7 February 1997.

129 *R. v. Wilson*; see also *R. v. Karalapillai*, [1995] OJ No. 2105 (QL) (Ct of Justice – Prov. Div.).

130 *R. v. Ingram and Grimsdale* (1977), 35 CCC (2d) 376 at 379. And in *R. v. Lelas* (1990), 74 OR (2d) 552 at 558, Houlden JA said: 'When mischief is racially or religiously motivated and is done to cause emotional injury or shock to a particular segment of Canadian society, it calls for a far more severe penalty than mischief which is done merely to damage property.'

131 *R. v. D.M.* (1990), 61 CCC (3d) 129 at 131 (Ont. CA).

132 Another, earlier instance of some, albeit rather faint, judicial recognition of the larger issue into which the gay bashing should be situated is the case of *R. v. Atkinson, Ing and Roberts* (1978), 43 CCC (2d) 342 (Ont. CA), wherein five youths set out to beat up 'queers' in a local park that 'had a reputation of being a place frequented by homosexuals.' See also *S.H.M. v. R.* (1989), 71 CR (3d) 257 (SCC), where a seventeen-year-old was charged with murder and possession of stolen property. The Court of Appeal ((1987), 52 Alta. LR 356) allowed the appeal of the lower court decision and directed the transfer. The Court of Appeal said that, contrary to what the Court of Queen's Bench said, there was a record of violence here – there were two counts of sexual assault against young boys. The court also considered 'the callous and brutal nature of the crime alleged and the insensitivity of the perpetrators as they sold the property while the victim lay dead in the basement' (per Laycroft JA). The Supreme Court of Canada said it would not interfere in the decision to transfer the case to adult court, in part because of the 'age of the accused and the inappropriateness of a 3-year sentence, given the heinous nature of the alleged crimes' (305). Also, in *R. v. Glode*, [1991] OJ No. 2651 (QL) (Gen. Div.), the accused was charged with murder. In sentencing, O'Driscoll J said: 'No reports [were put] before me that in any way ameliorate what has been alleged by Crown counsel that you are a very dangerous 25 year old male, especially when at large amongst male homosexuals. It is apparent that you think that these people are fair game to rob at your whim.' See also *R. v. Young,*

[1991] OJ No. 2210 (QL) (Gen. Div.). In these three cases, the judges note the element of homophobia involved, but little turns on it as a larger issue. The accused might deserve a harsh punishment but only because of the 'heinous' nature of the crime, not particularly because of the threat he represented to the homosexual community at large.

133 *R. v. McDonald*, [1995] OJ No. 2137 (QL) (Gen. Div.).

134 *Duval v. The Queen* (1970), 15 CR (NS) 140 (Que. CA).

135 *R. v. Benner,* [1989] OJ No. 2474 (QL) (Prov. Ct – Crim. Div.).

136 *R. v. A.J.-R.*, [1991] OJ No. 1978 (QL) (Prov. Div.).

137 The court decided not to raise him to adult court because of a number of factors. The accused was fifteen years old. *R. v. A.B.H.*, [1992] OJ No. 814 (QL) (Prov. Div.) is the case involving the other young offender involved in *R. v. A.J.-R.*, and this one was raised to adult court. In *R. v. Adam H.* (1992), 10 OR (3d) 683 (Gen. Div.); application for review dismissed (1993), 12 OR (3d) 634 (CA), the young offender in *R. v. A.J.-R.* appealed the decision to move him to ordinary court. The application was dismissed.

138 *R. v. D.J.M.*, [1990] OJ No. 514 (QL) (Prov. Ct – Youth Off. Ct).

139 Another example is *R. v. Pizzardi* (1994), 17 OR (3d) 623 (CA). There was a robbery of gold pieces from a gay man. According to Lacourcière JA: 'When asked by Levis whether there was any other way to raise money, the appellant allegedly told the group that he believed that Rickard (the complainant) was in possession of gold pieces, and that Rickard was an older gay person who lived alone and could be persuaded to give up the gold collection' (626). The 'homosexual' as an easy and natural target is also illustrated in the case of *R. v. Cooney* (1995), 98 CCC (3d) 196 (Ont. CA), where the accused told another person that he and a friend 'had placed an ad in a "fag" magazine to lure a homosexual victim. He said he had robbed the man of his bank card and "scared the shit out of him" to get his PIN number for the card. He then shot the man four times in the head.' See also *R. v. Pilgrim*, [1983] OJ No. 812 (QL) (HCJ). A final and tragic example of this association of bashing and robbery is *R. v. Schau*, [1987] MJ No. 363 (QL) (CA), where the accused and others were charged with a number of offences arising in part out of the following facts as set out by Twaddle JA:

At a very early hour in the morning of March 26, 1986, a young man aged 24 attended at the grounds of the Legislative Building in Winnipeg intent upon finding a partner for homosexual activity. He was approached by two men, one of whom was the respondent Schau, and an assignation was made. It was arranged that Schau and the other man in one car would follow the intended victim in his car to the place of assignation. En route, the victim became suspicious when he saw a third man accompanying Schau and his known companion. The victim stopped his automobile to find out what was happening. He walked towards the other automobile which had pulled up behind him. As he was looking into the back seat of the other automobile, he was hit on the back of the head with a beer bottle and robbed of his wallet. He then was subjected to a very severe beating.

The wallet of the vcitim contained identification which showed his home address. At about 3:00 a.m. in the same morning, three or four persons including the respondent Goffard broke into the previous victim's home then occupied by his mother and a brother who were in their beds asleep. Woken abruptly by men wearing masks, the occupants separately were terrorized and subjected to much personal violence and verbal abuse. The premises were ransacked and goods worth $8,500.00 taken. Amongst the goods taken was a solid gold watch subsequently pawned by Goffard.

It has been claimed by a Crown attorney that neo-Nazis in Winnipeg beat and rob homosexuals in what are called 'fund raisers.' See 'Neo-Nazis went after gay men, Crown says,' *Globe and Mail* (national edition), 13 August 1997, A7.

140 *Rose v. Société de transport de la Communauté urbaine de Montréal*, [1996] AQ No. 688 (QL) (Super. Ct).
141 Per Bilodeau J.
142 The court found that the alert system should have been put on from the start and that Montreal Transport was responsible for the damages.
143 Text accompanying note 138, above.
144 *R. v. Gallant* (1994), 95 Man. R (2d) 296 (CA).
145 Ibid., 297.
146 *R. v. MacFarlane* (1989), 55 Man. R (2d) 105 (CA).
147 Ibid., 106, per Monnin CJM.
148 Ibid., 113.
149 Ibid.
150 *R. v. Kluke*.
151 *R. v. Rutledge*, [1996] BCJ No. 755 (QL) (SC).
152 Per Miller Prov. Ct J.
153 See Robson, *Lesbian (Out)Law*, 147.
154 Petersen, 'A Queer Response to Bashing,' 239.
155 *R. v. Richard* (1982), 16 Man. R (2d) 355 (CA).
156 Ibid., 355–6.

157 *R. v. Longpre*, [1993] MJ No. 309 (QL) (Prov. Ct).

158 Per Devine Prov. Ct J.

159 The accused was sentenced to eight years in jail. The judge also noted a curious fact: 'Interestingly, according to the complainant, at least one of [the accused's] associates – one of the other step-daughters – was also motivated by jealousy, she also allegedly having a lesbian relationship with the complainant.'

160 See esp. s. 718.2 of the Criminal Code, RSC 1985, c. C-16, as amended by SC 1995, c. 22, s. 6, and SC 1997, c. 23, s. 17. See also Shaffer, 'Criminal Responses to Hate-Motivated Violence: Is Bill C-41 Tough Enough?'

161 Some forces now recruit homosexuals. See Mia Stansbury, 'Cautiously Coming Out,' *Vancouver Sun*, 4 November 1995, F11.

162 The police have historically been very active in attempting to root out homosexual activity to punish. See Gary Kinsman, *The Regulation of Desire: Homo and Hetero Sexualities* (Montreal: Black Rose 1996), esp. at 170*ff*. See, however, Janice L. Ristock, '"And Justice for All?" ... The Social Context of Legal Responses to Abuse in Lesbian Relationships,' *Canadian Journal of Women and the Law* 7 (1994), 415. This police desire to find homosexuality is perhaps limited to male homosexuality; police response to situations involving lesbians is in some cases at best disbelief.

163 *R. v. Goguen* (1977), 36 CCC (2d) 570 (BCCA).

164 Ibid., 572, per Branca JA. See also *R. v. K. and H.* (1957), 26 CR 186 (Alta. SC).

165 *R. v. White* (1975), 25 CCC (2d) 172 (Ont. CA).

166 See also *R. v. Lefebvre* (1978), 4 CR (3d) 164 (Que. Ct Sess.) Two men having sex in a car in a parking lot at 4:30 am does not constitute having sex in a public place.

167 *R. v. Mailhot* (1996), 108 CCC (3d) 376 at 384 (Que. CA).

168 Ibid.

169 *Re R.L.* [1981] OJ No. 382 (QL) (Co. Ct).

170 *R. v. Lupien*.

171 *R. v. Smith*.

172 *R. v. Lemoine* (1992), 113 NSR (2d) 361 at 363 (Prov. Ct); See similarly *R. v. Devereaux* (1996), 112 CCC (3d) 243 (Nfld. CA); *Newfoundland and Labrador (Human Rights Commission) v. Newfoundland and Labrador (Minister of Employment and Labour Relations)* (1995), 127 DLR (4th) 694 (Nfld. TD).

173 See Casswell, *Lesbians, Gay Men, and Canadian Law*, chap. 9 and Peter Rusk, 'Same-Sex Benefits and the Evolving Conception of Family,' *University of Toronto Faculty Law Review* 52 (1993), 170.

174 See Richard Green '"Give Me Your Tired, Your Poor, Your Huddled

Masses" (of Heterosexuals): An Analysis of American and Canadian Immigration Policy,' *Anglo-American Law Review* 16 (1987), 139 at 151.

175 See *Re Haig and The Queen in right of Canada* (1991), 86 DLR (4th) 617 (Ont. Ct – Gen. Div.), appeal dismissed (1992), 94 DLR (4th) 1 (Ont. CA); *Douglas v. Canada* (1992), 98 DLR (4th) 129 (FCTD).

176 See *Little Sisters Book and Art Emporium v. Minister of Justice* (1996), 131 DLR (4th) 486 (BCSC); affirmed [1998] BCJ No. 1507 QL (CA). An account of the trial of this case is contained in Janine Fuller and Stuart Blackley, *Restricted Entry: Censorship on Trial* (Vancouver: Press Gang 1995). See also Chapter 2.

177 See *Pizarro v. Canada (Minister of Employment and Immigration)* (1994), 75 FTR 120 (TD); *Dykon v. Canada (Minister of Employment and Immigration)* (1994), 25 Imm. LR (2d) 193 (FCTD); *Canada v. Ward*, [1993] 2 SCR 689; Nicole La Violette, 'The Immutable Refugees: Sexual Orientation in *Canada (A.G.) v. Ward*,' *University of Toronto Faculty Law Review* 55 (1997), 1. For a treatment of immigration/refugee decisions from the immigration and refugee boards, see Casswell, *Lesbians, Gay Men, and Canadian Law*, 575–603.

178 *789617 Ontario Inc. c.o.b. as The Spa on Maitland v. Toronto (City) and Nixon, Commissioner and Chief Building Official for Toronto (City)* (1990), 75 OR (2d) 475 (Dist. Ct).

179 Ibid., 478.

180 *Haig v. Durrell*, [1990] OJ No. 1350 (QL) (HCJ).

181 Related instances are dealt with in Casswell, *Lesbians, Gay Men, and Canadian Law*, 494–5.

182 Another example is the controversy in Red Deer about the local museum's intention to mount an exhibit on gays in Alberta. See 'Alberta opposes grant for gay study,' *Vancouver Sun*, 16 August 1997, A6.

183 *Trudel et Commission des droits de la personne du Québec v. Camping & Plage Gilles Fortier Inc.*, [1994] JTDPQ No. 32 (QL) (HR Trib Que.).

184 See Robert Wintemute, *Sexual Orientation and Human Rights: The United States Constitution, the European Convention, and the Canadian Charter* (Oxford: Oxford University Press 1995), chap. 8. See also Diana Majury, 'Refashioning the Unfashionable: Claiming Lesbian Identities in the Legal Context,' *Canadian Journal of Women and the Law* 7 (1994), 286. Cf. *Re Board of Governors of the University of Saskatchewan and Saskatchewan Human Rights Commission* (1976), 66 DLR (3d) 561 (Sask. QB); doubted in *Re CIP Paper Products Ltd. and Saskatchewan Human Rights Commission* (1978), 87 DLR (3d) 609 (Sask. CA).

185 *525044 Alberta Ltd. (c.o.b. Tony C's 21 Club & Restaurant) v. Triple 5 Corp.*, [1993] AJ No. 728 (QL) (QB).

186 *R. v. Humphrey*, [1984] OJ 218 (QL) (HCJ).

187 *R. v. Parks* (1993), 84 CCC (3d) 353 (Ont. CA) (leave to appeal denied, [1994] 1 SCR x) where the court allowed challenges for cause in jury selection based on allegations of racial bias.

188 *R. v. Alli* (1996), 110 CCC (3d) 283 (Ont. CA).

189 Ibid., 285.

190 *R. v. Musson* (1996), 3 CR (5th) 61 (Ont. Gen. Div.).

191 Ibid., 66.

192 Ibid.

193 *R. v. Benner*, [1989] OJ No. 2474 (QL) (Prov. Ct – Crim. Div.).

194 *R. v. Chaisson* (1995), 102 CCC (3d) 564 (NBCA); appeal allowed (1995), 99 CCC (3d) 289 (SCC).

195 Ibid., 569–70.

196 *Mercedes Homes Inc. v. Grace*, [1993] OJ No. 2610 (QL) (Gen. Div.).

197 *Layland v. Ontario (Minister of Consumer and Commercial Relations)* (1993), 104 DLR (4th) 214 (Ont. Ct – Gen. Div.).

198 Ibid., 222, per Southey J.

199 Ibid., 231.

200 *Egan v. Canada* (1993), 103 DLR (4th) 336 at 342 (FCA).

201 Ibid., 359.

202 *Egan v. Canada* (1995), 124 DLR (4th) 609 at 625 (SCC).

203 Ibid., 649.

204 *Brown v. British Columbia (Minister of Health)* (1990), 66 DLR (4th) 444 (BCSC).

205 Ibid., 457.

206 Ibid., 459.

207 Ibid.

208 Ibid. See also *Little Sisters; Haig v. Durrell.*

209 *R. v. Wilson.*

210 *R. v. Smith.*

211 *Andrews v. Law Society of British Columbia*, [1989] 1 SCR 143.

212 Ibid., 175.

213 *R. v. Keegstra*, 36–7.

214 Ibid., 37. See also Roberts, *Disproportionate Harm*, 3–4. This Report contains a good bibliography of works in this area.

215 *R. v. Wilson.*

Chapter 5: Outing

1 Michel Foucault, *The History of Sexuality,* vol 1, *An Introduction* (New York: Vintage 1990), 23.

2 Ibid., 35.
3 Ibid., 59.
4 Ibid., 101.
5 See Bruce Ryder, 'Straight Talk: Male Heterosexual Privilege,' *Queen's Law Journal* 16 (1991), 287.
6 See Didi Herman, *Rights of Passage: Struggles for Lesbian and Gay Legal Equality* (Toronto: University of Toronto Press 1994); Jeffrey Weeks, 'Capitalism and the Organisation of Sex,' Gay Left Collective, eds., *Homosexuality: Power and Politics*, chap. 1 (London: Allison & Busby 1980).
7 John Eastburn Boswell, 'Jews, Bicycle Riders, and Gay People: The Determination of Social Consensus and Its Impact on Minorities,' *Yale Journal of Law and the Humanities* 1 (1989), 205 at 206.
8 Boswell says there are many and no real reasons for this ebb and flow.
9 The presence or absence of a 'moral justification' for outing is discussed in Andrea Austen and Adrian Alex Wellington, 'Outing: The Supposed Justifications,' *Canadian Journal of Law and Jurisprudence* 8 (1995), 83. The authors conclude: 'Outing will rarely be morally justified as long as remaining closeted is necessary to avoid serious social disadvantage, harassment and violence' (105). The authors do not look at the appropriate legal response and this chapter does not examine general moral justifications.
10 Outing, of course, could have an even larger meaning and could have an impact on most people, covering their many secret characteristics or identities. Here it will be restricted to gay men, lesbians, and bisexuals, for the most part. In many matters the interests of these groups conflict. Be it in relation to same-sex spousal benefits, pornography, or children, the interests of gay men and lesbians often seem to diverge and indeed to be diametrically opposed. See Sharon Dale Stone, 'Introduction,' in Sharon Dale Stone, ed., *Lesbians in Canada* (Toronto: Between the Lines 1990), 9–10; Mary Eaton, 'Lesbians and the Law,' in ibid., chap. 8. However, at the risk of being rash, it can be said that with outing the issues relating to gay men, lesbians, and bisexuals are roughly similar.
11 See *The Sheaf* [University of Saskatchewan student paper] 19 May 1994, 1.
12 The process of coming out is made more complex if it is not just the sexual orientation of the person that society denigrates. If the person is a woman, a member of a racial or linguistic minority, or a disabled person, or such like, then there is double (or multiple) inferiorization and the person may be forced to 'choose her oppression' or at least deal with one issue at a time.
13 See Erving Goffman, *Stigma* (Englewood Cliffs, N.J.: Prentice-Hall 1963), chap. 2, 'Information Control and Personal Identity.'
14 Thus, courts sometimes find that in custody and access cases one parent

alleges (falsely) homosexuality on the part of the other parent in order to get custody. For example, *Hahn v. Stafford*, [1985] OJ No. 595 (QL) (HCJ); *Re O and O* (1980), 30 OR (2d) 588 (HCJ). See Chapters 2 and 3.

15 See John F. Hernandez, 'Outing in the Time of AIDS: Legal and Ethical Considerations,' *St Thomas Law Review* 5 (1993), 493. See also *Stiles v. Canada (Attorney General)* (1986), 3 FTR 234 (TD); and *Canada v. Thwaites*, [1994] 3 FC 38 (TD.); Lynne Pearlman, 'Theorizing Lesbian Oppression and the Politics of Outness in the Case of *Waterman v. Nat'l Life Assurance*: A Beginning in Lesbian Human Rights/Equality Jurisprudence,' *Canadian Journal of Women and the Law* 7 (1994), 454.

16 *R. v. Paterson*, [1995] BCJ No. 1032 (QL) (SC); affirmed, [1998] BCJ No. 126 (QL) (CA).

17 See *Parks v. H.H. Marshall Ltd.* (1984), 136 APR 172 (NSTD).

18 On being out at work, see Charlotte Gray, 'Out of the Closet and into the Fire?' *Chatelaine*, September 1995, 113.

19 See James D. Woods and Jay H. Lucas, *The Corporate Closet: The Professional Lives of Gay Men in America* (New York: Free Press 1993).

20 *Stiles v. Canada*; *Gallant v. The Queen* (1978), 91 DLR (3d) 695 (FCTD).

21 See Chapter 3.

22 One writer has said that when he is baited by homophobes, he 'even' says he is gay rather than pleading his heterosexuality. See Bruce Ryder, 'Straight Talk,' 303. Another writer, in an essay on 'Sexual Orientation and Equality Rights' makes sure to thank 'my wife' for reading his paper. Arnold Bruner, 'Sexual Orientation and Equality Rights,' in Anne F. Bayefsky and Mary Eberts, *Equality Rights and the Canadian Charter of Rights and Freedoms* (Toronto: Carswell 1985), at 457.

23 On the issues of homosexuality as a threat to national security in Britain and on the ideas of the state as Männerstaat, see L.J. Moran, 'The Uses of Homosexuality: Homosexuality for National Security,' *International Journal of Sociology of Law* 19 (1991), 149. Most blackmail and traitorous acts must be by straights, since they are in theory the only ones traditionally allowed in the military, police, and spy agency. Mohr gives the example of two U.S. Marines who were found to be spies and adds: 'Had these Marines been sleeping with each other rather than communists, our national security would be ever so much better off.' Richard D. Mohr, *Gays/Justice: A Study of Ethics, Society, and Law* (New York: Columbia University Press 1988), 199.1.

24 In England, the Criminal Law Amendment Act of 1885 was dubbed 'The Blackmailer's Charter' for the opportunities it gave the criminal to prey upon otherwise law-abiding members of the public. See Wayne R. Dynes,

ed., *Encyclopedia of Homosexuality* (Chicago: St James Press 1990), vol. 1, 'Blackmail,' 152.

25 In *Equality for All: Report of the Parliamentary Committee on Equality Rights*, October 1985, chaired by Patrick Boyer, the committee recommended that the Canadian Human Rights Act be amended to prohibit discrimination of the basis of sexual orientation.

26 Ibid., 31.

27 See Chapter 4.

28 See Goffman, *Stigma*, 30.

29 *R. v. Humphrey*, [1984] OJ 218 (QL) (HCJ).

30 *Re Canadian AIDS Society and Ontario* (1995), 25 OR (3d) 388 at 396 (Gen. Div.); affirmed (1996), 31 OR (3d) 798 (CA), leave to appeal to SCC refused, 8 May 1997. The judge, however, went on to find that the Charter challenges to disclosure failed.

31 Goffman, *Stigma*, 30.

32 Austen and Wellington, 'Outing: The Supposed Justifications,' 92.

33 William A. Henry III, 'Forcing Gays out of the Closet: Homosexual Leaders Seek to Expose Foes of the Movement,' *Time*, 29 January 1990, 67.

34 See also *Dykon v. Canada (Minister of Employment and Immigration)* (1994), 25 Imm. LR (2d) 193 (FCTD) for a more recent example: Ukraine. See Richard Plant, *The Pink Triangle: The Nazi War against Homosexuals* (New York: Henry Holt 1986).

35 The law in Canada is slowly changing on this point: *Leshner v. Ontario* (1992), 92 CCLC ¶17,035 (Ont. Bd Inq.): Leshner's same-sex partner was entitled to benefits (see similarly *Clinton v. Ontario Blue Cross* (1993), 93 CLLC ¶17,026 (Ont. Bd Inq.); *Knodel v. BC (Medical Services Comm.)* (1991), 58 BCLR (2d) 356 (SC): 'spouse' in the Medical Services Act regulations did not include a partner of the same sex and this infringed s. 15 of the Charter – the court accepted psychological evidence of homosexuality; cf. *Egan v. Canada* (1995), 124 DLR (4th) 609 (SCC); and *Re Attorney-General of Canada and Mossop* (1993), 100 DLR (4th) 658 (SCC). See Douglas Sanders, 'Constructing Lesbian and Gay Rights,' *Canadian Journal of Law and Society* 9 (1994) 99; Mary Eaton, 'Patently Confused: Complex Inequality and *Canada v. Mossop*,' *Review of Constitutional Studies* 1 (1994), 203; Robert Wintemute, 'Sexual Orientation Discrimination as Sex Discrimination: Same-Sex Couples and the *Charter* in *Mossop*, *Egan* and *Layland*,' *McGill Law Journal* 39 (1994), 429; Jody Freeman, 'Defining Family in *Mossop v. DSS*: The Challenge of Anti-essentialism and Interactive Discrimination for Human Rights Litigation,' *University of Toronto Law Journal* 44 (1994) 41.

36 *Anderson v. Luoma* (1986), 50 RFL (2d) 127 (BCSC); *Anderson v. Luoma* (1984),

42 RFL (2d) 444 (BCSC); *Layland v. Ontario (Minister of Consumer and Commercial Relations)* (1993), 14 OR (3d) 658 (Div. Ct). On same-sex marriages in history, see William N. Eskridge, Jr. 'A History of Same-Sex Marriage,' *Virginia Law Review* 79 (1993), 1419; John Boswell, *Same-Sex Unions in Premodern Europe* (New York: Villard Books 1994).

37 Except by circuitous routes.

38 *Thaarup v. Hulton Press Ltd.* (1943), LT 309 (CA).

39 On the issues of constructionism and essentialism, see Chapter 1.

40 The entertainer Liberace was called 'fruit-flavoured' in an article in the 26 September 1956 *Daily Mirror*. The court accepted that that designation would be understood as implying that he was homosexual and (truth, incredibly, not having been established) awarded damages to Liberace. See H. Montgomery Hyde, *Their Good Names: Twelve Cases of Libel and Slander with Some Introductory Reflections on the Law* (London: Hamish Hamilton 1970), chap. 12, 'The Limits of Criticism.'

41 *Thompson v. The King*, [1918] AC 221 (HL).

42 *Vancouver Sun*, 29 July 1994. Hatfield has been identified by newspapers as 'a well-known ... homosexual': *Globe and Mail*, 13 July 1994.

43 *Atlantic Canada Frank*, 5 July 1994, 3.

44 *Franck v. Webster*, [1994] MJ No. 242 (QL) (QB).

45 *In re Guardianship of Sharon Kowalski*, 478 NW 2d 790 (Minn. App. 1991); review denied 10 February 1992. Ruthann Robson discusses this case in *Lesbian (Out)law: Survival under the Rule of Law* (Ithaca, N.Y.: Firebrand Books 1992), 118–19.

46 This decision is extracted and discussed in Arthur S. Leonard, *Sexuality and the Law: An Encyclopedia of Major Legal Cases* (New York: Garland Publishing 1993), 377–82.

47 Outing can involve HIV status, itself. In many cases the outing of sexual orientation and HIV status will be simultaneous. It has been argued that the double outing could produce burdens for any particular individual to bear that would be 'too great': Hernandez, 'Outing in the Time of AIDS,' 503. On AIDS and outing, see Donald G. Casswell, 'Disclosure by a Physician of AIDS-Related Patient Information: An Ethical and Legal Dilemma,' *Canadian Bar Review* 68 (1989), 225; William F. Flanagan, 'Equality Rights for People with AIDS: Mandatory Reporting of HIV Infection and Contact Tracing,' *McGill Law Journal* 34 (1989), 530; Anne L. McBride, 'Deadly Confidentiality: AIDS and Rule 1.6(b),' *Georgetown Journal of Legal Ethics* 4 (1990), 435; Trudy Mauth, 'Charter Implications of Compelling Dentists to Reveal Their HIV Status,' *Health Law in Canada* 15 (1994), 97.

48 *Valiquette v. The Gazette* (1991), 8 CCLT (2d) 302 (Que. Super. Ct).

49 Ibid., 309, per Viau J. On the Quebec Charter, see Nicole Duplé, 'Homosexualité et droits à l'égalité dans les Chartes canadienne et québécoise,' *Cahiers de droit* 25 (1984), 801.

50 Ibid., 310.

51 'Situational' homosexuality occurs in same-sex situations such as prisons. See *Piche v. Canada (Solicitor General)*, [1984] FCJ No. 1008 (QL) (TD). Does participation in a homosexual act there make the person homosexual?.

52 Jon E. Grant, 'Note – "Outing" and Freedom of the Press: Sexual Orientation's Challenge to the Supreme Court's Categorical Jurisprudence,' *Cornell Law Review* 77 (1991), 103 at 130.

53 See *Sipple v. Chronicle Publishing Co.*, 201 Cal. Rptr. 665 (Ct App. 1984).

54 3 December 1993, Issue 8.

55 On gay male pornography, see Christopher N. Kendall, '"Real Dominant, Real Fun!": Gay Male Pornography and the Pursuit of Masculinity,' *Saskatchewan Law Review* 57 (1993), 21; Carl F. Stychin, 'Exploring the Limits: Feminism and the Legal Regulation of Gay Male Pornography,' *Vermont Law Review* 16 (1992), 857.

56 *Sunday Times*, 'Gays Say "Outing" Plot Was Not a Hoax,' 4 August 1991.

57 The outing issue might be rendered as the question: Does the interest of a particular group prevail over the rights of one of the members of that group? This question presents outing as a contest between an individual's right to privacy and the group's right to defend or advance its interests. There is, however, no particular reason to single out outing of sexual orientation as a group versus individual issue any more than a revelation of a person's heterosexuality, race, religion, and so on would be.

58 Arthur Schafer, 'Privacy: A Philosophical Overview,' in Dale Gibson, ed., *Aspects of Privacy Law: Essays in Honour of John M. Sharp*, chap. 1 (Toronto: Butterworths 1980), 5.

59 Warren Johansson and William A. Percy, *Outing: Shattering the Conspiracy of Silence* (New York: Harrington Park Press 1994), 241.

60 Ibid., 251.

61 See Schafer, 'Privacy: A Philosophical Overview.'

62 See Arthur Selwyn Miller, 'Privacy in the Modern Corporate State: A Speculative Essay,' *Administrative Law Review* 25 (1973), 231.

63 Article 12 of the *Universal Declaration of Human Rights* (1948) and Article 17 of the *International Covenant on Civil and Political Rights* (1966) (in force, including Canada 1976).

64 See the cases cited at note 35.

65 They say: 'The press is overstepping in every direction the obvious bounds of propriety and of decency. Gossip is no longer the resource of the idle and

the vicious, but has become a trade, which is pursued with industry as well as effrontery. To satisfy a prurient taste the details of sexual relations are spread broadcast in the columns of the daily papers. To occupy the indolent, column after column is filled with idle gossip, which can only be procured by intrusion on the domestic circle.' Samuel D. Warren and Louis D. Brandeis, 'The Right to Privacy,' *Harvard Law Review* 4 (1890), 193 at 196.

66 See John Elwood, 'Note: Outing, Privacy, and the First Amendment,' *Yale Law Journal* 102 (1992), 747.

67 American Law Institute, *Restatement of the Law Torts (Second)* (St Paul, Minn.: American Law Institute Publications, 1977), sec. 652D.

68 William Prosser, *Handbook of the Law of Torts*, 4th ed. (St Paul: West Publications, 1971), 807–14. See also William L. Prosser, 'Privacy,' *California Law Review* 48 (1960), 383; Vincent J. Samar, *The Right to Privacy: Gays, Lesbians and the Constitution* (Philadelphia: Temple University Press 1991), 29.

69 Gary L. Bostwick argues that privacy involves three concepts: 'the privacy of repose, the privacy of sanctuary, and the privacy of intimate decision.' Gary L. Bostwick, 'A Taxonomy of Privacy: Repose, Sanctuary and Intimate Decision,' *California Law Review* 64 (1976), 1447. See also Kenneth L. Karst, 'The Freedom of Intimate Association,' *Yale Law Journal* 89 (1980), 624; Barbara Moretti, 'Outing: Justifiable or Unwarranted Invasion of Privacy? The Private Facts Tort as a Remedy for Disclosures of Sexual Orientation,' *Cardozo Arts & Entertainment Law Journal* 11 (1993), 857; Frederick Davis, 'What Do We Mean by "Right to Privacy"?' *South Dakota Law Review* 4 (1959), 1; Louis Lusky, 'Invasion of Privacy: A Clarification of Concepts,' *Columbia Law Review* 72 (1972), 693; Richard B. Parker, 'A Definition of Privacy,' *Rutgers Law Review* 27 (1974), 275; William M. Beaney, 'The Right to Privacy and American Law,' *Law and Contemporary Problems* 31 (1966), 253; Milton R. Konvitz, 'Privacy and Law: A Philosophical Prelude,' *Law and Contemporary Problems* 31 (1966), 272; Arthur Schafer, 'Privacy: A Philosophical Overview'; Edward Shils, 'Privacy': Its Constitution and Vicissitudes,' *Law and Contemporary Problems* 31 (1996), 280 (this article contains a good examination of how our attitudes to privacy have changed over time and place); David A.J. Richards, 'Constitutional Privacy and Homosexual Love,' *New York University Review of Law and Social Change* 14 (1986), 895. On the privacy rights issue in the abortion context, see David J. Garrow, *Liberty and Sexuality: The Right to Privacy and the Making of Roe v. Wade* (New York: Macmillan 1994). On the issues that affect sexual orientation, see chap. 9. For an economic analysis of privacy law, see Richard A. Posner, 'The Right to Privacy,' *Georgia Law Review* 12 (1978), 393; Richard A. Posner, 'Privacy, Secrecy, and Reputation,' *Buffalo Law Review* 28 (1979), 1.

70 See *Victoria Park Racing and Recreation Grounds Co. Ltd. v. Taylor* (1937), 58
    CLR 479 at 496 (High Ct of Aust. per Latham CJ). Gerald Dworkin, 'The
    Common Law Protection of Privacy,' *Tasmanian University Law Review* 4
    (1967), 418.

71 The Wolfenden Committee (*The Report of the Committee on Homosexual
    Offences and Prostitution* ('The Wolfenden Report') (London: HMSO, CMND
    247 1957) was set up following two notorious cases of homosexuality in
    1954. As Alex Gigeroff says: '... Lord Winterton, supported by Lord Vansit-
    tart, introduced a debate in the House of Lords calling for an appointment
    of a committee on the "nauseating subject" of homosexuality. He was
    offended by what he regarded as a propaganda campaign in the weekly
    press, waged by those he termed "pansies" ...' Alex K. Gigeroff, *Sexual
    Deviations in the Criminal Law: Homosexual, Exhibitionistic, and Pedophilic
    Offences in Canada* (Toronto: Clarke Institute of Psychiatry 1968), 83. There
    were many views put forward. The Archbishop of Canterbury, influential
    in his moderation, said that in his view the threat to general public moral
    standards was less from homosexual acts done in private than by fornica-
    tion and adultery. Ibid., 85. The Lord Bishop of Rochester, however, said
    that there was a danger of contagion and that homosexuals should be 'kept
    on a leash.' Ibid., 86. Lord Denning thought the law should condemn the
    evil of homosexuality for the evil that it is, but that judges should be dis-
    creet in their punishment of it. Ibid.
        In the Authorized American edition (New York: Stein and Day 1963), the
    Introduction by Karl Menninger, MD, says: 'Prostitution and homosexual-
    ity rank high in the kingdom of evils. They have in common the fact that
    they exist illegally to provide relief for psychological and emotional ten-
    sions which, in theory, could and should find other outlets' (5). He also
    says: 'Homosexuality ruins the lives of millions and breaks the hearts of
    millions more ...'

72 On the tort of breach of confidence, see M.P. Thompson, 'Breach of Confi-
    dence and the Protection of Privacy in English Law,' *Journal of Media Law
    and Practice* 6 (1985), 5. On educational records, see Beverley M. McLach-
    lin, 'Educational Records and the Right to Privacy,' *UBC Law Review* 15
    (1981), 175. See also Leon Brittan, 'The Right of Privacy in England and
    the United States,' *Tulane Law Review* 37 (1963), 235; Brian Neill, 'The Pro-
    tection of Privacy,' *Modern Law Review* 25 (1962), 393; David J. Seipp,
    'English Judicial Recognition of a Right to Privacy,' *Oxford Journal of Legal
    Studies* 3 (1983), 325; Peter Burns, 'Privacy and the Common Law: A Tan-
    gled Skein Unravelling?' in Dale Gibson, ed., *Aspects of Privacy Law: Essays
    in Honour of John M. Sharp*, chap. 2 (Toronto: Butterworths 1980); and Peter

Burns, 'The Law and Privacy: The Canadian Experience,' *Canadian Bar Review* 54 (1976), 1.

73 See *Franck v. Webster*; Dale Gibson, 'Common Law Protection of Privacy,' in Lewis Klar, ed., *Studies in Canadian Tort Law* (Toronto: Butterworths 1977), chap. 12.

74 See *Krouse v. Chrysler Canada Ltd.*, [1970] 3 OR 135 (HC); *Saccone v. Orr* (1981), 34 OR (2d) 317 (Co. Ct); *Capan v. Capan* (1980), 14 CCLT 191 (Ont. HC); *R. v. Otto* (1984), 16 CCC (3d) 289 (BC Co. Ct); *Roth and Roth v. Roth, Roth and Stephens* (1991), 4 OR (3d) 740 (Ont. Ct – Gen. Div.).

75 See, *inter alia*, Privacy Act (RSBC 1996, c. 373, The Privacy Act, RSM 1987, c. P125; The Privacy Act, RSS 1978, c. P-24; The Privacy Act, RSN 1990, c. P-22; Freedom of Information and Protection of Privacy Act, RSO 1990, c. F.31; Privacy Act, RSC 1985, c. P-21. There are numerous other pieces of legislation dealing with financial information and credit information. See Ian Lawson, *Privacy and Free Enterprise: The Legal Protection of Personal Information in the Private Sector* (Ottawa: Public Interest Advocacy Centre 1993), chap. 3 'Legislated Privacy.' Quebec protects privacy through the Quebec Charter of Human Rights and Freedoms, ss. 4 and 5, which has been described as intended 'to protect either the solitude of the individual or his or her anonymity': H. Patrick Glenn, 'The Right to Privacy in Quebec Law,' in Dale Gibson, ed., *Aspects of Privacy Law: Essays in Honour of John M. Sharp* (Toronto: Butterworths 1980), at 44. The federal legislation and the Freedom of Information Acts only apply to governments. On the federal Act see Peter Burns, 'A Retrospective View of the Protection of Privacy Act: A Fragile Rede Is Recked,' *UBC Law Review* 13 (1979), 123. Another possible statutory recourse in Canada might be defamatory libel under ss. 300 or 301 of the Criminal Code (RSC 1985, c. C-46).

76 See, e.g. *Davis v. McArthur* (1970), 17 DLR (3d) 760 (BCCA); *Silber v. BCTV Broadcasting System Ltd.* (1985), 69 BCLR 34 (SC).

77 *Franck v. Webster.*

78 Sidney M. Jourard, 'Some Psychological Aspects of Privacy,' *Law and Contemporary Problems* 31 (1966), 307 at 308.

79 Charles Fried, *An Anatomy of Values: Problems of Personal and Social Choice* (Cambridge, Mass.: Harvard University Press 1970), 138.

80 See Schafer, 'Privacy: A Philosophical Overview.'

81 J.S. Mill, *On Liberty* (1859; New York: W.W. Norton 1975), chap. 3.

82 Vincent J. Samar, *The Right to Privacy: Gays, Lesbians and the Constitution* (Philadelphia: Temple University Press 1991), 96.

83 Ronald F. Wick, 'Out of the Closet and Into the Headlines: "Outing" and the Private Facts Tort,' *Georgetown Law Journal* 80 (1991), 413 at 424.

84 Exclamation mark added.

85 Wick, 'Out of the Closet and Into the Headlines,' 428.

86 Ibid., 430.

87 Richard Mohr, 'The Outing Controversy: Privacy and Dignity in Gay Ethics,' in *Gay Ideas: Outing and Other Controversies* (Boston: Beacon Press 1992), 30. See also Richard Mohr, 'The Perils of Postmodernity for Gay Rights,' *Canadian Journal of Law and Jurisprudence* 8 (1995), 5.

88 Grant, 'Note – "Outing",' 132. See also Carl J. Friedrich, 'Secrecy versus Privacy: The Democratic Dilemma,' in *Nomos XIII: Privacy*, chap. 6 (New York: Atherton Press 1971); Sissela Bok, *Secrets: On the Ethics of Concealment and Revelation* (New York: Pantheon 1982); Richard A. Posner, *Economics of Justice* (Cambridge, Mass.: Harvard University Press 1981), 299–309.

89 Mohr, 'The Outing Controversy,' 172. See also Mohr, *Gays/Justice*, 98–9. See also Richard A. Goreham, 'Le droit à la vie privée des personnes homosexuelles,' *Cahiers de droit* 25 (1984), 843.

90 Johansson and Percy reply to Richard Mohr's view (that sexual orientation is not private but sexual acts are) by saying that, on the contrary, a sexual orientation is 'an intrinsically and unalterably private matter just because it cannot be observed, but only experienced': Johansson and Percy, *Outing*, 253. A sex act, however, with the exception of masturbation, always involves at least one other person and so is not absolutely private and the other person cannot be depended on not to tell.

91 E.g., the doctrine of *ex turpi causa*, on which see Bruce MacDougall, '*Ex Turpi Causa*: Should a Defence Arise from a Base Cause?' *Saskatchewan Law Review* 55 (1991), 1.

92 Quoted in *The Sunday Age* (Melbourne), 3 April 1994, 7.

93 See also *Re Priape Enrg. and the Deputy Minister of National Revenue* (1979), 52 CCC (2d) 44 (Que. Super. Ct – Crim Div.), which I discussed in Chapters 2 and 4, where Hugessen ACJQ thought two men in a park kissing would cause a disturbance.

94 Ryder, 'Straight Talk: Male Heterosexual Privilege,' 293.

95 The Wolfenden Report.

96 See Wick, 'Out of the Closet,' 432.

97 Such as *Valiquette*; see note 48 and the text accompanying it.

98 Austen and Wellington, 'Outing: The Supposed Justifications,' 105.

99 See Gabriel Potello, 'Tactical Considerations,' *OutWeek*, 16 May 1990, 52–3.

100 The Supreme Court of Canada upheld publication bans on sexual assault complainants' names in *R. v. Canadian Newspapers Co. Ltd.* (1988), 52 DLR (4th) 690. The intrusion on freedom of expression was justified in the inter-

ests of 'foster[ing] complaints by victims of sexual assault by protecting them from the trauma of widespread publication resulting in embarrassment and humiliation' (695, per Lamer J).

101 Our society does sometimes prohibit publicity of a characteristic such as 'black' in the context of a 'criminal' report. This, however, is not because it is 'bad' to be black but because the law seeks to prevent the non-black majority from associating black with criminal (which is 'bad').

102 Bruce Ryder, 'Equality Rights and Sexual Orientation: Confronting Heterosexual Family Privilege,' *Canadian Journal of Family Law* 9 (1990), 39 at 43–4.

103 This situation applies not just to homosexuals. Marilyn Frye, for example, deals with the situation of women. Marilyn Frye, *The Politics of Reality: Essays in Feminist Theory* (Freedom, Cal.: Crossing Press 1983), chapter on 'Oppression.'

104 See Eve Kosofsky Sedgwick, *The Epistemology of the Closet* (Berkeley: University of California Press 1990).

105 See Suzanne Pharr, *Homophobia: A Weapon of Sexism* (Inverness, Cal.: Chardon Press 1988), 18 and Sylvia A. Law, 'Homosexuality and the Social Meaning of Gender,' *Wisconsin Law Review* [1988] 187.

106 E.g., Johansson and Percy, *Outing*, 232–3.

107 Hernandez, 'Outing in the Time of AIDS,' 495.

108 Sir Edward Coke, *Institutes of the Laws of England, Third Part*, chap. 10. He was just modifying the accusation found in the Bible in Ezekiel 16:49: 'Behold, this was the iniquity of thy sister Sodom, pride, fulness of bread, and abundance of idleness was in her and in her daughters, neither did she strengthen the hand of the poor and needy.' See Dynes, ed., *Encyclopedia of Homosexuality*, vol. 1, 'Aristocratic Vice, Homosexuality as,' 74.

109 See, generally, Weeks, 'Capitalism and the Organisation of Sex,' 11–20.

110 See James D. Woods and Jay H. Lucas, *The Corporate Closet: The Professional Lives of Gay Men in America* (New York: Free Press 1993), 121; Samar, *The Right to Privacy: Gays, Lesbians and the Constitution*, 111; Michelangelo Signorile, *Queer in America: Sex, the Media and the Closets of Power* (New York: Random House 1993).

111 *Central Canada Frank*, 7 July 1994, 5.

112 In any event, legal restrictions will not stop those who care from knowing in many cases. Haiman says: 'If a community is small enough for most people who read the name in the paper or hear it on radio or television to know and have contact with the victim, it is likely that the information will spread by word of mouth anyhow. In a large community the name would be meaningless to most people who are exposed to it, unless it is

that of a person or family of prominence, in which case we would be involved with what might fairly be considered a "name-crucial" situation.' Franklyn S. Haiman, *Speech and Law in a Free Society* (Chicago: University of Chicago Press 1982), 71.

113 See note 27 in Introduction.

114 For a judicial exposition on justifications for free expression, see Dickson CJC in *R. v. Keegstra* (1990), 61 CCC (3d) 1 at 46–52 (SCC).

115 See *Gay Law Students Assoc. v. Pacific Telephone & Telegram Co.*, 595 P 2d. 592 (1979), where the court recognized the political nature of speech in achieving gay equality.

116 Some writers would think that the term 'culture' or 'cultures' for the gay community would not be strong enough. Johansson and Percy prefer the term 'nation' (as in Queer Nation). Johansson and Percy, *Outing*.

117 The term 'culture' is much more satisfactory than 'subculture,' which has a negative overtone and implies subservience and a certain illegitimacy.

118 On the requisites of a 'culture,' see Clifford Geerz, *The Interpretation of Cultures* (New York: Basic Books 1973); Fern Johnson, 'Women's Culture and Communication: An Analytical Perspective,' in Cynthia M. Lont and Sheryl Friedley, eds., *Beyond Boundaries: Sex and Gender Diversity in Communication* (Fairfax, Va.: G. Mason University Press 1989); Ann Ferguson, 'Is There a Lesbian Culture?' in Jeffner Allen, ed., *Lesbian Philosophies and Cultures* (Albany, N.Y.: State University of New York Press 1990), 63–88; Derek Cohen and Richard Dyer, 'The Politics of Gay Culture,' in Gay Left Collective, eds., *Homosexuality: Power and Politics*, chap. 14 (London: Allison & Busby 1980), 172–86; Michael Bronski, *Culture Clash: The Making of Gay Sensibility* (Boston: South End Press 1984). That is not to say that there is *one* homosexual culture in Canada or anywhere else. (On the development of gay and lesbian communities in Canada, see Gary Kinsman, *The Regulation of Desire: Homo and Hetero Sexualities* (Montreal: Black Rose 1996), esp. chaps. 8 and 9.) Far from it. Lesbians, gays, and bisexuals have many things in common, but the most common element among them is their historical persecution and the fact that non-homosexuals lump them together. See Sharon Dale Stone and The Women's Survey Group, 'Lesbian Life in a Small Centre: The Case of St. John's,' in Stone, ed., *Lesbians in Canada*, chap. 7, 101–2. There is arguably more than one culture. (See Ed Cohen, 'Who Are "We?"': Gay "Identity" a Political (E)motion' in Diana Fuss, ed., *Inside/Out: Lesbian Theories, Gay Theories* (New York: Routledge 1991), at 72.) The culture of the gay aesthetes is quite different from the culture of the gay leatherman. There is, however, never any definitive delineation of any culture. Who is to say that there is a single American

culture, for instance? Homosexuals should not be denied cultural status on the basis that there is no definite bounds or delineation for their culture(s).

119 Richard Posner appears to believe that homosexuals think they are numerous, an odd proposition. He says that the public is under the impression that there are more homosexuals than in fact exist. He gives as a reason the fact that they are concentrated in large cities and the media are concentrated in one of those cities – New York. Richard Posner, *Sex and Reason* (Cambridge, Mass.: Harvard University 1992), 128. How he supports this proposition is not explained. Most gays are either hidden in cities or grouped in ghettos. Furthermore, the media habitually ignore or poke fun at gays.

120 See Dynes, ed., *Encyclopedia of Homosexuality*, vol. 1, 'Gesture and Body Language,' 474–5.

121 See ibid., vol. 1, 'Cruising,' 284–5.

122 See *Globe and Mail*, 8 August 1992, D5 by Peter Freedman, 'The Canadian Conspiracy.'

123 See *R. v. Keegstra*.

124 Larry Gross, *Contested Closets: The Politics and Ethics of Outing* (Minneapolis: University of Minnesota Press 1993). See also Larry Gross, 'Out of the Mainstream: Sexual Minorities and the Mass Media,' in Michelle A. Wolf and Alfred Kielwasser, eds., *Gay People, Sex, and the Media* (New York: Harrington Park Press 1991), 19–46 and Marc A. Fajer, 'Can Two Real Men Eat Quiche Together? Storytelling, Gender-Role Stereotypes, and Legal Protection for Lesbians and Gay Men,' *University of Miami Law Review* 46 (1992), 511.

125 See Vito Russo, *The Celluloid Closet: Homosexuality in the Movies*, rev. ed. (New York: Harper & Row 1987).

126 In *R. v. Butler*, 1992), 89 DLR (4th) 449 (SCC), Sopinka J said: 'Artistic expression rests at the heart of freedom of expression values and any doubt in this regard must be resolved in favour of freedom of expression' (471).

127 The Supreme Court of Canada appears to favour such a balancing of interests in *R. v. Butler*, at 470–1.

128 *BBC Music Magazine*, July 1994, at 11.

129 This article vastly oversimplifies what Rorem undoubtedly meant. Rorem has written: 'I'm less defensive than Isherwood – less "moralistic" – about queerdom than about musicality, for musicality in this world is queerer than any kind of sex.' And also: 'Is there a homosexual sensibility?, people still ask. Why yes, no doubt. But one would be hard put to show that sen-

sibility defined, say, by the homosexual's musical composition or poetry or law practice or medical notions, as distinct from the sensibility of one who screws too seldom or too often or is redheaded or over fifty or is more interested in microscopes than in Love or is dumb.' Ned Rorem, 'Being Alone,' extracted in Winston Leyland, ed., *Gay Sunshine Journal No. 47: Anthology of Fiction/Poetry/Prose* (San Francisco: Gay Sunshine Press 1982), quotations at 143–4. It is unlikely that many of the readers of *BBC Music Magazine* know of the writings of Rorem about homosexuality.

130 On Schubert's homosexuality, see Susan McClary, 'Constructions of Subjectivity in Schubert's Music,' in Philip Brett, Elizabeth Wood, and Gary C. Thomas, eds., *Queering the Pitch: The New Gay and Lesbian Musicology*, chap. 9 (New York: Routledge 1994), 205–33. She gives an excellent description of how the subject of Schubert's sexual orientation was met with real hostility by other musicians. People wanted to 'defend' Schubert's reputation.

131 DG 413 453–2.

132 For a refreshingly candid portrayal of a composer's homosexuality and how it affected his music, see Humphrey Carpenter, *Benjamin Britten: A Biography* (London: Faber and Faber 1992).

133 Richard Meyer, 'Rock Hudson's Body,' in Fuss, ed., *Inside/Out*, 279.

134 See Pearlman, 'Theorizing Lesbian Oppression.'

135 Note it is possible that homosexuality should be concealed by the legal system in some circumstances. For example in a court trial there is no reason why the trier of fact need know the sexual orientation of a party. But, this is only where it is as irrelevant as would be a person's religion or ethnicity. *Dagenais v. CBC* (1992), 99 DLR (4th) 326 (Ont. CA), holds that where freedom of expression and the right of an accused to a fair trial conflict, the latter value should prevail.

136 See Jonathan Dollimore, *Sexual Dissidence: Augustine to Wilde*, Freud to Foucault (Oxford: Clarendon Press 1991), 247.

137 See Law, 'Homosexuality and the Social Meaning of Gender,' Pharr, *Homophobia: A Weapon of Sexism*; Sedgwick, *The Epistemology of the Closet*; Carl F. Stychin, 'Unmanly Diversions: The Construction of the Homosexual Body (Politic) in English Law,' *Osgoode Hall Law Journal* 32 (1994), 503.

138 Wednesday, 4 August 1993, A10–A11. See also Kirk Bohls and Mark Wangrin, 'Athletes Revel in Being One of the Guys, Not One of the Gays,' *Globe and Mail*, national edition, 4 August 1993, A10 & A11.

139 Paedophilia, however, appears to have been rife in his organization. See, e.g., 'Ex-Garden Worker Admits Molesting 24 Boys,' *Vancouver Sun*, 9 September 1997, A4. But, then, such paedophiles were not avowed and, so, apparently, acceptable.

140 On the experience of one person see Makeda Silvera, 'Man Royals and
Sodomites: Some Thoughts on the Invisibility of Afro-Caribbean Lesbi-
ans,' in Stone, ed., *Lesbians in Canada*, 48–60. See also Joanne Doucette,
'Redefining Difference: Disabled Lesbians Resist,' in ibid., chap. 4, 61–72;
Kitty Tsui, 'Breaking Silence, Making Waves and Loving Ourselves: The
Politics of Coming Out and Coming Home,' in Jeffner Allen, ed., *Lesbian
Philosophies and Cultures* (Albany, N.Y.: State University of New York Press
1990), 49–61; Martha Rosenfeld, 'Jewish Lesbians in France: The Issue of
Multiple Cultures,' in *Lesbian Philosophies and Cultures*, 109–24; Edwina
Franchild, '"You Do So Well": A Blind Lesbian Responds to her Sighted
Sisters,' in *Lesbian Philosophies and Cultures*, 181–91; Vicky D'Aoust, 'Competency, Autonomy, and Choice: On Being Lesbian and Having Disabilities,' *Canadian Journal of Women and the Law* 7 (1994), 564. On the issues
relating to discrimination on more than one basis, see Nitya Iyer, 'Categorical Denials: Equality Rights and the Shaping of Social Identity,' *Queen's
Law Journal* 19 (1993), 179.
141 Dollimore, *Sexual Dissidence*, 345. See also Paulette Peirol, 'Minority
Homosexuals Invisible to Their World,' *Globe and Mail* (national edition),
21 May 1997, A1.
142 See Jewelle Gomez, 'Repeat after Me: We Are Different. We Are the Same,'
NYU Review of Law and Social Change 14 (1986), 935.
143 Although these groups are far from being treated in practice as equals by
all Canadians, the legal system has in recent years begun to respond to
their concerns. These groups are also useful for comparison purposes
because they are common targets of prejudice. According to Wayne
Dynes, Jews are like homosexuals in that they can both 'pass,' they have
both created their own self-deprecating humour and have a large share of
self-contempt, they both suffered at roughly the same times historically
and they are both accused of having undue influence financially and in
the media. See Dynes, ed., *Encyclopedia of Homosexuality*, vol. 1, 'Anti-
Semitism and Antihomosexuality,' 68–9.
144 Another possible tort action is for breach of confidence, e.g., *Franck v. Webster*, or for an injunction to restrain information acquired in a marriage,
e.g., *Argyll v. Argyll*, [1965] 1 All ER 611. On other actions to protect privacy, see Peter Burns, 'The Law and Privacy: The Canadian Experience,'
Canadian Bar Review 54 (1976), 1.
145 On defamation, see Raymond Brown, *The Law of Defamation in Canada*
(Scarborough, Ont.: Carswell 1987); *Gatley on Libel and Slander*, 8th ed.
(London: Sweet & Maxwell 1981); P.F. Carter-Ruck and R. Walker, *Carter-
Ruck on Libel and Slander*, 3rd. ed. (London: Butterworths 1985); Jeremy

S. Williams, *The Law of Libel and Slander in Canada*, 2nd ed. (Toronto: Butterworths 1988).

146 *Jones v. Jones*, [1916] 2 AC 481 (HL).

147 Ibid., 500.

148 See, e.g., *Cherneskey v. Armadale Publishers Ltd.*, [1979] 1 SCR 1067 at 1097, per Ritchie J.

149 Even reporting a rumour could be defamatory. Saying that 'there is a rumour' that a person has VD is an imputation of unchastity and is actionable per se and it does not matter if the speaker did not intend to impute unchastity or to imply that the disease was acquired otherwise than innocently. *Houseman v. Coulson*, [1948] 2 DLR 63 (Sask. KB).

150 *Kerr v. Kennedy*, [1942] 1 KB 409.

151 Ibid., at 412. However, in *Wetherhead v. Armitage* (1690), 83 ER 534, it was held that to call a female dancing teacher a 'hermaphrodite' was not actionable without special damages.

152 *R. v. Bishop*, [1975] 1 QB 274 (CA).

153 Ibid., at 281.

154 Ibid. See also *Thaarup v. Hulton Press Ltd.* There is copious U.S. authority for an allegation of homosexuality being slanderous per se. In *Schomer v. Smidt*, 170 Cal. Rptr. 662 (App. 1981), it was held that it was slanderous per se to say that someone had committed a homosexual act. See also *Matherson v. Marchello*, 473 NYS 2d 998 (A.D. 2 Dept. 1984); *contra Moricoli v. Schwartz*, 361 NE 2d 74 (App. Ct Ill., 1977) and *Stein v. Trager*, 232 NYS 2d 362 (Sup. Ct, 1962). On the issue of whether an imputation of homosexuality is slanderous per se, see 3 ALR 4th 752. See also John Elwood, 'Note: Outing'; *Mazart v. State*, 441 NYS 2d 600 (Ct Cl. 1981); *Buck v. Savage* 323 SW 2d 363 (Tex. Civ. App. 1959).

155 *Wlodek v. Kosko* (1974), 7 OR (2d) 611 at 612 (CA); appeal dismissed (1976), 65 DLR (3d) 383 (SCC).

156 *A.M.N. v. O'Halpin* ([1996] OJ No. 3576 (QL) (Gen. Div.).

157 *Clark v. Duncan*, (1923), 53 OLR 287 (Ont. CA).

158 *Lever v. George* ([1950] OR 115 (HCJ).

159 See also *Ralston v. Fomich* (1992), 66 BCLR (2d) 166 (SC). The words 'son of a bitch' were just an insult and not capable of bearing a defamatory meaning. However, the addition of 'sick' before the phrase added a 'libellous colour.'

160 *Culhane v. Rawlings*, [1987] OJ No. 1562 (QL) (Dist. Ct).

161 See Wick, 'Out of the Closet,' 415.

162 *Alexander v. North Eastern Railway Co.* (1865), 122 ER 1221.

163 See note 40, above. Note that in the United States it is possible that a case

could be defamatory even if the facts are true, so long as they are embarrassing. See *Melvin v. Reid*, 299 SW 967 (1931); and see Ian Lawson, *Privacy and Free Enterprise: The Legal Protection of Personal Information in the Private Sector* (Ottawa: Public Interest Advocacy Centre 1993), 253–5.

164 It has been noted that 'Given the dramatic change in attitudes regarding homosexuality during the past decade, it is difficult to envision any proliferation of decisions in favour of the Asquith view.' Brown, *The Law of Defamation in Canada*, 1:346, note 581.

165 *Gatley on Libel and Slander*, 25. There is some U.S. authority for saying that calling a white person black is defamatory. According to *50 Am. Jur. 2d* 583: 'According to a number of cases, [omitted] a written statement that a white person is a Negro or mulatto, or is tainted with Negro blood, is actionable per se. Even since the enactment of the Thirteenth, Fourteenth, and Fifteenth Amendments to the Federal Constitution, it has been held that such written charges are actionable per se, because these amendments in no way affect the social relationships between the white and the Negro races.'

166 *Brotherhood of Maintenance of Way Employees v. Canadian Pacific Ltd.*, [1997] QJ No. 466 (QL) (SC – Civil Div.).

Chapter 6: Conclusion

1 *R. v. J.A.F.*, [1997] BCJ No. 2503 QL (Prov. Ct).

2 *Trinity Western University v. College of Teachers (BC)* (1997), 41 BCLR (3d) 158 (SC).

3 Ibid., 187.

4 Ibid., 188.

5 *United States of Mexico v. Hurley* (1997), 35 OR (3d) 481 (CA).

6 Ibid., 497–8. The court actually agreed that the extradition in that case was not in error, even though there was strong evidence that the person being extradited, as an openly homosexual man, would be subject to abuse by state authorities in Mexico because of his homosexuality. In Mexico, once extradited, the accused was convicted of murder and sentenced to fifteen years in prison: 'Canadian to Spend 15 Years in Jail for Murder of Lover,' *Vancouver Sun*, (22 July 1998, A16. See also *United States of America v. Cobb* ([1997] OJ No. 4362 QL (Gen. Div.).

7 *Rosenberg v. Canada (Attorney General)*, (1998), 158 DLR (4th) 664 (CA).

8 Ibid., 674.

9 *Buist v. Greaves*, [1997] OJ No. 2646 QL (Gen. Div.).

10 *R. v. Roy*, [1998] AQ No. 935 QL (CA).

11 *Little Sisters Book and Art Emporium v. Canada (Minister of Justice)*, [1998] BCJ No. 1507 QL (CA).

12 *Kane v. Ontario (Attorney General)*, [1997] OJ No. 3979 QL (Gen. Div.).

13 *Vriend v. Alberta* (1998), 156 DLR (4th) 385 (SCC).

14 Ibid., 417.

15 Ibid., 423.

16 Ibid., 428.

17 Ibid., 432.

Cases Cited

A. (C.) v. Critchley [1997] BCJ No. 1020 (QL) (SC).

Adams v. Woodbury, [1986] BCJ No. 2735 (QL) (SC).

Alexander v. North Eastern Railway Co. (1865), 122 ER 1221.

Alli, R. v. (1996), 110 CCC (3d) 283 (Ont. CA).

Anderson v. Luoma (1984), 42 RFL (2d) 444 (BCSC).

Anderson v. Luoma (1986), 50 RFL (2d) 127 (BCSC).

Andrews and Minister of Health for Ontario, Re (1988), 49 DLR (4th) 584 (Ont. HCJ).

Andrews v. Law Society of British Columbia, [1989] 1 SCR 143.

Argyll v. Argyll, [1965] 1 All ER 611.

Association (L') A.D.G.Q. v. Catholic School Commission of Montreal (1979), 112 DLR (3d) 230 (Que. Super. Ct).

Atkinson, Ing and Roberts, R. v. (1978), 43 CCC (2d) 342 (Ont. CA).

Attis v. Board of Education of District No. 15 (1993), 142 NBR (2d) 1 (CA).

Attorney-General of Canada and Mossop, Re (1990), 71 DLR (4th) 661 (FCA); appeal dismissed (1993), 100 DLR (4th) 658 (SCC).

Austin v. Austin, [1986] NBJ No. 547 (QL) (QB – Fam. Div.).

B. (J.E.) v. B. (R.G.), [1996] BCJ No. 2717 (QL) (SC).

B. (L.) R. v. (1989), 98 AR 259 (Prov. Ct – Youth Div.).

Barkley and Barkley, Re (1980), 28 OR (2d) 136 (Prov. Ct – Fam. Div.).

Before and After, R. v. (1982) Ltd. (1982), 111 APR 17 (Nfld Dist. Ct).

Benner, R. v., [1989] OJ No. 2474 (QL) (Prov. Ct – Crim. Div.).

Berger, R. v. (1975), 27 CCC (2d) 357 (BCCA); leave to appeal to SCC refused (1975), 27 CCC (2d) 357n.

Bernhardt v. Bernhardt (1979), 10 RFL (2d) 32 (Man. QB).

Bertrand v. Hôpital Général Juif, [1994] JTDPQ No. 19 (QL) (H.R. Trib. Mtl).

Bezaire v. Bezaire (1980), 20 RFL (2d) 358 (Ont. CA).

Bishop, R. v., [1970] 5 CCC 387 (Ont. Prov. Ct).

Bishop, R. v., [1975] 1 QB 274 (CA).

Board of Governors of the University of Saskatchewan and Saskatchewan Human Rights Commission, Re (1976), 66 DLR (3d) 561 (Sask. QB).

Boardman v. DPP, [1974] 3 All ER 887 (HL).

Bowers v. Hardwick, 92 L. Ed. 2d 140 (USSC 1986).

Brand v. College of Physicians and Surgeons of Saskatchewan, [1989] 5 WWR 516 (Sask. QB): affirmed [1990] 3 WWR 272 (Sask. CA).

Brodie, Dansky and Rubin v. The Queen, [1962] SCR 681.

Brotherhood of Maintenance of Way Employees v. Canadian Pacific Ltd., [1997] QJ No. 466 (QL) (SC – Civil Div.).

Brown, R. v., [1993] 2 All ER 75 (HL).

Brown v. British Columbia (Minister of Health) (1990), 66 DLR (4th) 444 (BCSC).

Buck v. Savage, 323 SW 2d 363 (Tex. Civ. App. 1959).

Buist v. Greaves, [1997] OJ No. 2646 QL (Gen. Div.).

Butler, R. v. (1992), 89 DLR (4th) 449 (SCC).

Butler, R. v. (1995), 104 CCC (3d) 198 (BCCA), leave to appeal to SCC refused, 23 May 1996.

C. (L.) v. C. (C.) (1992), 10 OR (3d) 254 (Ont. Ct – Gen. Div.).

C., R. v. (1981), 84 APR 451 (Nfld Dist. Ct Judge's Crim. Ct).

C. Coles Co. Ltd. R. v., [1966] 2 OR 777.

Caldwell and Stuart, Re (1980), 114 DLR (3d) 357 (BCSC); appeal allowed (1982), 132 DLR (3d) 79 (BCCA); appeal dismissed (1984), 15 DLR (4th) 1 (SCC).

Canada v. Thwaites, [1994] 3 FC 38 (TD).

Canada v. Ward, [1993] 2 SCR 689.

Canadian AIDS Society and Ontario, Re (1995), 25 OR (3d) 388 (Gen. Div.); affirmed (1996), 31 OR (3d) 798 (CA), leave to appeal to SCC refused 8 May 1997.

Canadian Civil Liberties Association v. Ontario (Minister of Education) (1990), 65 DLR (4th) 1 (Ont. CA).

Canadian Newspapers Co. Ltd., R. v. (1988), 52 DLR (4th) 690.

Capan v. Capan (1980), 14 CCLT 191 (Ont. HC).

Carifelle, R. v. (1988), 90 AR 316 (CA).

Carolan, R. v. (1995), 163 AR 238 (Prov. Ct).

Caskenette, R. v. (1993), 80 CCC (3d) 439 (BCCA).

Cavanagh and Donaldson, R. v. (1976), 15 OR (2d) 173 (CA).

Chaisson, R. v. (1995), 102 CCC (3d) 564 (NBCA); appeal allowed (1995), 99 CCC (3d) 289 (SCC).

Charest, R. v., [1990] AQ No. 405 (QL) (CA).

Cherneskey v. Armadale Publishers Ltd., [1979] 1 SCR 1067.

Children's Aid Society of the District of Thunder Bay v. T.T., [1992] OJ No. 2975 (QL) (Prov. Div.).

Children's Aid Society of the Regional Municipality of Waterloo v. R. (T.), [1990] OJ No. 766 (QL) (Prov. Ct – Fam. Div.).

Cinema International Canada Ltd., R. v. (1982), 13 Man. R. (2d) 335 (CA).

CIP Paper Products Ltd. and Saskatchewan Human Rights Commission, Re (1978), 87 DLR (3d) 609 (Sask. CA).

Clark v. Duncan (1923), 53 OLR 287 (Ont. CA).

Clinton v. Ontario Blue Cross (1993), 93 CLLC ¶17,026 (Ont. Bd Inq.).

Cloutier v. Trudel, [1982] CS 951.

Collin v. Kaplan, [1983] 1 FC 496 (TD).

Cooney, R. v. (1995), 98 CCC (3d) 196 (Ont. CA).

Cribben, R. v. (1994), 17 OR (3d) 548 (CA).

Cromer v. BC Teachers' Federation, [1986] 5 WWR 638 (BCCA).

Culhane v. Rawlings, [1987] OJ No. 1562 (QL) (Dist. Ct).

D. v. D. (1978), 88 DLR (3d) 578 (Ont. Co. Ct).

Dagenais v. CBC (1992), 99 DLR (4th) 326 (Ont. CA); appeal allowed, [1994] 3 SCR 835.

Davis v. McArthur (1970), 17 DLR (3d) 760 (BCCA).

DeBattista, R. v. (1986), 26 CCC (3d) 38 (Man. CA).

Delius, Re, [1957] Ch. 299.

Devereaux, R. v. (1996), 112 CCC (3d) 243 (Nfld. CA).

Donoghue, R. v. (1978), 42 CCC (2d) 40 (Ont. CA).

Douglas v. Canada (1992), 98 DLR (4th) 129 (FCTD).

Douglas/Kwantlen Faculty Association v. Douglas College (1990), 77 DLR (4th) 95 (SCC).

Droit de la famille – 31, [1983] CS 69.

Dubois, R. v. (1982), 69 CCC (2d) 494 (Alta. CA).

Dubois, R. v. (1987), 83 AR 161 (CA).

Dudgeon v. UK (1982), 4 EHRR 149.

Duthie Books Ltd., R. v., [1967] 1 CCC 254 (BCCA).

Dutton, R. v. (1996), 6 OTC 371 (Gen. Div.).

Duval v. The Queen (1970), 15 CR (NS) 140 (Que. CA).

Duvivier, Kowalchuk and Hollingsworth, R. v. (1990), 75 OR (2d) 203 (HCJ); affirmed (1991), 3 OR (3d) 49 (CA).

Dykon v. Canada (Minister of Employment and Immigration) (1994), 25 Imm. LR (2d) 193 (FCTD).

E. (T.D.), R. v. (1991), 116 AR 382 (Prov. Ct).

Edwards Books & Art Ltd. v. The Queen, [1986] 2 SCR 713.

Egan v. Canada (1991), 87 DLR (4th) 320 (FCTD); appeal dismissed (1993),

103 DLR (4th) 336 (FCA), appeal dismissed (1995), 124 DLR (4th) 609 (SCC).

Elliott v. Elliott, [1987] BCJ No. 43 (QL) (SC).

F. (J.A.), R. v., [1997] BCJ No. 2503 QL (Prov. Ct).

Five Accused Persons, R. v., 12 July 1961, Criminal Law Quarterly 4 (1961–62), 124).

Fournier, R. v. (1982), 70 CCC (2d) 351 (Que. CA).

Franck v. Webster, [1994] MJ No. 242 (QL) (QB).

Fraser, R. v. (1980), 55 CCC (2d) 503 (CA).

Fricke v. Lynch, 491 F Supp. 381 (US Dist Ct, 1980).

Gallant, R. v. (1994), 95 Man. R (2d) 296 (CA).

Gallant v. The Queen (1978), 91 DLR (3d) 695 (FCTD).

Gauthier, R. v. (1975), 34 CCC (2d) 266 (Que. CA).

Gaveronski v. Gaveronski (1974), 45 DLR (3d) 317 (Sask. QB).

Gay Law Students Assoc. v. Pacific Telephone & Telegram Co., 595 P 2d. 592 (1979).

Gay Students Organization v. Bonner, 509 F 2d 652 (1st Circ. 1974).

Gaylord v. Tacoma School District No. 10, 559 P 2d 1340 (Wash. 1977).

Gillis, R. v. (1994), 134 NSR (2d) 119 (CA).

Glad Day Bookshop Inc. v. Canada (Deputy Minister of National Revenue, Customs and Excise – M.N.R.) (1992), 90 DLR (4th) 527 (Ont. Ct Just. – Gen. Div.).

Glode, R. v., [1991] OJ No. 2651 (QL) (Gen. Div.).

Goel, R. v. (1986), 27 CCC (3d) 438 (Dist. Ct).

Goguen, R. v. (1977), 36 CCC (2d) 570 (BCCA).

Guardianship of Sharon Kowalski, In re, 478 NW 2d 790 (Minn. App. 1991), review denied 10 February 1992.

Guay v. The Queen (1978), 42 CCC (2d) 536 (SCC).

Guerard v. Parent, [1986] BCJ No. 1836 (QL) (SC).

H., R. v. (1985), 43 Alta. LR (2d) 250 (Prov. Ct – Youth Div.).

H. (A.B.), R. v., [1992] OJ No. 814 (QL) (Prov. Div.).

H. (Adam), R. v. (1992), 10 OR (3d) 683 (Gen. Div.); application for review dismissed (1993), 12 OR (3d) 634 (CA).

H. (E.), R. v., [1987] NWTJ No. 3 (QL) (SC).

H. (G.B.), R. v., [1985] OJ No. 702 (QL) (Prov. Ct – Fam. Div.).

H. (J.), R. v. (1996), 15 OTC 380 (Gen. Div.).

H. (R.A.), R. v., [1989] OJ No. 604 (QL) (Youth Ct).

Hahn v. Stafford, [1985] OJ No. 595 (QL) (HCJ).

Haig and The Queen in right of Canada, Re (1991), 86 DLR (4th) 617 (Ont. Ct – Gen. Div.); appeal dismissed (1992), 94 DLR (4th) 1 (Ont. CA).

Haig v. Durrell, [1990] OJ No. 1350 (QL) (HCJ).

Halm v. Canada (Minister of Employment and Immigration), [1995] 2 FC 331 (TD).

Hansford, R. v. (1987), 33 CCC (3d) 74 (Alta. CA), leave to appeal to SCC refused (1987), 56 CR (3d) xxviii.

Harrison v. UBC (1990), 77 DLR (4th) 55 (SCC).

Hawkins, R. v., [1986] BCJ No. 1115 (QL) (CA).

Healy v. James, 408 US 169 (1972).

Hennessey, Williams and Kumka, R. v., [1969] 2 CCC 372 (Man. CA).

Hicklin, R. v. (1868), LR 3 QB 360.

Hill, R. v. (1982), 32 CR (3d) 88 (Ont. CA); appeal allowed (1985), 51 CR (3d) 97 (SCC).

Homma, R. v., [1989] BCJ No. 793 (QL) (CA).

Houseman v. Coulson, [1948] 2 DLR 63 (Sask. KB).

Hoyt, R. v., [1991] YJ No. 176 (QL) (Terr. Ct).

Humphrey, R. v., [1984] OJ 218 (QL) (HCJ).

Hyde v. Hyde and Woodmansee (1866), LR 1 P&D 130.

Inaudi, Re (unreported), 9 April 1992, IRB, No. T91-04459.

Ingram and Grimsdale, R. v., (1977), 35 CCC (2d) 376 (Ont. CA).

Irwin Toy Ltd. v. Quebec (Attorney-General) (1989), 58 DLR (4th) 577 (SCC).

J.-R. (A.) R. v., [1991] OJ No. 1978 (QL) (Prov. Div.).

Johnston v. Rochette, [1982] CS 407.

Jolicoeur, R. v., (unreported), BC Prov. Ct, 7 February 1997.

Jones v. Jones, [1916] 2 AC 481 (HL).

Jones v. The Queen (1986), 31 DLR (4th) 569 (SCC).

K. v. K. [1976] 2 WWR 462 (Alta. Prov. Ct).

K. and H., R. v. (1957), 26 CR 186 (Alta. SC).

Kane v. Ontario (Attorney General), [1997] OJ No. 3979 QL (Gen. Div.).

Karalapillai, R. v., [1995] OJ No. 2105 (QL) (Ct of Justice – Prov. Div.).

Keegstra, R. v. (1990), 61 CCC (3d) 1 (SCC).

Kendall, R. v., [1987] OJ No. 388 (QL) (CA).

Kerr v. Kennedy, [1942] 1 KB 409.

King v. King, [1985] OJ No. 432 (QL) (HCJ).

Klippert v. The Queen, [1968] 2 CCC 129 (SCC).

Kluke, R. v., [1987] OJ No. 766 (QL) (CA).

Knodel v. British Columbia (Medical Services Commission) (1991), 58 BCLR (2d) 356 (SC).

Korn v. Potter (1996), 134 DLR (4th) 437 (BCSC).

Krouse v. Chrysler Canada Ltd., [1970] 3 OR 135 (HC).

L. (G.E.), R. v., [1988] BCJ No. 860 (QL) (Co. Ct).

L. (R.), Re [1981] OJ No. 382 (QL) (Co. Ct).

Lavigne v. O.P.S.E.U. (1991), 81 DLR (4th) 545 (SCC).

Layland v. Ontario (Minister of Consumer and Commercial Relations (1993), 104 DLR (4th) 214, (Ont. Div. Ct).

LeBeau and Lofthouse, R. v. (1988), 41 CCC (3d) 163 (Ont. CA), appeal quashed (1990), 149 NR 236 (SCC).

Ledinski, R. v. (1991), 95 Sask. R 1 (QB); affirmed (1995), 134 Sask. R 256 (CA).

Lee, R. v. (1985), 166 APR 387 (NSSC, App. Div.).

Lee v. Canada (Armed Forces, Chief of Defence Staff) (1992), 51 FTR 136 (TD).

Lefebvre, R. v. (1978), 4 CR (3d) 164 (Que. Ct Sess.).

Lelas, R. v. (1990), 74 OR (2d) 552 (Ont. CA).

Lemoine, R. v. (1992), 113 NSR (2d) 361 (Prov. Ct).

Leshner v. Ontario (1992), 92 CCLC ¶17,035 (Ont. Bd Inq.).

Lever v. George, [1950] OR 115 (HCJ).

Little Sisters Book and Art Emporium v. Minister of Justice (1996), 131 DLR (4th) 486 (BCSC); affirmed [1998] BCJ No. 1507 QL (CA).

Longpre, R. v., [1993] MJ No. 309 (QL) (Prov. Ct).

Lupien, R. v., [1969] 1 CCC 32 (BCCA); appeal allowed, [1970] 2 CCC 193 (SCC).

Luxton, R. v., [1990] 2 SCR 711.

M. v. H. (1996), 27 OR (3d) 593 (Gen. Div.); appeal dismissed (1996), 31 OR (3d) 417 (CA).

M. (A.J.), R. v. (1986), 29 CCC (3d) 418 (Alta. QB).

M. (C), R. v. (1995), 41 CR (4th) 134 (Ont. CA).

M. (D.), R. v. (1990), 61 CCC (3d) 129 (Ont. CA).

M. (D.J.), R. v., [1990] OJ No. 514 (QL) (Prov. Ct – Youth Off. Ct).

M. (G.J.), R. v. (1992), 130 AR 33 (QB), reversed (1993), 135 AR 204 (CA).

M. (H.I.) v. M. (W.A.) [1994] BCJ No. 2824 (QL) (Prov. Ct).

M. (S.H.), R. v. (1987), 52 Alta. LR 356 (CA); appeal dismissed (1989), 71 CR (3d) 257 (SCC).

MacFarlane, R. v. (1989), 55 Man. R (2d) 105 (CA).

Magliaro, R. v. (1981), 45 NSR (2d) 504 (Co. Ct).

Mailhot, R. v. (1996), 108 CCC (3d) 376 (Que. CA).

Martini v. Martini, [1987] BCJ No. 2757 (QL) (SC).

Marzan and The Queen, Re (1981), 131 DLR (3d) 370 (Man. CA); appeal allowed (1982), 131 DLR (3d) 370n (SCC).

Mason, R. v. (1981), 59 CCC (2d) 461 (Ont. Prov. Ct – Crim. Div.).

Matherson v. Marchello, 473 NYS 2d 998 (A.D. 2 Dept. 1984).

Mattais, R. v., [1970] 5 CCC 344 (Que. CA).

Mazart v. State, 441 NYS 2d 600 (Ct Cl. 1981).

McAleer v. Canada (Canadian Human Rights Commission) (1996), 132 DLR (4th) 672 (FCTD).

McDonald, R. v., [1995] OJ No. 2137 (QL) (Gen. Div.).

McKinney v. University of Guelph (1990), 76 DLR (4th) 545 (SCC).

Melvin v. Reid, 299 SW 967 (1931).

Mercedes Homes Inc. v. Grace, [1993] OJ No. 2610 (QL) (Gen. Div.).

Monette v. Sylvestre, [1981] CS 731.

Moore, R. v. (1996), 81 BCAC 153 (CA).

Moore, R. v., [1987] BCJ No. 2734 (QL) (Co. Ct).

Morgentaler v. Wiche, [1989] OJ No. 2582 (QL) (HCJ).

Moricoli v. Schwartz, 361 NE 2d 74 (App. Ct Ill., 1977).

Morrison v. Morrison (1972), 2 Nfld & PEIR 465 (PEI SC).

Munster, R. v. (1960), 129 CCC 277 (NSSC).

Murphy v. Little Memphis Cabaret Inc. (1996), 20 OTC 313 (Gen. Div.).

Musson, R. v. (1996), 3 CR (5th) 61 (Ont. Gen. Div.).

N. (A.M.) v. O'Halpin, [1996] OJ No. 3576 (QL) (Gen. Div.).

N. (R.K.), R. v. (1997), 32 OR (3d) 537 (CA).

National News Co. Ltd., R. v., [1953] OR 533 (CA).

Neil, R. v. (1957), 26 CR 281 (SCC).

Neve, R. v. (1994), 160 AR 255 (QB).

Newfoundland and Labrador (Human Rights Commission) v. Newfoundland and Labrador (Minister of Employment and Labour Relations) (1995), 127 DLR (4th) 694 (Nfld TD).

Nielsen v. Canada, [1992] 2 FC 561 (TD).

North and Matheson, Re (1974), 52 DLR (3d) 280 (Man. Co. Ct).

Noyes, R. v. (1986), 6 BCLR (2d) 306 (BCSC); affirmed (1987), 22 BCLR (2d) 45 (CA), leave to appeal to SCC refused 16 May 1988, 27 BCLR (2d) xxxv.

O and O, Re (1980), 30 OR (2d) 588 (HCJ).

Obey, R. v. (1973), 11 CCC (2d) 28 (BCSC).

Ontario English Catholic Teachers Asociation and Essex County Roman Catholic School Board, Re (1987), 58 OR (2d) 545 (HCJ – Div. Ct); leave to appeal to SCC refused (1988), 51 DLR (4th) vii.

Otto, R. v. (1984), 16 CCC (3d) 289 (BC Co. Ct).

P. (P.A.) v. P. (M.B.), [1986] NSJ No. 492 (QL) (Fam. Ct).

P.-B. (D.) v. P.-B. (T.), [1988] OJ No. 2398 (QL) (Prov. Ct – Fam. Div.).

Paquette, R. v., [1988] BCJ No. 1624 (QL) (Co. Ct).

Parks, R. v. (1993), 84 CCC (3d) 353 (Ont. CA); leave to appeal denied [1994] 1 SCR x.

Parks v. H.H. Marshall Ltd. (1984), 136 APR 172 (NS TD).

Partland v. Partland (1960), 24 DLR (2d) 576 (Ont. HC).

Paterson, R. v., [1995] BCJ No. 1032 (QL) (SC); affirmed [1998] BCJ No. 126 (QL) (CA).

Patterson, R. v. (1972), 9 CCC (2d) 364 (Ont. Co. Ct).

Penthouse Int'l Ltd., R. v. (1979), 96 DLR (3d) 735 (Ont. CA); leave to appeal refused (1979), 96 DLR (3d) 735n (SCC).

Pereira-Vasquez, R. v. (1988), 43 CCC (3d) 82 (BCCA).

Piche v. Canada (Solicitor General), [1984] FCJ No. 1008 (QL) (TD).

Pilgrim, R. v. (1981), 64 CCC (2d) 523 (Nfld CA).

Pilgrim, R. v., [1983] OJ No. 812 (QL) (HCJ).

Pinard and Maltais, R. v. (1982), 5 CCC (3d) 460 (Que. CA).

Pink Triangle Press, R. v. (1979), 45 CCC (2d) 385 (Ont. Prov. Ct); reversed (1980), 51 CCC (2d) 485 (Ont. Co. Ct).

Pisces Health Spa Ltd., R. v. (1981), 63 CCC (2d) 427 (Alta. CA).

Pizarro v. Canada (Minister of Employment and Immigration) (1994), 75 FTR 120 (TD).

Pizzardi, R. v. (1994), 17 OR (3d) 623 (CA).

Plessey v. Ferguson, 163 US 537 (1896).

Plato, R. v., [1987] AJ No. 903 (QL) (CA).

Prairie Schooner News Ltd. and Powers, R. v. (1970), 1 CCC (2d) 251 (Man. CA); leave to appeal refused, [1970] SCR x.

Priape Enrg. and the Deputy Minister of National Revenue, Re (1979), 52 CCC (2d) 44 (Que. Super. Ct – Crim Div.).

R. (S.), R. v., [1989] OJ No. 1487 (QL) (Youth Ct).

Ralston v. Fomich (1992), 66 BCLR (2d) 166 (SC).

Reference re An Act to Amend the Education Act (Ontario) (1987), 40 DLR (4th) 18 (SCC).

Reference re Child Welfare Act (Nfld) (1990), 48 CRR 281 (Nfld SC – Unified Family Court).

Richard, R. v. (1982), 16 Man. R (2d) 355 (CA).

Robertson, R. v. (1979), 46 CCC (2d) 573 (Ont. CA).

Robertson v. Geisinger (1991), 36 RFL (3d) 261 (Sask. QB).

Roestad, R. v. (1971), 19 CR (NS) 190 (Ont. Co. Ct); leave to appeal refused (1971), 19 CR (NS) 235n (Ont. CA).

Romer v. Evans, 134 L. Ed. 2d 855 (USSC, 1996).

Rose v. Société de transport de la Communauté urbaine de Montréal, [1996] AQ No. 688 (QL) (Super. Ct).

Rosenberg v. Canada (Attorney General), (1998) 158 DLR (4th) 664 (CA).

Roth and Roth v. Roth, Roth and Stephens (1991), 4 OR (3d) 740 (Ont. Ct – Gen. Div.).

Roy, R. v., [1998] AQ No. 935 QL (CA).

Ruby, R. v., [1986] NJ No. 154 (QL) (CA).

Russow v. British Columbia (Attorney-General) (1989), 62 DLR (4th) 98 (BCSC).

Rutledge, R. v., [1996] BCJ No. 755 (QL) (SC).

Ryznar, R. v. (1986), 43 Man. R (2d) 143 (CA); leave to appeal to SCC refused (1986), 46 Man. R (2d) 160n.

S. (E.), R. v., [1991] AJ No. 873 (QL) (Prov. Ct).

S. (Guy), R. v. (1991), 5 OR (3d) 97 (CA); leave to appeal to SCC refused (1992), 6 OR (3d) xiii.

S. (W.), R. v., [1989] OJ No. 65 (QL) (CA).

S. (W.B.), R. v.; R. v. P. (M.) (1992), 73 CCC (3d) 530 (Alta. CA).

Saccone v. Orr (1981), 34 OR (2d) 317 (Co. Ct).

St Paul's Roman Catholic Separate School (District No. 20) v. C.U.P.E, Local 2268, [1987] SJ No. 209 (QL) (CA).

Salida, R. v., [1969] 1 OR 203 (Mag. Ct).

Saunders v. Saunders (1989), 20 RFL (3d) 368 (BC Co. Ct).

Schau, R. v., [1987] MJ No. 363 (QL) (CA).

Schomer v. Smidt, 170 Cal. Rptr. 662 (App. 1981).

Section 24, B.N.A. Act, Re, [1930] 1 DLR 98 (PC).

Serup v. School District No. 57 (1987), 14 BCLR (2d) 393 (SC); appeal allowed in part (1989), 54 BCLR (2d) 258 (CA).

Silber v. BCTV Broadcasting System Ltd. (1985), 69 BCLR 34 (SC).

Silva, R. v. (1995), 26 OR (3d) 554 (Gen. Div.).

Sipple v. Chronicle Publishing Co., 201 Cal. Rptr. 665 (Ct App. 1984).

Smith, R. v., [1989] MJ No. 394 (QL) (Prov. Ct – Crim. Div.).

Stein v. Trager, 232 NYS 2d 362 (Sup. Ct, 1962).

Stewart, R. v. (1995), 41 CR (4th) 102 (BCCA).

Stiles v. Canada (Attorney General) (1986), 3 FTR 234 (TD).

Swann v. Charlotte-Mecklenburg Board of Education, 402 US 1 (1971).

T. v. T. and W. (1975), 24 RFL 57 (Man. QB).

T. (R.R.) v. T. (G.), [1994] OJ No. 2453 (QL) (Prov. Div.).

Tanner, R. v. (1994) 19 OR (3d) 259 (CA) reversed (1995), 97 CCC (3d) 289 (SCC).

Taylor, R. v. (1982), 66 CCC (2d) 437 (Ont. CA).

Templeman v. Templeman, [1986] BCJ No. 1426 (QL) (SC).

Tetley, R. v. (1985), 40 Alta. LR (2d) 409 (CA).

Thaarup v. Hulton Press Ltd. (1943), LT 309 (CA)..

Thibaudeau v. M.N.R., [1994] 2 FC 189 (CA); appeal allowed (1995), 12 RFL (4th) 1 (SCC).

Thompson v. The King, [1918] AC 221 (HL).

Tremblett, R. v. (1975), 8 APR 482 (Nfld Mag. Ct).

Trinity Western University v. College of Teachers (B.C.) (1997), 41 BCLR (3d) 158 (SC).

Trudel et Commission des droits de la personne du Qc v. Camping & Plage Gilles Fortier Inc., [1994] JTDPQ No. 32 (QL) (HR Trib Que.).

United States of America v. Cobb, [1997] OJ No. 4362 QL (Gen. Div.).

United States of Mexico v. Hurley (1997), 35 OR (3d) 481 (CA).

University of Manitoba and Deputy Minister, Revenue Canada, Customs & Excise, Re (1983), 4 DLR (4th) 658 (Man. Co. Ct).

Valiquette v. The Gazette (1991), 8 CCLT (2d) 302 (Que. Super. Ct).

Valley, R. v. (1986), 26 CCC (3d) 207 (Ont. CA), leave to appeal to SCC refused, 22 April 1986.

Veysey, R. v., [1989] OJ No. 1015 (QL) (CA).

Veysey v. Canada (Correctional Service), [1990] 1 FC 321 (TD); varied (1990), 43 Admin. LR 316 (FCA).

Victoria Park Racing and Recreation Grounds Co. Ltd. v. Taylor (1937), 58 CLR 479.

Video World Ltd., R. v. (1985), 22 CCC (3d) 331 (Man. CA); affirmed (1987), 35 CCC (3d) 191 (SCC).

Vriend v. Alberta, [1994] 6 WWR 414 (Alta. QB); appeal allowed (1996), 132 DLR (4th) 595 (Alta. CA); reversed (1998), 156 DLR (4th) 385 (SCC).

Waldie, R. v., [1987] BCJ No. 2291 (QL) (Co. Ct).

Wetherhead v. Armitage (1690), 83 ER 534.

White, R. v. (1975), 25 CCC (2d) 172 (Ont. CA).

White, R. v. (1990), 88 Sask. R 54 (QB); appeal dismissed, (1991), 91 Sask. R 225 (CA).

White v. The Queen (1964), 44 CR 75 (NBSC App. Div.).

Whyte v. Whyte (1991), 101 NSR (2d) 249 (SC TD).

Wilson, R. v. (1990), 59 CCC (3d) 432 (BCCA).

Wilson, R. v., [1991] OJ No. 1746 (QL) (Prov. Div.).

Wlodek v. Kosko (1974), 7 OR (2d) 611 (CA); appeal dismissed (1976), 65 DLR (3d) 383 (SCC).

Worby v. Worby (1985), 48 RFL (2d) 369 (Sask. QB).

Young, R. v., [1991] OJ No. 2210 (QL) (Gen. Div.).

Young v. R. (1980), 27 CR (3d) 85 (BCCA).

Zylberberg v. Sudbury Board of Education (Director) (1988), 52 DLR (4th) 577 (Ont. CA).

525044 Alberta Ltd. (c.o.b. Tony C's 21 Club & Restaurant) v. Triple 5 Corp., [1993] AJ No. 728 (QL) (QB).

789617 Ontario Inc. c.o.b. as The Spa on Maitland v. Toronto (City) and Nixon, Commissioner and Chief Building Official for Toronto (City) (1990), 75 OR (2d) 475 (Dist. Ct).

Bibliography

Adams, Henry E., Lester W. Wright, Jr, and Bethany A. Lohr. 'Is Homophobia Associated with Homosexual Arousal?' *Journal of Abnormal Psychology* 105 (1996), 440.

Alexander, Michael. 'Censorship and the Limits of Liberalism.' *University of Toronto Faculty of Law Review* 47 (1988), 58.

American Law Institute. *Restatement of the Law Torts* 2nd ed. St. Paul, Minn.: American Law Institute 1977.

Arnup, Katherine. '"Mothers Just Like Others": Lesbians, Divorce, and Child Custody in Canada.' *Canadian Journal of Women and the Law* 3 (1989), 18.

Arons, Stephen. 'Constitutional Litigation and Education Reform: Canada's Opportunity.' In Michael E. Manley-Casimir and Terri A. Sussel, eds., *Courts in the Classroom: Education and the Charter of Rights and Freedoms*, chap. 8. Calgary: Detselig 1986.

Auger, Jeanette A. 'Lesbians and Aging: Triple Trouble or Tremendous Thrill.' In Sharon Dale Stone, ed., *Lesbians in Canada*, chap. 1. Toronto: Between the Lines 1990.

Austen, Andrea, and Adrian Alex Wellington. 'Outing: The Supposed Justifications.' *Canadian Journal of Law and Jurisprudence* 8 (1995), 83.

Bagnall, Robert G., Patrick C. Gallagher, and Joni L. Goldstein. 'Burdens on Gay Litigants and Bias in the Court System: Homosexual Panic, Child Custody, and Anonymous Parties.' *Harvard Civil Rights – Civil Liberties Law Review* 19 (1984), 497.

Banks, N. Kathleen ('Sam'). Comment on the *Knodel v. B.C. (Medical Services Commission)* (1991), 58 BCLR (2d) 356 (SC) case. *Canadian Journal of Family Law* 11 (1993), 287.

Bannerji, Himani. *Thinking Through: Essays on Feminism, Marxism and Anti-racism*. Toronto: Women's Press 1995.

Barendt, Eric. *Freedom of Speech*. Oxford: Clarendon Press 1985.

Bartee, Wayne C., and Alice Fleetwood Bartee. *Litigating Morality: American Legal Thought and Its English Roots*. New York: Praeger 1992.

Bateman, Margaret. 'Lesbians, Gays and Child Custody: An Australian Legal History,' *Australian Gay and Lesbian Law Journal* 1 (1992), 47.

Bates, Frank. 'Child Law and the Homosexual Parent – Recent Developments in the United States.' *Australian Gay and Lesbian Law Journal* 1 (1992), 21.

– 'Child Law and the Homosexual Parent: Some Further Developments in Australia and the United States.' *Australian Gay and Lesbian Law Journal* 2 (1992), 1.

Baudoin, Jean-Louis. 'La vérité et le droit des personnes: aspects nouveaux.' *Revue géneral de droit* 18 (1987), 801.

Beaney, William M. 'The Right to Privacy and American Law.' *Law and Contemporary Problems* 31 (1966), 253.

Beaudoin, Gérald-A., and Errol Mendes, eds. *The Canadian Charter of Rights and Freedoms*. 3rd ed. Scarborough, Ont. Carswell 1996.

Bell, John. 'The Judge as Bureaucrat.' In John Eekelaar and John Bell, eds., *Oxford Essays in Jurisprudence*, 3rd Series, Oxford: Oxford University Press 1987.

– *Policy Arguments in Judicial Decisions*. Oxford: Oxford University Press 1983.

Bentham, Jeremy. 'An Essay on "Paederasty."' *Journal of Homosexuality* 3 (1978), 389.

Black, William. '*Vriend*, Rights and Democracy.' *Constitutional Forum* 7 (1996), 126.

Blair, Justice D.G. 'The Charter and the Judges: A View from the Bench.' *Manitoba Law Journal* 13 (1983), 445.

Bok, Sissela. *Secrets: On the Ethics of Concealment and Revelation*. New York: Pantheon 1982.

Bostwick, Gary L. 'A Taxonomy of Privacy: Repose, Sanctuary and Intimate Decision.' *California Law Review* 64 (1976), 1447.

Boswell, John. 'Categories, Experience and Sexuality.' In Edward, Stein, ed., *Forms of Desire: Sexual Orientation and the Social Constructionist Controversy*, chap. 7. New York: Garland 1990.

– *Christianity, Social Tolerance and Homosexuality: Gay People in Western Europe from the Beginning of the Christian Era to the Fourteenth Century*. Chicago: University of Chicago Press 1980.

– 'Jews, Bicycle Riders, and Gay People: The Determination of Social Consensus and Its Impact on Minorities.' *Yale Journal of Law and the Humanities* 1 (1989), 205.

– *Same-Sex Unions in Premodern Europe*. New York: Villard 1994.

Boyd, Neil. 'Censorship and Obscenity: Jurisdiction and the Boundaries of Free Expression.' *Osgoode Hall Law Journal* 23 (1985), 37.

Boyle, Christine. 'Custody, Adoption and the Homosexual Parent.' *Reports of Family Law* 23 (1976), 129.

Brittan, Leon. 'The Right of Privacy in England and the United States.' *Tulane Law Review* 37 (1963), 235.

Britton: An English Translation, F.M. Nichols, ed. Washington, D.C.: John Byrne & Co.

Brockman, Joan. 'A Difference without a Distinction?' *Canadian Journal of Law and Society* 8 (1993), 149.

Bronski, Michael. *Culture Clash: The Making of Gay Sensibility.* Boston: South End Press 1984.

Brown, Raymond. *The Law of Defamation in Canada.* Scarborough, Ont. Carswell 1987.

Bruner, Arnold. 'Sexual Orientation and Equality Rights.' In Anne F. Bayefsky and Mary Eberts, eds., *Equality Rights and the Canadian Charter of Rights and Freedoms*, chap. 10. Toronto: Carswell 1985.

Burns, Peter. 'The Law and Privacy: The Canadian Experience.' *Canadian Bar Review* 54 (1976), 1.

- 'A Retrospective View of the Protection of Privacy Act: A Fragile Rede Is Recked.' *UBC Law Review* 13 (1979), 123.

- 'Privacy and the Common Law: A Tangled Skein Unravelling?' In Dale Gibson, ed., *Aspects of Privacy Law: Essays in Honour of John M. Sharp*, chap. 2. Toronto: Butterworths 1980.

Butler, Judith. 'Imitation and Gender Insubordination.' In Diana Fuss, ed., *Inside/Out: Lesbian Theories, Gay Theories*, chap. 1. London: Routledge 1991.

Byron, Stuart. 'The Closet Syndrome.' In Karla Kay and Allen Young, eds., *Out of the Closets: Voices of Gay Liberation.* New York: Douglas 1972, 58–65.

Calhoun, Cheshire. 'Denaturalizing and Desexualizing Lesbian and Gay Liberation.' *Virginia Law Review* 79 (1993), 1859.

Canada. *Equality for All: Report of the Parliamentary Committee on Equality Rights.* ('Boyer Report') October 1985.

Canadian Judical Council. *Commentaries on Judicial Conduct.* Cowansville, Que.: Yvon Blais 1991.

Caron, Michèle L. 'Variations sur le thème de l'invisibilisation.' *Canadian Journal of Women and the Law* 7 (1994), 271.

Carpenter, Humphrey. *Benjamin Britten: A Biography.* London: Faber and Faber 1992.

Carter-Ruck, P.F., and R. Walker. *Carter-Ruck on Libel and Slander.* 3rd ed. London: Butterworths 1985.

Casswell, Donald G. 'Disclosure by a Physician of AIDS-Related Patient Information: An Ethical and Legal Dilemma.' *Canadian Bar Review* 68 (1989), 225.
- *Lesbians, Gay Men, and Canadian Law.* Toronto: Emond Montgomery 1996.
Chapman, Pamela A. 'The Politics of Judging: Section 1 of the *Charter of Rights and Freedoms.*' *Osgoode Hall Law Journal* 24 (1986), 867.
Chapman, T.L. 'Male Homosexuality: Legal Restraints and Social Attitudes in Western Canada, 1890–1920.' In Louis A. Knafla, ed., *Law and Justice in a New Land: Essays in Western Canadian Legal History.* Toronto: Carswell 1986.
- 'An Oscar Wilde Type: The "Abominable Crime of Buggery" in Western Canada, 1890–1920.' *Criminal Justice History* 4 (1983), 97.
Chinn, Sarah, and Kris Franklin. '"I Am What I Am" (Or Am I?): The Making and Unmaking of Lesbian and Gay Identity in *High Tech Gays,'* *Discourse* 15.1 (Fall 1992), 11.
Chotalia, Shirish. 'The *Vriend* Decision: A Case Study in Constitutional Remedies in the Human Rights Context,' *Alberta Law Review* 32 (1994), 825.
Clark, Lorenne M.G. 'Liberalism and the Living-Tree: Women, Equality, and the Charter.' *Alberta Law Review* 28 (1990), 384.
Clarke, Paul T. 'Free Speech and Canada's Public School Teachers: An Employment Law and Constitutional Law Analysis.' Unpublished PhD dissertation, University of Saskatchewan 1997.
Cohen, Derek, and Richard Dyer. 'The Politics of Gay Culture.' In Gay Left Collective, eds. *Homosexuality: Power and Politics,* chap. 14. London: Allison & Busby 1980.
Cohen, Ed. 'Who Are "We?": Gay "Identity" a Political (E)motion.' In Diana Fuss, ed. *Inside/Out: Lesbian Theories, Gay Theories.* New York: Routledge 1991.
Coke, Edward. *Institutes of the Laws of England.* Third Part, chap. 10, 'Of Buggery, or Sodomy.' 1658–9; London: Clarke 1823.
Collier, Richard. *Masculinity, Law and the Family.* London: Routledge 1995.
Cossman, Brenda, and Bruce Ryder. 'Customs Censorship and the *Charter*: The *Little Sisters* Case.' *Constitutional Forum* 7 (1996), 103.
Crenshaw, Kimberle. 'Mapping the Margins: Intersectionality, Identity Politics, and Violence against Women of Color,' *Stanford Law Review* 43 (1991), 1241.
Crompton, Louis. 'The Myth of Lesbian Impunity: Capital Laws from 1270 to 1791,' *Journal of Homosexuality* 6 (1980–1), 11.
D'Aoust, Vicky. 'Competency, Autonomy, and Choice: On Being Lesbian and Having Disabilities,' *Canadian Journal of Women and the Law* 7 (1994), 564.
Davis, Frederick. 'What Do We Mean by "Right to Privacy"?' *South Dakota Law Review* 4 (1959), 1.
Day, Dian. 'Lesbian/Mother.' In Sharon Dale Stone, ed. *Lesbians in Canada,* chap. 2. Toronto: Between the Lines 1990.

Day, Shelagh, and Gwen Brodsky. 'The Duty to Accommodate: Who Will Benefit?' *Canadian Bar Review* 75 (1996), 433.

De Coste, F.C. 'Case Comment. *Vriend v. Alberta*: Sexual Orientation and Liberal Policy,' *Alberta Law Review* 34 (1996), 950.

de Lauretis, Teresa. 'Queer Theory: Lesbian and Gay Sexualities – An Introduction,' *Differences* 3 (1991), 111.

Deleury, Édith. 'L'union homosexuelle et le droit de la famille,' *Cahiers de droit* 25 (1984), 751.

Devlin, Patrick. *The Enforcement of Morals*. London: Oxford University Press 1965.

Dollimore, Jonathan. *Sexual Dissidence: Augustine to Wilde, Freud to Foucault*. Oxford: Clarendon Press 1991.

Doucette, Joanne. Redefining Difference: Disabled Lesbians Resist. In Sharon Dale Stone, ed. *Lesbians in Canada*, chap. 4. Toronto: Between the Lines 1990.

Dressler, Joshua. 'Survey of School Principals Regarding Alleged Homosexual Teachers in the Classroom: How Likely (Really) Is Discharge?' *University Dayton Law Review* 10 (1984), 599.

Dubick, Keith. 'Freedom to Hate: Do the Criminal Code Proscriptions against Hate Propaganda Infringe the *Charter*?' *Saskatchewan Law Review* 54 (1990), 149.

Duclos, Nitya. 'Some Complicating Thoughts on Same-Sex Marriage,' *Law & Sexuality* 1 (1991), 31.

Duplé, Nicole. 'Homosexualité et droits à l'égalité dans les Chartes canadienne et québécoise,' *Cahiers de droit* 25 (1984), 801.

Dutile, Fernand N. *Sex, Schools and the Law: A Study of the Legal Implications of Sexual Matters Relating to the Public School Curriculum (With a Separate Chapter on Sex Education), the Public School Library, the Personal Lives of Teachers and Students, and the Student Press*. Springfield, Ill.: Charles Thomas 1986.

Dworkin, Gerald. 'The Common Law Protection of Privacy,' *Tasmanian University Law Review* 4 (1967), 418.

Dworkin, Ronald. *Taking Rights Seriously*. London: Duckworth 1977.

Dyer, Richard. *The Matter of Images: Essays on Representation*. London: Routledge 1993.

Dynes, Wayne R., ed. *Encyclopedia of Homosexuality*. Chicago: St James Press 1990.

Dyzenhaus, David. 'Regulating Free Speech,' *Ottawa Law Review* 23 (1991), 289.

Eagleton, Terry. *Ideology: An Introduction*. London: Verso 1991.

Eaton, Mary. 'Homosexual Unmodified: Speculations on Law's Discourse, Race, and the Construction of Sexual Identity.' In Didi Herman and Carl

Stychin, ed. *Legal Inversions: Lesbians, Gay Men, and the Politics of Law.* Philadelphia: Temple University Press 1995.

– 'Lesbians and the Law.' In Sharon Dale Stone, ed. *Lesbians in Canada,* chap. 8. Toronto: Between the Lines 1990.

– 'Lesbians, Gays and the Struggle for Equality Rights: Reversing the Progressive Hypothesis,' *Dalhousie Law Journal* 17 (1994), 130.

– 'Patently Confused: Complex Inequality and *Canada v. Mossop,' Review of Constitutional Studies* 1 (1994), 203.

Elman, Bruce P. 'Combatting Racist Speech: The Canadian Experience,' *Alberta Law Review* 32 (1989), 623.

Elwood, John P. 'Note: Outing, Privacy, and the First Amendment,' *Yale Law Journal* 102 (1992), 747.

Eskridge, William N., Jr. 'A History of Same-Sex Marriage,' *Virginia Law Review* 79 (1993), 1419.

Esson, William A. 'The Judiciary and Freedom of Expression,' *University of Western Ontario Law Review* 23 (1995), 159.

Faderman, Lillian. *Surpassing the Love of Men: Romantic Friendship and Love between Women from the Renaissance to the Present.* New York: William Morrow 1991.

Fajer, Marc A. 'Can Two Real Men Eat Quiche Together? Storytelling, Gender-Role Stereotypes, and Legal Protection for Lesbians and Gay Men,' *University Miami Law Review* 46 (1992), 511.

Ferguson, Ann. 'Is There a Lesbian Culture?' In Jeffner Allen, ed. *Lesbian Philosophies and Cultures.* Albany, N.Y.: State University of New York Press 1990.

Finnis, John. 'Law, Morality, and "Sexual Orientation".' *Notre Dame Journal of Law, Ethics and Public Policy* 9 (1995), 11.

Flanagan, William F. 'Equality Rights for People with AIDS: Mandatory Reporting of HIV Infection and Contact Tracing,' *McGill Law Journal* 34 (1989), 530.

Fleta H.G. Richardson and G.O. Sayles, ed. London: Selden Society 1985.

Forbidden Passages: Writings Banned in Canada. Pittsburgh: Cleis 1995.

Forsythe, Gail H. 'Sexual Orientation – Two Professional Experiences,' Law Society of BC *Benchers' Bulletin.* April 1997, 6.

Foucault, Michel. *The History of Sexuality.* Vol 1. *An Introduction.* New York: Vintage 1990.

Franchild, Edwina. '"You Do So Well": A Blind Lesbian Responds to Her Sighted Sisters.' In Jeffner Allen, ed. *Lesbian Philosophies and Cultures.* Albany, N.Y.: State University of New York Press 1990.

Freeman, Jody. 'Defining Family in *Mossop v. DSS*: The Challenge of Anti-

Essentialism and Interactive Discrimination for Human Rights Legislation,' (1994), *University of Toronto Law Journal* 44 (1994), 41.

Fried, Charles. *An Anatomy of Values: Problems of Personal and Social Choice.* Cambridge, Mass.: Harvard University Press 1970.

Friedland, Martin L. *A Place Apart: Judicial Independence and Accountability in Canada.* Canadian Judicial Council 1995.

Friedrich, Carl J. 'Secrecy versus Privacy: The Democratic Dilemma.' In *Nomos XIII: Privacy,* chap. 6. New York: Atherton Press 1971.

Frye, Marilyn. *The Politics of Reality: Essays in Feminist Theory.* Freedom, Cal.: Crossing Press 1983.

Fuller, Janine, and Stuart Blackley. *Restricted Entry: Censorship on Trial.* Vancouver: Press Gang 1995.

Fuller, Lon L. *The Morality of Law.* New Haven: Yale University Press 1964.

Furedy, John J. 'Academic Freedom, Opinions and Acts: The Voltaire-Mill Perspective Applied to Current Canadian Cases,' *UNB Law Journal* 44 (1995), 131.

Fuss, Diana, ed. 'Introduction.' In *Inside/Out: Lesbian Theories, Gay Theories.* London: Routledge 1991.

Gammon, Carolyn, et al. 'Organizing Lesbian Studies at Concordia.' In Sharon Dale Stone, ed., *Lesbians in Canada,* chap. 15. Toronto: Between the Lines 1990.

Garrow, David J. *Liberty and Sexuality: The Right to Privacy and the Making of Roe v. Wade.* New York: Macmillan 1994.

Gatley on Libel and Slander, 8th ed. London: Sweet & Maxwell 1981.

Gavigan, Shelley A.M. 'A Parent(ly) Knot: Can Heather Have Two Mommies?' In Didi Herman and Carl Stychin, eds., *Legal Inversions: Lesbians, Gay Men, and the Politics of Law.* Philadelphia: Temple University Press 1995.

Geerz, Clifford. *The Interpretation of Cultures.* New York: Basic Books 1973.

Geiser, R. *Hidden Victims: The Sexual Abuse of Children.* Boston: Beacon Press 1979.

Gibbons, John, ed. *Language and the Law.* London: Longman 1994.

Gibson, Dale. 'Common Law Protection of Privacy.' In Lewis Klar, ed. *Studies in Canadian Tort Law,* chap. 12. Toronto: Butterworths 1977.

Gigeroff, Alex K. *Sexual Deviations in the Criminal Law: Homosexual, Exhibitionistic, and Pedophilic Offences in Canada.* Toronto: Clarke Institute of Psychiatry 1968.

Gilbert, Arthur N. 'Conceptions of Homosexuality and Sodomy in Western History,' *Journal of Homosexuality* 6 (1980–1), 57.

Girard, Philip. 'From Subversion to Liberation: Homosexuals and the Immigration Act, 1952–1977,' *Canadian Journal of Law and Society* 2 (1987), 1.

- 'Sexual Orientation as a Human Rights Issue in Canada 1969–1985,' *Dalhousie Law Journal* 10 (1986), 267.

Givan, David. 'The Ross Decision and Control in Professional Employment,' *UNB Law Journal* 41 (1992), 333.

Glenn, H. Patrick. 'The Right to Privacy in Quebec Law.' In Dale Gibson, ed. *Aspects of Privacy Law: Essays in Honour of John M. Sharp*, chap. 3. Toronto: Butterworths 1980.

Goffman, Erving. *Stigma*. Englewood Cliffs, N.J.: Prentice-Hall 1963.

Gomez, Jewelle. 'Repeat after Me: We Are Different. We Are the Same,' *NYU Review of Law and Social Change* 14 (1986), 935.

Goreham, Richard A. 'Le droit à la vie privée des personnes homosexuelles,' *Cahiers de droit* 25 (1984), 843.

Grace, Elizabeth. 'Professional Misconduct or Moral Pronouncement: A Study of "Contentious" Teacher Behaviour in Quebec,' *Education and the Law Journal* 5 (1993), 99.

Graham, Jack. 'AIDS in Schools: A Model of Enlightenment and Tolerance?' (1990), *Education and the Law Journal* 2 (1990), 299.

Grant, Jon E. 'Note – "Outing" and Freedom of the Press: Sexual Orientation's Challenge to the Supreme Court's Categorical Jurisprudence,' *Cornell Law Review* 77 (1991), 103.

Green, Maurice A., and Margaret Correia. 'Comment: Freedom of Speech and Teachers' Duties: *Ross* Revisited,' *Education and the Law Journal* 5 (1993), 361.

Green, Richard. '"Give Me Your Tired, Your Poor, Your Huddled Masses"' (of Heterosexuals): An Analysis of American and Canadian Immigration Policy,' *Anglo-American Law Review* 16 (1987), 139.

- 'The Immutability of (Homo)sexual Orientation: Behavioral Science Implications for a Constitutional (Legal) Analysis,' *Journal of Psychiatry and the Law* 16 (1988), 537.

- *Sexual Science and the Law*. Cambridge, Mass.: Harvard University Press 1992.

Greenberg, David F. *The Construction of Homosexuality*. Chicago: University Chicago Press 1988.

Greenland, Cyril. 'Dangerous Sexual Offenders in Canada,' *Canadian Journal of Criminology and Corrections* 14 (1972), 44.

Greschner, Donna. 'Judicial Approaches to Equality and Critical Legal Studies.' In Sheilah L. Martin and Kathleen E. Mahoney, eds. *Equality and Judicial Neutrality*. Scarborough, Ont.: Carswell 1987.

Groarke, Leo. 'Pornography, Censorship, and Obscenity Law in Canada,' *Windsor Review of Legal and Social Issues* 2 (1990), 25.

Gross, Larry. *Contested Closets: The Politics and Ethics of Outing*. Minneapolis: University of Minnesota Press 1993.

- 'Out of the Mainstream: Sexual Minorities and the Mass Media.' In Michelle A. Wolf and Alfred P. Kielwasser, eds. *Gay People, Sex, and the Media*. New York: Harrington Park Press 1991.

Gross, Wendy L. 'Judging the Best Interests of the Child: Child Custody and the Homosexual Parent,' *Canadian Journal of Women and the Law* 1 (1986), 505.

Haiman, Franklyn S. *Speech and Law in a Free Society*. Chicago: University of Chicago Press 1982.

Halley, Janet E. 'The Politics of the Closet: Towards Equal Protection for Gay, Lesbian, and Bisexual Identity,' *UCLA Law Review* 36 (1989), 915.

Halperin, David. et al. *Before Sexuality: The Construction of Erotic Experience in the Ancient Greek World*. Princeton, N.J.: Princeton University Press 1990.

Harbeck, Karen M., ed. *Coming Out of the Classroom Closet: Gay and Lesbian Students, Teachers and Curricula*. New York: Harrington Park Press 1992.

Hart, H.L.A. *Law, Liberty and Morality*. Oxford: Oxford University Press 1963.

Hartman, Rhonda. 'Revitalizing Group Defamation as a Remedy for Hate Speech on Campus,' *Oregon Law Review* 71 (1992), 855.

Harvard Law Review editors. *Sexual Orientation and the Law*. Cambridge, Mass.: Harvard University Press 1989.

Heger, Heinz. *The Men with the Pink Triangle*. Boston: Alyson 1980.

Herek, Gregory M. 'The Social Psychology of Homophobia: Toward a Practical Theory,' *NYU Review of Law & Social Change* 14 (1986), 923.

Herman, Didi. 'Are We Family? Lesbian Rights and Women's Liberation,' *Osgoode Hall Law Journal* 28 (1990), 789.

- *Rights of Passage: Struggles for Lesbian and Gay Legal Equality*. Toronto: University of Toronto Press 1994.

Hernandez, John F. 'Outing in the Time of AIDS: Legal and Ethical Considerations,' *St Thomas Law Review* 5 (1993), 493.

Herzer, Manfred. 'Kertbeny and the Nameless Love,' *Journal of Homosexuality* 12 (1985), 1.

Hocquenghem, Guy. *Homosexual Desire*. Durham, N.C.: Duke University Press 1993.

Hogarth, John. *Sentencing as a Human Process*. Toronto: University of Toronto Press 1971.

Hogg, Peter. *Constitutional Law of Canada*. 4th ed. Scarborough, Ont.: Carswell 1996.

Hopcke, Robert H. *Jung, Jungians and Homosexuality*. Boston: Shambhala 1991.

Hurlbert, E.L., and M.A. Hurlbert. *School Law under the Charter of Rights and Freedoms*. Calgary: University of Calgary Press 1992.

Hutchins, Loraine, and Lani Kaahumanu. *Bi Any Other Name: Bisexual People Speak Out*. Boston: Alyson 1991.

Hyde, H. Montgomery. *Their Good Names: Twelve Cases of Libel and Slander with Some Introductory Reflections on the Law.* London: Hamish Hamilton 1970.

Iyer, Nitya. 'Categorical Denials: Equality Rights and the Shaping of Social Identity,' *Queen's Law Journal* 19 (1993), 179.

Jefferson, James E. 'Gay Rights and the *Charter,*' *University of Toronto of Faculty Law Review* 43 (1985), 70.

Johansson, Warren, and William A. Percy. *Outing: Shattering the Conspiracy of Silence.* New York: Harrington Park Press 1994.

Johnson, Fern. 'Women's Culture and Communication: An Analytical Perspective.' In Cynthia M. Lont and Sheryl Friedley, eds. *Beyond Boundaries: Sex and Gender Diversity in Communication.* Fairfax, Va.: G. Mason University Press 1989.

Jones, Randall W., and John E. Bates. 'Satisfaction in Male Homosexual Couples.' In John DeCecco, ed., *Gay Relationships.* New York: Haworth 1988.

Jourard, Sidney M. 'Some Psychological Aspects of Privacy,' *Law and Contemporary Problems* 31 (1966), 307.

Kalen, Evelyn. 'Never Again: Target Group Responses to the Debate Concerning Anti-Hate Propaganda Legislation,' *Windsor Yearbook of Access to Justice* 11 (1991), 46.

Kaplan, Morris B. 'Constructing Lesbian and Gay Rights and Liberation,' *Virginia Law Review* 79 (1993), 1877.

– *Sexual Justice: Democratic Citizenship and the Politics of Desire.* New York: Routledge 1997.

Karst, Kenneth L. 'The Freedom of Intimate Association,' *Yale Law Journal* 89 (1980), 624.

– *Law's Promise, Law's Expression: Visions of Power in the Politics of Race, Gender, and Religion.* New Haven: Yale University Press 1993.

Kendall, Christopher N. '"Real Dominant, Real Fun!" Gay Male Pornography and the Pursuit of Masculinity,' *Saskatchewan Law Review* 57 (1993), 21.

Kennedy, Duncan. 'Freedom and Constraint in Adjudication: A Critical Phenomenology,' *Journal of Legal Education* 36 (1986), 518.

Keohane, Kieran. *Symptoms of Canada: An Essay on the Canadian Identity.* Toronto: University of Toronto Press 1997.

Khayatt, Didi. 'In and Out: Experiences in the Academy.' In M. Oikawa, D. Falconer, and A. Decter, eds. *Resist: Essays against a Homophobic Culture.* Toronto: Women's Press 1994.

– 'Lesbian Teachers: Coping at School.' In Sharon Dale Stone, ed., *Lesbians in Canada,* chap. 6. Toronto: Between the Lines 1990.

Kinsey, Alfred. et al. *Sexual Behavior in the Human Female.* Philadelphia: W.B. Saunders 1953.

– *Sexual Behavior in the Human Male*. Philadelphia: W.B. Saunders 1949.

Kinsman, Gary. *The Regulation of Desire: Homo and Hetero Sexualities*. Rev. ed. Montreal: Black Rose Books 1996.

Kirk, Marshall, and Hunter Madsen. *After the Ball: How America Will Conquer Its Fear and Hatred of Gays in the 90s*. New York: Doubleday 1989.

Kitzinger, Celia. *The Social Construction of Lesbianism*. London: Sage Publications 1987.

Konvitz, Milton R. 'Privacy and Law: A Philosophical Prelude,' *Law and Contemporary Problems* 31 (1966), 272.

Koppelman, Andrew. 'Note. The Miscegenation Analogy: Sodomy Law as Sex Discrimination,' *Yale Law Journal* 98 (1988), 145.

Kroll, Ian T., and Lorne B. Warneke. *The Dynamics of Sexual Orientation and Adolescent Suicide: A Comprehensive Review and Developmental Perspective*. Calgary: University of Calgary and University of Alberta 1995.

La Violette, Nicole. 'The Immutable Refugees: Sexual Orientation in *Canada (A.G.) v. Ward*,' *University of Toronto of Faculty Law Review* 55 (1997), 1.

Lamrock, Kelly. 'Free Speech on Campus: The Principle Beyond the Crucible,' *UNB Law Journal* 44 (1995), 103.

Law Commission (of England). *Consent in the Criminal Law* (Consultation Paper no. 139). London: Law Commission 1995.

Law, Sylvia A. 'Homosexuality and the Social Meaning of Gender,' *Wisconsin Law Review* [1988], 187.

Lawson, Ian. *Privacy and Free Enterprise: The Legal Protection of Personal Information in the Private Sector*. Ottawa: Public Interest Advocacy Centre 1993.

Lefebour, Patricia. 'Same Sex Spousal Recognition in Ontario: Declarations and Denials: A Class Perspective,' *Journal of Law and Social Policy* 9 (1993), 272.

Leonard, Arthur S. 'Homophobia, Heterosexism and Judicial Decision Making,' *Journal of Gay and Lesbian Psychotherapy* 1 (1991), 65.

– *Sexuality and the Law: An Encyclopedia of Major Legal Cases*. New York: Garland Publishing 1993.

Leopold, Margaret, and Wendy King. 'Compulsory Heterosexuality, Lesbians, and the Law: The Case for Constitutional Protection,' *Canadian Journal of Woman and the Law* 1 (1985), 163.

Lewes, Kenneth. *The Psychoanalytic Theory of Male Homosexuality*. New York: Simon and Schuster 1988.

L'Heureux-Dubé, Claire. 'Nomination of Supreme Court Judges: Some Issues for Canada,' *Manitoba Law Journal* 20 (1991), 600.

Lieberman, Marcia K. '"Someday My Prince Will Come": Female Acculturation through the Fairy Tale,' *College English* 34. Urbana, Ill.: National Council of Teachers of English 1972.

Lusky, Louis. 'Invasion of Privacy: A Clarification of Concepts,' *Columbia Law Review* 72 (1972), 693.

MacDougall, Bruce. 'Outing: The Law Reacts to Speech about Homosexuality,' *Queen's Law Journal* 25 (1995), 79.

– '*Ex Turpi Causa*: Should a Defence Arise from a Base Cause?' *Saskatchewan Law Review* 55 (1991), 1.

MacGuigan, Mark R. 'Sources of Judicial Decision Making and Judicial Activism.' In Sheilah L. Martin and Kathleen E. Mahoney, eds. *Equality and Judicial Neutrality.* Toronto: Carswell 1987.

MacKay, A. Wayne. 'The Canadian Charter of Rights and Freedoms: A Springboard to Students' Rights,' *Windsor Yearbook of Access to Justice* 4 (1984), 174.

– *Education Law in Canada.* Toronto: Emond-Montgomery 1984.

– 'Judicial Free Speech and Accountability: Should Judges Be Seen But Not Heard?' *National Journal of Constitutional Law* 3 (1993), 159.

MacKinnon, Catherine. *Feminism Unmodified.* Cambridge, Mass.: Harvard University Press 1987.

MacKinnon, Martha. 'Aids and Schools.' In William F. Foster, ed. *Education & Law: A Plea for Partnership,* chap. 10. Welland, Ont.: Soleil 1992.

Magsino, Romulo. 'Denominational Rights in Education.' In Michael E. Manley-Casimir and Terri A. Sussel, eds. *Courts in the Classroom: Education and the Charter of Rights and Freedoms.* Calgary: Detselig 1986.

– 'Institutional Responses to Teacher Misconduct in the Atlantic Provinces,' *Education and the Law Journal* 5 (1993), 143.

– 'Institutional Responses to Teacher Misconduct in Manitoba,' *Education and the Law Journal* 5 (1993), 71.

Mahoney, Kathleen. 'Case Comment. *Vriend v. Alberta*: A Victory for Discrimination,' *Canadian Labour and Employment Law Journal* 4 (1996), 389.

Major, Marie-France. 'American Campus Speech Codes: Models for Canadian Universities?' *Education and the Law Journal* 7 (1995), 13.

– 'Sexual-Orientation Hate Propaganda: Time to Regroup,' *Canadian Journal of Law and Society* 11 (1996), 221.

Majury, Diana. 'Refashioning the Unfashionable: Claiming Lesbian Identities in the Legal Context,' *Canadian Journal of Women and the Law* 7 (1994), 286.

Manley-Casimir, Michael. 'Teaching as a Normative Enterprise,' *Education and the Law Journal* 5 (1993), 1.

Manley-Casimir, Michael E., and Stuart M. Piddocke. 'Teachers in a Goldfish Bowl: A Case of "Misconduct".' *Education and the Law Journal* 3 (1991), 115.

Martin, Robert. 'Criticising the Judges,' *McGill Law Journal* 28 (1982), 1.

Martin, S.L. 'Women as Lawmakers,' *Alberta Law Review* 30 (1992), 738.

Martin, Sheilah L., and Kathleen E. Mahoney, eds. *Equality and Judicial Neutrality*. Toronto: Carswell 1987.

Mauth, Trudy. 'Charter Implications of Compelling Dentists to Reveal Their HIV Status,' *Health Law in Canada* 15 (1994), 97.

McArdle, David. 'A Few Hard Cases? Sport, Sadomasochism and Public Policy in the English Courts,' *Canadian Journal of Law and Society* 10 (1995), 109.

McBride, Anne L. 'Deadly Confidentiality: AIDS and Rule 1.6(b),' *Georgetown Journal of Legal Ethics* 4 (1990), 435.

McClary, Susan. 'Constructions of Subjectivity in Schubert's Music.' In Philip Brett, Elizabeth Wood, and Gary C. Thomas, eds., *Queering the Pitch: The New Gay and Lesbian Musicology*. New York: Routledge 1994.

McCormick, Peter. 'Judicial Career Patterns and the Delivery of Reasons for Judgment in the Supreme Court of Canada 1949–1993.' *Supreme Court Law Review* 5 (1994), 499.

McCormick, Peter, and Ian Greene. *Judges and Judging*. Toronto: Lorimer 1990.

McCormick, Peter, and Twyla Job. 'Do Women Judges Make a Difference? An Analysis by Appeal Court Data,' *Canadian Journal of Law and Society* 8 (1993), 135.

McEvoy, J.P. 'The *Charter* and Spousal Benefits: The Case of the Same-Sex Spouses,' *Review Constitutional Studies* 2 (1994), 39.

McIntosh, Mary. 'The Homosexual Role,' *Social Problems* 16 (Fall 1968), 101.

McKenna, Ian B. 'Canada's Hate Propaganda Laws – A Critique,' *Ottawa Law Review* 26 (1994), 159.

McLachlin, Beverley M. 'Educational Records and the Right to Privacy,' *UBC Law Review* 15 (1981), 175.

McLeod, Donald W. *Lesbian and Gay Liberation in Canada: A Selected Annotated Chronology, 1964–1975*. Toronto: ECW Press 1996.

Meyer, Richard. Rock Hudson's Body. In Diana Fuss, ed. *Inside/Out: Lesbian Theories, Gay Theories*, chap. 11. New York: Routledge 1991.

Mill, J.S. *On Liberty*. 1859, New York: W.W. Norton 1975.

Millbank, Jennie. 'Lesbian Mothers, Gay Fathers: Sameness and Difference,' *Australian Gay and Lesbian Law Journal* 2 (1992), 21.

Miller, Arthur Selwyn. 'Privacy in the Modern Corporate State: A Speculative Essay,' *Administrative Law Review* 25 (1973), 231.

Minow, Martha. *Making All the Difference: Inclusion, Exclusion, and American Law*. Ithaca, N.Y.: Cornell University Press 1990.

Mohr, Richard D. *Gays/Justice: A Study of Ethics, Society, and Law*. New York: Columbia University Press 1988.

– 'The Perils of Postmodernity for Gay Rights,' *Canadian Journal of Law and Jurisprudence* 8 (1995), 5.

- 'The Outing Controversy: Privacy and Dignity in Gay Ethics.' In *Gay Ideas: Outing and Other Controversies*, chap. 1. Boston: Beacon Press 1992.

Money, John. *Gay, Straight, and In-Between: The Sexology of Erotic Orientation*. New York: Oxford University Press 1988.

Montesquieu. *De l'esprit des lois*. 1748; Paris: Garnier 1973.

Moon, Richard. 'Drawing Lines in a Culture of Prejudice: *R. v. Keegstra* and the Restriction of Hate Propaganda,' *UBC Law Review* 26 (1992), 99.

- 'The Supreme Court of Canada on the Structure of Freedom of Expression Adjudication,' *University of Toronto Law Journal* 45 (1995), 419.

Moran, Leslie J. *The Homosexual(ity) of Law*. London: Routledge 1996.

- 'Sexual Fix, Sexual Surveillance: Homosexual in Law.' In Simon Shepherd and Mick Wallis, eds. *Coming on Strong: Gay Politics and Culture*, chap. 10. London: Unwin Hyman 1989.

- 'The Uses of Homosexuality: Homosexuality for National Security,' *International Journal of Sociology of Law* 19 (1991), 149.

Moran, Mayo. 'Talking about Hate Speech: A Rhetorical Analysis of American and Canadian Approaches to the Regulation of Hate Speech,' *Wisconsin Law Review* [1994-] 1424.

Moretti, Barbara. 'Outing: Justifiable or Unwarranted Invasion of Privacy? The Private Facts Tort as a Remedy for Disclosures of Sexual Orientation,' *Cardozo Arts and Entertainment Law Journal* 11 (1993), 857.

Morton, W.L. *Canadian Identity*. 2nd ed. Toronto: University of Toronto Press 1972.

Neill, Brian. 'The Protection of Privacy,' *Modern Law Review* 25 (1962), 393.

Nordahl, Richard. 'Ronald Dworkin and the Defense of Human Rights,' *Canadian Journal of Law and Jurisprudence* 8 (1995), 19.

Nowlin, Christopher. 'The Relevance of Stereotypes to s. 15 Analysis – *Little Sisters Book and Art Emporium et al. v. The Minister of Justice et al*, *UBC Law Review* 30 (1996), 333.

O'Byrne, Shannon K., and James F. McGinnis. 'Case Comment: *Vriend v. Alberta*: *Plessy* Revisited: Lesbian and Gay Rights in the Province of Alberta,' *Alberta Law Review* 34 (1996), 892.

Ortiz, Daniel R. 'Creating Controversy: Essentialism and Constructivism and the Politics of Gay Identity,' *Virginia Law Review* 79 (1993), 1833.

Parker, Richard B. 'A Definition of Privacy,' *Rutgers Law Review* 27 (1974), 275.

Parker-Jenkins, Marie, and Judith A. Osborne. 'Rights in Conflict: The Case of Margaret Caldwell,' *Canadian Journal of Education* 10 (1985), 66.

Pearlman, Lynne. 'Theorizing Lesbian Oppression and the Politics of Outness in the Case of *Waterman v. National Life Assurance*: A Beginning in Lesbian

Human Rights/Equality Jurisprudence,' *Canadian Journal of Women and the Law* 7 (1994), 454.

Perry, Michael J. 'The Morality of Homosexual Conduct: A Response to John Finnis,' *Notre Dame Journal of Law, Ethics and Public Policy* 9 (1995), 41.

Petersen, Cynthia. 'Envisioning a Lesbian Equality Jurisprudence.' In Didi Herman and Carl Stychin, eds., *Legal Inversions: Lesbians, Gay Men, and the Politics of Law*. Philadelphia: Temple University Press 1995.

– 'Living Dangerously: Speaking Lesbian, Teaching Law,' *Canadian Journal of Women and the Law* 7 (1994), 318.

– 'A Queer Response to Bashing: Legislating against Hate,' *Queen's Law Journal* 16 (1991), 237.

Pharr, Suzanne. *Homophobia: A Weapon of Sexism*. Inverness, Cal.: Chardon Press 1988.

Piddocke, Stuart. 'Settling Disputes between School Boards and Teachers: A Review of Formal Procedures and Some Provincial Variations,' *Education and the Law Journal* 5 (1993), 23.

Plant, Richard. *The Pink Triangle: The Nazi War against Homosexuals*. New York: Henry Holt 1986.

Posner, Richard A. *Economics of Justice*. Cambridge, Mass.: Harvard University Press 1981.

– 'Privacy, Secrecy, and Reputation,' *Buffalo Law Review* 28 (1979), 1.

– 'The Right to Privacy,' *Georgia Law Review* 12 (1978), 393.

– *Sex and Reason*. Cambridge, Mass.: Harvard University Press 1992.

Pothier, Dianne. 'M'Aider, Mayday: Section 15 of the *Charter* in Distress,' (1996), *National Journal of Constitutional Law* 6 (1996), 295.

Prosser, William. *Handbook of the Law of Torts*. 4th ed., St Paul: West Publications 1971.

– 'Privacy,' *California Law Review* 48 (1960), 383.

Raymaker, Derek, and David Kilgour. 'The Freedom to Promote Hate: What We Learned from Jim Keegstra and Malcolm Ross,' *UNB Law Journal* 41 (1992), 327.

Rayside, David M. 'Homophobia, Class and Party in England,' *Canadian Journal of Political Science* 25 (1992), 121.

Réaume, Denise. 'Individuals, Groups, and Rights to Public Goods,' *University of Toronto Law Journal* 38 (1988), 1.

Regel, Alan R. 'Hate Propaganda: A Reason to Limit Freedom of Speech,' (1984), 49 *Saskatchewan Law Review* 303.

Reinig, Timothy W. 'Sin, Stigma and Society: A Critique of Morality and Values in Democratic Law and Policy,' *Buffalo Law Review* 38 (1990), 859.

Renke, Wayne N. 'Case Comment. *Vriend v. Alberta*: Discrimination, Burden of Proof, and Judicial Notice,' *Alberta Law Review* 34 (1996), 925.

Reyes, Allison. 'Freedom of Expression and Public School Teachers,' *Dalhousie Journal of Legal Studies* 4 (1995), 35.

Richards, David A.J. 'Constitutional Privacy and Homosexual Love,' *New York University Review of Law and Social Change* 14 (1986), 895.

Riley, Marilyn. 'Note: The Avowed Lesbian Mother and Her Right to Child Custody: A Constitutional Challenge That Can No Longer Be Denied,' *San Diego Law Review* 12 (1975), 799.

Riordan, Michael. *The First Stone*. Toronto: McClelland and Stewart 1990.

Ristock, Janice L. '"And Justice for All?" ... The Social Context of Legal Responses to Abuse in Lesbian Relationships,' *Canadian Journal of Women and the Law* 7 (1994), 415.

Roberts, Julian V. *Disproportionate Harm: Hate Crimes in Canada – An Analysis of Recent Statistics*. Ottawa: Department of Justice 1995.

Robinson, Svend. 'The Collision of Rights,' *UNB Law Journal* 44 (1995), 61.

Robson, Ruthann. *Lesbian (Out)Law: Survival under the Rule of Law*. Ithaca, N.Y.: Firebrand 1992.

Rofes, Eric E. *'I Thought People Like That Killed Themselves': Lesbians, Gay Men and Suicide*. San Francisco: Grey Fox 1983.

Rorem, Ned. 'Being Alone.' Extracted in Winston Leyland, ed., *Gay Sunshine Journal No. 47: Anthology of Fiction/Poetry/Prose*. San Francisco: Gay Sunshine Press 1982.

Rosenfeld, Martha. 'Jewish Lesbians in France: The Issue of Multiple Cultures.' In Jeffner Allen, ed. *Lesbian Philosophies and Cultures*. Albany, N.Y.: State University of New York Press 1990.

Ross, Becki. 'Sexual Dis/Orientation or Playing House: To Be or Not to Be Coded Human.' In Sharon Dale Stone, ed. *Lesbians in Canada*, chap. 9. Toronto: Between the Lines 1990.

Ruby, Clayton. *Sentencing*. 3rd ed. Toronto: Butterworths 1987.

Rule, Jane. 'Lesbian and Writer: Making the Real Visible.' In Margaret Cruikshank, ed., *New Lesbian Writing*. San Francisco: Grey Fox Press, 1984, 96–9.

Ruse, Michael. *Homosexuality*. Oxford: Blackwell 1988.

Rusk, Peter. 'Same-Sex Benefits and the Evolving Conception of Family,' *University of Toronto Faculty Law Review* 52 (1993), 170.

Russell, Peter H. *The Judiciary in Canada: The Third Branch of Government*. Toronto: McGraw-Hill Ryerson 1987.

Russo, Vito. *The Celluloid Closet: Homosexuality in the Movies*. Rev. ed. New York: Harper & Row 1987.

Ryder, Bruce. 'Becoming Spouses: The Rights of Lesbian and Gay Couples.' [1993] *Special Lectures of the Law Society of Upper Canada – Family Law*, 399.

- 'Equality Rights and Sexual Orientation: Confronting Heterosexual Family Privilege,' *Canadian Journal of Family Law* 9 (1990), 39.
- 'Family Status, Sexuality and "The Province of the Judiciary"': The Implications of *Mossop v. Attorney-General Canada*,' *Windsor Yearbook of Access to Justice* 13 (1993), 3.
- 'Straight Talk: Male Heterosexual Privilege,' *Queen's Law Journal* 16 (1991), 287.
Samar, Vincent J. *The Right to Privacy: Gays, Lesbians and the Constitution.* Philadelphia: Temple University Press 1991.
Sanders, Douglas. 'Constructing Lesbian and Gay Rights,' *Canadian Journal of Law and Society* 9 (1994), 99.
Saunders [*sic*], D. E., Note in (1967), 10 *Criminal Law Quarterly* 25.
Scales, Ann. 'Avoiding Constitutional Depression: Bad Attitudes and the Fate of *Butler*,' *Canadian Journal of Women and the Law* 7 (1994), 349.
Scanlon, T. 'A Theory of Freedom of Expression.' In R.M. Dworkin, ed. *The Philosophy of Law.* Oxford: Oxford University Press 1977, 153–71.
Schafer, Arthur. 'Privacy: A Philosophical Overview.' In Dale Gibson, ed. *Aspects of Privacy Law: Essays in Honour of John M. Sharp*, chap. 1. Toronto: Butterworths 1980.
Schauer, Frederick. *Free Speech: A Philosophical Enquiry.* Cambridge: Cambridge University Press 1982.
Schaum, Melita, and Connie Flanagan, ed. *Gender Images: Readings for Composition.* Boston: Houghton Mifflin 1992.
Schippers, Jan. 'Homosexual Identity, Essentialism and Constructionism.' In Dennis Altman et al., eds., *Homosexuality, Which Homosexuality?* London: GMP 1989.
Schmeiser, Douglas A., and Roderick J Wood. 'Student Rights under the Charter,' *Saskatchewan Law Review* 49 (1984), 49.
Schwartz, Bryan. 'On Choosing Judges – Oracles and Performers; or Philosophers and Sages?' *Queen's Law Journal* 17 (1992), 479.
Sedgwick, Eve Kosofsky. *The Epistemology of the Closet.* Berkeley: University Calif. Press 1990.
Seipp, David J. 'English Judicial Recognition of a Right to Privacy,' *Oxford Journal of Legal Studies* 3 (1983), 325.
Shaffer, Martha. 'Criminal Responses to Hate-Motivated Violence: Is Bill C-41 Tough Enough?' *McGill Law Journal* 41 (1995), 199.
Shils, Edward. 'Privacy: Its Constitution and Vicissitudes,' *Law and Contemporary Problems* 31 (1966), 280.
Siegel, Paul. 'Second Hand Prejudice, Racial Analogies and Shared Showers: Why "Don't Ask, Don't Tell" Won't Sell,' *Notre Dame Journal of Law, Ethics and Public Policy* 9 (1995), 185.

Signorile, Michelangelo. *Queer in America: Sex, the Media and the Closets of Power.* New York: Random House 1993.

Silvera, Makeda. 'Man Royals and Sodomites: Some Thoughts on the Invisibility of Afro-Caribbean Lesbians.' Sharon Dale Stone, ed. *Lesbians in Canada*, chap. 3 Toronto: Between the Lines 1990.

Simon, Barbara Levy. *Never Married Women.* Philadelphia: Temple University Press 1987.

Sissons, C.B. *Church and State in Canadian Education: An Historical Study.* Toronto: Ryerson 1959.

Smith, William J. 'Rights and Freedoms in Education: The Application of the *Charter* to Public School Boards,' *Education and the Law Journal* 4 (1993), 107.

Sokhansanj, Banafsheh. 'Our Father Who Art in the Classroom: Exploring a *Charter* Challenge to Prayer in Public Schools,' *Saskatchewan Law Review* 56 (1992), 47.

Sproat, John R. *Equality Rights and Fundamental Freedoms.* Scarborough, Ont. Carswell 1996.

Stein, Edward, ed. *Forms of Desire: Sexual Orientation and the Social Constructionist Controversy.* New York: Garland 1990.

Stephenson, Carol A. 'Religious Exercises and Instruction in Ontario Public Schools,' *University of Toronto Faculty of Law Review* 49 (1991), 82.

Stewart, James B. 'Death of a Partner,' *The New Yorker*, 21 June 1993.

Stone, Julius. *Precedent and Law: Dynamics of Common Law Growth.* Sydney: Butterworths 1985.

Stone, Sharon Dale. 'Introduction.' In Sharon Dale Stone, ed. *Lesbians in Canada*. Toronto: Between the Lines 1990.

Stone, Sharon Dale, ed. *Lesbians in Canada*, Toronto: Between the Lines 1990.

Stone, Sharon Dale, and the Women's Survey Group. 'Lesbian Life in a Small Centre: The Case of St. John's.' In Sharon Dale Stone, ed., *Lesbians in Canada*, chap. 7. Toronto: Between the Lines 1990.

Stoppard, Tom. *The Invention of Love.* London: Faber and Faber 1997.

Stratas, David. *The Charter of Rights in Litigation: Direction from the Supreme Court of Canada.* Aurora, Ont.: Canada Law Book 1997.

Stychin, Carl. 'Essential Rights and Contested Identities: Sexual Orientation and Equality Rights Jurisprudence in Canada,' *Canadian Journal of Law and Jurisprudence* 8 (1995), 49.

– 'Exploring the Limits: Feminism and the Legal Regulation of Gay Male Pornography,' *Vermont Law Review* 16 (1992), 857.

– *Law's Desire: Sexuality and the Limits of Justice.* London: Routledge 1995.

– 'A Postmodern Constitutionalism: Equality Rights, Identity Politics and the Canadian National Imagination,' *Dalhousie Law Journal* 17 (1994), 61.

- 'Unmanly Diversions: The Construction of the Homosexual Body (Politic) in English Law,' *Osgoode Hall Law Journal* 32 (1994), 503.
Sussel, Terri A. *Controversies in School Law: A Handbook for Educational Administrators*. Vancouver: EduServ 1990.
- 'Schoolrooms of a Lesser God: The Fundamentalist Challenge to Public Education,' *Education Law Journal* 1 (1989), 72.
Sussel, T.A., and M.E. Manley-Casimir. 'The Supreme Court of Canada as a "National School Board": The Charter and Educational Change.' In Michael E. Manley-Casimir and Terri A. Sussel, eds. *Courts in the Classroom: Education and the Charter of Rights and Freedoms*, chap. 11. Calgary: Detselig 1986.
Symposium entitled: 'Language as Violence v. Freedom of Expression in the Candian and American Perspectives on Group Defamation,' *Buffalo Law Review* 37 (1988), 337.
Taylor, Eddie. 'Hanging up on Hate: Contempt of Court as a Tool to Shut Down Hatelines,' *National Journal of Constitutional Law* 5 (1995), 163.
Thompson, Cooper. 'A New Vision of Masculinity.' Extract published in Melita Schaum and Connie Flanagan, eds., *Gender Images: Readings for Composition*. Boston: Houghton Mifflin 1992, 77.
Thompson, M.P. 'Breach of Confidence and the Protection of Privacy in English Law,' *Journal of Media Law and Practice* 6 (1985), 5.
Trakman, Leon. 'Group Rights: A Canadian Perspective,' *International Law and Politics* 24 (1992), 1579.
Tripp, C.A. *The Homosexual Matrix*. New York: McGraw-Hill 1975.
Troiden, Richard R. *Gay and Lesbian Identity: A Sociological Analysis*. Dix Hills, N.Y.: General Hall 1988.
Tsui, Kitty. 'Breaking Silence, Making Waves and Loving Ourselves: The Politics of Coming Out and Coming Home.' In Jeffner Allen, ed. *Lesbian Philosophies and Cultures*. Albany, N.Y.: State University of New York Press 1990.
Vagelos, Ellen. 'The Social Group That Dare Not Speak Its Name: Should Homosexuals Constitute a Particular Social Group for Purposes of Obtaining Refugee Status? Comment on *Re: Inaudi*,' *Fordham International Law Journal* 17 (1993), 229.
Valois, Martine. 'Hate Propaganda, Section 2(b) and Section 1 of the Charter: A Canadian Constitutional Dilemma,' *Revue juridique Thémis*, 26 (1992), 373.
van den Boogaard, Henk. 'Blood Furious Underneath the Skins ...: On Anti-Homosexual Violence: Its Nature and the Needs of the Victims.' In *Homosexuality, Which Homosexuality?* London: GMP 1989.
Warren, Samuel D., and Louis D. Brandeis. 'The Right to Privacy,' *Harvard Law Review* 4 (1890), 193.

Watney, Simon. 'School's Out.' In Diana Fuss, ed. *Inside/Out: Lesbian Theories, Gay Theories*, chap. 17. New York: Routledge 1991.

Watson, Jack. 'Badmouthing the Bench: Is There a Clear and Present Danger? To What?' *Saskatchewan Law Review* 56 (1992), 113.

Webber, Jeremy. 'The Limits to Judges' Free Speech: A Comment on the Report of the Committee of Investigation into the Conduct of the Hon. Mr Justice Berger,' *McGill Law Journal* 29 (1984), 369.

Weeks, Jeffrey. 'Capitalism and the Organisation of Sex.' In Gay Left Collective, eds. *Homosexuality: Power and Politics*, chap. 1. London: Allison & Busby 1980.

– 'Discourse, Desire and Sexual Deviance: Some Problems in a History of Homosexuality.' In Kenneth Plummer, ed., *The Making of the Modern Homosexual*, chap. 4. London: Hutchinson 1981.

– *Invented Moralities: Sexual Values in an Age of Uncertainty*. New York: Columbia University Press 1995.

– 'Necessary Fictions.' In Jacqueline Murray, ed. *Constructing Sexualities*. University of Windsor Working Papers in the Humanities I (1993).

Weinberg, George. *Society and the Healthy Homosexual*. New York: St Martin's Press 1972.

Wick, Ronald F. 'Out of the Closet and Into the Headlines: "Outing" and the Private Facts Tort,' *Georgetown Law Journal* 80 (1991), 413.

Williams, Diane. 'Who's That Teacher? The Problems of Being a Lesbian Teacher of Colour.' In M. Oikawa, D. Falconer, and A. Decter, eds. *Resist: Essays against a Homophobic Culture*. Toronto: Women's Press 1994.

Williams, Jeremy S. *The Law of Libel and Slander in Canada*. 2nd ed. Toronto: Butterworths 1988.

Wilson, Bertha (Madame Justice). 'Will Women Judges Really Make a Difference?' *Osgoode Hall Law Journal* 28 (1990), 508.

Wine, Jeri Dawn. 'Outsiders on The Inside: Lesbians in Canadian Academe.' In Sharon Dale Stone, ed. *Lesbians in Canada*, chap. 11. Toronto: Between the Lines 1990.

Wintemute, Robert. 'Recognising New Kinds of Direct Sex Discrimination: Transsexualism, Sexual Orientation and Dress Codes,' *Modern Law Review* 60 (1997), 334.

– 'Sexual Orientation Discrimination as Sex Discrimination: Same-Sex Couples and the *Charter* in *Mossop, Egan* and *Layland*,' *McGill Law Journal* 39 (1994), 429.

– *Sexual Orientation and Human Rights: The United States Constitution, the European Convention, and the Canadian Charter*. Oxford: Oxford University Press 1995.

('Wolfenden') Report of the Committee on Homosexual Offences and Prostitution. London: HMSO, CMND 247 1957. Authorized American edition New York: Stein and Day 1963.

Woods, James D., and Jay H. Lucas. The Corporate Closet: The Professional Lives of Gay Men in America. New York: Free Press 1993.

Woolley, Alice. 'Excluded by Definition: Same-Sex Couples and the Right to Marry,' University of Toronto of Law Journal 45 (1995), 471.

Yogis, John A., Randall R. Duplak, and J. Royden Trainor. Sexual Orientation and Canadian Law: An Assessment in the Law Affecting Lesbian and Gay Persons. Toronto: Emond Montgomery 1996.

Index